THE
EISENHOWER
DIARIES

THE
EISENHOWER
DIARIES

EDITED BY

ROBERT H. FERRELL

W·W·NORTON & COMPANY·NEW YORK·LONDON

Copyright © 1981 by Robert H. Ferrell
Published simultaneously in Canada by George J. McLeod Limited, Toronto.
Printed in the United States of America
First Edition

Library of Congress Cataloging in Publication Data
Eisenhower, Dwight David, Pres. U.S., 1890–1969.
The Eisenhower diaries.
Bibliography: p.
Includes index.
1. Eisenhower, Dwight David, Pres. U.S., 1890–1969.
2.Presidents—United States—Biography. I. Ferrell,
Robert H. II. Title.
E836.A3155 1981   973.921'092'4 [B]   80-27866
ISBN 0-393-33180-6

Book design by Antonina Krass

W.W. Norton & Company, Inc. 500 Fith Avenue, New York, N.Y. 10110
W.W. Norton & Company Ltd. 25 New Street Square, London EC4A 3NT

1 2 3 4 5 6 7 8 9 0

CONTENTS

Contents

ACKNOWLEDGMENTS

I do want to thank the historian Neal H. Petersen of the Department of State, who first told me of the diaries in the Dwight D. Eisenhower Library in Abilene. A few days after talking with Neal I drove out that bleak highway, Interstate 70, to the one-time cattle town of Kansas to investigate. For assistance during that early visit to Abilene and subsequent visits, let me express my warm appreciation to the staff of the Eisenhower Library—the director, John Wickman; the senior archivist, James Leyerzapf; achivists Rod Soubers, Thomas Branigar, and David Haight; librarian Robert Bohanan; and photo archives technician Hazel Hartman. General J. Lawton Collins, former U.S. Army chief of staff, the "Lightning Joe" of the Normandy breakout, read the 1944 diary and pointed out confusions in the editing. Forrest C. Pogue clarified for me the several versions of the January–July 1942 diary. General Eisenhower's assistant over many years, Kevin McCann, related his chief's delightfully human qualities. John S.D. Eisenhower, who is his father's literary executor and a well-known military historian, was kind enough to give permission to publish. Dwight David Eisenhower II spoke of memories of his grandfather and of his own remarkable understanding of "the Eisenhower Era."

As for the putting together of the book, I have many people to thank. My copy editor at W.W. Norton, Sue Lowe, caught most of my errors with a tactful query or glancing comment that took any possible sting out of the point. Jim Mairs, friend and editor, asked questions with his customary directness, which didn't sting either. John M. Hollingsworth was the able cartographer, and Antonina Krass designed with imagination and skill. I am again grateful to Donald S. Lamm, the president of Norton. Of course, once more, a thank you to Lila and Carolyn.

EDITORIAL NOTE

The habit of editors is to explain the obvious, and in introductions to the various parts of *The Eisenhower Diaries*—to the main sections, as well as in headnotes, footnotes, and occasional summaries—I have tried to present the issues as simply as possible. Where the diary does not stand by itself I have sought to explain without relating too much. My comments appear in a contrasting, oblique type-face.

The same practice has been applied to the style of the text. Styling changes have been kept to a minimum, but where necessary they have been made without fuss—without brackets or "sics." A special problem in regard to the editing is Eisenhower's somewhat prim use of dashes in place of full expletives, as in d---. Occasionally, he wrote out the words. I have retained this inconsistency. Eisenhower was an excellent speller, so there was little to correct; the very occasional lapses have been corrected without notice, on the theory that the diarist was in a hurry and deserves consideration from posterity. Likewise, Eisenhower's tendency to use dashes for commas. Eisenhower had a military habit of capping nouns, and these now appear lowcapped. The considerable number of exclamation marks and underlinings, which are mostly unnecessary and would distract the attention of present-day readers, have been reduced. I have also spelled out the many abbreviations which would otherwise have required an overabundance of footnotes. And, finally, I have replaced the few instances of illegible handwriting with ellipses.

INTRODUCTION

The diaries of the late Dwight D. Eisenhower are unique documents, in that they alone, in the mass of Ike's prose, reveal the innermost thoughts of the soldier-statesman. In his books—the memoir of the Second World War, the two large volumes on the presidency, the incomplete autobiography written near the end of his life—Eisenhower related the course of events over the years, with descriptive detail and frequently with humor, but he usually stayed away from analysis. In his many private letters to friends and acquaintances, some of which have been published, he was more frank, but he still held back. And the public record of his military career and of his presidency does not reflect many open, frank statements, proofs that the soldier-president thought long and deeply about issues, personal or public; it has given substance to the speculation by many of his contemporaries and by some later students of Eisenhower that he was essentially a public relations man and that his life was all outward—an expression of assent and agreement or at least of forebearance, of a man who never had an idea or, if he did, would quickly chase it out of sight. Ike had advanced in the military because he exhibited the proper feelings toward his fellow officers—he was ambitious, but not overambitious, and always thoughtful about his friends. He was companionable and conciliatory. When he had any spare time in the military he devoted it to bridge and to reading "Westerns"; as a politician, he also took up golf. Eisenhower was the friend of everyone—the man of judgment amid men of passion, the American from Abilene who somehow had risen high in the army and had done the same thing in politics and who, therefore, wanted people everywhere to get along with each other rather than oppose and quarrel and fight. To the American people he seemed a boyish, enthusiastic figure and no militaristic army officer. But in the diaries another Eisenhower appears—a man who carefully masked his shrewdness, his purposes. The general-president knew what he was doing. Contrary to the critics who said that what seemed thoughtlessness was indeed so, there was an active mind at work, not shuffling through issues and crises but determined to get to the essentials; it is this analytical mind that presents itself in the diaries.

If the diaries have a second quality, apart from the writer's ability to analyze, that quality might well be described as a quiet ambition—this despite the army's feeling that its officers should not be overambitious. The army's accepted system of behavior undoubtedly played down ambition among its inner membership— the West Pointers and such of the outlanders as George C. Marshall, who although he attended Virginia Military Institute was admitted to the inner circle. But the playing down was largely a matter of form rather than reality. In Eisenhower's case, the hardworking officer in the Philippines—the diaries begin in 1935, when Ike was under the thumb of the imperious Douglas MacArthur, trying to organize a Philippine army—dearly wanted to do well and gain authority, as would anyone in any other walk of life, or almost all the other walks of life. Throughout the diaries we see Eisenhower looking for tasks that would challenge him.

A third quality so evident in the diary entries of the years after 1945 is that Eisenhower saw himself not merely as a conciliator and mover of men but, to use the word, a politician. He believed that anyone who made it to the top in the United States Army could handle men politically. It seems a quaint belief, for the work of being a politician involved so many more activities than were necessary in the army. But Eisenhower believed that he possessed all the qualities necessary to analyze American political life. Involved in his new political being was the need to reevaluate his political philosophy, for it was well known (or so the successful general appears to have convinced himself) that political leaders could articulate their beliefs. The general decided that he was in favor of free enterprise and balanced federal budgets. Also necessary was the need to know your enemy, in this case communism, and Ike made some elementary attempts to understand the philosophy of the people in Moscow; his speculations on the nature of communism would not have been impressive to any professional student of the subject, but they were impressive to the Republicans of his day who, after a few Eisenhower extrapolations, were willing to believe that if the general mentioned the word communism, he had been studying it. And lastly Ike, as a politician, sought to enlist the good will of the businessmen of the country, the controllers of enterprise, who had been under a cloud ever since the beginning of the Great Depression in 1929. Eisenhower sensed that the businessmen of his time were different individuals from the speculators and bankers of the earlier era, the supporters of Herbert Hoover in the late 1920s. He had seen businessmen patriotically at work during the war, enlarging their factories in miraculous ways and making the country the great arsenal of democracy. Businessmen seemed devoted to the national welfare, and Ike believed they could be marshalled in politics; given half a chance, they could turn the Republican party into an instrument for the national good.

The diaries thus show that Eisenhower could be frank with himself, that he was attracted to power, and that he saw himself as a politician. The last point is of special interest and raises a question of reality—did the general-president really master politics? Or was he deluded, as so many men (generals perhaps least) have been deluded, by the heady notice, attention, publicity, that comes to both good and bad politicians—the hero worship that comes to anyone who reaches high public office—especially the office of president of the United States?

Here it is necessary to say that Eisenhower proved himself a marvelous politician. He not merely wanted to move men politically but he showed he could do it. As the years of the presidency wore on, and somewhat against his will he served a second term—by 1956 his policies were not yet achieved, not yet secure, and no other member of the Republican party had begun to approach his vote-getting abilities—he sometimes remarked modestly that he was a better politician than the professionals. There is every reason to believe this statement, for the president's popularity was ineradicable, invincible, simply not subject to the erosions or buffetings that have knocked down so many American political reputations throughout the country's history. Eisenhower was a success, in the largest possible way, in American politics; no politician of his time did nearly as well. The professionals were dazzled by his virtuosity. If the philosophy of free enterprise and balanced budgets did not find universal approval and met the guffaws of the sophisticated of his time, it did appeal to the masses of Americans; it would not have encountered guffaws among the chastened sophisticates of the stagflation 1980s. Eisenhower's views on communism perhaps were simplistic, but they were as good as those many of his contemporaries produced. As for his political effort to enlist the businessmen of the United States in upholding the best qualities of the capitalistic system, no rational American of the 1980s would disagree either with the goal or with many of Eisenhower's methods, which if they did not produce miracles, were at least as miraculous as the economic wonderworks of the 1960s and 1970s.

Eisenhower was a phenomenon in American politics, and there never has been anything quite like him. No American today can fail to take his presidency seriously. And many Americans are now looking back to the Eisenhower fifties, as they are called, with a feeling of real nostalgia, a sense that here was a time that one would like to relive, if it were only possible.

In looking at Eisenhower's career it is a fascinating task to compare the qualities—the capacity for high public office—of the two leading political personalities of the period after the Second World War, Dwight D. Eisenhower and Harry S. Truman. As Richard Rovere pointed out many years ago, here were two individuals who came from very much the same backgrounds, small towns of the Middle West, actually two small towns that were less than two hundred miles apart. Truman as a young bank clerk just after the turn of the century lived for a short time in a rooming house in Kansas City with another young man named Arthur Eisenhower—Ike's brother. If circumstances had been slightly different for Truman, he would have been a graduate of West Point. (He tried hard to get in and failed because of poor eyesight.) Similarly, Eisenhower might have followed the paths of his brothers into banking or into agricultural education and eventually have become vice-president of some Western big city bank or president of one of the Midwestern colleges.

There were other points of similarity. Both men were scrupulously honest. Truman was never grazed by the Pendergast machine, and after he served in public office for fifteen years including a term as United States senator he was still so poor that he could not raise the money to save his mother's farm from foreclosure. In the first years after his presidency and despite the writing of his memoirs, his expenses ran ahead of income, and he kept his head above water only by selling off acreage from his mother's inheritance to a developer who wanted to build a shopping center, now known as Truman Corners. Likewise, Eisenhower never profited greatly from what must have been many opportunities. He was scrupulous about small matters; in one of his diary entries in 1938 he remarked that he had taken Mamie with him on a trip to the East—the American East—and paid for all her accommodations and avoided staying in better-than-average places. After the war he managed to come into more than four hundred thousand dollars of tax-free royalties from his book, *Crusade in Europe*, because of a special tax deal negotiated with federal authorities. But in extenuation one has to point out that the arrangement was entirely open and public and seemed in a sense a gift from the American people to a great military figure who otherwise, before the book came out, could hardly make ends meet on his military salary. The responsibilities of large public figures are many; they are expected to contribute to worthy causes and undertake other public duties and keep up their correspondence, whatever the cost. Eventually, Eisenhower, as a general of the army, received a federal stipend that allowed him a staff and clerical help, and some years later Truman as an ex-president received a similar arrangement. But both men could have gone into private industry or accepted corporation directorships or taken on lucrative literary arrangements like—in the 1970s and 1980s—former Secretary of State Henry A. Kissinger, or even have fixed up deals whereby they could endorse this or that. They could have become hugely rich. Neither chose to do so.

In the backgrounds of the two men were similarities, but there the resemblance ended. Eisenhower fitted into the mold of the army, the mold of team play, of no intruding, or at least apparent, ambition; whereas Truman from the outset was a boisterous, openhearted man who did what was necessary to get ahead and made no bones about it. Eisenhower became smooth in human relationships, able to say the right thing in an innocuous way. He looked for ways to finesse problems, to smother them in good humor or good spirits or maybe it was team play. Truman could become scrappy and irritable and pointed. In private Truman was a straightshooter, just as in public. The politics of the two men went different ways almost at the outset. Truman had to be a Democrat to get elected to any public office in Missouri, and his whole family background was Democratic; whereas Eisenhower, as an inhabitant of the Kansas farm belt, drifted easily toward Republicanism. Truman found it easy to take interest in the problems of cities, for Independence was next door, and increasingly so, to Kansas City. Eisenhower never appears to have liked cities; his army experience drew him away; the social problems of cities were almost foreign to him.

One interesting aspect of the Eisenhower diaries is the devotion that Ike evidenced toward his wife, Mamie. This point needs emphasis at a time when many Americans are willing to believe that their public leaders often are dissolute, two-faced in public and private. The assertions of Eisenhower's automobile driver in the European theater during the Second World War, the late Kay Summersby Morgan, have been so explicit *(Past Forgetting: My Love Affair with Dwight D. Eisenhower)*, and the rumors that ran through American politics for so many years so plausible, that it has become a matter of belief that Eisenhower and Mamie were incompatible, at least during their later years. Mamie's obvious trouble with her physical balance, the result of a malady of the inner ear, was attributed to alcohol, and likewise her trouble with an asthmatic condition. Her visits to a Western health spa were quietly defined as efforts to dry herself out. Nothing in the diaries supports these allegations.

Eisenhower wrote most of his diaries by hand. For a time or two, notably when the business machine magnate Thomas J. Watson gave him a new IBM typewriter in 1949, he tried to type the entries, but his typing was not up to the task and he abandoned the machine. The handwriting has a tendency to scrawl, but even at worst it is approximately readable. The presidential years allowed the secretarial services of Mrs. Ann C. Whitman, who usually typed up the handwritten diary entries in a single copy and destroyed the originals. The president also dictated entries to Mrs. Whitman. Occasionally he would dictate memoranda of conversations, "Memoranda for the Record" as he entitled them, which he would then put into the diaries.

The coverage of the diaries is, unfortunately, sporadic—sometimes for several years Eisenhower did not keep a diary. Entries for the Philippine tour began in December 1935 and are quite detailed into 1936 and 1937 and for part of 1938. The diary-keeping then stops until January 1942, when it continues until July. About three-fourths of this 1942 diary was published in Alfred D. Chandler, Jr., ed., *The Papers of Dwight David Eisenhower: The War Years*, volume I.* Chandler was unable to find the rest of the diary—which in fact had been removed by its author, Eisenhower, who sensed that he had written too frankly. The existence of an unexpurgated version of the diary for January–July 1942 came to light in 1979 when Francis L. Loewenheim of Rice University obtained a copy from the Eisenhower Library and quoted a few selections from it in two articles in the Houston *Chronicle*. The gist of his articles was picked up by newspapers and magazines around the country. Loewenheim found interesting items about General Douglas MacArthur and Admiral Ernest J. King—entries in which Eisenhower expressed deep concern over President Franklin D. Roosevelt's decision in February 1942 to order MacArthur out of the Philippines and also opined

---

*The project to publish Eisenhower's papers is a large one and perhaps will total twenty volumes or more. The war years required five volumes. A sixth volume on the occupation of Germany in 1945 was edited jointly by Chandler and his successor editor, Louis P. Galambos, who has followed with three volumes on Eisenhower's term as army chief of staff in 1945–1948 (Baltimore, 1979).

offhandedly that (because of King's bullying behavior) one thing that might help win the European war during those dismal months of defeat was to get someone to shoot the admiral. The entire diary for January–July 1942 is published in the present book for the first time. From the summer of 1942 through late 1944, General Eisenhower dictated occasional diary accounts for his friend Captain Harry C. Butcher, USNR, who kept a headquarters diary. After the war, Butcher published part of his own diary under the title of *My Three Years with Eisenhower*, but did not include Ike's entries, which appeared in Chandler's volumes published in 1970. Those entries are republished in the present book, together with one entry that Chandler missed. The entries for 1942–1944 that appear in Chandler constitute the only portion of Eisenhower's diaries that has been published to date (with one very minor exception—several paragraphs for 1946 and 1947 that appear in Kevin McCann, *Man from Abilene*, pp. 156–60). After a gap for the period from December 1944 until December 1945, during which time Eisenhower was helping to end the war in Europe and involved in the occupation of Germany, the entries pick up when Ike became chief of staff. They continue through the years when he was president of Columbia University and commander of NATO forces, until the spring of 1952, when the work of gaining the Republican presidential nomination and later the election appears to have made diary keeping impossible. After the election the diaries resume and cover the first administration in detail. The second administration has less coverage, perhaps because the president was not in the best of health; he suffered his first heart attack in 1955, an attack of a digestive disorder from which he long had suffered, known as ileitis, in 1956, and a stroke in 1957.* The diaries as presently published have only a few entries for the post-presidential period, between 1961 and 1969. The papers in Abilene for this era have been closed. Eisenhower's few years of retirement, however, were afflicted by illness, and surely the ex-president found it very difficult to write much more than about matters concerning his health.†

---

*At the present writing (1981) some diary entries for the presidential years remain closed, mostly for reasons of security, a few because their release would violate the donor's deed of gift. Withdrawals for security reasons can be lifted only after special request to the Washington agency of origin. Withdrawals under the donor's deed can be appealed. There is every reason to believe, however, that for the presidential years little from the Eisenhower diary has been withheld. Withdrawn items often are short, seldom more than a page. Withdrawal sheets in the archival boxes usually give the subject of closed items, and it is evident that some entries were withheld because they dealt with personalities. In the withdrawal sheets a total of thirty-two diary entries are listed.

†The processing of Eisenhower's post-presidential papers in the library in Abilene has begun, but it will be a long time indeed, almost an incalculable time, before all of them will be available to students of the era. The papers are in the order they were kept at Gettysburg and elsewhere and will have to be organized by the archivists so as to exclude anything with a security classification or anything that is donor-restricted. This is a tedious process, as the post-presidential papers are full of classified or donor-restricted material. Classified items will have to be declassified, a tedious business in the extreme. Despite presidential efforts of recent years to hurry declassification there has been foot dragging in the lower echelons, and many classified papers also require interagency scrutiny. The State Department, the national security council, and the military agencies are all reluctant to release papers. Students may ask for declassification of individual classified items through requests for

Here, then, is no massive daily accounting that takes its subject from morning to night, month by month, year by year. But the Eisenhower diaries have much to offer. They extend through all the major portions of Eisenhower's adult life in a way that no other contemporary documents could have done. The keeping of diaries as a record of introspection, as a measure of the moment, a calculation of the future, is of course a unique way of holding one's life to the glass. In the case of a man whose life turns into public importance and reaches the pinnacle of military and political renown, diaries are precious documents, for they not merely are the personal measure of their writer but they explain our own past.

"mandatory review" under the presidential orders, but the requests move slowly. As for donor-restricted material in the post-presidential files, much of it will remain closed until Eisenhower's contemporaries pass from the scene.

THE
EISENHOWER
DIARIES

I

THE PHILIPPINES

By the time that Major Dwight D. Eisenhower, in October 1935, arrived in the Philippines for duty with the special mission headed by General Douglas MacArthur, the future president of the United States must have thought that the United States Army might not be taking his lifetime hopes in any clearly discernible direction and that, generally speaking, life was not going to hold too many surprises and certainly no large future. In the mid-1930s about all he could look forward to was retirement, probably as a full colonel. This after years of duty as a football coach, an aide to then Brigadier General Fox Conner, and, in 1935, an aide to General MacArthur. No war in Europe or Asia beckoned; in the Far East the Japanese had taken Manchuria away from China in the early 1930s but momentarily seemed to be satisfied; in Europe the new ruler of Germany, Chancellor Adolf Hitler, was speaking loudly to his fellow Germans and to his fellow Austrians about the importance of the new Germany, which he was pleased to call the Third Reich, but his actions thus far had been much less strenuous than his words. Only in Africa, where the Italians invaded Ethiopia in the summer of 1935, did war threaten, but it was a kind of tribal war on the side of the Ethiopians and not much of a conflict from the point of view of the Italians— one could draw few lessons from it in the year 1935. And so for Eisenhower, a military man since his entrance into West Point in 1911, no war seemed imminent. And not much of fascinating interest was going to happen to him in the Philippines; he could be sure of that. If anything happened in the Philippines that would add cubits to his military stature, all the credit would promptly be taken by his chief, the imperious MacArthur.

For Dwight Eisenhower the assignment to duty in the Philippines came in mid-career, and it was cause for reflection. In his mind's eye he might have gone back over the years to his birth in Denison, Texas, October 14, 1890, to his

The senior class of Abilene High,
1909. Dwight Eisenhower is top
row left.

Mr. and Mrs. David Eisenhower
and three of the boys, c. 1909. L.
to r., Earl, Dwight, Milton; at
bottom, Ike's dog "Flip."

Lt. Eisenhower with Mamie in.
San Antonio, Texas, 1916.

Doud Dwight (Icky) Eisenhower
was born early in 1918 and died
of scarlet fever at Christmastime
1920. His death was probably the
most tragic occurrence in
Eisenhower's life.

With John and Mamie in
Washington, D.C., during the
MacArthur era, c. 1934–35.

Panama, with John, c. 1924.

upbringing in the cow town of Abilene, Kansas, at the turn of the century, where his parents worked hard to find the wherewithal to bring up their six sons, of whom Dwight was the third. It had been the difficulty of going to college, short of government support, that had driven the young Dwight to apply to West Point, and he was grateful for the opportunity. His luck momentarily held when he graduated in 1915, for two years later the United States entered the First World War. But then his luck changed and he never got out of the country. His classmates and many of the older graduates of the Point went to France to lead the big square divisions of twenty-eight thousand men, the divisions so much in need of officers with any kind of training; some of these graduates of the academy were killed, but most of them came back—and not a few of them were cited for bravery under fire. The war distributed increased rank to academy graduates, young and old, those who went to the war in Europe and those who stayed home; Eisenhower obtained the rank of lieutenant colonel by training tank troops at Camp Meade in Maryland and at Camp Colt in the middle of Pennsylvania. Then his rank, like that of his friends and acquaintances, was lost with the armistice and peace, and he reverted to captain, rose back again to major, and held the latter rank for sixteen years.

In the 1920s and early 1930s the opportunity to get ahead did not seem to be present in the United States Army, and many of the best men left—men like Robert E. Wood, who reached the rank of brigadier general in the wartime army and would have reverted to major; he preferred to go into civilian life and head Sears, Roebuck in Chicago. Eisenhower stayed on, for not having had the chance to rise high he could not have fallen far.

In the early 1920s he was posted to Panama, where he began to learn many of the lessons he should have been taught at West Point, lessons that were taught to him by General Conner, one of the most remarkable officers ever to grace the ranks of the United States Army. Conner was Pershing's righthand man at Chaumont, and then the coming of peace brought an end to his opportunities; by the time of the Second World War he was too old for leadership. He did, however, indoctrinate young Dwight Eisenhower in 1922–1924 during Dwight's service in Panama, and got Eisenhower back to reading—he had read omnivorously in high school but did little thereafter, especially at West Point. Under Conner's careful tutelage he read U.S. Grant's memoirs and the memoirs of the other Civil War greats, such as W.T. Sherman, and he read the literature of warfare that had arisen in Europe. In this way Conner educated him to future leadership. When, at Conner's urging, Dwight Eisenhower went to the Command and General Staff School at Fort Leavenworth, Kansas, in the mid-1920s, he came out first in his class, and did so easily, for Conner had taught him all that he needed to know.

Despite the sponsorship of Fox Conner, young Eisenhower had to wait his turn in the peacetime army, and that turn had not yet come by the year 1935, when he was posted to Manila with MacArthur. Indeed it seemed as if he was moving into a dead end. After duty at various tasks in the latter 1920s he had been picked by MacArthur as special assistant in 1932, after MacArthur became army chief *of staff, and that had seemed a plus. The minus came when the general wore out his welcome with President Franklin D. Roosevelt, who sent MacArthur out to survey the military needs of the Philippine commonwealth, in anticipation of the commonwealth's full independence in 1946; once MacArthur got to Manila, the president arranged for him to stay there—a suitable distance for the man whom Roosevelt privately had denominated one of the two most dangerous men in the United States, the other being Senator Huey Long, who was felled by an assassin's bullet the same year that MacArthur went to the Philippines. By accompanying MacArthur, Eisenhower was entering upon a duty that was not looked upon in a friendly way by the Roosevelt administration, glad to get MacArthur out of the country. And the United States Army's leaders after MacArthur were just as pleased as President Roosevelt to get MacArthur a good distance away from the State, War and Navy Building in Washington. During MacArthur's years as chief of staff it was said that he had disliked the so-called Chaumont crowd, the officers such as Fox Conner who had helped Pershing create the forty-two full divisions of the AEF. MacArthur had given the impression that Pershing's friends had had too much leeway in the United States Army after the end of the World War in 1918, and hence that he was unfriendly to the Chaumont officers. They in turn reciprocated what seemed to be his dislike. By going to Manila with him, Eisenhower was in danger of isolating himself from his friends at home. He was tying his kite to an officer whose career was finished.*

Such thoughts surely crossed the mind of Dwight D. Eisenhower as the throb of engines aboard his ship took him the long eight thousand miles out to the Philippine Islands. Hawaii was three thousand miles off the West Coast, and that was far enough, but the Philippines were a continent away—they were, practically speaking, an appendage of Asia. It was symbolic of their distance that everyone going to the Philippines in those days took ship first to one of the great ports of Japan, and then transshipped to the Islands. The backwater of the Philippines was a considerable distance even from Japan.

There is something about the army that says that whatever the problems, the hardships, one must do his duty, and it was a tight-lipped Eisenhower who faced up to his duty on December 27, 1935, when he made the first entry in his Philippine diary.

1935

DECEMBER 27, 1935

The first entry in this book is made as of December 27, 1935. The military mission, headed by General MacArthur, landed in Manila two months ago, on October 26. It has been the intention from the start to keep a brief narrative record of the principal recommendations and activities of the mission. Due to unsettled conditions, there has been, up to this time, no opportunity to make a methodical record of events. The first installment, therefore, is intended to summarize briefly the outstanding incidents of the past two months, with the intention that hereafter this journal will represent a daily running account of the mission's activities.

The group is so organized that the detailed work connected with the development of the Philippine defense plan falls principally upon Major James B. Ord (in this narrative referred to as "Jimmy") and myself.[1] Captain T.J. Davis serves as General MacArthur's aide, is the administrative officer for the whole group, and is in charge of such matters as motor transportation, clerical assistance, normal administrative contacts with the Philippine department, and so on.[2] Major Howard J. Hutter, medical corps, is specifically charged with the development of a sanitary plan for the Philippine army and in addition serves as personal physician for the group.

General MacArthur is the head of the mission and is officially designated as the military adviser to the Philippine government. He directs policy and, except

The military mission landed in Manila in October 1935.

in matters of detail, does all the contact work with the president of the common-wealth.

The principal features of the Philippine defense plan were developed in Washington, beginning about the first of November, 1934. General MacArthur announced that the defense system should be based primarily upon universal conscription and should be so devised as to require the minimum of expenditure. He gave as the basic mission of the plan the development of a defensive force that would assure maximum local protection in every island, district, and province of this country.

Specifically, he recognized, from the beginning, the impossibility of developing a defensive force in the Philippines capable of concentrating its full potential power at any threatened point of attack. In other words, from a strategic viewpoint, a cordon system of defense was practically forced upon the islands due to the impracticability of developing naval forces to preserve inter-island communications against any powerful attack by water. The objective, then, of the defense plan is to ensure such an excellent defense of each portion of Philippine territory that the cost of its subjugation would exceed the potential rewards accruing to any aggressor.

Manifestly, such a system cannot protect any island nation against the consequences of a blockade by sea. However, it represents the ultimate that a small and relatively poor nation can hope to accomplish and at the very minimum gives to such a nation the hope that through preservation of territorial integrity it may, in the event of prolonged blockade, acquire powerful allies before the moment of final starvation arrives.[3]

In addition, the plan contemplates the development of an air corps, the threat of which will be sufficient to keep major portions of a hostile navy completely outside these territorial waters.[4]

Based upon these conceptions, the details of the original plan were worked out by Ord. He had intermittent assistance from personnel in the War College, where he was then on duty, and kept in close contact with General MacArthur and with myself.

It included tables of administrative and tactical organization; progress charts showing in detail the anticipated growth of the new army; and maps showing the location of each unit to be raised. It included also drafts of laws prescribing the army's basic organization and methods for registering and inducting trainees into the army; establishing a system of military instruction in public schools; and appropriating necessary funds for the development.

Cost estimates were prepared on the following basis: Ord first prepared a plan based upon maximum practicable results, taking into consideration only such elements as population strength and local geographical and climatic conditions, with only a secondary purpose of minimizing expense.

General MacArthur then directed Ord to revamp the plan with the idea of attaining the same results so far as ultimate strength in personnel was concerned but making cost the predominating factor otherwise.[5] On this basis, Ord and I worked for some time. We cut the period of training; cut down on pay and allowances; eliminated particularly costly elements of the army, and substituted conscripts for professional wherever we considered it safe to do so. We retained as the minimum strength of the professional force 1,500 officers and 19,000 enlisted men. On this basis we arrived at a minimum yearly estimate of 22 million pesos.[6] The general then decided that this figure must be cut to 16 million pesos, still without reducing the total number of trained men finally to be incorporated into the army. We reduced the regular force to 930 officers and about 7,000 enlisted men, substituting for the enlisted men so eliminated an equal number of conscripts that are to be retained in the service one year; we extended the munitions procurement program to attain fruition in twenty instead of ten years, made important deferments in the development of an artillery corps, and so on. While Ord and I expressed the conviction that with this kind of organization it would be difficult to sustain efficiency because of the lack of professional personnel, it was the basis adopted because of the savings represented. The cost estimates were thus reduced to 16 million pesos annually.

We landed in the Philippines with the various portions of the defense plan prepared as completely as was possible before gaining an intimate knowledge of local conditions. Among other things, we had written for the president a long explanatory address, intended for delivery to the national assembly upon submission to that body of the plan. This speech was delivered by Mr. Quezon about November 22.[7] The language of the address committed the president to enthusiastic support of the basic features of the plan.

Before landing, General MacArthur was very hopeful that the proposed bills we had prepared would be accepted practically as written and could be enacted into law no later than November 20, that is, within a very few days of the inauguration of the commonwealth government. It soon became evident that the bill would have to be rewritten insofar as arrangement and much of its language was concerned. Its basic provisions were, however, retained intact; that is to say, universal service, a stabilized budget of 16 million pesos, and the proposed scheme of organization were fully accepted by the president and the assembly. A series of conferences, beginning even before November 15, were held with officials of the insular government and, later, with the national defense committee of the assembly. The bulk of this contact work fell upon Ord. The plan, somewhat revised as to detail, was finally approved on December 21, 1935.

A question arising soon after our arrival was that of devising a practicable method whereby Philippine Scout officers could be incorporated into the new army.[8] Many factors were involved and these became the subject of frequent conferences between Ord, myself, and individual Scout officers. To date (January 1, 1936) the question has not been completely and satisfactorily settled.[9]

Soon after our arrival also, General MacArthur announced his intention to secure the appointment of Colonel Paulino Santos as the chief of staff and of Brigadier General Valdez as deputy chief of staff. We based all plans and conferences on this understanding until about December 28, 1935, when we received information that this arrangement might prove unacceptable to the president. For political, personal, or other reasons the tentative slate on which we are now working is to appoint José de los Reyes as brigadier general and acting chief of staff and Colonel Santos, General Valdez, and Colonel Francisco as his immediate assistants. No formal appointments to this effect have as yet been made.[10]

Another question requiring much study was that of planning for the organization of the regular division, provided for in the Basic Defense Act. Originally we had hoped to locate this unit as a well-concentrated force in the island of Luzon. For two reasons we were forced to abandon this idea temporarily. The first reason involved the lack of quarters and other accommodations in the island of Luzon. The second was the necessity for supporting constabulary elements in other sections of the Philippines, where existing units must be substantially reduced in order to form the nuclei of the new army. Tentatively, therefore, we propose to organize one regiment at Camp Murphy, just outside of Manila; one at Camp Keithly in Mindanao; and one in the island of Cebu.

We have had many conferences concerning such subjects as the preparation of a suitable building for the central general staff and other elements of a war department; the pushing of construction at Camp Murphy to establish a satisfactory flying field and providing quarters for a considerable body of troops; the selection of officers to fill key positions in the war department and tactical units; and the procurement of armament, particularly rifles, with which to equip new units as they are formed. In this connection, we are very hopeful that the United States government will agree to sell to us, at a nominal price, three hundred thousand of the Enfield rifles left over from the World War. A radio request to this effect has been submitted to the war department.

To sum up: The first of the year, 1936, finds us with less definite accomplishment to our credit than we had hoped to attain by this time, when we landed more than two months ago. The Philippine war department is not yet organized, and responsible officials have not been set up to undertake the many planning, administrative, and organizational tasks with which the commonwealth army is faced. Necessary proclamations have not been drawn up, regulations have not been prepared, and, under present conditions, it is even impracticable to use any of the money that has been appropriated for the development and maintenance of the army.

On the other hand, the mission itself has become better acquainted with local conditions and personalities and is much better prepared to go ahead with the work, once the various developments indicated above can be initiated. Since the first registration of manpower is scheduled to take place in early April, these many problems must soon be solved or the schedule of development contemplated in the law and in the plan will require drastic revision.

We—at least Jimmy and myself—have learned to expect from the Filipinos with whom we deal a minimum of performance from a maximum of promise. Among individuals there is no lack of intelligence, but to us they seem, with few exceptions, unaccustomed to the requirements of administrative and executive procedure. When any detail is under discussion, they seem to grasp the essentials of the problem and readily agree to undertake accomplishment of whatever decision may be arrived at in conference. But thereafter it is quite likely that nothing whatsoever will be done. Moreover, it often develops that the decision itself has not really been accepted by them, even though at the time they appeared to be in full agreement. The whole matter must then be gone over again. These peculiar traits we are learning to take into account, but obviously they impede progress.

Jimmy and I have worked a great deal with General Valdez and Colonel Santos. With the possible exception of the president, they are the two most able executives we have met here. We earnestly hope they both will accept positions in the army headquarters.

We have prepared a succession of slates for the important subordinate positions in the war department. Each one so prepared was supposed, at the time, to make the best possible use of available personnel and to conform to the ideas and desires of the president. Each, in turn, has proven unsatisfactory. This must be settled soon. . . . staff.[11] It is around this nucleus we are attempting to develop and organize a general staff.)

The development of rules and regulations to govern the new army as well as to establish the processes of registration and induction into the service has been turned over to the staff for study. This is a matter of primary importance, and considerable progress has been made on it. Forms for registration cards, military register, and general instructions to registering officers have been approved by this office, and proof copies have already been printed. The president has issued a proclamation directing the registration of young men of military age during April, but there have as yet been no effective steps taken to organize the administrative machinery to accomplish registration. This must be done within the next few weeks or the registration in April will be a failure.

1936

The year 1936 proved to be a signal, indeed crucial, year in the coming of the Second World War, for this was the year when the new leader of Germany not merely violated the Treaty of Versailles in an open way—he had done this with the collusion of the British government in 1935 when the British signed a naval agreement allowing the Germans warships not permitted under the treaty—but violated it in a manner that ensured his strategic control of both Western and Eastern Europe. In the retrospect of later years, especially France's abject defeat by Germany in 1940, it is clear that the occupation of the Rhineland by German troops in 1936, contrary to the Treaty of Versailles, separated France from her eastern allies, namely, Czechoslovakia, Rumania, and Yugoslavia, allowing the German government to take on the Austrians and Czechoslovaks piecemeal in 1938 and so endangering European peace that the British and French had to go to war the next year.

The untoward developments in Europe were virtually lost upon the man who was to preside over Germany's defeat in 1944–1945, as he struggled to find some sort of formula by which the Philippine commonwealth's leaders might convince themselves that they were arranging a defense of their country. The American mission had an enormous task, since the Philippine government had neither the will nor the means to defend itself. Always in the background, perhaps, was the thought that the Pacific fleet would come booming out from Pearl Harbor, and an army contingent would appear from the United States—much as Commodore Dewey in 1898 had arrived from Mirs Bay, while Major General Wesley Merritt brought eleven thousand troops out from the West Coast. The task of the 1930s, as Eisenhower knew full well, was vastly different, for the Japanese were hardly to be considered in the same breath with the inept Spanish of over a generation before. Dewey's little flotilla had no competition in 1898; the opposing Spanish squadron anchored in shallow water, so that when Dewey's guns sank the ships they did not have to go down very far. Merritt's troops had little more than their side arms and a few artillery pieces, and when they arrived they persuaded the Spanish to arrange a mock defense of Manila, to protect Spanish honor, and then the war was over. Still it was possible that if some kind of local defense plan was put together that was acceptable to the Filipino leadership, and if the people of the Philippines began to see the importance of their own defense, something more effective could be produced. And one had to start somewhere.

Begin at the beginning—so said one of the rules in the race held in Alice in Wonderland. *In the year 1936 the beginning was rifles—Enfields left over from the World War.*

JANUARY 20, 1936

At this moment the mission is engaged principally with questions that have arisen out of our request to the American government to furnish the Philippine army with Enfield rifles at nominal cost. Knowing that this item of equipment is considered an obsolescent one in the American army, we supposed, at the time the request was submitted, that the only question that would arise would be one involving unit cost. Actually, when the request was received in Washington, it was apparently looked upon as one involving major policy and was referred to the president for decision. We are at a loss to determine exactly what the question of policy may be, whether it involves domestic politics or whether it is supposed to have somewhat of an international tinge. For example, the president may be concerned as to the effect upon the pacifistic group in the United States of announcing a decision to furnish considerable quantities of arms to the Philippine commonwealth. Again, it may be that he has some fear of disaffection among important groups in the islands and would look upon a distribution of arms throughout the various provinces as an opportunity for these groups to revolt against the central government. It has even been suggested that the Filipinos as a nation would in a crisis turn against the United States, and we would have the spectacle of a people who had been armed and equipped by American effort and largely at American expense becoming an active opponent of the United States. It has been suggested also that the administration at home might fear the effect upon American relationships with Japan should our government show real determination to assist the Filipinos in becoming relatively strong defensively in this region. Finally, there is the possibility that with arms embargo and neutrality legislation attracting so much congressional attention, the announcement of the sale of obsolete arms to the Philippine government might be construed as a flagrant violation of the spirit of congressional intent.[1]

All these questions, upon analysis, fail to furnish any satisfactory explanation of what seems to us to be a shortsighted policy on the part of the administration. The matter is purely a domestic one, involving relationships between the United States and one of its own political subdivisions. It conforms entirely to the announced policy of making the Filipino capable of independent government within ten years. It does not concern the munition industry in the United States since the items requested are now in storage and are, generally speaking, useless for future American use. Whether or not disaffection in the islands will finally grow to a point where a major revolt might take place is a question that should have been settled before the passage of the Tydings-McDuffie Act. It is too late now to consider such a possibility as a decisive factor in preventing the Filipino people from arming themselves in accordance with a sound and economical plan for defending their future independence.

Regardless, however, of the motives actuating Washington, or of the soundness of our own views in the matter, the pertinent fact is that the question has been referred to the high commissioner by the president, and the general has been instructed to confer with the commissioner as to the necessity for the amounts of munitions requested in our telegrams to the war department.[2] The high commissioner is, of course, a politician—not a soldier. His views as to the political and international aspects in the matter will be particularly valuable to the president, as also his conclusions as to the danger of general revolt of the Filipinos against constituted authority. However, when it comes to the question of the number of rifles and automatic rifles furnished to the army, there seems to be no reason for making the high commissioner the arbiter in the matter.

In this situation, we can only do our best to secure some favorable expression of opinion out of the high commissioner and hope that the language of his report to Washington will be such as to secure substantial approval of the proposition we have already submitted. At the minimum, if we are successful in obtaining some forty or fifty thousand rifles during the current calendar year, there is no reason to despair as to ultimate success. There may be a change of administration after next November and in any event, even if the present administration is reelected, there may be a definite change in attitude toward this matter. We must never forget that every question is settled in Washington today on the basis of getting votes next November. To decide this matter completely in our favor would gain no votes, while to disapprove the request and give the matter some publicity might be considered as a vote-getting proposition among the pacifists and other misguided elements of the American electorate.[3]

Our attitude now should be that we have given our best professional advice on the subject and that, no matter what decision is rendered, we stand ready to make the best of it for the time being. If need arises, the general can always find reasonable excuse for going to Washington and attempting through personal persuasion to straighten the matter out and secure the announcement of a definite and favorable policy in this regard.

FEBRUARY 6, 1936

Authority was finally received from Washington to purchase one hundred thousand Enfield rifles during the current year, with a statement of policy to the effect that in the absence of drastic change in the general situation an additional three hundred thousand rifles could be made available to this government over a period of eight years. This decision was undoubtedly influenced by the cable report submitted by the high commissioner to the war department. We held several conferences with the high commissioner and with members of the staff, and his office became convinced that our request was entirely reasonable. The only real disappointment for us in the decision rendered by Washington was the price fixed for the Enfield rifles. We had hoped to obtain them at a price of about eight pesos laid down in Manila. Actually they will cost us about eighteen pesos. Even so, the saving represented is a very considerable one when compared to the price of the Springfield, which is approximately sixty-five pesos each, delivered in Manila. The mechanical difference between the two rifles is far too small to justify any such differences in price.

We have encountered many difficulties already, mainly occasioned by an almost total lack of administrative ability in the higher officials of the government and of the army. From the president down, each official seems to act individually and on the spur of the moment with respect to any detail in which he is interested and without regard for possible effects upon other activities or upon the army as a whole. Moreover, the orders given by the president at the time he installed General Reyes as acting chief of staff, and General Valdez as his principal assistant, have caused additional trouble. Those instructions required General Reyes to act as provost marshal general and to supervise only in a most general way the processes of organizing the Philippine army. In actual practice, however, General Reyes has issued specific orders involving assignment and reassignment of personnel, which practice has at times rather badly handicapped current work. General Valdez has been resentful and even went so far as to report one incident to General MacArthur. The president, during a visit to the military academy at Baguio, issued such sharp reprimands to the faculty, in the presence of the student body, there was no other recourse than to replace the superintendent and all his assistants, since, under the circumstances, their usefulness in that school was obviously ended. This morning, February 6, we have word that the president has, in company with the chief of staff, gone to southern Luzon with the idea of establishing an entirely new site for the military academy. We have no idea as to the reason for this move nor what the result will be, but the fact remains that if any major construction project of this kind is undertaken with the funds now available, all other building will have to stop. This will be a calamity.[1]

Jimmy and I still stick to the conclusion we formed as long ago as early November, last year, which is that Colonel Santos is the only logical person to serve as chief of staff of the Philippine army. He understands organization and the necessity for systematic procedure in handling an army. He appears to us to be essentially an energetic worker who has a sound, logical head and who always keeps the main objective in view. General MacArthur agrees with this conclusion but appreciates also that the time is not yet ripe when a change of the kind indicated can be insistently urged upon the president.

I have recently completed a speech for the president to be delivered before the faculty and students of the Philippine University. The draft was accepted by the president and upon delivery of the speech the plan is to distribute copies to every unit in the public school system of the islands. Its purpose is educational and was written in the hope that through its wide distribution a better understanding of the defense plan and of the duties and obligations of private citizens will obtain. I am now engaged in writing a talk along similar lines to be given before the teachers' convention in Baguio in March or April.

Jimmy is principally engaged in assisting Colonel Aguilar and Colonel Francisco in the development of studies and plans applying to procurement, financing, preparation and revision of regulations, construction, and final distribution of available troops.

FEBRUARY 15, 1936

Recently a subject that has been much discussed among members of the mission is the advisability of accepting higher rank for each of us under the provisions of the National Defense Act. To any such thought I have been unalterably opposed from the start and have, in fact, gone so far as to inform the general that I personally would decline at this time to accept any such appointment from the Philippine army in the event it were tendered to me. Although in one of the early discussions of this matter Captain Davis informed the general, in my presence, that his action in the matter would be governed by the general's personal desire, he has since then swung around definitely to my view of the matter and now stands with me in direct opposition to the proposal. Jimmy also, though in somewhat less positive fashion, stands with Captain Davis and myself.[1]

The principal reasons for our opposition are two. In the first place, we believe that in a locality where we are serving with so many American officers, most of whom believe that the attempt to create a Philippine army is somewhat ridiculous, the acceptance by us of high rank in an army which is not yet formed would serve to belittle our effort. Moreover, it would seriously handicap every effort on our part to secure necessary cooperation from commanders and staffs in the American army. Secondly, we believe that in dealing with Philippine army headquarters our position is unassailable as long as we purport to be nothing but assistants to the military adviser. If, however, we should accept military titles in the Philippine army, the authority and soundness of our advice would be measured, in the minds of Philippine army officers, by the rank held. We believe this would create an anomalous situation and would handicap our efforts to assist, advise, and direct the efforts of army headquarters and subordinate officials.

Captain Davis and I have in addition strongly advised General MacArthur to decline, for the present, the acceptance of the title tendered him as field marshal.

Recently Jimmy and I have been urging upon General MacArthur the advisability of his making an early trip to Washington. It is becoming more and more evident that there is no basic appreciation in the War Department of the local defense problem, at least as we see it. The Tydings-McDuffie Act so clearly contemplates the employment of the Philippine army by the president of the United States, in the event of a national emergency, that we believe the American war department could make a definite effort to develop the strength and efficiency of this military adjunct. For the next ten years complete responsibility for Philippine defense resides in the American government, and since weakness in the local defenses would involve extreme embarrassment in the event of war, it seems to us to be the part of wisdom for the American government to take positive and appropriate action in the matter. Specifically, we believe that the local reserves of the American army in weapons and ammunition should be substantially increased and the stocks so accumulated should be made available for the training of the Philippine army. We believe such a policy should apply particularly with respect to those weapons in the possession of the American army that are becoming obsolescent from the viewpoint of the American army. In this category are such things as Enfield rifles, hand weapons of the revolver type, Lewis machine guns, infantry mortars, and British-type 75-mm. guns.[2] Jimmy and I believe that if this whole matter were clearly explained to the American chief of staff and secretary of war, very substantial and effective assistance would be forthcoming. Such assistance would not involve any weakening of the United States defenses at home, would materially strengthen them in this outpost, and would not involve any straining of international relationships. In addition to the reasons given above for the making of a personal visit to Washington by General MacArthur is the fact that department headquarters has shown a disposition to question the legality and propriety of the letter of September 18, written by the acting secretary of war to department headquarters. That letter directs the department commander to cooperate with the military adviser in every possible way to insure the rapid development of the Philippine army. Under it the department commander is authorized to use personnel and property to accomplish this end, and if the legality of the order is to be called into question, it is highly necessary that the whole subject be completely clarified in Washington.

All these views have been presented to General MacArthur, but he has stated that he has no intention of going to Washington before the late fall of this year.

MARCH 1, 1936

General MacArthur has been considering the various reasons advanced by Jimmy and myself in urging him to go to Washington at an early date. In lieu of such a visit, he has determined to have prepared a rather exhaustive treatise on the whole subject of the Philippine army. While the document is to be labeled a report, it will actually constitute a comprehensive argument to support the efficiency and soundness of the Philippine defense plan and the idea that the American war department should cooperate efficiently toward its development. I have been assigned the duty of preparing this paper.

In the following entry a note of exasperation creeps into the diary. The reader has the impression that Eisenhower had begun the diary as a semi-official account, a headquarters diary such as was standard operating procedure during the World War of 1917–1918; in such a diary the aide's task was to write it up and thereby register, for any future need, the progress of affairs and the possible remedies if things were going wrongly; the diarist, being an aide, had to be careful in his appraisals, as who would know when the general might ask to see some prose? One can guess that in the case of Ike's Philippine diary he already had gone off the deep end by referring to undiplomatic issues and the opinions thereon of himself and his friends Jimmy and TJ. By the time of the following entry he may have decided that, well, to hell with diplomacy, he'd never show the diary to the general. And if he did not make such a decision in the pages that immediately follow, he made it within a few hours thereafter.

MAY 29, 1936

Registration was carried out during the month of April, and the total number registering was considerably in excess of our original estimate. Jimmy and I are quite doubtful, however, that all of the 150,000 who registered are actually twenty years old this year. We are inclined to the belief that many men both younger and older than this entered their names on the rolls. Only future registrations can establish the accuracy of this estimate.

As a result of the large registration General MacArthur has quite suddenly decided to make a material change in the plan for the year 1937. He has decided to take in the full quota of forty thousand conscripts during the year instead of the total of six thousand contemplated under the original plan. This decision, of course, tremendously increases the estimated outlays for immediate construction and procurement of supplies. Its general effect is to increase, during the next four years, our training program by approximately ninety-four thousand individuals. Disregarding entirely the cost of arms and ammunition for these men after they have been trained, the additional training and maintenance cost involved will be about ten million pesos. In other words, a ten-million-peso additional cost has been placed upon the ten-year plan while no additional revenues have been provided. Another acute embarrassment arises from the fact that we have no money whatsoever immediately available for construction. Before January 1, 1937, we must have selected something over 125 sites for training cadres, erected the necessary buildings, and procured the additional amounts of supplies that will be required. Since sums for all these things were not included in the 1936 budget, there is nothing to do but to await the meeting of the national assembly in June and secure from them the necessary authorization to go ahead. Other new problems created by this decision are those of providing and training instructional staffs for training cadres and of establishing an expanded overhead to take care of administration and maintenance.

The purpose of increasing the number of men to be trained in 1937 had been previously advanced by General MacArthur, who at first thought this could be accomplished through the American army. As early as January we initiated detailed conferences with the department staff in an effort to have officers and enlisted men in considerable numbers trained in 1937 at the various army posts. General MacArthur was of the opinion that as many as fifteen thousand could be trained during the year under a suitable arrangement. After exhaustive study of the proposition by the department staff it was found that a very complicated administrative arrangement would be involved, that the number possible to be trained would be limited to some five or six hundred enlisted men, and that the per capita cost would be high. For these reasons General MacArthur advised the department commander that the proposal would be dropped. In lieu of that plan it was requested that a considerable number of Philippine Scout enlisted men be detailed for duty under the direction of the military adviser. It was recommended that they serve as instructors in training cadres. This request was approved in principle, and plans are now developing to train, in our own stations, forty thousand men in 1937, beginning with the first contingent of twenty thousand on January 1.

The matter of higher organization in the Philippine army was finally brought to a head upon the insistence of Jimmy and myself in early May. The president finally accepted the slate as recommended by General MacArthur and issued the necessary orders to appoint Santos, Valdez, and De los Reyes as major generals and Francisco as a brigadier general. This was a slight change from our recommendations as we did not contemplate the promotion of De los Reyes. Santos is now serving as chief of staff.

In the long negotiations with Philippine Scout officers a definite plan was evolved in early April setting forth the various conditions under which a scout officer might serve with the Philippine army. Several acceptable sets of conditions were developed and stated as follows: (1) Any native-born officer of the Philippine Scouts electing to retire from the American army would be tendered a commission by the president of the Philippines on the day of his retirement (radiograms received from the War Department state that a retired Philippine Scout officer who accepts a commission in the Philippine army could continue to draw retired pay from the American government as long as the commonwealth status of government exists. After termination of the commonwealth form of government, the individual, under existing law, will either surrender his retired status in the American army or his commission in the Philippine army). (2) Any Philippine Scout officer who desires to remain for some time in the American army in order to acquire retirement privileges may either remain on duty with the American army or may take a detail with the Philippine army pending his retirement. (3) Any officer resigning from the American army will be immediately commissioned in the Philippine army.

In all these cases it is understood that no additional compensation is to be paid such officers from the military appropriation of the commonwealth, no officer is to be detailed for duty with the Philippine army except with his own consent, and each is to be informed prior to his retirement of the exact place on the Philippine promotion list that he will occupy. In addition, General MacArthur stated that officers of this group accepting commissions in the Philippine army would be credited for pay purposes with the amount of service each has to his credit in the American army, but that his retirement credit will begin from the moment he accepts his commission in the Philippine army. In this last connection, the general has agreed to support legislation to the effect that whenever any officer of this group should lose his retired status in the American army because of his commission in the Philippine army he will then be credited for retirement purposes from the Philippine army with all service performed in both organizations.

MAY 29, 1936 (SECOND ENTRY)

Jim and I undertook to get the general to modify his order to call twenty thousand men next January. We insisted further than the general thought we should, and he gave us one of his regular shouting tirades. He seemed particularly bitter toward me. Jim knows the objections as well as I. We cannot possibly get the money for some time yet. We cannot select each site carefully and provide proper technical supervision for each construction project. There are 128 of them. Each needs water, roads, lights, drainage, etc., etc. Camp Murphy, plus about ten well-selected sites, should be all that we try to develop this year. We have no officer corps to supervise organization on such a scale, and officers cannot be produced out of thin air. We have no comprehensive supply system, and we've not yet had a chance to develop the overhead that can absorb, train, segregate, organize, and maintain reserve units. I argue these points with more heat and persistency than does Jim—consequently I come in for the more severe criticism.

We've tried also, time and again, to get the general to stay in closer contact with Q [Quezon]. Things happen, and we know nothing of them. We're constantly wondering whether the president will approve or disapprove. We ought to know. We could if the general would take the trouble to see Q weekly—but he apparently thinks it would not be in keeping with his rank and position for him to do so.

JULY 1, 1936

The report of the military adviser already referred to in this diary was published in June. It obtained considerable space in the local press and quite a good bit of favorable comment. Simultaneously with its submission to the national assembly, the president also designated General MacArthur as a field marshal in the local army. The question of local rank for General MacArthur's assistants was happily not again brought up, and we sincerely hope that the action in the case of the general will not create any unfavorable impression. By this time the general himself had become very reluctant to accept the title, although originally, of course, he was very determined to do so. He feels now, however, that he could not decline it without offense to the president. Anyway he is tickled pink—and feels he's made a lot of "face" locally.

In this situation we have sent urgent messages to the American War Department recommending that the reserve stocks of the Philippine department be materially increased by the addition of Enfield rifles, Lewis machine guns, Stokes mortars, and British-model 75-mm. field cannon. From the standpoint of the American army all this equipment is obsolete or obsolescent. If the War Department agrees to this suggestion (which recommendation has been strongly supported by the department commander), we will undertake to revise the armament plans for the whole Philippine army so as to take advantage of the availability of this materiel. In this way more money would be available for the purchase of ammunition both for training and reserve purposes.

Recently some adverse comment in the newspapers has disturbed General MacArthur very considerably. Jimmy, TJ, and myself have not taken these items very seriously and have constantly recommended against any attempt to answer them. The general, however, has taken an opposite view, believing that by circulating favorable publicity we can neutralize criticism directed against the soundness and efficiency of the defense plan. In line with this, we prepared one rather lengthy document which was released as an address by General MacArthur and sent it to the states. It was also released locally. The general has also made one or two shorter statements which he has furnished to the local press.

Recently a report appeared in the papers that the Appropriation Committee of the assembly was investigating alleged corruption in the purchase of army supplies. The chief of staff promptly appeared before the committee with a complete analysis of all army purchases so far made; he fully satisfied the committee that army headquarters had been guilty of nothing irregular or illegal in the procurement of supplies—on the contrary, had been very solicitous in protecting the interests of the government. While we do not know what inspired the chairman of the committee to initiate the investigation or to make any statement concerning it, it would appear from surface indications that his actions were governed by nothing else than ignorance and stupidity and possibly some hope for publicity. Jimmy studied the reports rendered by army headquarters and is convinced that the supply division is operating efficiently and properly.

SEPTEMBER 26, 1936

TJ and I came in for a terrible bawling out over a most ridiculous affair. The general has been following the *Literary Digest* poll and has convinced himself that Landon is to be elected, probably by a landslide. I showed him letters from

Arthur Hurd,[1] which predict that Landon cannot even carry Kansas, but he got perfectly furious when TJ and I counseled caution in studying the *Digest* report. I don't believe it reaches the great mass of people who will vote for the incumbent. We couldn't understand the reason for his almost hysterical condemnation of our stupidity until he suddenly let drop that he had gone out and urged Q to shape his plans for going to the United States on the theory that Landon will be elected. Possibly he will. I don't know. But I hear the general is trying to bet several thousand pesos on it. He'll look fine, both here and at home, if his calculations, based on his ravings about "least squares" and the accuracy of the *Digest* figures as a proper index, are proved unfounded. But why should he get sore just because we say, "Don't be so d--- certain and go out on a limb unnecessarily." Both of us are "fearful and small-minded people who are afraid to express judgments that are obvious from the evidence at hand." Oh hell.

NOVEMBER 15, 1936

Boy, did the general backpedal rapidly. I hear he walked out to Q on the first or second and "took back" what he had said at first. Accused the *Literary Digest* of "crookedness" when he heard Wall Street odds had gone up to 4–1 on Roosevelt against Landon. Now he's scared Roy Howard will *"tell on him"* in Washington, for his former views were well advertised by H. But he's never expressed to TJ or to me any regret for his awful bawling out of a couple of months ago.[1]

1937

The year 1937 was not a time of obvious change in Europe but it indeed was so in the Far East, and whatever Eisenhower missed in observing the changing international scene during the preceding year he caught up close at hand in the new. For this was the time when the Japanese government, having taken the opportunity to seize Manchuria during the so-called Manchurian incident of 1931–1933, decided to go farther and take over all of China. Perhaps the decision was not immediate, for the incident that broke out on July 7 at the Marco Polo Bridge near Peking may have had its origins in a scuffle rather than a plan. Once the action began it quickly enlarged, and in subsequent months the Japanese army attacked the major coastal cities such as Shanghai and Tientsin and occupied them, with large loss of life to the Chinese. At the end of the year, on December 12, Japanese planes attacked the American river gunboat Panay, obviously a foreign warship flying the American flag, and sank the Panay in the Yangtze, with loss of two men killed and thirty wounded. Two days later the United States government demanded apology, reparations, and guarantees, and the Japanese rushed to comply. On Christmas Day, Secretary of State Cordell

Hull announced this favorable response, and the incident—that is, the American incident—was closed. The China incident was not, and in the months after the Marco Polo Bridge affair the Japanese occupied large sections of China in a war that, once begun, lasted on until August 1945.

Always in the background was the possibility of more German action in Europe, which came the next year, 1938. In the year 1937, the annus terribilis for the government of Chiang Kai-shek, which was quickly driven to the inland city of Chungking, about all that was visible was the danger of Far Eastern aggression.

Lieutenant Colonel Eisenhower (he had been promoted in 1936) and his chief MacArthur realized the approach of danger and did what they could to ensure against its spreading to the Philippines. But the old debates about the size of the Philippine army, its cost, and the business of finding new places for cantonments and then putting up the buildings preoccupied the Americans. Always present was what a governor general of the 1920s, later a secretary of state, Henry L. Stimson, had described as the Malay tendency to backslide. Never could Eisenhower and MacArthur be sure that a program once started would go forward rather than backward.

JANUARY 23 – MAY 30, 1937

General MacA, with TJ and H, accompanied Q to states in spring of 1937.[1] They were absent about four months, during which time we simply carried on plans and policies previously laid down by MacA.

JUNE 21, 1937

General MacA decided the budget must be revised to provide sufficient money for mobilization equipment for complete class of 1936 and first half of 1937. This means a total (average of various estimates) of approximately 4,500,000 pesos, whereas budget, as at present constituted, sets up only 1,150,000 for this purpose. Mobilization equipment, according to General MacA, must take precedence over all other charges except those that are fixed, such as pay of personnel. He said that to fail to do this was to defeat his whole plan.

JUNE 23, 1937

Showed general how we could rearrange budget to obtain maximum amount in item "Mobilization Equipment." This consists in (1) elimination of principal ordnance items, including eight howitzers, 75-mm.—approximately 600,000 pesos; (2) cutting down signal corps—approximately 300,000 pesos; (3) revision of savings estimates in purposes I and II to add—approximately 900,000 pesos; and (4) reduction of purpose III by 100,000 pesos.

It was explained to General MacA that nothing was to be gained in reduction of construction costs, since under present arrangement with B of B these costs are to be charged against surplus, and assembly will not be asked to appropriate for this item.[1]

This situation would place a total of about 3,000,000 pesos in mobilization equipment.

General rejected that part of ordnance savings involving 75-mms. by saying this equipment is equally necessary with mobilization equipment. This cuts down projected shift of amounts to about 500,000 from that item. It was explained to him that by making maximum estimates on this year's savings in purposes I and II we ran the risk of going broke in those two items before end of 1938—which would require discharge of trainees and relief of reserve officers. In this connection, however, I am not listing these estimates of savings at anything like the amounts given in a statement from Victoria. I am making a compromise between his figures and the ones we used originally, which were vastly smaller.

Altogether I think I'll add to the "mobilization" item by 1.5 million. The general frankly said this mobilization is for psychological reasons—giving this answer to silence my strenuous objections, on account of cost.

JUNE 24, 1937

1. In a conference with General Grunert agreed that twenty McKinley trainees will be instructed in motor transport work.[1]

2. General MacA read Ord's preliminary study on November 15 concentration. Agreed to it except that we instead of improvised staffs must do the work. Ordered an immediate beginning, so I gave the paper to Harrison and told him to go ahead.

3. Agreed with Colonel Hodges and General Humphrey on composition of next camp at Davi.[2] General H (artilleryman) has authority, during first six weeks of camp, to transfer up to one hundred men, if he finds this necessary.

JUNE 25, 1937

General MacA disturbed by some criticism in local press and says that all misstatements must be answered. I am to prepare a statement at once showing that we've fed men well and that this army has very low proportion of professional officers, particularly in higher grades.

JUNE 26, 1937

Boy Scout argument up again, with the general seriously concerned about it. Has appointed me, Santos, Segundo as representatives of army to meet Boy Scout executives in conference.[1] Mr. Vargas, upon hearing of this, said to lay off conferences until Stevens returns.[2]

JUNE 28, 1937

1. General has directed me to get up estimates on total needs in mobilization equipment for next two years, to end of 1939. This amount, he says, he's going to get Mr. Quezon to donate from "oil" money. If this is so, then we ought to return to original composition of budget. Says he's been promised minimum of thirty million extra to finance plan.

2. General Santos has shown again that he will not stand fast on any project when appeals are made to him by subordinates. He agreed to assignment of Garcia as district commanding officer, then weakened under maudlin appeal from Garcia and promised him he could stay as G-3 [operations officer]. He also came up with a plea to send school officers to states via tourist accommodations on *Coolidge* instead of dormitory accommodations on transport. He had a dozen reasons, but the real one is, as usual, "face." I'm weary trying to save money when everyone else wants to spend it, so I said, "Do as you please."

3. General MacA wants to get at construction of addition to this office for use of engineers that are to come over in October. He said, "My real purpose in having them here under my thumb is that, though paid by funds of the Power Development Corporation, I can use them to help us out whenever they are not busy on other work. I am to go get Mr. Vargas's permission to build the addition in the old wall."

JULY 1, 1937

Prepared the statement on accomplishments of the Philippine army during past six months. My original intent was to write it as a summarized report from chief of staff to Malacañan and to furnish copies to papers for their use. When the general read it he liked the tone and immediately said he'd issue it in his own name. With this purpose in view he desired an expansion of the paper to include additional subjects—air corps, off-shore patrol, tributes to American army and navy, etc. I protested that the paper lost all value and became just another report. He insisted, so today he is to give it as an "interview" to the *Herald*. I fear that one of these days some editor will flatly refuse to take such statements for publication, because of little or no news value.

We have not yet gotten permission to increase revolving fund by two million pesos with which to buy mobilization kits.

Have told Harrison that he could have Bailey for a while to help prepare plans for concentration in Manila on November 15.

Finally authorized Hutter to send his detachment to Corregidor for training. Against my better judgment, but haven't the time myself to conduct the research and investigations necessary to establish the facts as to whether or not the expenditure is justified.

Big conference at army headquarters on June 29 of all staff officers and district commanders (ten). I talked at meeting on duties, responsibilities, and importance

of new district commanders. Answered questions for an hour and did all I could
to get these officers to take hold of job and carry it through. Informed conference
of general's decision to eliminate Scout enlisted instructors next January.

JULY 9, 1937

Informed this morning by TJ that the general called him in for a long talk.
Subject was the general's readiness to dispense, at a moment's notice, with the
service of any or all members of mission. The occasion for the conversation was
speculation on Ord's possible permanent stay in United States and the general's
expressed irritation at what he termed the "conceit and self-centered" attitudes
of various members of the mission. Said too many individuals were acting as if
they were indispensable and remarked that each was selfishly "looking out only
for himself."

It begins to look as if we were resented simply because we labor under the
conviction, and act on it, that someone ought to know what is going on in this
army and help them over the rough spots. However, from the beginning of this
venture I've personally announced myself as ready and willing to go back to an
assignment in the United States Army at any moment. The general knows this
if he knows anything, so I guess I don't have to make an issue of the matter by
busting in and announcing it again.

JULY 20, 1937

Army headquarters is moving into its new building. A week or so ago the general
called for a detailed statement of expenditure from military adviser fund. After
going over it he directed that all Scout noncommissioned officers be dropped as
of next January 1. They cost us fifty thousand pesos per year, and this drain on
the fund cannot be longer sustained. I've given orders to this effect, hoping that
cadres will be able to function without Scout enlisted men next year.

Because of current expenses the general directed that Whatly be given only
$5.00 per day, instead of the $8.50 that all other liaison officers get, and that we
attempt to get the services of a signal officer at $3.00 per day.

1938

*The last full year before the outbreak of war in Europe, the year 1938, showed
something less than the preceding year's full budget of Japanese aggression—but
one could arrive at no final conclusion as to what the Japanese were trying to do.
Quite possibly the China incident, following upon the Manchurian incident, was
going to end the same way, namely, with the complete conquest of China, as the
earlier affair had ended with the taking of all Manchuria. In that case the*

Japanese would persist to the bitter end. Whether the vast Chinese hinterland, more difficult to take and hold than the coastal areas, would prove so awkward for the Japanese that they would tie themselves up in years of warfare along the rivers and across the mountains and thus have no time to give attention to the Philippines must have proved an interesting subject in Manila, in American army camps, and in other establishments on the islands. Undoubtedly Eisenhower and his friends thought about these matters.

A more thought-provoking subject that year could have been Europe, where Hitler's Germany took Austria in a bloodless occupation, and then, in the autumn —after extraordinary discussions culminating in a conference in the south German city of Munich—representatives of Britain and France gave in to German demands and allowed the western part of Czechoslovakia, known as the Sudetenland, to pass under German control. It was almost impossible to defend Czechoslovakia without the Sudetenland, and occupation of the entire country the next spring was ridiculously easy.

In 1938 it was not yet clear that a Second World War would break out in Europe, even if hostilities already had begun on a considerable scale in China. The European scene was opaque that year, and Prime Minister Neville Chamberlain put his faith in the words of the German Fuehrer, who said that the Sudetenland was his last European demand. Eisenhower, in the distant Philippines, must have wondered what he should do about his remote assignment, more diplomatic than military, an assignment made almost impossible by the headstrong beliefs and actions of his military senior, MacArthur. He evidently was uncertain, for after a trip back to the United States that took more than four months he returned to the islands. He had enough connections in the army to have maneuvered a stateside assignment, if he had felt he should do it. Duty brought him back, a compound of feeling that he still could work with MacArthur and that a large war in Europe or Asia, perhaps both, involving eventually the United States, was not yet certain.

JUNE 26, 1938

Sailed from Manila on time, 5:00 P.M. Quarters 105–107. Sitting at Captain Ahlin's table. Deposited with purser cash $360, traveler's checks, two packages, $3,000 and $1,010, also watch and chain.

JUNE 28, 1938

Docked at Hong Kong at 8:00 A.M. Went to Repulse Bay Hotel. One large room for the three of us. Forty Mexican dollars per day. Exchange rate equals 3.20 Mexican dollars for 1 American dollar. Scheduled to leave here at 9:00 P.M., June 30.

JUNE 29, 1938

Wrote notes to General MacA,· bridge club, Bill Z, Santos, Garcia, Lim, Segundo, Ajula.

JUNE 30, 1938

Left Hong Kong 9:00 P.M., June 30. Have written to TJ, Lewis, Valdez. (Must write to Mrs. Kuppel.)

JULY 4, 1938

Arrived Kobe, 1:00 P.M. Left Kobe, 10:00 P.M.

JULY 5, 1938

Arrived Yokohama, 5:45 P.M. Left Yokohama, 12:00 midnight.

JULY 13, 1938

Arrived Honolulu, 9:00 A.M. Left Honolulu, 6:00 P.M.
    General Herron made available to us his private car and driver.[1] We looked over Hickam Field, Pearl Harbor, new ordnance storage tunnels and visited spots of natural scenic beauty. Pali pass was particularly interesting.

Hong Kong, 1938.

JULY 17, 1938

Settled laundry bills on ship. Took receipt for ten dollars of my personal laundry, as it appears from regulations that I may be able to get that much back from government.

JULY 18, 1938

Landed at San Francisco at 3:00 P.M. Found there a radio from General MacA directing me to examine situation at Fort Mason with respect to shipments of rifles, gun slings, etc. Sent him a long radio on subject, copy of which is in my papers.
    Purchased tickets for Denver. My ticket and berth cost $51.95. Took receipt.
    Spent three dollars for baggage transfer (my own baggage), arranged by Colonel Hodgson while I was attending to business above described, so that receipt was not obtained.[1] Have retained checks.

JULY 21, 1938, DENVER

Sent the general an air mail letter in further explanation of the Fort Mason situation. Last evening I sent him an amateur radio [message] requesting he send a personal letter of appreciation to Colonel Harvey.

JULY 22, 1938

Wired Lieutenant Lee to arrange conference at Wichita; commanding officer, Picatinny Arsenal, to arrange visit at that arsenal.[1] Personal wires to Colonel Darst and my dad.
    Received a radiogram from General MacA regarding Fort Mason situation, with instructions to communicate with Colonel Harvey at once by telegraph. In compliance therewith I sent following by night letter: . . . Cost, $1.35.[2]

JULY 24, 1938

Received night letter (collect) from Colonel Harvey ($1.68) and immediately repeated the gist of it to signal officer, San Francisco, asking him to radio my message to the commanding general, Philippine Department, for General MacArthur ($1.35).
    My message informed General MacA that we would probably get some of our Fort Mason equipment on the August trip, but that Colonel Harvey could make no prophecy as to November possibilities.
    Wire from Lee suggests conference at Wichita next Thursday or Friday, which is OK.

JULY 27, 1938

Last evening sent General MacA clipper letter enclosing a message from Colonel Harvey regarding Fort Mason situation. Unreceipted bill for stamp, fifty cents.
    This morning am taking off for Wichita, Kansas, to talk to Stevenson and Beechcraft people.

JULY 28, 29, 30, 1938

Made full inspection of airplane plants in Wichita. Arranged trip so as to cost government nothing except one-way ticket from Abilene-Denver, making rest of journey in private plane.
    Beech is confident his plane can be modified for military purposes.[1] In fact he is now designing one for a South American government to use . . . [illegible] and be somewhat bigger than present ship. Latest cost around fifty thousand dollars.
    Ample guns, etc. Speed 220, cruising, all other characteristics as to handling, etc., as good as present ship, of which eleven are in service. All reports good.
    Lee and Parker much impressed.[2]

JULY 31, 1938

Sent General MacArthur long radio telling him of changed schedule because of Mamie's operation. Also advised him to have Dick go ahead with permanent program, reserving funds allotted to American armament items.[1]
    Must write to Lee, Parker, Beech, etc.

AUGUST 3, 1938

Wrote Mr. H.D. Fairweather, vice-president, Colt's Patent Firearms Company, Hartford, and Mr. Oliver E. Nelson, Winchester Repeating Arms Company, New Haven, explaining that my visit to their plants would be after September 1. I must ask the War Department for passes to visit Winchester and Colt plants. Wrote to Schaefer, J.E., Stevenson Aircraft; Walter Beech, Beechcraft Company. In Beech Aircraft Company are Mr. Gates, sales; Mr. Wells, engineer; Mr. Rankin, pilot. Wrote to Parker.

AUGUST 4, 1938

Mamie went to hospital (Pueblo). Wrote Brent School, American Armament, and Everett.

AUGUST 5, 1938

American Armament Corporation, 6 East Forty-fifth Street, New York. (Plant at Rahway, N.J.)

AUGUST 11, 1938 (EN ROUTE TO YELLOWSTONE PARK)

Left Denver at 6:00 A.M. and headed north on York Street, which runs into main road to Cheyenne. Dad drove to Cheyenne without incident. Roads paved. Distance, 104 miles. Time, two and a half hours.

Continued north and west from Cheyenne to Casper, 185 miles. Considerable portions of the road under repair, the rest rather rough gravel. Stopped for lunch under a cottonwood. Mother and Auntie fixed us a "swell" repast which we thoroughly enjoyed and saved some for next day.

Traveled west from Casper to Shoshoni, where we stopped at the Shawnee Hotel for the night. Rooms two dollars apiece. Supper and breakfast forty cents each per person.

Shoshoni is 390 miles from Denver. Reached it at 5:30 P.M.

The most interesting sights of the day were (1) Hell's Half Acre. About thirty to forty miles east of Shoshoni. It is a great sunken tract that was originally a volcano, then was filled with geysers, all now extinct. The solid salts from the geysers remain in all types of weird shapes. (2) The oilfields just west of Casper and the adjacent refineries. In one large tract there seems to be a well every 150 yards. Not many are pumping now. Very hot and dirty day.

AUGUST 12, 1938

Left Shoshoni at 6:15 and struck north through the Wind River Canyon. Reached Thermopolis at 7:15 (34 miles), and Dad got himself a little more breakfast, as we fared poorly at Shoshoni. He also got me some doughnuts.

We continued north to Greybull through a country not quite so barren as east of Shoshoni, and then turned west to Cody and then through a canyon to Shoshone Dam. Built 1910. Height 320 feet. Width at bottom 110; at top, 10. Built on an arch and dams up the Shoshone River to form a lake 10 miles long, 225 feet deep.

Ate lunch just above the dam. The road runs through tunnels in places.

We then entered a national forest and another canyon that continued practically to the entrance gate to the park. It was a wooded rocky canyon, very pretty and interesting.

At the park entrance we paid $3 and then came on about twenty-seven miles over a winding road under repair to Lake Lodge (fishing bridge). $3.50 each for bed, breakfast, and supper. Tomorrow morning we expect to go fishing.

Both of us feel well, but as we don't go in much for the type of entertainment put on here for the guests, I suppose we'll just go to bed tonight. We will get supper, our first meal in the park, in twenty minutes. Hot dog!

AUGUST 13, 1938

Cold rainy day.

Intended going fishing at bridge, but about 9:45 A.M. started off on loop to see park. Saw grand canyon and falls of Yellowstone. Climbed down wooden steps into canyon twice—once 502 steps. Oh boy. Falls and canyon most beautiful sight I have seen. Canyon 1,200 feet deep, 2,000 feet across.

Continued north toward Twin Falls, 180-foot drop of small creek into Yellowstone River. Miserable road under repairs. Then went west to Mammoth, Paintpots, deposits from warm springs.

South along a valley of steaming springs and geysers, stopping tonight at Old Faithful Lodge.

Traveled about 105 miles today.

AUGUST 14, 1938

Early this morning I made a trip to the principal geysers. Emerald Pool and Black Sand Pool were the most interesting I thought. At 8:20 we started for Thumb, about twenty miles. There we hired a guide and boat ($1.50 per hour) and went fishing. We trolled in lake with spinners. Each caught one nice trout (cut throat).

At 12:00 we started home via south gate. Got into rain and, due to bad reports concerning roads to east and south, stopped at Jackson at 3:00 P.M. for the night. This is the famous Jackson Hole country and is bounded on the east by the Grand Teton mountains. These peaks tower over the valley, no foothills intervening between them and the valley floor. We are stopping at a funny little hotel where both Wyoming United States senators are spending the night. Kendrick and Carey.

AUGUST 15, 1938

Were ready to leave town at 6:00, but in order to get breakfast and get chains put on car (together with losing gas tank cap) it was 7:10 when we left. I drove 80 miles to Pinedale over a muddy winding road. Pinedale is 104 miles from Rock Springs, the nearest railroad. Dad drove to Rock Springs (100 miles) in 2.10 minutes. We drove 410 miles today, although the first 78 miles took us three hours, and the last 20 took another hour.

Stopping at Laramie.

AUGUST 16, 1938

Up at 5:20. Left Laramie at 6:30, via Fort Collins. Home at 10:10 A.M. Total distance, 1,378 miles.

AUGUST 21, 1938

On August 18 I received (at Pueblo) written instructions to proceed on an emergency trip (by air) to the War Department to prevent adoption of policy that might limit our use of government property (United States) on loan basis. Today I got reservations on UAL and will be in Washington tomorrow night.

AUGUST 25, 1938

Returned from Washington this evening. Trip entirely successful. Contrary to impression in our office at Manila, General H. has not sent any communication to Washington advocating limitations on his authority to lend us property. He has asked for additional property, which he wants to let us have for *temporary* use on other islands.

I contacted and had long talks with the chief of staff, deputy chief of staff, adjutant general, War Plans Division, G-4 [Supply Division], Chief of the Bureau of Insular Affairs [in the Department of the Interior], Colonel Sparkes, G-4 Division, executive officer, G-4.

Secretary of war and assistant secretary out of town.

AUGUST 26, 1938

Spent two dollars in air mail stamps for official letters to Manila.

SEPTEMBER 7, 1938

Left for Washington, stopping first at Leavenworth to go over school prospects. Exec (Gilbreath) believes . . . [illegible] a better man than Garcia.

Arrived Washington thirteenth, called on all principal officials of department.

Wired General MacA, army director OK. Merritt report? Had long conversations with Sparkes (G-4). We should request more ammunition at $8.50 price. 1906 can be obtained new at possibly $20 per m. Ask for price in letter.

G-4 has approved shipment of sixteen 2.95s to Philippine Islands as well as a number of 3-inch mortars. Have been promised that G-4 will see how cheap ammunition for latter can be sold.

Ordnance can sell us 81-mm. and 60-mm. But some delay in these items will probably ensure better prices.

Talked to air corps, ordnance, infantry, adjutant general, etc.

Following sent special messages to General MacA.: Craig, Adams, Embick, Tyner, Marshall, Lynch, Arnold (Westover not in town).[1] (Hardenberg, office of the chief of infantry wants to be remembered to Hughes.)

Not yet certain Lewis is going to Maxwell, but probabilities are affirmative. Air Corps is delighted to help us out.

Discussed our problems with Colonel Clarke (Philippine Projects section, WPD, also Perkins), Sparkes, Tyner, Marshall, Embick, Lynch, Booth (ordnance), adjutant general.

The chief of staff is against . . . [illegible] detail, but answer has not finally been determined. Ordnance will give thorough test to Molex [illegible]. They are not hopeful, suspicious that this explosive is dangerous to handle.

SEPTEMBER 19, 1938

Many conferences with Sparkes. G-4 has authorized shipment of guns and mortars. Question of ammunition comes up, since the department commanding officer feels it inadvisable to sell from stores.

My solution is to defer purchase of mortars, buy now (for storage under facilities of commanding general, Philippine department) about five years requirement in artillery ammunition. In this connection G-4 believes they have a few more million rounds of stuff they will sell at $8.50 per thousand. Also they are manufacturing a considerable amount of new 1906 caliber 20. We can purchase for $20–22 per thousand as compared to $30 per thousand for M1 (Boat tail).

SEPTEMBER 23, 1938

Left Washington September 20. Sent radio to General MacA concerning all questions he had forwarded to me. Jim Ulio is writing him a personal letter reference Merritt report.

Sent to Newark, $1.35. Receipt obtained.
Arranged for following trips:
1. Picatinny reference powder tests.
2. New Haven and Hartford . . . [illegible] Winchester and Colt products.
3. Rahway, American Armament products. (Malcolm out of city for week.)
Flood conditions terrible. Communications will not be reestablished for some days to Hartford, consequently Connecticut trip had to be confined to Winchester plant at New Haven.

Cost of New Haven trip. Receipts not available, except for Pullman seat. All tickets inter-urban type, collected and no receipt given. See certificate and statement of witness.

We should carefully check net costs in ammunition from United States Ordnance and from Winchester, etc.

Mr. Nelson says we paid more for .22 ammunition than his company would have charged us.

SEPTEMBER 25, 1938

Visit to American Armament and Rahway factory was instructive. Fine plant. Company apparently resented by certain people in United States Army. Took Colonel Hughes, Ordnance, with me to inspect plant. Both much impressed.

Did my best to unearth underlying cause of any antagonism to company.

The engineer (Brayton) acknowledged by all to be expert. Fifteen years with ordnance department. Unpopular.

All problems that have been bothering ordnance, such as fin assembly, capsule form, fuses (deformation of point), etc., have been attacked by company and a solution found. Have asked for latest prices, to compare in detail with ordnance department. Spent long time here.

Mamie accompanied me on trip east, but all expenses, of all kinds for her, were paid from personal funds. I habitually bought minimum accommodations for myself, no matter what I bought for her.

OCTOBER 8, 1938

Our scare over John's appendix was apparently useless. Fitzsimons surgeons say there is no indication that operation is necessary. Repeated kidney tests show those organs normal.

OCTOBER 10, 1938

Left Denver 5:45 P.M.

Arrive Portland at 7:30 A.M. on second morning. Left Portland one hour later, arriving Tacoma at 1:00 P.M. Spent day with Edgar there, calling on General Sweeney at Fort Lewis. Wayne Clark is on the general staff there. Also Hills in the adjutant general's office wants to be remembered to Stuart [illegible], adjutant general's office at Stotsenberg.[1]

OCTOBER 14, 1938

Arrived at Vancouver, B.C. by ferry at 8:00 A.M., October 14, and sailed from Vancouver at 11:45 A.M., October 14, and from Victoria at 6:00 P.M.

OCTOBER 20, 1938

Arrived Honolulu at 10:30 A.M., October 19. Sailed at 10:15 A.M., October 20.

OCTOBER 28, 1938

Arrived Yokohama, 7:00 A.M. Left Yokohama, 3:00 P.M.

OCTOBER 29, 1938

Arrived Kobe, 9:00 A.M. Left Kobe, 6:00 P.M.

OCTOBER 31, 1938

Shanghai. Arrived 6:00 P.M.

NOVEMBER 2, 1938

Left Shanghai on November 2 at 1:30 P.M.

NOVEMBER 3, 1938

Arrived Hong Kong, 8:00 A.M. Left Hong Kong, 10:00 P.M.

NOVEMBER 5, 1938

Landed at Manila at 10:00 A.M. Paid table steward $10.00 and room steward $10.00 as personal tips for voyage from Vancouver. Both being Chinese, made no attempt to secure receipts.

THE WAR DEPARTMENT
IN CRISIS

Dwight Eisenhower's departure from the Philippines was arranged by himself, not by Douglas MacArthur—with whom his relations had become admittedly awkward, but who, nonetheless, did not realize how low Eisenhower's confidence in him had dropped. MacArthur's life in the Philippines was one of aloofness, from both the Americans and the Filipinos, a life that was led almost in seclusion, in hotel suites in Manila or in carefully managed offices, a life apart from the heat and sticky inconvenience endured by the American officers as they worked away, day after day, month after month, with their conscript Filipino army that was to stand up to the Japanese if war ever came. The general had proved willing to countenance Eisenhower's promotion to lieutenant colonel, but then that would have been difficult to avoid, as Eisenhower's quality performance was no secret, even to the War Department in faraway Washington. Beyond formal contacts —such as the ever-present questions and concerns that Eisenhower was forced to bring to the general for some sort of decision or, as was the case frequently, some sort of delay or papering over after consultation with the Filipino political leaders—Eisenhower and MacArthur shared little camaraderie. The time came, shortly after the declaration of war by Britain and France upon Germany on September 1, 1939, when Eisenhower asked MacArthur for release from the Philippine duty.

"General," Ike said, "in my opinion the United States cannot remain out of this war for long. I want to go home as soon as possible. I want to participate in the preparatory work that I'm sure is going to be intense."

MacArthur said that Eisenhower, having spent four years in the Philippines, and knowing the work there, was making a mistake. That work, he said, was far more important than what Eisenhower could do as a mere lieutenant colonel in the American army.

Eisenhower doughtily reminded MacArthur that because the War Department had decided he was more useful as an instructor in the United States than as a fighting man in the First World War, he had missed combat in that earlier conflict. He was now determined to do everything he could to make sure he would not miss the new crisis.

President Quezon was far more emphatic than MacArthur in insisting that Ike remain, and handed him a blank contract, saying, "We'll tear up the old contract. I've already signed this one and it is filled in—except what you want as your emoluments for remaining. You will write that in."

"Mr. President," said Eisenhower, "your offer is flattering. But no amount of money can make me change my mind. My entire life has been given to this one thing, my country and my profession. I want to be there if what I fear is going to come about actually happens."

After a beautiful farewell luncheon in the Malacañan Palace, the Eisenhowers —the lieutenant colonel, Mamie, young John—departed for San Francisco by liner, spent Christmas 1939 in Hawaii, and celebrated New Year's in their home country. The noise and glitter, as Eisenhower wrote long afterward, the celebration of what might have been the good year 1940 (but proved to be the appallingly bad year 1940), was the last of what had been a peaceful decade of family life together. John would go off to West Point. Mamie, after a year or two, would find herself an army widow, ensconced in a Washington hotel while her husband, by then a general, was overseas.

The year 1940 saw a change in the European war from Sitzkrieg, as the wags described the apparently stable trench war, to Blitzkrieg; it saw the Nazi invasion of Denmark and Norway, and then the lightning strike down through the Netherlands and Belgium into France, followed by the abject capitulation of the French government and the evacuation of the British expeditionary force from Dunkirk —during this dismal year the Eisenhowers were in a dead-end assignment at Fort Lewis in the state of Washington. Ike again was with troops, and this made him happy. But not much was going on with the 15th Infantry at Lewis, and reading the newspapers about the excitement in Europe made him nervous, unsure if MacArthur and Quezon perhaps had been right in urging him to remain in the Philippines, where the action really might be. Training troops in the United States, with the rank of lieutenant colonel, was not altogether attractive.

In the summer of 1940, however, came the Draft Act, the first peacetime draft in American history, and in the autumn of that year the army began to get transfusions of new blood. The regular officers had been good men for the most part, but the enlisted men frequently had left something to be desired; they were men of the sort that later were to be described by the novelist James Jones, who encountered these dregs of humanity during his own service in the Second World War. These men were accustomed to heavy drinking and malingering; their major concerns were payday and goofing off, with a secondary interest in the remote occasion when, having served sufficient hitches, they could be pensioned off and retire in out-of-the-way places, raise vegetable gardens, or maybe just drink up their paychecks and throw the vegetables away. With the Draft Act the peacetime army was about to be transformed, and Eisenhower's hope not to be a perennial training officer was to be fulfilled in ways he never could have imagined.

In the autumn of 1940 word came to Eisenhower of assignment to duty as chief of staff, Third Division, Fort Lewis. At the beginning of March 1941 came a new assignment, albeit still at Fort Lewis: chief of staff to the IX Army Corps, comprising all of the northwestern part of the United States. A few days after the transfer Ike was promoted to full colonel and for the first time in his years with the army he began to see the possibility of a generalship, with all the responsibility that would go along with such rank. The conscripts were pouring into Lewis, and the post was noisily alive day and night with construction crews hard at work.

In the summer of 1941 came orders transferring Ike to headquarters, Third Army, in San Antonio, where he became deputy and then chief of staff to Lieutenant General Walter Krueger, whose command stretched all the way from New Mexico to Florida, with a strength of 240,000 officers and men: shades of the old days in the Philippines, when Ike was counting hundreds or, at best, a few thousands and had to work with MacArthur and Quezon, who were counting pesos.

The assignment as Krueger's chief of staff at Third Army made Eisenhower's reputation, for that summer the great maneuvers in Louisiana brought him into prominence. His plans for the maneuvers, compounded from the instruction of Conner years before, succeeded brilliantly, even though the troops that summer were conducting mock warfare and didn't even have the equipment to handle the "mock" end of it, having to label trucks as "tanks" and in other ways pretend they really were on maneuvers. At the end of the exercise Dwight D. Eisenhower became a brigadier general.

It was just in time, for only a few months remained until the United States suddenly, on December 7, went to war.

The months passed in a rush of training and activity. One Sunday noon the general was eating lunch and found himself so sleepy he decided to take a long nap; he ordered his aide under no circumstances to awaken him. When the aide nonetheless came in, the reason was transparently clear.

Five days later came the telephone message from Washington: "The Chief [General George C. Marshall, chief of staff] says for you to hop a plane and get up here right away." The War Department was in near-total confusion, and Marshall desperately needed Eisenhower.

1942

JANUARY 1, 1942

I arrived in Washington December 14, 1941.
Telephone call from office of chief of staff.
I've been insisting Far East is critical, and no other sideshows should be
undertaken until air and ground are in satisfactory state. Instead, we're taking on
Magnet, Gymnast, etc.[1] The chief of staff told me to pay special attention to the
Philippine Islands, Hawaii, Australia, Pacific islands, China.

JANUARY 2, 1942

Unity of command in ABDA [American, British, Dutch, Australian] area seems
assured. Good start, but what an effort. Talk, talk, talk.

JANUARY 3, 1942

Becoming increasingly evident that something must be done in China. War
effort lagging there, and China shows signs of being willing to quit. Apparently
the British don't take this seriously. They should.

JANUARY 4, 1942

Tempers are short. There are lots of amateur strategists on the job, and prima
donnas everywhere. I'd give anything to be back in the field.
    It's hard to get anything done in Australia. Dive bombers arrived minus
essential parts; base facilities are meager; other expeditions, directed by politicians, interfere, notably Magnet and Gymnast. But we're getting some things on
the road to Australia. The air plan is 4 pursuit, 2 heavy bomber, 2 medium
bomber, 1 light bombardment groups. We're trying to ship staff and personnel
needed. But we've got to have ships and we need them now.

JANUARY 5, 1942

Ham is to go to a division soon as assistant.[1] Then later he gets a division to
command. This War Department is cockeyed. Ham is one of our ablest, but he,
at fifty-two or fifty-three, must serve an apprenticeship before getting a division.
The conversations with the British grow wearisome. They're difficult to talk to,
apparently afraid someone is trying to tell them what to do and how to do it.
Their practice of war is dilatory.[2]

At the end of the Louisiana maneuvers Dwight D. Eisenhower became a brigadier general.

The Eisenhowers at Fort Lewis, Washington, c. 1941. Ike enjoyed serving as a chef.

JANUARY 6, 1942

Chief of staff out of town one day. Would be a relief except that we've so much work we can't catch up anyway. So we'll go home at 10:00 P.M. as usual. Secretary of war with General Drum.[1] Secretary of war with General Gerow and General Arnold.[2] [The Japanese were threatening the Burma Road, lifeline to China, and Secretary of War Henry L. Stimson was looking for a Burma-China commander.]

JANUARY 7, 1942

Have been attempting to arrange better effort for China. Chief of staff wanted to send Drum to organize air effort, Burma Road, etc.
Two days of feeling bum. Hope it's only flu. Afraid it may be shingles coming back.

JANUARY 8, 1942

Still trying to get navy to run the blockade (by submarine) into MacArthur with some anti-aircraft ammunition. Admiral King has issued orders, but I'm still not sure we'll get it done. May merely lose another sub.

JANUARY 9, 1942

Still working on China problem. Looks like Drum runs out of it. He wants none of it because he doesn't like the looks of the thing. He seemingly cannot understand that we've got to do the best we can with what we've got.

JANUARY 10, 1942

Every day the same, 7:45 A.M. to 11:45 P.M. Attended conference this afternoon with combined chiefs of staff. Subject: China, Burma. British, as usual, are scared someone will take advantage of them even when we furnish everything.

JANUARY 11, 1942

Everybody has suddenly decided Far East is critical. Now we've all got to find some way to rush troops there, but political situation won't let us give up Magnet.

JANUARY 12, 1942

Told Spaatz about trigger motors for A-24s in Australia on basis of MacArthur's radio.[1] Said he hadn't heard of this before.
Somervell (G-4) did a good job finding boats.[2] We'll get off twenty-one thousand men on January 21 to Australia; but I don't know when we can get all their

equipment and supplies to them. Ships! Ships! All we need is ships! Also ammunition, anti-aircraft guns, tanks, airplanes, what a headache!

JANUARY 13, 1942

Another day. Yesterday finished and got off long telegrams breaking off command connection between Philippine Islands and Australia so Brereton, in latter place, could operate directly under Wavell, commanding general of ABDA area.[1] Today a wire from MacArthur saying fine. But I've got my fingers crossed. I still think he might have made a better showing at the beaches and passes, and certainly he should have saved his planes on December 8, but he's still the hero.[2]

JANUARY 15, 1942

Looks like Stilwell may be selected for China.[1] That leaves Gymnast command open. Recommend three major generals and three brigadiers. Gerow at top of brigadiers.

I feel that the laborious nature of the procedure for sending a message to ABDA will drive us crazy. On routine and personnel matters, we should have direct channels.

General headquarters wants to start a campaign as far south as Freetown, Africa, working north. I disagree.

JANUARY 17, 1942

Colonel Hurley, former secretary of war, is on his way to X [Australia].[1] He was inducted at noon today and at 1:00 tonight starts by plane via Pacific. He was equal to the quick transition, and I'm hopeful he can do something in organizing blockade running for MacArthur. The whole Far East situation is critical. My own plan is to drop everything else—Magnet, Gymnast, replacements in Ireland —and make the British retire in Libya. Then scrape up everything everywhere and get it into NEI [Netherlands East Indies] and Burma. We mustn't lose NEI, Singapore, Burma line; so we ought to go full out saving them. We've been struggling to get a bunch of heavy bombers into NEI, but the whole movement seems bogged down. The air corps doesn't have enough men that will do things.

JANUARY 18, 1942, (SUNDAY)

Just another day. Grind away.

JANUARY 19, 1942

Told Magruder yesterday to get busy on inducting AVG [American Volunteer Group] in China and Burma.[1] The AVG needs planes badly, and we're trying to land fifty on the west coast of Africa and fly them over.[2] Wonder how many will arrive? I prepare about six cables a day. In many ways MacArthur is as big a baby as ever. But we've got to keep him fighting.

JANUARY 20, 1942

One hell of a day.

JANUARY 21, 1942

Catching a cold. Hope I can ward it off.
   Sent a long cable to Wavell asking advice on Dutch request for six hundred pursuit planes.

JANUARY 22, 1942

Hurry-up call to go to state department. Saw Secretary Hull, in conference with navy files, Ridgway.[1] Wanted a bribe to give Chile in way of defense materials, so as to get a favorable vote on breaking off relations with Axis.
   Scraped up a bunch of coast artillery corps and small items of lend-lease aid. Arnold promised 50 A-6s and 17s for distribution in South American countries.
   The struggle to secure the adoption by all concerned of a common concept of strategical objectives is wearing me down. Everybody is too much engaged with small things of his own, or with some vague idea of larger political activity, to realize what we are doing, rather, not doing.
   We've got to go to Europe and fight, and we've got to quit wasting resources all over the world, and still worse, wasting time. If we're to keep Russia in, save the Middle East, India, and Burma, we've got to begin slugging with air at West Europe, to be followed by a land attack as soon as possible. (May 7. The above plan, which finally won official approval in April, is called Bolero.) [On May 7, 1942, Eisenhower turned back in his diary to the January 22 entry to make this parenthetical comment.]

JANUARY 23, 1942

Chief says to "get behind communication system." Looks like WPD has to kick everybody in the pants.
   Today, in a most flamboyant radio, MacArthur recommends successor in case of "my death." He picked Sutherland, showing that he still likes his boot lickers.[1]
   General Stilwell pushed for China job. He's a soldier.

JANUARY 24, 1942

ABDA area boundaries changed some for the better. Wavell now responsible for Darwin area. But what a job to work with allies. There's a lot of big talk and desk hammering around this place, but very few doers. They announce results in advance in a flashy way and make big impressions, but the results often don't materialize, and then the workers get the grief.

Went to Bill Somervell this A.M. to find out what he knows about this landing craft business. He has known nothing of it to date, but is having matter looked up.

Mamie will soon be coming up here. I get weary of going all the way out to Falls Church at 10:30 P.M.

JANUARY 25, 1942

Spent the morning arguing with air corps and G-4 [Supply Division], showing them how B-26s can get to X a lot faster than planned. Sold them the idea, and if we can get a little drive behind the thing, maybe we can get some fighting strength in ABDA. For same reason have been plaguing Arnold about B-25s for Dutch.

Saw Royce for a minute.[1] Back from England.

Had dinner with the Clarks this evening.[2] Had to come back and go to work. Since I took a couple of old-fashioneds, I got d----- sleepy.

JANUARY 26, 1942

Australia-New Caledonia shipments supposedly leaving Charleston today. Part leaves West Coast in couple days. Have never had much faith in New Caledonia garrison arriving there under current conditions. It goes via X. My own opinion is that the whole works will be so badly needed by ABDA, we'll never get this gang to Caledonia. However, we'll see. In the meantime, I'm going to start making up another shipment for Far East.

Got navy and air force together on question of getting torpedoes to X for B-26s and making sure crews were trained in use. None of the people I talked to seemed to know anything about the matter, but now everything possible seems done.

JANUARY 27, 1942

A navy officer (McDowell) is trying to act as "United States Secretary on Collaboration." His duties are to clear to British all messages that require combined chiefs of staff action. We sent to him, on twenty-first, an important message to Wavell, asking advice on six hundred pursuit ships. This morning we learn it has not yet even gone to British here in Washington. My God, how I hate to work by any method that forces me to depend on someone else. It's typical navy stuff.

Tom Handy and I stick to our idea that we must win in Europe.[1] Joe McNarney not only agrees but was the first one to state that the French coast could be successfully attacked.[2] It's going to be one h--- of a job, but, so what? We can't win by sitting on our fannies and giving our stuff in driblets all over the world, with no theater getting enough. Already we're probably too late in Burma, and we'll have to hurry like hell in Ceylon. The British have to get moving.

JANUARY 29, 1942

MacArthur has started a flood of communications that seem to indicate a refusal on his part to look facts in the face, an old trait of his. He has talked about big naval concentrations; he has forwarded (probably inspired) letter from Mr. Quezon; statements (Quisling) from Aguinaldo; he complains about lack of unity of command, about lack of information.[1] He's jittery!

JANUARY 30, 1942

The news from Wavell is all bad. Troops in Malay [peninsula] giving up and going back to Singapore Island tonight. The British still don't want Chinese. Wrote a memo today trying to smoke out Chinese situation. What a mess. We're going to regret every damn boat we sent to Ireland, etc. Damn 'em, I tried, but I don't wear 45s. So the hotshots can sneer at me. Anyway I got the Ireland movement largely postponed; but not all, and the boats actually moved there could have taken a bunch of anti-aircraft to Australia.[1] It now lies on the dock. Hell.

FEBRUARY 1, 1942

Events move too fast and keep me too busy to permit the writing of notes. Day by day the case looks worse in ABDA; it is becoming clear that Jap damage to Sumatra airfields is making it impossible for our B-17s to jump from Bangalore (India) to a satisfactory field in Java. Consequently, our air strength is not building up as expected. The navy made a raid in the Marshalls and Gilberts. Some damage was done to shipping and local defenses. One cruiser and one aircraft carrier of ours sustained minor damage.

FEBRUARY 2, 1942

Yesterday, listened to a talk by Bullitt, just back from Near East and Africa.[1] I liked his presentation. He knows, or he doesn't; no quibbling. Doesn't think much of Gymnast except on a one hundred thousand [-man] basis.

FEBRUARY 3, 1942

Looks like MacArthur is losing his nerve. I'm hoping that his yelps are just his way of spurring us on, but he is always an uncertain factor.

    The Dutch want planes; the Australians want planes; ABDA has to have planes; China must get them; the British need them in Near East. What a mess!

FEBRUARY 4, 1942

We've decided to shift a group of pursuits from ABDA to Australia, for use in NEI against Jap attack. Hope it does some good. Alerted the second group to be ready for action to Australia. Hope it is in time. We made clear we wanted the arrangement to be temporary, so ABDA could get its planes back.

FEBRUARY 5, 1942

Had to change our priorities in sending planes to Australia. ABDA is desperate. Fields getting bombed. Lost four B-17s on ground; also seven pursuits. We rarely lose a ship in the air, but my God, how they do catch us on the ground. Burma situation not quite so gloomy, but God knows whether or not we can save the place. Gerow and I have been yelling for the British to ask for Chinese help; but they (B) are certainly stiff-necked.   ·

FEBRUARY 6, 1942

Information that Chinese and British are finally getting together. We may save Burma yet. The joint and combined staff work is terrible. Takes an inconceivable amount of time. Fox Conner was right about allies. He could well have included the navy. We are faced with a big reorganization of the War Department. We need it. The general staff is all to be cut down, except the War Plans Division, which now has all joint and combined work (a terrible job), all plans, and all operations so far as active theaters are concerned. We need help.

FEBRUARY 7, 1942

Mamie came yesterday. Living at Wardman.

FEBRUARY 8, 1942

Another long message on "strategy" to MacArthur. He sent in one extolling the virtues of the flank offensive. Wonder what he thinks we've been studying for all these years. His lecture would have been good for plebes. Today another long wail from Quezon. I'll have to wait though, because it is badly garbled. I think he wants to give up.[1]
    Navy asks for command over our air forces on the coasts.

FEBRUARY 9, 1942

Spent the entire day preparing drafts of president's messages to MacArthur and Quezon. Long, difficult, and irritating. Both are babies. But now we'll see what happens. Tonight at 6:45 I saw the president and got his approval to sending the messages.

FEBRUARY 10, 1942

Attended "liaison meeting," State Department, undersecretary of state, Brazilian, Chile, Argentine questions, 10:00 A.M.

Six weeks ago Gerow and I predicted to ourselves navy would demand "unity of command" over coastlines of United States. They have already done so, only they have limited it to air forces, so far. We're telling them what is plain fact, defense of continental United States is army responsibility, and navy forces assisting should be under our command. What a gang to work with.

FEBRUARY 16, 1942

Took charge today of War Plans Division after having been here since December 14 on special work in the section. As "Gee" walked out, he said, "Well, I got Pearl Harbor on the book; lost the Philippine Islands, Singapore, Sumatra, and all the NEI north of the barrier. Let's see what you can do."[1]

FEBRUARY 17, 1942

The navy wants to take all the islands in the Pacific, have them held by army troops, to become bases for army pursuit and bombers. Then the navy will have a safe place to sail its vessels. But they will not go farther forward than our air (army) can assure superiority.[1] The amount of air required for this slow, laborious, and indecisive type of warfare is going to be something that will keep us from going to Russia's aid in time. Moreover, the navy wants us to give it (between now and June 1944) thirteen hundred heavy and medium bombers, land-based. If the navy is so helpless without air, and its sea operations are going to depend upon air, I wonder why it does not quit building battleships and start on carriers, and more carriers.

FEBRUARY 19, 1942

Had a meeting with the navy. One encouraging sign was that they have come to recognize the need for cargo ships. But they'd like us to stop building armament and equipment so they can have more battleships, etc., etc. Wonder how they finally expect to win this war. We've got to go on a harassing defensive west of Hawaii; hold India and Ceylon; build up air and land forces in England; and, when we're strong enough, go after Germany's vitals, and we've got to do it while Russia is still in the war, in fact, only by doing it soon can we keep Russia in. The trickle of supplies we can send through Basra and Archangel is too small to help her much.

FEBRUARY 22, 1942

Went to General Marshall's for Sunday dinner in honor of General Chu and Dr. T.V. Soong, both Chinese.[1] Longest I've been out of the office in daytime since coming here ten weeks ago today.

ABDA area is disintegrating. We have concocted a message to MacArthur directing him to start south to take command of Australian area, etc. I've always been fearful of this plan. I think he's doing a better job in Bataan than he will anywhere else. (Draft of message went to FDR.)

We've dilly dallied along about Burma, India, and China. Now, with Singapore gone, the NEI practically gone, and the Japs free to move as they please, we're getting scared. Again, I think, too late. Circumstances are going to pull us too strongly to the Australian area. We've got to keep Russia in the war and hold India. Then we can get ready to crack Germany through England.

FEBRUARY 23, 1942

Message to MacArthur was approved by president and dispatched. I'm dubious about the thing. I cannot help believing that we are disturbed by editorials and reacting to "public opinion" rather than to military logic. "Pa" Watson is certain we must get MacArthur out, as being worth "five army corps."[1] He is doing a good job where he is, but I'm doubtful that he'd do so well in more complicated situations. Bataan is made to order for him. It's in the public eye; it has made him a public hero; it has all the essentials of drama; and he is the acknowledged king on the spot. If brought out, public opinion will force him into a position where his love of the limelight may ruin him. We're having our troubles in joint army-navy problems. Admiral King, commander in chief of United States fleet, and directly subordinate to the president, is an arbitrary, stubborn type, with not too much brains and a tendency toward bullying his juniors.[2] But I think he wants to fight, which is vastly encouraging. In a war such as this, when high command invariably involves a president, a prime minister, six chiefs of staff, and a horde of lesser "planners," there has got to be a lot of patience—no one person can be a Napoleon or a Caesar. And certainly there's no room for a Pope or a Gates.[3] It's a backbreaking job to get a simple battle order out, and then it can't be executed for from three to four months.

FEBRUARY 24, 1942

MacArthur says, in effect, "Not now." I think he is right. This psychological warfare business is going to fall right into the lap of WPD, principally for the reason that no one else will lead with his chin. We'll probably take it on.

FEBRUARY 28, 1942

I wonder when we're going to get the dope on landing craft. I've got McCarthy trying it now.[1] But no one seems to give a damn.

MARCH 8, 1942

ABDA area is gone. Java is occupied almost completely. The task of reorganizing a command in SW Pacific is under study. Australians have made a proposal, through London, that United States take supreme command. The navy will probably not agree. Proposal contained in chiefs of staff No. (W) 109. What a headache this combined stuff is. We spend our time figuring out how to keep from getting in each other's way rather than in how to fight the war.[1]

MARCH 9, 1942

General McNaughton (commanding Canadians in Britain) came to see me.[1] He believes in attacking in Europe (thank God). He's over here in an effort to speed up landing craft production and cargo ships. Has some d----- good ideas. Sent him to see Somervell and Admiral Land.[2] How I hope he can do something on landing craft.

MARCH 10, 1942

Father died this morning. Nothing I can do but send a wire.
    One thing that might help win this war is to get someone to shoot King. He's the antithesis of cooperation, a deliberately rude person, which means he's a mental bully. He became Commander in Chief of the fleet some time ago. Today he takes over, also, Stark's job as chief of naval operations. It's a good thing to get rid of the double head in the navy, and of course Stark was just a nice old lady, but this fellow is going to cause a blow-up sooner or later, I'll bet a cookie.[1]
    Gradually some of the people with whom I have to deal are coming to agree with me that there are just three "musts" for the Allies this year: hold open the line to England and support her as necessary; keep Russia in the war as an active participant; hold the India-Middle East buttress between Japs and Germans. All this assumes the safety from major attack of North America, Hawaii, and Caribbean area.
    We lost eight cargo ships yesterday. That we must stop, because any effort we make depends upon sea communication.

MARCH 11, 1942

I have felt terribly. I should like so much to be with my Mother these few days. But we're at war. And war is not soft, it has no time to indulge even the deepest and most sacred emotions. I loved my Dad. I think my Mother the finest person

I've ever known. She has been the inspiration for Dad's life and a true helpmeet in every sense of the word.

I'm quitting work now, 7:30 P.M. I haven't the heart to go on tonight.

MARCH 12, 1942

My father was buried today. I've shut off all business and visitors for thirty minutes, to have that much time, by myself, to think of him. He had a full life. He left six boys, and, most fortunately for him, mother survives him. He was not quite seventy-nine years old, but for the past year he has been extremely old physically. Hardened arteries, kidney trouble, etc. He was a just man, well liked, well educated, a thinker. He was undemonstrative, quiet, modest, and of exemplary habits—he never used alcohol or tobacco. He was an uncomplaining person in the face of adversity, and such plaudits as were accorded him did not inflate his ego.

His finest monument is his reputation in Abilene and Dickinson County, Kansas. His word has been his bond and accepted as such; his sterling honesty, his insistence upon the immediate payment of all debts, his pride in his independence earned for him a reputation that has profited all of us boys. Because of it, all central Kansas helped me to secure an appointment to West Point in 1911, and thirty years later it did the same for my son, John. I'm proud he was my father. My only regret is that it was always so difficult to let him know the great depth of my affection for him.

DAVID J. EISENHOWER 1863 – 1942

MARCH 14, 1942

Lest I look at this book sometime and find that I've expressed a distaste for some person, and have put down no reason for my aversion, I record this one story of Admiral King.

One day this week General Arnold sent a very important note to King. Through inadvertence, the stenographer in Arnold's office addressed it, on the outside, to "Rear Admiral King." Twenty-four hours later the letter came back, unopened, with an arrow pointing to the "Rear," thus: [Here a long, heavy arrow has been drawn in a diagonal line underneath and pointing to the word "Rear."] And that's the size of man the navy has at its head. He ought to be a big help winning this war.[1]

MARCH 19, 1942

MacArthur is out of Philippine Islands. Now supreme commander of "Southwest Pacific Area." The newspapers acclaim the move—the public has built itself a hero out of its own imagination. I hope he can do the miracles expected and predicted; we could use a few now. Strange that no one sees the dangers. Some

[52] THE EISENHOWER DIARIES

apply to MacArthur, who could be ruined by it. But this I minimize; I know him too well. The other danger is that we will move too heavily in the Southwest. Urging us in that direction now will be: Australians, New Zealanders, our public (wanting support for the hero), and MacArthur. If we tie up our shipping for the SW Pacific, we'll lose this war. Already committed are

Air
    2 heavy bomber groups
    2 medium groups
    3 pursuit groups
    1 light group
    4 pursuit squadrons, on island bases
Ground
    2 divisions, Australia
    1 division, New Zealand
    1 division, New Caledonia
    1 division, among islands

This is too much, but I agreed to one in Australia and one in New Zealand to get those people to leave equal numbers in Middle East, which must be saved. More than this will be terrible.

MARCH 21, 1942

Yesterday I got very angry and filled a page with language that this morning I've "expurgated." Anger cannot win, it cannot even think clearly. In this respect Marshall puzzles me a bit. I've never seen a man who apparently develops a higher pressure of anger when he encounters some piece of stupidity than does he. Yet the outburst is so fleeting, he returns so quickly to complete "normalcy," that I'm certain he does it for effect. At least he doesn't get angry in the sense I do—I blaze for an hour! So, for many years I've made it a religion never to indulge myself, but yesterday I failed.

MARCH 28, 1942

I was made a major general yesterday. Took the oath of office today. Still a permanent lieutenant colonel, but the promotion is just as satisfactory as if a permanent one.[1] I suppose one could call it the official "stamp of approval" of the War Department.

I've been trying for some weeks to get some force in the Middle East and India. I want to help the British as much as possible, but avoiding use of our ground troops (except possibly one armored division). But I'm scared. We must save that region or run the risk of losing the war.

MARCH 30, 1942

Paragraph 1, Special Orders 79, War Department, announced me as major general (temporary) Army of the United States, dating from March 28; ranking from March 27. This should assure that when I finally get back to troops, I'll get a division.

Wainwright's position is getting bad, food and medicine required, and except for sub there's not much chance.[1]

MARCH 31, 1942

For many weeks—it seems years—I've been searching everywhere to find any feasible way of giving more help to the Philippine Islands. We've literally squandered money; we wrestled with the navy, we've tried to think of anything that might promise even a modicum of help. I'll go on trying, but daily the situation grows more desperate.

APRIL 20, 1942

MacArthur is getting rid of Quezon, apparently he no longer needs the president. Have had some difficulty answering MacArthur's message due to absence of president (Hyde Park). He approves but wants Ickes and Welles to concur.[1]

The generalissimo, Stilwell, American Volunteer Group, Tenth Air Force question has been in somewhat of a mess. Have tried to straighten it out, I hope successfully.

General Marshall returned from London last evening. He looks fine. I hope that, at long last, and after months of struggle by this division, we are all definitely committed to one concept of fighting. If we can agree on major purposes and objectives, our efforts will begin to fall in line and we won't just be thrashing around in the dark.

MAY 5, 1942

Bolero is supposed to have the approval of the president and prime minister.[1] But the struggle to get everyone behind it and to keep the highest authority from wrecking it by making additional commitments of air, ships, troops, elsewhere is never ending.

The actual fact is that not one man in twenty in the government (including the war and navy departments) realizes what a grisly, dirty, tough business we are in. They think we can buy victory.

MAY 6, 1942

This morning I attended a committee meeting on "landing craft" at which were discussed questions on which I begged the answers last February: (1) Who is responsible for building landing craft? (2) What types are they building? (3) Are they suitable for cross-Channel work? (4) Will the number of each type be sufficient? etc.?

How in hell can we win this war unless we can crack some heads?

Corregidor surrendered last night. Poor Wainwright! He did the fighting in the Philippine Islands, another got such glory as the public could find in the operation. Resistance elsewhere in the P.I. will quickly close, so it lasted five months.

General MacArthur's tirades, to which TJ and I so often listened in Manila, would now sound as silly to the public as they then did to us. But he's a hero! Yah.

NORTH AFRICA
AND ITALY

A half year of confusion in Washington could not cover over the fact that the United States, despite passage of the Draft Act in the summer of 1940, was still —two years later—quite unprepared to take part in the war in Europe. The trouble, although the War Department's high officials hesitated to diagnose it openly, was that the troops were without experience of almost any sort.

What to do? The situation of Russian troops that summer of 1942 was almost desperate. The Germans were attacking deep into Russian territory, and nothing seemed capable of stopping them. The planners of the United States Army could find some comfort in the fact that the situation of the Russians a year before, in the summer of 1941, also had been desperate, and the Soviet Army had survived. But the Russians pressed hard upon the American government to do something against the Germans during the year 1942, so as to take the pressure off the eastern front, and when Foreign Minister Vyacheslav Molotov came through Washington that spring President Roosevelt had promised a second front, presumably in France. The task of the American army's leaders then was to arrange the front, and it was some task, especially when the British army's leaders, who possessed the only battle-trained troops among the Anglo-Americans, virtually refused from the outset to take part in any invasion of the Continent through France.

As the weeks and months of 1942 began to pass, without any clear indication of what ought to be done, or could be done, messages went back and forth between London and Washington; General Marshall found himself pushed into a corner and so sent Eisenhower off to survey the prospects in England to see

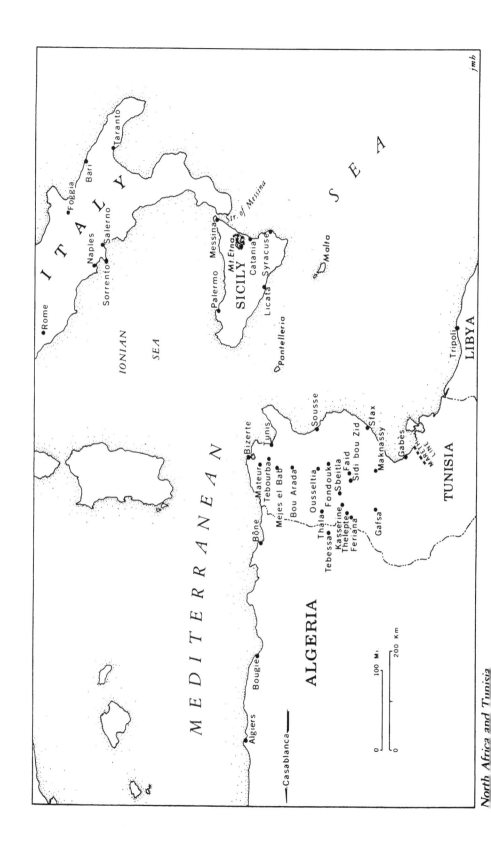

North Africa and Tunisia

if the American troops already sent to England, along with contingents that would come across that summer, would suffice (together with British forces, presumably working enthusiastically with the Americans) to invade the Continent and take the pressure off the Russians. Eisenhower went to Europe and did not find a serious sense of urgency either among the British or the Americans. The task seemed so large. Eventually a modus vivendi was arrived at—a decision taken to go into North Africa rather than Europe.

The decision to invade French North Africa had some considerable military justification, for quite apart from offering the necessary training to raw American troops and giving experience to Allied commanders in Anglo-American joint operations, there would be an opportunity not merely to ensure Africa against German penetration but to trap the German and Italian troops already there. In a series of desert campaigns that had moved back and forth across the top of Africa, from the very border of Egypt back into Libya as far as Bengasi, the British had been fighting the Italians since the latter had entered the war in 1940. But the Germans had gone into Africa in strength and furnished the remarkable leadership of General Erwin Rommel, the Desert Fox as he became known. The infusion of German troops among the Italians had stiffened up the campaigning, which was conducted sometimes according to the haunting strains of the only remarkable melody to come out of the Second World War, the tune entitled "Lili Marlene." In the spring of 1942, Rommel penetrated into Egypt; there was danger that a renewal of the fighting might roll up the British and allow Rommel to take Cairo and then move on into the oilfields of Saudi Arabia, Iraq, and Iran and maybe pass on to India as a second Alexander the Great. Prime Minister Winston Churchill's distaste for a cross-Channel attack into France was joined with concern for his beleaguered troops in Egypt. He began to urge a pincers attack in Africa, with Anglo-American troops coming down from England and crossing the Atlantic from America to occupy Morocco and Algeria at the same time that British troops in Egypt opened a counterattack and began to push Rommel's troops back through Libya.

Politically, the North African invasion also had its advantage, for President Roosevelt, a wily politician if ever there was one, told General Marshall that in the year 1942 it was essential to have American troops attacking somewhere, that they could not just sit and do nothing when the Russians were imploring the Americans for help and when the American people, two years after the Draft Act, were thinking that their own troops should surely be doing something. Congressional elections were coming up in November 1942, and Roosevelt did not want to lose them.

As mentioned, Eisenhower's first trip to England was in the role of his position as head of war plans, for he needed to see what the plans were producing. Marshall, however, may well have sensed from the outset that his assistant was the ideal man to command in England and, therefore, to command whatever attack was to be made by American troops that year.

MAY 21, 1942

I'm taking off on the twenty-third with General Arnold and others for a trip to England. We want to see how things are going there on our offensive plan, also Arnold wants to make a deal with the British to effect some kind of reallocation in airplanes. Under present arrangements we cannot build an air force; all our planes are taken up so rapidly that we cannot train.

My own particular reason for going is an uneasy feeling that either we do not understand our own commanding general and staff in England or they don't understand us. Our planning for Bolero is not progressing. We'll be gone about a week.

MAY 23, 1942

Landed at Montreal 10:10 A.M. Took off at 11:30 A.M., landing at Goose Lake, Labrador. Left Goose Lake late afternoon for United Kingdom. Three hours out had to turn back because of the weather, landing at Gander, Newfoundland, about midnight.

MAY 24, 1942

Spent the day at Gander. Skeet shooting. Left 5:30 P.M. Landed at Prestwick, Scotland, next day.

MAY 25, 1942

Had a late breakfast at the airfield. Then with Clark and Dykes visited activities in connection with an amphibian exercise that had just been called off.[1]

We saw assault landing craft and tank landing craft in operation. One of the tank landing crafts unloaded two heavy tanks (Churchills) and other equipment onto a ramp that was built in imitation of a beach. The British report themselves as well pleased with the "R" boat (our Higgins-Y boat), except that it carries no armor and is too noisy. Their assault-landing craft and tank-landing craft run very noiselessly but are not particularly suitable. They could cross the Channel only in very calm weather. The large tank-landing craft we saw was about 150 feet over-all and with 127 feet usable space.

We conferred with General Hawkesworth, commanding the Fourth Division, and with the captain in charge of the large landing craft.

During the day we passed the birthplace of Robert Burns and saw one of the spots where Robert Bruce was supposed to have spent considerable time.

MAY 26, 1942

We left Glasgow late Monday evening for London by train, arriving at 7:30 Tuesday morning. We spent the morning in conferences with General Chaney and his staff.[1] In the afternoon conferences were carried on with Colonel Truscott, some British officers, and in the evening went to a dinner given by Air Marshal Portal.[2]

MAY 27, 1942

Spent the day visiting a large field exercise in the Kent-Sussex area. The purpose of the exercise was to test out the new divisional organization of the British. General Montgomery, army commander in the southeast, was director and explained the exercises to us. General Montgomery is a decisive type who appears to be extremely energetic and professionally able. I would guess his age at fifty-eight years.[1]

During the day we met General Burrows of the tank corps and General Creagh. The latter officer has just returned from Egypt after almost two years of fighting in that region. He has positive and definite ideas on tank fighting, and we were particularly pleased to find him free from all inhibitions. He is a radical thinker and apparently a very good man.[2]

The new divisional organization of the British army is notable for two reasons. First, a tank brigade is included in each infantry division; second, it has an organized reconnaissance regiment. This regiment has considerable mobility and striking power. The British believe that it is absolutely essential as part of an infantry division.

The armored division has been reorganized by eliminating one of the mechanized brigades. Its total strength in tanks is now about 330. The tank regiment of the infantry division uses a very heavy Churchill type carrying a six-pounder and two machine guns. It is rather slow but is especially designed to take a terrific amount of punishment.

The tanks of the armored division are lighter and faster. In the British concept, the armored division must depend largely on maneuvers (soft spots) in tactics while the infantry division and its equipment should be organized for powerful blows.

MAY 28, 1942

In the morning attended meeting of the combined chiefs of staff. American officers present: General Somervell, General Chaney, and myself.

The main subject for discussion was the over-all command organization for Roundup.[1] The British submitted two diagrammatic outlines, one of which contemplated a supreme commander, the other did not.

General Brooke outlined the British viewpoint in detail, emphasizing the need for agreeing now on the basic outline of eventual command. He first stated that the supreme commander should be named at an early date.[2]

I outlined the American position, as explained to me by General Marshall before I left Washington, so far as it applied to the subject of discussion. I stated that in principle the Americans believed that single command was essential and that committee command could not conduct a major battle. I explained that our own organization was ideally adapted to this idea, since the operation would involve the American forces—principally air and ground. The navy part would be to bring the troops to England.

It was explained that although this was the American view it was believed that there was no necessity at present for naming the supreme commander for Roundup. As General Marshall has already stated, if any emergency operation takes place this year it will be under British command, with our forces attached to the British in suitable capacities. The eventual operation must of necessity be carried out by someone whose views will coincide closely with those of the British and American chiefs of staff, and consequently, planning can go ahead definitely and progressively without incurring the danger of the commander in chief having to scrap the plan and initiate a new one when operations begin.

I discovered that the British were puzzled as to the identity of the office with which their planners should cooperate. I flatly stated that this office was General Chaney's, that he was the American theater commander, and that through him representation would be accomplished on every joint committee involved.

This idea had apparently never occurred to the British chiefs of staff; they have looked on Chaney as something other than a theater commander. I took pains to make clear that the commander of the United States forces in Great Britain was the representative here of General Marshall and is the operational and administrative commander of all United States troops in the United Kingdom.

I suggested the thought that possibly the assault echelon of Bolero should be under a single commander, who would be a direct subordinate of the supreme commander.[3] To this idea General Brooke took exception and argued somewhat on it. I dismissed the subject with the statement that it should be studied and intimated that General Marshall might be prepared to accept Mountbatten as the commander concerned.[4] I definitely stated that the thought was one that had occurred to me because of the very special nature of this operation but that the only matter of principle involved was that of assuring unity of command on each particular section of the beach attacked.

The meeting broke up with my promise to see Lord Mountbatten on Thursday afternoon and General Brooke on Friday afternoon for further discussion.

It is quite apparent that the question of high command is the one that is bothering the British very much and some agreement, in principle, will have to be reached at an early date in order that they will go ahead wholeheartedly to succeeding steps. Attached hereto is a suggested diagram for higher organization, which I shall show to General Brooke.[5]

Attached to these notes are the diagrams submitted by the British chief of staff.[6]

At 4:30 P.M., meeting with Lord Mountbatten and his staff. The whole question of combined operations was discussed at length, as was also the future operations of commandos. There was no disagreement developed at the meeting. Lord Mountbatten believes that his particular mission is to develop the training and tactical doctrine applying to the assault echelon. The question of a single commander for the assault echelon was discussed briefly—it was agreed that this matter would be settled at a future date and that any one of several solutions would probably be acceptable. General Clark agreed with Lord Mountbatten to exchange staff officers in order to assure that training for this particular task would be homogeneous in both armies.

Landing craft came in for a considerable discussion, conducted mainly by Lord Mountbatten. He pointed out that British insistence upon the larger type of craft was not due entirely to the length of the run across the Channel. The British believe that very strong ground formations must strike the beaches suddenly and simultaneously. This cannot be accomplished in small boats because the required density cannot be achieved. They agree that the tactics cannot be the same on all beaches because of different characteristics and differences in the tactical situations. They foresee the need of employing, along with the giant type of personnel and tank carriers, a considerable number of troop ships, which will unload into small boats, somewhat according to the normal pattern.

Lord Mountbatten has an engagement to meet General Somervell to discuss possibilities in landing craft procurement.

At 8:30 P.M., conference was held with the plans section of General Chaney's office. The conference was for the purpose of discussing the conception of the invasion task, as the plans division here so far visualizes it. The plan was worked up in collaboration with General Paget's office.[7]

The plan contemplates the American forces on the western portion of the invasion front, the British on the eastern. It has been calculated that if eighteen or nineteen American divisions are in England on "D" day then the American army can have twenty-seven divisions in France by "D" day plus eighty or ninety.

All plans are worked up under a series of assumptions, most of which involve the Russian situation and the consequent readiness of the Germans to oppose invasion. A copy of the tentative estimate is attached to these notes.[8]

MAY 29, 1942

Conference in the morning with Dr. Evatt.[1] The conference lasted considerable time, but Dr. Evatt requested nothing specific except that we not forget our commitments in the Pacific.

At three o'clock had a conference with General Brooke. Only the two of us were present. The general plan of attack, the question of high command, and the general organization of the American forces in the near future were the subjects chiefly discussed.

After the meeting with General Brooke, had a conference with General Kennedy, who is director of military plans and operations. Much the same subjects were discussed with him as were previously discussed with General Brooke.

Had a conference with the joint secretariat and arranged Nevins's position and status.[2]

Conference with General Arnold and General Somervell at 7:00 P.M. They agreed that we must be particularly careful to impress the British with the responsibility resting upon General Chaney, together with his complete authority to act for American forces in Europe. Dinner with Admiral Stark in the Dorchester.[3]

MAY 30, 1942

Visited the Dover defenses under command of Brigadier Harding. Returned to London at 4:30 P.M. and held conference with General Paget. Others present were General Clark, Colonels Barker, Sheetz, and Hamblen, and members of General Paget's staff.[1] General Paget's idea is that the Americans should assault with the idea of capturing Le Havre; and the British, Boulogne and Calais, each with a force of about three divisions. Immediately thereafter each force should be built up to six divisions and General Paget believes that this reports the maximum that could be placed across the Channel until port facilities begin to be usable.

The question of inland transportation from the bridgehead was discussed at length and the British believe that it is going to be at least a three-to-four-month task to secure the necessary ports and extended communications inland to the point where we can really begin a major advance.

The British are setting up twenty-one divisions for the whole operation including Canadian and one Polish. Eight of these divisions will be armored.

General Paget is very anxious to have an additional staff officer immediately to serve as an intelligence officer.

JUNE 4, 1942

Returned yesterday from England. I've recommended McNarney to replace Chaney. Also, I've recommended Wayne Clark to command the first corps to be sent to England. I talked with many people in England—chiefs of staff (Pound, Portal, Brooke, Mountbatten), Paget, Montgomery, Nye, and our own commander and staff.[1] Our own people are able but do not quite understand what we want done. It is necessary to get a punch behind the job or we'll never be ready by spring, 1943, to attack. We must get going.

JUNE 8, 1942

The chief of staff told me this morning that it's possible I may go to England in command. It's a big job; if the United States and the United Kingdom stay squarely behind Bolero and go after it tooth and nail, it will be the biggest American job of the war. Of course, command now does not necessarily mean command in the operation, but the job before the battle begins will still be the biggest outside of that of the chief of staff himself.

JUNE 11, 1942

The chief of staff says I'm the guy. He also approves Clark for corps commanding general in England and gives us the II Corps. Now we really go to work. Hope to leave here by plane on twenty-second.

JUNE 20, 1942

The president of the Philippines visited me at 10:00 A.M. today. His purpose was to tender to me an honorarium for services rendered during the period I was acting as General MacArthur's chief of staff in Manila, where he (MacArthur) went as military adviser to the Philippine government. (Certain American officers were detailed to that task, by direction of the president of the United States, under authority of a law passed in 1926 and amended in 1934 or 1935.)

President Quezon brought with him to my office a draft of a citation which he had written to accompany the presentation to me of the honorarium.

I carefully explained to the president that I deeply appreciated his thought and was grateful for his expressions of gratitude, but that it was inadvisable and even impossible for me to accept a material reward for the services performed.

I explained that while I understood this to be unquestionably legal, and that the president's motives were of the highest, the danger of misapprehension or misunderstanding on the part of some individual might operate to destroy whatever usefulness I may have to the allied cause in the present war. My government has entrusted me with important tasks, carrying grave responsibility. We agreed that the only matter that is now important is for everyone to do his best in the war effort, and any gossip on such a matter might reflect upon the army and the War Department.

In view of the representations I made, the president accepted my explanations and stated that the matter was ended once and for all.

He then said he wanted to do something that could not possibly embarrass me. It developed that this plan was to present to me, in official form, the citation he had written to accompany the honorarium he had in mind. I stated that I not only had no objection but that I would be highly honored in the receipt of a commendation from him, which I explained would be supplementary to the flattering citation he gave me two years ago. I told him that such a citation would be of great and more lasting value to me and my family than any amount of money his government could possibly present to me.

The matter was dropped on this basis, with the president stating that he honestly believed that in the same circumstances he would probably have given the same answer that I did. He obviously accepted my decision without resentment and without loss of face—this latter point was one that had given me tremendous concern. To refuse a gift from anyone raised in the Far East, especially if a point of ethics has to be pled, is quite apt to develop into a serious personal matter. I'm certain that President Quezon feels I did the right thing and that he has respect for my decision. (In contemplating my decision, which I had opportunity to do in advance because of a telephone call from General Valdez, my method of declining gracefully became clearer after a short talk with General Marshall on the subject.)[1]

JUNE 22, 1942

General Clark and I had an appointment with the president and the prime minister at noon. Mr. Hopkins was present.[1] Matters discussed were of a general nature pertaining to Bolero and the exact nature of the assignments for General Clark and myself in England. The president had been informed of an appointment General Clark and I had with the prime minister for 5:30 that same evening, so after a brief visit the meeting broke up.

The president commented to me personally that he was having a small inter-bureau war because of requests from four governmental departments for the services of my brother Milton. He jokingly remarked that it was taking all his time to decide the merits of the case. I merely observed that my brother was a very able man, and the president retorted that he was well aware of the fact, that that was the whole reason for the war.[2]

JUNE 23, 1942

General Clark and I, accompanied by a group of staff officers, left Washington at 9:00 A.M. on a stratoliner, Captain Campbell commanding. We landed at Gander about 3:30 P.M. Washington time and took off about two hours later. We landed at Prestwick and, after remaining there an hour and a half, came on to London without incident.

General Bolté, members of the headquarters staff, General Lee, and Lord Louis Mountbatten with members of his staff met us at the plane. Conference that night at the hotel with Lee, his chief of staff, General Clark, General Bolté, and General Littlejohn.[1]

Time of arrival was 7:00 P.M., June 24.

JUNE 25, 1942

Conferences all day with members of the headquarters staff and with General Lee. Points stressed to the staff were (1) that each section must bear its share of responsibility and push incessantly toward the attainment of the objective, which is to have an army in the field, ready to attack by early spring, 1943; (2) that each staff section contribute its part toward assuring a readiness to fight before that time with whatever might be available at the moment such a fight might be ordered; that plans for this emergency fight would be largely prepared by the II Corps commander, but with the full collaboration of this staff and the SOS [Service of Supply]; (3) that an atmosphere of the utmost earnestness coupled with determined enthusiasm and optimism characterize every member of this staff and every subordinate command in England; that pessimism and defeatism not be tolerated, and that any person who could not rise above the recognized obstacles and bitter prospects that lie in store for us has no recourse but to ask for instant release from this theater; and (4) that all staff work be characterized by an absence of formality—that we are not operating or writing for the record but to win the war. Staff officers are free to see the chief or the commander at any moment to bring to their attention such matters as are necessary or desirable. They are free to solve their own problems wherever possible and not to get in the habit of passing the buck up.

Press release drafted in Washington given out at first press conference, which was held today. Notes of the conference are kept in separate file, "Minutes of Press Conferences."[1]

I have been assigned to command the European theater for United States forces. The formal establishment of a European theater is a logical step in coordinating the efforts of Great Britain and the United States.

Six months ago the prime minister of Great Britain and the president of the United States heartened the people of the United Nations by moving swiftly to merge the military and economic strength of Britain and the United States for a common effort. At that Washington conference they set a more effective pattern for unqualified partnership than has ever before been envisaged by allied nations in pursuit of a common purpose. Only recently they have met again to bring combined action into even closer coordination.

The presence here in the British Isles of American soldiers and pilots in rapidly increasing numbers is evidence that we are hewing to the line of that pattern. [Press release.]

Announcement was made of an intention to move the headquarters outside of the middle of London, and the headquarters commandant was given the task of finding suitable accommodations so that a common mess and living accommodations could be established for all of us. A place called Wentworth was suggested as a likely one. General Ismay has promised to help us out in this task.[2] The staff was further informed that all policy making applying to this theater lay with this headquarters. All subordinate commands are executive and operating agencies, with their functions of planning and policy making applying only to their respective spheres of responsibility and action. It was emphasized that no set scheme of organization, training, or concept of command was to prevail over common sense in adjusting our means to meet our needs. Absolute freedom in planning to meet our requirements has been granted this headquarters, and this imposes a corresponding responsibility to act decisively and promptly and with no alibis to offer.

Arrangements have been made for a group of us to go to Ireland on Wednesday next, returning Thursday. Tonight a group of us are meeting with Lord Louis Mountbatten to hear a lecture given by an officer who participated in the Madagascar operation. Tomorrow afternoon I am to call on the three chiefs of staff of the British army. Colonel Stirling (of the war cabinet secretariat) visited me this afternoon and, among other things, stated that he would arrange for me to pay my duty call on the king.

I explained to Summers my reason for sending him home.

I am living temporarily at the Claridge Hotel.

JUNE 26, 1942

This morning I called on the British chiefs of staff, Admiral Pound, Air Chief Marshal Portal, and General Nye (General Brooke has not yet returned from Washington). Immediately thereafter I called on the American ambassador, Winant, and had a long talk with him.[1] This afternoon I had conferences with General Spaatz, General Clark, and General Davison.[2] Questions discussed included many applying to the Eighth Air Force, construction of airdromes, and air support for the II Corps. General agreements and understanding were reached on all questions raised.

I have made arrangements with Lord Louis Mountbatten to go with him next Tuesday night on a special exercise to witness the landing of tanks during hours of darkness. The following day Lord Louis will put me down in Ireland where I have a date with Lee, Hartle, Clark, and Spaatz.[3] This coming Sunday I go to dinner as General Lee's guest and the following Thursday as the guest of General Bolté.

JUNE 27, 1942

General Clark went to the Southern Defense Command to make preliminary arrangements for the establishment of his headquarters and to agree in principle upon defense missions that would be assigned to his troops.

I held a morning conference with the heads of all special staff sections and later a special conference with General Lyon, head of the technical air staff. This last conference developed the fact that a number of functions pertaining to the old "military observer" are still being performed by this headquarters. We are quite ready to serve as an agency for the War Department in any manner deemed necessary or desirable, but it would appear essential that a new definition of duties in this respect should be given us so that we do not cross wires with the Munitions Assignment Committee and similar bodies.

Conference was held with the anti-aircraft officer and G-3 [Operations] division concerning our requirements in anti-aircraft for airdromes in England and for the actual problems of invasion. Anti-aircraft units required for the first purpose must to a large extent meet those of the second, since limitations both in production of units and in shipping will not permit the fulfillment of the entire requirements as calculated by the staff. A compromise solution is being reached at once, and preliminary telegram is going to the War Department this afternoon.

I go to Scotland on Tuesday to witness a special exercise; I go to Ireland on Wednesday and Thursday to see the troops there; Friday I go to the south of England for a special purpose, which I will record in more detail after the event. This evening I go to a little affair given in my honor by the military attaché. Afterwards I have an informal dinner with my old friend Everett Hughes.[1]

Colonel Summers requested today that I revoke his orders for returning to the states. I declined but promised that I would carry him over for about a month so as to avoid the implication that I relieved him immediately upon arrival.

JUNE 29, 1942

Conversations with a number of staff officers during the day. Principal topics for discussion involve the organization of theater and SOS headquarters so as to promote efficiency in the use of the technical services. This matter was fought all the way through the World War, has been the subject of much bitter discussion ever since, and is still a tough one to handle. Most advice is, of course, colored by individuals who subsconsciously think of their own power or opportunities for advancement. Even without these difficulties there seems to be no perfect solution. Fortunately, I have in Lee one of the best officers of the army and I am confident that he and I together can work out a practical answer that will meet the requirements of the particular problems in this theater.[1]

Another matter that we have discussed all day long is that of promotions to the grade of general officer. General Chaney has previously recommended a number of colonels for promotion, but these were held up by the War Department pending my comment. In addition, I have two officers of General Clark's staff who were more or less promised promotion in Washington—to become effective upon their arrival in this theater.

This morning a representative of Colonel Donovan's named Shepardson called on me. His purpose was to explain the situation of the chief of intelligence branch here with respect to the theater. It appears that he fully understands the necessity for the theater commander controlling all activities of a military nature on this front, and I have every confidence that his operations will be conducted accordingly.[2]

General Truscott reports that the First Ranger Battalion is now moving to its new station and will start intensive training at once.

This afternoon I visited General Ismay, head of the War Cabinet Secretariat. I assured him that if the British undertook definite planning for Sledgehammer, we would cooperate to the extent of our available resources and on the basis of attachment to their commander.[3] He also offered to help in securing a satisfactory site for a new headquarters.

General Ismay is taking personal charge of making arrangements for my call on the prime minister and on the king. I requested him to postpone this until the beginning of next week, due to my crowded schedule of the next few days. He replied that this would be particularly satisfactory from the standpoint of the prime minister, who is busily engaged in preparing an important speech to be delivered before the Parliament.

JUNE 30, 1942

In the morning called on General Paget, accompanied by General Clark and General Bolté. The conversation dealt largely with means and methods for pushing the planning for Roundup. General Paget remarked that "If we could only have your organization, this whole thing would be easy."

General Paget is to keep my staff informed in advance as to meetings of the commanders in chief so that I may attend such meetings with members of my staff.

The chiefs of staff are likewise to keep me informed in advance concerning meetings at which "Roundup" operations will be discussed. I am to attend those meetings.

In the afternoon Major Forester, British army, called to see me. He is press relations officer and works in Washington in close liaison with General Surles.[1]

Left at 4:30 P.M. for Scotland with General Clark and Lord Louis Mountbatten.

JULY 1, 1942

Went as a member of Lord Louis's party to witness some secret exercises in Scotland, north of Prestwick. The exercises were over about 5:00 P.M. Went to bed on Lord Louis's yacht and got up at eight. Visited a combined signal school run by Lord Louis's group and then went on to Prestwick. Left Prestwick at 11:00 A.M. by plane and landed at Longkesh. Spent the day with General Hartle, General Ward, General Ryder, General Lee, General Clark, and members of their respective staffs.[1] Discussed problems affecting the whole theater as well as those applying to Northern Ireland. Hartle and Lee are to work out a directive under which Lee will take over ordinary functions of the SOS in Ireland. Visited a number of troops of the First Armored Division and had dinner with the headquarters staff of the First Armored Division that evening.

Spent the night at the Grand Central Hotel in Belfast.

JULY 2, 1942

Returned to London this morning. During the day had discussions with members of the staff and with General McClure.[1] The latter had brought back with him from Washington a suggested directive for the placing of the office of the military attaché under the theater commander. He suggests a slightly different wording in one or two places, and I have accepted his recommendations. These suggestions are now being cabled to Washington with the expectation that they will be approved and the consolidation will take place soon.

I am a bit undecided as to the identity of my G-2.[2] I would personally prefer McClure, but this would probably mean the return of Case to the states.[3] Case is a very valuable man, and I would like to keep him here. Mr. Matthews, counselor at the embassy, called but discussed only general matters of cooperation between the two offices.[4]

At 8:15 P.M. went to a small dinner given by General Bolté. Present, aside from senior American officers, were the British chiefs of staff, General Ismay, and Lord

Louis Mountbatten. After dinner, drove with Mountbatten to his home near Southampton, where I spent the night.

JULY 3, 1942

Early this morning Mountbatten and I visited a ship called the *Prince Charles*, just ready to leave the port of Southampton as a part of the flotilla carrying a small expedition on a secret mission. On the ship were a few Americans, officers and men, participating in the operation. I had an intimate chat with all of them and found them to be the very finest types of soldier. I was unable to see the entire American contingent as they were scattered among a number of ships, some of which had already departed.

On leaving Southampton, I went to the airport at Worthy Downs, where I met General Eaker.[1] He flew me to an airport in the Huntingdon area, a hundred miles north of London. There were collected the men of six bomber groups who are to take part in an operation tomorrow. I had a chat with all of them and enjoyed the opportunity to say good luck to them.

While at the airport I inspected a heavy Wellington bomber that had just returned from a raid on Bremen. It had a Polish pilot whose name I do not know. The remainder of the crew were British. He came in with the airplane full of small-caliber bullet holes, with every member of the crew wounded except himself, with one wheel shot entirely away, and the other hanging uselessly with a punctured tire—the bomb doors hanging down, the exit door of the airplane shot away, and two or three heavy shots in the wings and engine sections. All pilots examining the plane were amazed that he could fly home. He landed the ship safely, and while it will probably be salvaged instead of repaired, he did not cause any further injury to any of his crew.

When authority is obtained for giving American awards to officers of other countries it is my intention to confer a suitable award upon this officer.

This evening I am having Commander Butcher, Colonel Davis, George Allen, and a number of others to dinner. Davis and Butcher arrived last evening.[2]

JULY 4, 1942

Attended formal opening of the Washington Club, a club for service personnel established by the Red Cross. Admiral Stark accepted for the navy; I accepted for the army.

In the afternoon, at the insistence of Ambassador Winant, I attended a reception at his house, standing in the receiving line. I had understood that it was to be a rather small reception, principally for service personnel. Actually, only a few military individuals attended, but a total number of 2,650 passed the receiving line.

In the evening had dinner alone with General Lee and discussed serious problems concerning organization of the SOS and the division of functions between the special staff officers and his headquarters and my own. Both of us are in substantial agreement, and it is entirely possible that we will abolish the title of "chief of service" in this theater.

JULY 5, 1942

Most of the day in the office, going to Chequers in the evening. General Clark and I went there at the invitation of the prime minister. We were due for eight o'clock dinner, arrived there at 7:45. We were met by Commander Thompson, the prime minister's naval aide, who entertained us until the prime minister made his appearance. We spent the early part of the evening on the lawn in front of the house, and when the prime minister appeared, took a walk with him into the neighboring woods, discussing matters of general interest in connection with the war.

The house at Chequers dates from about 1480 and is on the site of an earlier building of which records are kept dating from 1060. It is rather unpretentious but a very good type of English brick architecture of that time. The principal feature of the house is an enormous living room with the ceiling running completely to the roof, around which are built various offices, dining rooms, and dens. On the second floor is a nice movie theater at which the prime minister entertains not only his guests, but all of the retainers of the household. Dinner was at nine with Lady Portal as another guest and Mrs. Churchill present. General Ismay and Commander Thompson were the only other persons at dinner.

In the evening we saw a movie, *The Tuttles of Tahiti*, an American picture starring Charles Laughton. Fortunately it was in the lighter vein and was hilariously funny. All of us, including the prime minister, had a thoroughly good time.

After the movie, the prime minister and the rest of us talked until about 2:30 A.M. We were interrupted frequently to receive reports coming from all corners of the world, principally the Middle East and naval reports concerning the convoy off north Norway. Whenever these reports were of a favorable nature the prime minister's conversation would glow for the next thirty minutes or so. Conversely, a pessimistic report would get him in the dumps. Upon going to bed at 2:30, I found in my room a book that dealt exclusively with the history of Chequers, together with the furniture and objects of art all over the place. I could not go to sleep without reading that part applying to my own room. I slept in an enormous oak bed, four poster, with enormous bulges on the posts at intervals, each elaborately carved, the whole surmounted by a canopy, which instead of being of fabric was solid oak, apparently about six inches thick. The oak was black, either from coloring or from age, and elaborately carved as well. This room was supposed to have been frequently used by Cromwell, whose daughter had married the then owner of the house. Cromwell's picture hung in the room where I slept. Also there was a desk of inlaid wood that was reported to have been one of his favorites.

We rose at 7:45 in the morning, went downstairs to a breakfast that was typically American. Wayne and I each had two fried eggs and plenty of fried ham. Immediately after breakfast I inspected a guard of honor made up of a detachment of the Coldstream Guards. General Clark accompanied me, and both of us were impressed by the very elaborate drill, manual of arms, and ceremonies that the British have set up for this kind of performance. They were a magnificent body of men, the shortest being at least six feet.

We left Chequers at ten o'clock and arrived in London a bit after eleven.

The subjects discussed in our conversation with the prime minister really covered all the theaters of war. We talked generally about the Pacific, Australia, India, China, and so on, but, in general, our conversation was directed toward the western part of Europe and of Africa. It is plain to see that the prime minister strongly favors an operation this year in northwest Africa, called in our code name Gymnast. As a secondary operation or attempt, he favors an effort at northern Norway. He is quite averse to attempting anything on Western Europe between Norway and the Brest Peninsula. He believes it would be slaughter because we are not strong enough, either in the air, on the ground, or with landing craft to make the operation a success and stay on the Continent this year. I pointed out to him many of the disadvantages of Gymnast[1] and raised the question as to whether such an operation would divert from the Russian front a single German division or a single German airplane. He is quite confident that the Germans would come to meet such a movement the second it started and is also quite confident that the French would not fight the Americans. I cannot share his optimism on either of these points. I do not mean to say that I believe he is wrong but I do think that it is wrong to count on these two matters being as he believes.

JULY 6, 1942

Important conference this morning with General Paget and with members of his staff and the air staff. Principal questions discussed were (1) projected frontage for Roundup;[1] (2) considerations applying to a 1942 operation; (3) arrangements for insuring progress in planning and in concrete preparations involving joint British-American effort; and (4) agreement as to the meaning of the expression "deterioration in German morale," which is so often used in British discussions of the Roundup operation. Upon my suggestion it was agreed that this term means only that the Russian army will be in the field at the time of the beginning of Roundup, as a fighting force—it does not include a necessity that the Germans shall have suffered serious tactical reverses.

On recommendation of General Spaatz sent a telegram to General Handy asking him to release Colonel Hansell for service in this theater.[2]

Conferences with staff officers during the afternoon.

JULY 20, 1942

General Marshall arrived in London Saturday morning and immediately held a conference at the Claridge at which were present: Admiral King, General Clark, Admiral Stark, General Spaatz, General Lee, various staff officers, and myself. The subject discussed was the possibility of conducting an attack in this theater this year. The British attitude and our own findings on the thing were thoroughly discussed. The reasons for such an attack involve primarily help for Russia. The paper that I had prepared in advance of General Marshall's visit attempted to point out that the real questions to be settled were: first, exactly how desperate the Russian situation was, and second, whether or not Sledgehammer would contribute anything in assistance of the Russians.

Conferences revolving around this general subject were held throughout the day and were resumed on Sunday morning. Opinion gradually crystallized in favor of a Cherbourg operation if any should be undertaken at all.

General Marshall is due to see the prime minister and the British chiefs of staff today (Monday). He will present to them a memorandum which insists upon immediate preparation for a September attack if conditions then are such as to make it appear desirable.

Our immediate job is to push for the adequate organization of the II Corps (General Clark). This will require some change in shipping schedules and an immediate initiation of intensive planning, training, and organization.

The Thirty-fourth Division would necessarily be used, and I am sending at once for General Ryder, commanding that division, to make sure that he has the necessary officers, particularly in the senior grades.

The decisions to be made are not only highly secret but momentous. There is an atmosphere of tension that will disappear once the decisions are completed and we actually know what we are to do.

JULY 22, 1942

The last few days have been tense and wearing. We have had numerous conferences with General Marshall and Admiral King on the subject of the Sledgehammer attack. The British have placed themselves on record time and again as being definitely against this attack. First, because they believe it would have no beneficial effect on the Russian situation, and second, because the chances of tactical disaster are very great. The chances for tactical disaster arise out of the disparity between ourselves and the Germans in available military formations and out of the terrible weather conditions that prevail over the Channel during the fall.

The burden of stating, for the American side, whether or not the capture of Cherbourg is a feasible military operation has been placed upon General Clark and myself. It is a tough decision to make because so many imponderables are involved and because the time required for mounting the attack is so long. We had always understood that the British staff believed they could mount an attack of this description within sixty days after receipt of notice—they now demand four months, with an absolute minimum of three. This makes the earliest date for the attack October 15. We feel that in many respects the October 15 attack is a much more highly dangerous affair than the September 15; this due to weather and to strengthening of German defenses as well as to the possibility of their transferring troops from the Russian front. Moreover, if the attack is to help the Russians, it ought to be delivered at the earliest possible date.

Clark and I finally told the general that if he thought the Russians were in bad shape and that an attack on the French coast would have a material effect in assisting the Russians, we should attempt the job at the earliest possible date—regardless. We do not say that the thing will be a tactical success, but we do say that with wholehearted cooperation all the way round we have a fighting chance. As a result, we advised to fight for the proposition and to insist on making the attack. This was a tough recommendation to make, and I sincerely hope that it works out with reasonable success.

We have sat up nights on the problems involved and have tried to open our eyes clearly to see all the difficulties and not to be blinded by a mere passion for doing something. However, this last factor alone is worth something. The British and American armies and the British and American people need to have the feeling that they are attempting something positive. We must not degenerate into a passive and mental attitude.

Today, Wednesday, the twenty-second of July, the decision between General Marshall and Admiral King, representing the United States, and the prime minister and the British chiefs of staff, on the other side, should be reached. If that decision is to attack, we intend to do our utmost to have ready a small corps under Clark, comprising two divisions and auxiliary troops with the armored division in reserve.

JULY 26, 1942

On July 22 the British chiefs of staff and the prime minister definitely rejected our proposals that any offensive operation of this year should be directed against the French coast. We supported our recommendations with a brief outline of a plan for attacking Cherbourg, which we believe could be done rather effectively and with good chance of sustaining ourselves there.

Since both the British and Americans have been directed to conduct an offensive operation somewhere this year, the rejection by the British of our proposition forces the employment of additional United States troops in some theater other than this. Consequently, the British decision of July 22 may become one of the most far-reaching import on the future conduct of the war.

In effect, it rejects the thought that the allies can do anything to help the Russians remain in the war as an effective fighting force and compels action toward improving our own defensive situation in anticipation of a Russian collapse.

It is quite clear that Roundup may never come off, even with the most intensive and concentrated effort on our part, since the execution of Roundup must depend upon the existence of an effective Russian army, but the action of the British in rejecting Sledgehammer (offensive action against France this year) practically acknowledges that Roundup can never be executed, unless and until the whole German position experiences a very great deterioration. Our only effort to bring about that deterioration is a waiting one, rather than a positive one.

Upon the announcement of their decision by the British chiefs of staff, the problem became one of determining the proper action for the allied forces for the remainder of 1942. The old Gymnast operation was revived for consideration, as was the proposition of reinforcing the Middle East with American divisions. In this dilemma, it appeared that the Gymnast operation was the better one of the two, in that it was less passive in character, while the line of communications involved is only one-third as long. The decision was made to start intensive preparation for Gymnast, but with the determination to prosecute Round-up whenever this should become possible. The British do not agree with the Americans that the Gymnast operation means a practical death knell for Roundup.

The above decisions have been reached; the staff decisions centered around the proper command set up for the allied and the American armies. First of all, it was believed proper to get the same individual in charge of preparing for both Roundup and Gymnast, in order that there would not be two agencies competing for the resources of both missions. It was further agreed that such a commander might have to have a deputy in England, which deputy would later, in the event of the execution of Gymnast, be the commander of that operation. According to General Marshall's understanding of the agreement, I am to be that deputy and that future commander. This apparently places upon me the following tasks: (1) to command the American army forces in Europe; (2) to continue prepara-tions for the Roundup operation (including in this the task also of preparing for Sledgehammer, if by some good fortune we should get an unexpected opportunity to execute that operation under favorable circumstances); (3) to prepare the American forces for Roundup; and (4) to be in complete charge of preparing the Gymnast operation.

Obviously, at least three separate staffs, other than General Clark's in the II Corps, will be necessary for these jobs. The first one will be the present theater staff; the second one will be the supreme commander's staff for Gymnast; the third one will be the supreme commander's staff for Roundup.

The British have informed me (Ismay, Mountbatten, Stirling) that they con-sider all these agreements and understandings to be definitely attained, awaiting only formal, although secret, announcement by the two governments.[1] In the meantime, however, nothing can be done because the duties outlined above will place me in a position of controlling and directing staffs and commanders, among whom will be many individuals senior to me. I expect some kind of directive this week.

JULY 27, 1942

The first memorandum submitted by the chiefs of staff to the British chiefs of staff strongly urged the mounting of Sledgehammer.[1] It gave a number of reasons and possibly you [Commander Butcher was keeping the headquarters diary and this entry was going into it] might summarize these briefly by getting a copy from Captain Lee.[2] The British chiefs of staff and their prime minister finally and definitely rejected the proposal for mounting Sledgehammer.

General Marshall then asked me, with such of my assistants as I desired to bring into the picture, to prepare for him a statement of the strategy that should be applied in the Atlantic theater, to be considered with the possibility of reinforcing the Middle East—mounting of Gymnast—and the eventual fate of Roundup.[3] Out of all this, we finally evolved a plan which insisted upon retaining Roundup as the principal strategic aim of the United Kingdom–United States. We proposed to prepare for both Sledgehammer and Gymnast in the thought that one might become necessary this fall.

I believe that, for the sake of the record, you should get Captain Lee's file of papers pertaining to General Marshall's visit and summarize in the briefest possible fashion some of the principal arguments developed.

There are also papers dealing with the final agreements reached by the United States and United Kingdom staffs. As explained to me by General Marshall, it is now contemplated that I occupy three positions: (1) commanding general for

Along the road in North Africa. Ike is eating out of a messkit, a frying pan with a collapsible handle.

the United States forces in this theater, (2) deputy commander or the supreme commander over the whole Bolero-Roundup-Gymnast conception, (3) supreme commander of Gymnast, if that operation should actually be staged.

SEPTEMBER 2, 1942

On July 24 general agreement was reached by the combined chiefs of staff, meeting in London, to undertake the operation Torch.[1] I think the records clearly show the reasons why General Marshall finally became convinced that this decision must be accepted and implemented.

In agreeing to this proposition, General Marshall understood that there was available to the allies a sufficient amount of air, ground, and naval strength to execute strong attacks simultaneously at Casablanca, Oran, and Algiers. It was originally calculated that it might take to December 1 to mount this attack.

Even before General Marshall left London, on July 26, the president had approved the proposition tentatively but insisted upon an attack date of no later than October 30. All the agreements contained the proviso that I was to be commander in chief of the operation and that the whole expedition would be combined British-American land, air, and sea forces.

Delay in preparation was encountered immediately when some time elapsed before official word was received from Washington confirming command arrangements. For a period of about ten days the matter was kept most secret and not even the various commanders in chief in the British services were informed. This resulted in my being able to do nothing but make discreet studies of a G-2 [Intelligence] nature. Finally this authorization was secured and planning started with the early organization of a combined British-American staff. Admiral King sent to the United Kingdom members of his planning group, but these representatives were not authorized to make any commitments from the American naval strength. They stated they were here merely to learn.

It was quickly discovered that there was not in sight sufficient naval strength to support three major landings simultaneously. Various expedients were studied hurriedly, and I finally decided, in view of the very ambitious objectives prescribed by the combined chiefs of staff, to make the entire attack inside the Mediterranean. The Casablanca attack was abandoned because of the necessity for pushing rapidly into Tunis and because all reports showed that a very bad surf would probably be encountered in any attempt to land on the Atlantic coastline.

This solution awakened grave anxiety in the War Department at home. However, study had conclusively shown that it was impossible to build up a force of sufficient strength to make tactical considerations the governing ones in undertaking this operation. The capacity of the ports and the relative slowness of the buildup made it clear that if the French forces in North Africa should oppose the landing as a unit and with their full strength, there would be little hope of carrying out the great purpose of sweeping to the eastward to gain control of the whole of North Africa. Consequently, the whole campaign had to be considered as depending entirely upon political factors—that is, upon the accuracy with which our political leaders could foresee the reactions of the French and Spanish armies in North Africa to this landing.

Without going into the details of the various plans proposed, it is sufficient to say that, measured purely from a military standpoint, the risks of the projected operation were so great as to condemn it if military factors alone were considered.

Finally, about the middle of August, the chiefs of staff in Washington proposed to the British chiefs of staff that the directive be rewritten on the basis of attacking only at Casablanca and Oran. The purpose was to secure the landline of communications running from Casablanca to Oran and so to decrease the dependence upon the hazardous route through the straits of Gibraltar. This, of course, was highly desirable, but the fact remained that if the French resisted at all, the damage that could be caused the long and insecure line of communications—between the two cities named—would be so great as to prevent its use until after some months of rehabilitation and new construction. This fact again brought to the fore the certainty that success depends upon nonresistance on the part of the French army.

A considerable number of telegrams passed back and forth between the War Department and this headquarters and between the Washington chiefs of staff and the British chiefs of staff. The president and the prime minister likewise began corresponding on the matter. The general result of all this was that no firm plan could be made. It became necessary to prepare for a number of contingencies, hoping that not too much time would be lost—no matter what the nature of the final decision. During all this time, both the prime minister and the president were pressing for an early date of the attack, apparently not realizing that failure to reach firm decisions as between themselves and firm decisions as between the two groups of chiefs of staff made it impossible to prepare definitely for any operation.

On August 29 the president proposed that all British land forces be dropped from the calculations, that the attacks be directed at Casablanca and Oran, and that the whole project be entirely American except for supporting naval forces and shipping—possibly also some air. This plan contemplated the preparation of an American force in the United Kingdom for the attack at Oran. On our part it required a vast amount of hurried training, improvisation of units, and resort to expedients of various kinds. This inevitably meant also more time in order to prepare reasonably well for the attack. Moreover, by placing at least half the force against Casablanca, it involved the risk of being able to attack on any given date at Oran only—this because of a very great uncertainty as to weather conditions on the west coast. However, the president has manifestly been swayed by two considerations which he considers conclusive. First, that if the attack is wholly American, the French will probably not resist. If this is true, no other factors amount to anything because the first great prize, possession of the three principal French ports of northwest Africa, will come about automatically. The second great reason apparently influencing the president was the desire to secure the Casablanca base and the line of communications extending from there to Oran.

The British have been studying this proposal and have already replied to the president. They announced themselves as ready to go along with the president on any plan he approves, since under his current proposal the United States is shouldering the responsibility almost exclusively. However, they consider the failure to go into Algiers, simultaneously with the attacks at the other two points, a very great error. Their contention is that almost certainly weather would permit an attack at Oran and Algiers on any given day—almost as certainly they believe the attack at Casablanca must be flexible as to time and will probably have to wait for a considerable period to be favored by the necessary weather conditions. Today, September 2, we are awaiting the final outcome of these negotiations.

It would be quite impossible to give an account of—even in outline form—the numerous arguments and discussions that have taken place during the past six weeks. General Clark and I have had many meetings with the British chiefs of staff, with the prime minister, and with individuals of our own joint staff. A vast amount of statistics and factual data has come to light and much of this will be valuable no matter what the final decision. Nevertheless, we have been living for the past six weeks under conditions of strain, uncertainty, and tension that we can only hope will soon be terminated by a definite decision.

Our own conviction is that we are undertaking something of a quite desperate nature and which depends only in minor degree upon the professional preparations we can make or upon the wisdom of our own military decisions. In a way it is like the return of Napoleon from Elba—if the guess as to psychological reaction is correct, we may gain a tremendous advantage in this war; if the guess is wrong, it would be almost as certain that we will gain nothing and will lose a lot. The extent of the unfavorable potentialities is vast, including not only the chances of a very bloody repulse but a bringing into the ranks of our active enemies both France and Spain, which are now classed as neutrals. If it were possible to prepare and take into the region such a strong force in land and air and sea components that the rapid crushing of resistance in northwest Africa could be practically guaranteed, it would unquestionably be a good operation—so long as the Allies have practically abandoned hope for a 1943 Roundup. Since, however, such a force cannot be provided, we are simply sailing a dangerous political sea, and this particular sea is one in which military skill and ability can do little in charting a safe course.

SEPTEMBER 13, 1942

Besides the prime minister, the meeting [at Chequers, September 11–12] was attended by the CIGS [Chief of the Imperial General Staff], the First Sea Lord, Lord Leathers, and others.[1] Subjects discussed mainly revolved around question of date for the initial attack in Torch.[2] The prime minister has accepted November 4 as the earliest possible date, but is now concerned about a date which would represent the latest at which we may reasonably expect to get started. Should this latest date be after November 15, he believes he must undertake to run PQ-19.[3] I gave him as my best guess the date of November 8.

Another subject taken up was that of securing for the United States forces a number of P-39s now in England and set up for Russian use. The United States wants these planes so badly that they have engaged themselves to replace them to Russia by the Alaskan route. The prime minister and Lord Leathers immediately jumped into the thing seriously, and shipment of P-39s to boats was stopped. Incidentally, we are getting 176 of these planes.

I had a chance to talk to the people running the commercial vessels for England. There is a great story in the undemonstrative heroism of the British merchant sailors. Some day soon I will write a memorandum on the subject.

SEPTEMBER 15, 1942

On Tuesday morning I held a conference with Generals Clark, Spaatz, Lee, Thiele, and Smith present.[1] The purpose of the conference was to impress upon all the principal officers of the theater the importance of devoting everything to preparations for Torch. I informed them that success or failure in this task will be, so far as I am concerned, the measure of the individual's value. More than this, I stated that if each of these officers were successful in carrying out the mission given, there would be no limit to the representations I would make the War Department in his behalf; on the other hand, failure would mean only that the officer's usefulness was ended. I urged them particularly to impress this idea on all subordinates. I tried to make the point that this was not an ordinary task in which reasonable effort and reasonable measures had any application. On the contrary, it must be considered as a major crisis; and that as long as any preparatory purpose lay within the realm of human possibility, it had to be accomplished.

Each man present expressed himself as understanding what his own particular mission comprises, and, so far as I am concerned, there can be no excuses for failure except insofar as are involved matters over which none of us in this theater can exercise any possible influence.

Aside from the above, I discussed again with all these commanders the disciplinary problem and demanded that they institute immediately instructional programs that would insure a knowledge of elementary discipline and military courtesy on the part of all officers. I dwelt on this subject at some length and pointed out that the time had arrived when commanders of such units as are not coming up to standard must be relieved. The time has passed for dillydallying. We must demand satisfactory performance.

Planning the North African attack after the events of the spring and summer of 1942 must have been confusing in the extreme, for so many calculations previously made were now useless and, in effect, the planners, never much sure of their facts, had to start all over again. But then it must have been simplifying to be able to concentrate one's mind, as Dr. Johnson once said.

The decision, once taken, was to invade North Africa, which to Eisenhower meant three major ports, all in French possession. On the Atlantic was Casablanca, the entryway to French Morocco. And past the straits of Gibraltar lay, to the east, Oran and Algiers in French Algeria. Deciding to take three large ports at once was complicating to the enterprise of invasion, for the attacks would have to be simultaneous, never an easy task when one is moving on land, doubly difficult by sea. The arrangement therefore was that convoys from the United States and from England would concentrate in the Atlantic in the vicinity of Gibraltar and then move off to their tasks with proper timing. The moving off toward Oran and Algiers was easier said than done, for the moment the convoys passed the Straits of Gibraltar they would be exposed to Axis air attack, as well as assault by submarines attacking in wolf packs. The hope was that the Germans would think the Allied forces were headed for ports to the east beyond Algeria, perhaps in Tunisia, or, more likely, Sicily or Italy and that their defending planes and submarines would wait for the convoys' entrance into the narrow waters of the central Mediterranean. By that time, so Allied planning went, the attacks would have commenced on Oran and Algiers, and the Atlantic force would be moving on Casablanca.

The hundreds of ships, divided into fast and slow convoys, duly converged, rendezvousing in the Atlantic from two directions: one force carrying Lieutenant General George S. Patton, Jr.'s corps from the American East Coast came in from the west; the other, from England. The attacks opened on time, on November 8. A few days later the Allies seized three smaller ports to the east of Algiers —Bougie on November 11, Bône on November 12, and a port in-between named Djidjelli on November 13. Bône was close to the Algerian-Tunisian border. On November 15 the Allies sent parachutists to the south of Bône, to a place named Youks, thereby forming a north-south line that was seven hundred miles from Casablanca on the Atlantic coast.

The reason for setting up a line of defense at the eastern edge of Algeria was the presence of Axis troops in Tunisia—mainly Italian troops, but with a stiffening of Germans under the command of General Juergen von Arnim. And far to the east were the Italian-German forces of the Desert Fox himself, General Rommel, momentarily in retreat after the attack, within the boundary of Egypt, of the British Eighth Army under General Bernard L. Montgomery. The Germans under Rommel were battle-hardened and desert-wise and would be no easy adversaries of the Americans if they were pushed back by Montgomery and then combined with Arnim's forces to attack Eisenhower's American-British contingents. There was a special danger in the possibility of a German consolidation and attack before the Anglo-Americans could consolidate their far-flung positions, virtually port positions, and get up reserves and essential supplies.

The day before the taking of the three major ports on November 8, Eisenhower spent much of his precious time arguing with a French general, Henri Giraud, a tall, thin, extremely proud officer of the old school who had been spirited out of Vichy France with great difficulty—by submarine and plane—and who upon arrival in Gibraltar, Eisenhower's momentary headquarters, was to be persuaded to assert his personality upon the French commanders and civil governors in Morocco and Algeria, convincing them to welcome the Anglo-Americans. Giraud had the quaint idea that he was to command the Anglo-American forces himself, *instead of serving as a diplomat, and told Eisenhower so in thousands upon thousands of words, all in impeccable French logic.*

NOVEMBER 8, 1942

Worries of a Commander:

1. Spain is so ominously quiet that Governor of Gibraltar reports himself uneasy. No word from any agent or ambassador.
2. No news from task forces. Reports few and unsatisfactory.
3. Defensive fighting, which seemed halfhearted and spiritless this morning, has blazed up, and in many places resistance is stubborn.
4. No Frenchman immediately available, no matter how friendly toward us, seems able to stop the fighting. (Mast, et al.)[1]
5. Giraud is in Gibraltar, manifestly unwilling to enter the theater so long as fighting is going on.
6. Giraud is difficult to deal with—temperamental, wants much in power, equipment, etc., but seems little disposed to do his part to stop fighting.
7. Giraud wants planes, radios.
8. We are slowed up in eastern sector when we should be getting toward Bône-Bizerte at once.
9. We don't know whereabouts or conditions of airborne force.
10. We cannot find out anything.

NOVEMBER 9, 1942

Inconsequential thoughts of a commander during one of the interminable "waiting periods."

War brings about strange, sometimes ridiculous situations. In my service I've often thought or dreamed of commands of various types that I might one day hold—war commands, peace commands, battle commands, administrative commands, etc. One I now have could never, under any conditions, have entered my mind even fleetingly. I have operational command of Gibraltar. The symbol of the solidity of the British Empire, the hallmark of safety and security at home, the jealously guarded rock that has played a tremendous part in the trade development of the English race! An American is in charge, and I am he. Hundreds of feet within the bowels of the Rock itself I have my command post. I simply must have a grandchild or I'll never have the fun of telling this when I'm fishing, gray-bearded, on the banks of a quiet bayou in the deep South.

Again, what soldier ever took the trouble to contemplate the possibility of holding an allied command and, of all things, an allied command of ground, air, and naval forces? Usually we pity the soldiers of history that had to work with allies. But we don't now, and through months of work we've rather successfully integrated the forces and the commands and staffs of British and American contingents. Now we have to get together with the North African French. Just how the French angle will develop only the future can tell, but I am proud of this British-United States command. The final result I don't know, but I do know that every element of my command—all United States and British services—are working together beautifully and harmoniously. That's something. . . .[1]

How I'd like a few reports. I'm anxiously waiting word of: West Coast operations, Oran operations, Giraud's movements and intentions, Darlan's proposals, movements of Italian air, and intentions of Spain.

DECEMBER 10, 1942

This operation has been in progress just slightly over a month.

To compare the picture as it exists today with what was anticipated before we came in here, it is necessary to recall the differing assumptions upon which our calculations were made. These assumptions were three. *First,* that there might be definite opposition from the French, continuing as long as their forces were capable of fighting. *Second,* that we might from the outset obtain active and effective cooperation from the French all the way from Casablanca to Tunis, and especially in Algiers and Tunis. *Third,* that opposition from the French might not be severe but that we would get little in the way of effective help from them.

Under the first conception, we figured that it would be at least two months after D-day before we could move much to the eastward of Bougie and that thereafter we would have a rather laborious campaign, with a great number of troops actually immobilized on our lines of communication. Under the second assumption, we felt that we might, even with only a few parachute forces and some light ground troops, be in Tunis and Bizerte in a matter of ten days or so after landing at Algiers. Under the third assumption, we felt that the going would be pretty slow and that we would meet German resistance in western Tunisia. It was felt that within thirty days our general battle line might be along the western boundary of that province.

Actually, the situation we have encountered contained elements of all three of these basic assumptions. We had some pretty tough fighting against the French in the west and some of shorter duration in the center, and this reacted to make our eastward advance somewhat less strong. Moreover, after our landings were firmly established, some days elapsed before we could get any active help from the French. Within the last two weeks, this help has been of inestimable value to us but, even so, is no longer decisive because the enemy was allowed by the French forces in Tunis and Bizerte to enter the country in considerable force. The French under the control of Giraud seem to be perfectly willing to fight, but their forces are very light and lacking in the special equipment necessary to modern warfare.

In any event, we started for Tunis, pell mell, as soon as we got our leading troops ashore at Algiers. We went first to Bougie and Bône and overland from there. The situation developed so rapidly that we hoped very much to be able to make a rather strong attack by November 19 with two British brigade groups and the so-called "Blade" force—about a regiment of mixed armor.

Enemy opposition, particularly by air, became more effective from the beginning, and as the rains came on and made our mud fields unusable, and as our ground troops pushed well ahead of the most advanced landing fields we could employ, the situation gradually became such as to compel a halt. Conditions were aggravated by the impossibility of getting up supplies.

It takes time to organize a line of communications extending through four or five hundred miles of mountainous country, and time was something we did not have. We finally had docks, sidings, and even main lines of our poor little railroad all clogged up with supplies of all sorts, and these not even sufficiently catalogued so that it was possible to determine what was what—and where.

South af Anderson's main line in the vicinity of Mateur-Tebourba, the French, aided by small detachments of American troops, undertook to cover a very wide front and not only protect our flank but make the enemy believe that an attack was coming from that direction.[1] As it became apparent that there was not enough strength in Anderson's front to drive home an attack, all effort was turned toward correcting conditions along the L of C [line of communication] and so to produce a flow forward in supplies, which was difficult to do without any motor transport to clear sidings, and to bring up the forces and munitions necessary to put real weight behind the attack. In the meantime, we hoped, by bringing in additional bomber units, to keep pounding on the Axis supply lines and ports, so as to interfere with his reinforcement.

One of our worst enemies has been the weather, which has not only prevented full use of our fighter planes in forward areas but has so covered the enemy positions that effective bombing has been impossible for days at a time. Moreover, the logistics situation was so bad that it has been impossible to push to the front such additional reinforcements as we have been able to make available from other portions of the area. So far we have shoved forward the entire Seventy-eighth Division of the British and about 7,500 replacements to make good the losses we suffered during the early days of the campaign. In addition, we have put forward General Oliver's armored force from Oran, one battalion of the Twenty-sixth Infantry, and some odd units of anti-tank and anti-aircraft.[2] At this moment, there is waiting at Algiers a completely motorized infantry regiment from the Oran force ready to go up and join the battle line as soon as some method can be found for supplying it.

It is difficult out of this whole affair to evaluate the situation. Manifestly, if we cannot supply more troops at the front than we now have, we cannot make a strong attack. While this situation will improve as we can get motor transport into the area and make use of the one main road leading to the front, that prospect is rather a long-term one in view of our expected rate of buildup in motor transport. In the meantime, with a continuation of current weather conditions, there seems to be no prospect of denying the enemy even better opportunity for reinforcement than ourselves. Moreover, every day he is enabled to organize more highly the Tunis area, his capture will be more difficult from that aspect.

In this situation I am working everybody to the utmost to rush forward articles of supply and establish dumps, so that we can get numbers of reserves forward.

I believe this can be done and am now strongly hoping to put on a quite powerful attack about December 20, which attack has been put off from about November 20, then to December 2, then to December 9, and now again for another ten days.

Through all this, I am learning many things: (1) that waiting for other people to produce is one of the hardest things a commander has to do; (2) that in the higher positions of a modern army, navy, and air force, rich organizational experience and an orderly, logical mind are absolutely essential to success. The flashy, publicity-seeking type of adventurer can grab the headlines and be a hero in the eyes of the public, but he simply can't deliver the goods in high command. On the other hand, the slow, methodical, ritualistic person is absolutely valueless in a key position. There must be a fine balance—that is exceedingly difficult to find. In addition to the above, a person in such a position must have an inexhaustible fund of nervous energy. He is called upon day and night to absorb the disappointments, the discouragements, and the doubts of his subordinates and to force them on to accomplishments, which they regard as impossible. The odd thing about it is that most of these subordinates don't even realize that they are simply pouring their burdens upon the next superior and that when they receive orders to do something, they themselves have been relieved of a great load of moral responsibility. To find a few persons of the kind that I have roughly described above is the real job of the commander. Occasionally, because of governmental practices and difficulties as to rank, he cannot place them in actual command, but he can frequently bolster up an otherwise weak situation by getting one of these men into a position where, by personality and ability, he is the actual though not the nominal leader.

Two British officers that I have met have these qualifications to a marked degree—Admiral Cunningham and Air Marshal Tedder. I regard them both as top-flight leaders. I am sorry that Tedder is not an actual member of this organization. Among the American commanders, Patton I think comes closest to meeting every requirement made on a commander. Just after him I would, at present, rate Fredendall, although I do not believe the latter has the imagination in foreseeing and preparing for possible jobs of the future that Patton possesses. Clark is an unusual individual and is particularly strong in his organizational ability and orderliness of his mind. Unfortunately, I have not yet seen him in a position where he has had to carry the responsibility directly on his own shoulders, but there seems to be no reason why he should not measure up in this respect. . . . [3] I think, however, that for the next several months he will deliver well for several reasons. First, he is getting command of the Fifth Army, for which he has begged and pleaded for a long time. Second, the job, for the moment, is one largely of organization and training, and in these fields I think Clark has no superior. Moreover, such burdensome responsibilities as we attached to the job can well be shifted to these headquarters, since it will involve some sort of political contact with the French. Also, I have recently got him promoted to three-star rank.

All in all, I would rate our prospects for the present as good. We are having our troubles; so is the enemy. If we can make up our minds to endure more and go farther and work harder than he does, and provided only that the comparative logistics of the situation does not favor him too much, we can certainly win.

December 15, 1942

The offensive operation which we are now striving to mount in Tunisia should, according to present calculations, be fought with the following Allied ground forces: (1) British. The Seventy-eighth Infantry Division at approximately full strength. The Sixth Armored Division at approximately full strength. Two Commandos. Total, about twenty thousand. (2) American. Eighteenth Regimental Combat Team (which has in it one battalion of 105 howitzers). Reorganized combat Team B (portion of First Armored Division reinforced by 20 Mark IV tanks from the Second Division). The force will consist, primarily, of about 55 medium tanks, including the Mark IVs; 55 light tanks; 9 105-howitzers; some 25–30 self-propelled 75s (anti-tanks); and other small detachments. One battalion 155-mm. howitzers. One battalion 155-mm. guns. Total, about 11,000. In addition to the above, we have some three or four infantry companies (Thirty-ninth Infantry) on the British line of communications. One battalion of Twenty-sixth Infantry, one company of anti-tanks, one company of tanks, and a few parachutists (Colonel Raff's command, which works under French control, near Tebessa). (3) French. In the area south of Mejes el Bab and stretching all the way down below Tebessa, the French have approximately thirty thousand combat troops. However, they are poorly armed and equipped and have no means of combatting tanks or aircraft.

In the air we have in the whole theater a substantial superiority, but our strength on the Tunisian battlefront has constantly been inferior to the enemy's. This is because of his possession of two all-weather airfields, one at Tunis and one at Bizerte, and the location of the battle line, which is very close to his fields and far from ours. Our fields are unimproved, and a little rain makes them unusable. The enemy has in ground troops in the whole area possibly some 30,000 to 35,000, of which about 25,000 appear to be combat troops. Small detachments of 1,500 to 2,000 are apparently in Gabes, Sfax, and Sousse, but the bulk is concentrated to the westward of Tunis, covering the Bizerte-Tunis bridgehead. The enemy has a considerable number of anti-aircraft guns, all of which are apparently usable against ground targets, particularly tanks. He is strong in tanks, having at least 100 of his Mark III and Mark IVs, which are more powerful than anything we have except the 50 American mediums. On the other hand, he seems to be rather weak in field artillery, and our preponderance in this branch, if skillfully used, should make up for our deficiency in relative tank strength. Likewise, if our 155 guns are skillfully used, they should be able to knock out any located 88-mm. weapons the enemy has and cover the operations of our tanks. The German-Italian forces described are now on the ground; they have been steadily reinforced since their first landing on November 9. There is every indication that they will continue to grow stronger (in spite of our bombing operations against their ports), particularly in tanks. Our forces are not yet on ground. They cannot all be there before December 22.

We run three risks: (1) that Axis will be reinforced to point we cannot attack successfully; (2) that while our additional forces are coming up, we will get pounded enough that we have to use resources piecemeal (this has happened during past weeks) and cannot build up enough to attack; and (3) that weather may bog us down.

JANUARY 19, 1943

The past week has been a succession of disappointments. I'm just writing some down so as to forget them.

1. The French began showing signs of complete collapse along the front as early as the seventeenth. Each day the tactical situation has gotten worse. We will be pushed to make a decent front covering Tunisia.

2. The aggressive action and local attack I had so laboriously planned for the twenty-fourth and following days have had to be abandoned.

3. The newspapers want my scalp for "political censorship," but there is none. Has not been for two weeks. Why the yell?

4. Peyrouton's appointment to succeed the worthless Châtel has been received

Luncheon with the commander in chief, winter of 1942–43.

with howls of anguish at home.[1] Who do they want? He is an experienced administrator, and God knows it's hard to find many of them among the French in Africa.

5. We've had our railroad temporarily interrupted twice. I'm getting weary of it, but can't move the troops (even if I had enough) to protect the lines.

FEBRUARY 25, 1943

Some time between December 10 and 15 it began to look as if an attack by the Fifth British Corps in the north might well become impossible for two reasons. The first of these was that weather would prohibit movement off the roads, and we believed that our sole chance of quick victory at that date lay in the use of concentrated artillery fire, which in turn meant that the artillery had constantly to be able to maneuver to support every advance made. Even at that time the Germans had a superiority in tanks, but our own preponderance in artillery was marked. The second reason was that between November 19 and the middle of December the rate of Axis buildup was such, and the opportunity offered him for a defensive preparation was so great, that it began to appear that we would no longer have a chance to capture Tunisia with the light forces we had so far been able to push up to the front. It was felt that unless the attack could be staged in good order by Christmas, there was no chance whatsoever for the early rush to succeed.

In anticipation of a stalemate in that region, and because of the continued progress of the Eighth Army toward the west from Egypt, it became a definite possibility that some of Rommel's forces might try a quick combination with the enemy in Tunisia to deal us a damaging blow on the right flank. The only forces available for establishing a strategic flank guard in the great region running south of the Dorsale were American, and since the region to be covered was very wide, and in many instances featureless, the employment of mobile mechanized forces was clearly indicated. For this reason studies were started in mid-December to determine whether the First United States Armored Division could be concentrated in the Tebessa area and supported by sufficient infantry to allow it to act aggressively against the hostile line of communications.

As planning for the concentration of supplies and troops proceeded, both General Fredendall and the AFHQ [Allied Forces Headquarters] planning staff became convinced that a definite advance against a coastal city was possible, with Sfax indicated as the most logical objective.[1] This city was being used at the time as a port of embarkation for Tripoli through which Rommel's force was drawing the supplies necessary for combatting the Eighth Army.

The Allied commander in chief agreed to this plan but with the proviso that no geographical objective was to be held to the point of endangering the garrison; that only in so far as the concentrated First Armored Division could guarantee the safety and success of any such advance force would we tie ourselves down to an advance position. With this definite understanding, planning for an attack of this kind was authorized.

As these studies went forward, the question of command of the American organization in the Tebessa region was brought up. It was first decided to establish an American task force in the region under General Clark. He started planning at once for the moving of a headquarters to that region and began studies to determine the strength of the forces that could be maintained there with the indifferent lines of communication that exist. To build up the task force staff, General Clark used large parts of the II Corps staff.

In the meantime, American reinforcements in some strength had been pushed up to the [British] V Corps, and General Anderson was instructed to use them, so far as possible, as a unified whole. Particularly, he was instructed to use them in accordance with American doctrine in defensive situations, to keep tanks and mechanized forces out of the lines and to hold them in the rear, concentrated for powerful counterattacks. He was also told that in the event that an early Allied attack in the north might be called off, he must be prepared to release American troops for service in the south, although he was authorized to retain the 18th Regimental Combat Team until the 46th British Division should arrive on his front.

By the night of December 24 the Allied commander in chief had decided that, owing to the appalling weather conditions, attack in the north was not feasible. The Axis rate of buildup was such that an attack at that late date would have to depend for success on skillful use of artillery, in which we had a real preponderance. An outline of the plan as described herein was sent to the combined chiefs of staff by the commander in chief on December 26, 1942, by radio.[2]

In the meantime, General Clark had represented to the Allied commander in chief that the American command in the south could never be larger than a small mobile corps and that since he had already been set up as the commanding general of the American Fifth Army, it was appropriate to turn over the command in the southeast to the II Corps commander. He pointed out also that he had been engaged, from the beginning of Torch, in the broad study of necessary action on our western flank in case the enemy should ever attempt to penetrate the Iberian Peninsula. He felt, therefore, that his real job was in the west and that the II Corps commander should take over the southeastern front.

This presented a question as to a choice between General Fredendall and General Patton for command. The personal choice of the commander in chief was General Patton because of particular qualifications and his experience in desert work, and also because of his experience with mechanized troops. However, General Patton commanded the only forces in the west that were immediately available for use in that region in the event of trouble; moreover, almost the entire staff of the southeastern force, which was now on the ground, came from the II Corps, as did most of the troops. Consequently, it was determined to give Fredendall command in the southeast. He was brought up at once to Allied force headquarters, and the commander in chief in person explained to him the concept under which these forces were being organized there.

All during this period the question of over-all command in the theater had been a vexing one. The single line of communication leading eastward to Tunisia indicated the necessity for single command of the battlefront, and although AFHQ was in complete charge of this line of communications, the First British Army had the only communications set-up capable of controlling the extended battlefront. Attempt was made to place the whole battlefront under the First British Army, but an absolute refusal on the part of the French was encountered. In this situation the alternative solutions were to override the French refusal or for the Allied commander in chief to take personal charge of the battlefront. The latter alternative was decided upon and an advance command post at Constantine was established. The other alternative was not possible at the moment because of our complete dependence upon French protection of our vulnerable lines of communication and for continued defensive action in the Dorsale region. The period was one of comparative quiet so far as actual fighting was concerned, and the concentrations proceeded with the hope of being able to make the first important raid on about January 20.

In the meantime, the Allied commander in chief made a trip to Anfa and upon learning there of the schedule of advance planned by the Eighth Army, made the decision to avoid all attacks that would have for their purpose the holding of any geographical objective beyond the Faid-Gafsa line. The original concept of a strong mobile highly concentrated strategic flank guard was retained with the idea of operating aggressively against any targets that might be important.

On January 18, a fairly strong attack against the French front resulted in complete demonstration of the inability of French troops to hold the mountainous Dorsale region. The French had been furnished with a number of anti-tank and anti-aircraft weapons from both the British and American forces, and both the French and ourselves had believed that with a concentration of available means at the passes, and the employment of French infantry through the hilly regions, that area would be safe from assault. We made a bad error in this conclusion.

It became immediately necessary to hold the central region by rushing American and British troops to the area. This prevented the buildup of a central reserve and interfered with the concentration of the Fredendall force to the south. However, because of the necessity of American and British troops taking over defensive responsibility in the central Tunisian area, and because the seriousness of the situation had caused the French to withdraw their objections, the Allied commander in chief decided on the spot to place the whole force under General Anderson so as to attain instant coordination.

Directives to General Anderson emphasized the need for immediate sorting out of forces and using troops as units rather than as small packets and in keeping the First Armored Division so disposed as to permit concentrated action at any time. General Anderson was, however, seriously handicapped in that he had to take over command of a very extended front at a critical stage of the operations.

Toward the end of January it became evident that the enemy was preparing for an assault against our widely held line, and faulty G-2 [Intelligence] estimates placed the direction of attack as westward from Fondouk and possibly southwestward through the Ousseltia valley. Part of the First Armored Division under

General Robinett had already been used in the counterattack to restore the positions lost by the French between January 18 and 23, and General Anderson held this force west of Ousseltia. The First Armored Division immediately began the construction of a temporary road joining up its own position with that of General Robinett's, so that, in the event of attack, the whole force could be rapidly concentrated for the use prescribed by the commander in chief.

General Anderson, in the meanwhile, issued an order placing General Robinett's force in army reserve—that is, not to be employed except upon his specific orders.

While the British Sixth Armored Division would probably have been best fitted for this role, it was felt that this division could not be employed at the moment because we were about to start rearming the Sixth Armored Division with American Sherman tanks. Moreover, there still remained a considerable tank threat in the Bou Arada area.

On February 14 the enemy attacked westward through and around Faid. General Anderson did not wish to commit the whole of his reserve, and consequently the First Armored Division was never used as a complete unit. When finally it became apparent that the situation was serious near Sidi Bou Zid, he released one of Robinett's battalions and a day or so later released the rest of that force. All of this resulted in piecemeal action, and the enemy's advance succeeded in overwhelming our tank strength—one packet at a time. We were pushed back behind Feriana-Sbeitla, and the enemy's attack finally broke through the Kasserine pass. American troops succeeded in holding onto the ridge of Djebel el Hamra, and Americans and British held Thala and to the east thereof. The bulk of the United States First Armored and the First and Thirty-fourth Infantry Divisions were used. Also of the Thirty-ninth Infantry and of the Ninth Division, as well as many smaller units of artillery, anti-tank and anti-aircraft. On the night of February 22–23 the enemy started to retire through the Kasserine gap.

Meantime, General Alexander had finally arrived on February 17 and, on the eighteenth, went to the front to take charge, under the general direction of the commander in chief. He actually assumed command of the Eighteenth Army Group at 0001 hours of February 20, 1943.

General Alexander and I see the essentials of this situation eye to eye. We agree that the first thing is the concentration of all troops into nationalistic components and the immediate rehabilitation of the divisions, particularly those that have been partially used up. We will make absolutely sure of the ground we now hold, organize the passes into small fortresses, and from them make sorties with the particular hope of recovering advance airfields at Thelepte that were lost during the German advance. During all this period the Allied Forces Headquarters has been straining every nerve to bring into the battle area reinforcements and artillery, personnel and tanks. Units everywhere else have been stripped, and necessary messages have been sent to the United States and England for shipment of necessary equipment.

The air force is now better organized, is well sorted out and operating efficiently.

We will resume the offensive as soon as possible, most likely in the II Corps area so as to help the Eighth Army through the Mareth line.

JUNE 11, 1943

Now that the first phase of operations in this theater has been completed, I am recording herein my opinions and impressions concerning several senior officers, for reference when I may need them at a later date.

Admiral Sir Andrew Browne Cunningham. He remains in my opinion at the top of my subordinates in absolute selflessness, energy, devotion to duty, knowledge of his task, and in understanding of the requirements of allied operations. My opinions as to his superior qualifications have never wavered for a second.

Air Chief Marshal Sir Arthur William Tedder. He ranks close to Admiral Cunningham in qualifications, except in the one thing of broad vision. I believe that the history of the establishment of the Royal Air Force is reflected somewhat in his way of thinking and that, therefore, he is not quite as broad-gauged as he might be.[1] I do not register this opinion as a fixed conclusion, but I sometimes have the feeling I have just expressed. Certainly in all matters of energetic operation, fitting into an allied team, and knowledge of his job, he is tops. Moreover, he is a leader type. His deputy assistant is a man named Wigglesworth.

Air Vice-Marshal H.E.P. Wigglesworth. I think very highly of this officer and consider that in the very highest echelons of our air force leadership we are well fortified.

General Harold R.L.G. Alexander. He has a winning personality, wide experience in war, an ability to get along with people, and sound tactical conceptions. He is self-effacing and energetic. The only possible doubt that could be raised with respect to his qualifications is a suspected unsureness in dealing with certain of his subordinates. At times it seems that he alters his own plans and ideas merely to meet an objection or a suggestion of a subordinate, so as to avoid direct command methods. This, I must say, is only a feeling. I have no proof that in the cases where he has apparently changed his mind rather radically that he was swayed by anything except further reflection on the problem.

General Bernard L. Montgomery. General Montgomery is a very able, dynamic type of army commander. I personally think that the only thing he needs is a strong immediate commander. He loves the limelight but in seeking it, it is possible that he does so only because of the effect upon his own soldiers, who are certainly devoted to him. I have great confidence in him as a combat commander. He is intelligent, a good talker, and has a flare for showmanship. Like all other senior British officers, he has been most loyal—personally and officially—and has shown no disposition whatsoever to overstep the bounds imposed by allied unity of command.

Lieutenant General Kenneth A.N. Anderson. A very hardworking, sincere man who is an earnest fighter and completely devoted to duty. My own belief is that his one weakness is an inability to think in terms that an army commander should employ. His mind instinctively turns to battalions and brigades rather than to

With Admiral Cunningham,
the British officer who
perhaps impressed
Eisenhower more than did
any other, save Air Marshal
Tedder.

With Monty in North
Africa, Bedell Smith in
background.

Churchill loved Algeria and loved to be surrounded with generals and admirals; l. to r., Anthony Eden, foreign secretary; Sir Alan Brooke, chief of the imperial general staff; standing, Air Marshal Tedder, Admiral Cunningham, General Alexander; seated, General Marshall, Ike; standing, Monty.

divisions and corps. This leads him to prescribing the details of tactical movements that would better be left to subordinates. He has a real field of usefulness
but, if he is used as an army commander, he should be under the rather close
supervision of a man like Alexander.

Air Marshal Sir Arthur Coningham. This officer has been in command of our
tactical air force and has done a very fine job. He is impulsive, quick, earnest, and
sincere. He knows his job and, under the British system of cooperation, performs
it well.

Major General H.M. Gale. One of the ablest officers in the logistic field I have
ever seen. He is not disturbed by difficulties, is energetic, resourceful, and has a
fine personality. He is a real administrator.

Major General J.F.M. Whiteley. This officer has been my deputy chief of staff
since the beginning of Torch. I consider him one of the best, particularly in his
disinterested viewpoint toward all problems presented to him and in his willing-
ness to take responsibility on his own shoulders. He is cheerful, hardworking, and
devoted to duty.

Lieutenant General Mark W. Clark, Fifth Army commander. He is the best
organizer, planner, and trainer of troops I have yet met in the American army.
He thinks in an orderly and logical fashion and is energetic in carrying an adopted
plan into execution. While at one stage of the operations it seemed that he was
becoming a bit consumed with a desire to push himself, all that has disappeared
—if it ever existed—and he is certainly one of the very best we have.[2] His only
drawback now is a lack of combat experience in a high command position. This
I tried to give him in the early days of organizing an American task force in the
central Tunisian front. He rather resented taking any title except that of army
commander; and since I could not at that time establish an American army
command on the Tunisian front, I had to place another in charge of the American effort. This was a bad mistake on Clark's part, but I still think that he could
successfully command an army in operations.

Lieutenant General George S. Patton, Jr. A shrewd soldier who believes in
showmanship to such an extent that he is almost flamboyant. He talks too much
and too quickly and sometimes creates a very bad impression. Moreover, I fear
that he is not always a good example to subordinates, who may be guided by only
his surface actions without understanding the deep sense of duty, courage, and
service that make up his real personality. He has done well as a combat corps
commander, and I expect him to do well in all future operations.

Lieutenant General Omar N. Bradley. This officer is about the best rounded,
well balanced senior officer that we have in the service. His judgments are always
sound, and everything he does is accomplished in such a manner as to fit in well
with all other operations. He is respected by British and Americans alike. I have
not a single word of criticism of his actions to date and do not expect to have
any in the future. I feel that there is no position in the army that he could not
fill with success.

Lieutenant General Carl Spaatz. A fine technician, popular with his subordinates, who fits into an allied team very well indeed. I have had an impression that

he is not tough and hard enough personally to meet the full requirements of his high position. He is constantly urging more promotions for subordinates and seeking special favors or special consideration for his forces. For example, he wants all his second lieutenants made first lieutenants upon completion of a certain number of missions; he wants a liquor ration provided for the air force and wants additional grades and ratings for all his units, so that he may have a surplus of high-ranking noncommissioned officers. My belief in this regard is further strengthened by the type of staff he has accumulated around him. He has apparently picked officers more for their personal qualifications of comradeship and friendliness than for their abilities as businesslike, tough operators. I have been watching him very carefully and have urged him and pleaded with him to adopt a tougher attitude. While it is possible that his methods are correct for his particular job, the fact is that I never have great confidence in his recommendations for promotion of personnel and for the special favors he seeks for his own forces. This weakness is his only one. He does not seek personal glory or publicity, and he is a most loyal and hardworking subordinate.

Development of a plan for Husky, the seizure of Sicily, had begun in February, 1943, well before the end of the North African campaign, and although in the retrospect of greater seaborne expeditions, notably the invasion of France in June 1944, Husky seemed a small affair, it was large at the time, if only because of the inexperience of the Allied high command. The North African ports had been occupied without much planning. Lucky indeed it was that resistance there had proved so slight, for in North Africa the American harbor masters were confused, and ships milled about, with troops wondering what they were supposed to do. Everyone eventually got ashore, but it was every bit as confused as the famed landings in Cuba at Siboney and Daiquiri in 1898. (In case present-day readers have forgotten, these latter names represent the Cuban beaches where American troops heaved their horses overboard, in preparation for landing; the horses did not know where the beaches were and many of them swam off in the opposite direction.)

By the time of the landings in Sicily there had been at least a sensing of the difficulties, as a result of the landings in North Africa. More and better equipment was at hand. Landing craft became available in fairly large numbers along with the so-called ducks, amphibious trucks. Parachutists now were ready to get in first and hold the area behind the beaches so troops would not immediately encounter hostile fire.

The little island of Pantelleria, lying between Sicily and the northeastern coast of Tunisia, was taken on June 11; and its capture proved so easy that it heartened the attacking force for Husky. Pantelleria could have proved a tough nut, for it was topographically unsuited to airborne attack and required bringing in troops under the guns of the defenders. No one knew how strong were its defenses, and the island seemed a small Gibraltar. But the defenders, Italians all, had no stomach for naval bombardment, and after Eisenhower sent in a half-dozen cruisers and ten destroyers to shoot up the fortress, the defenders—some eleven-

thousand—surrendered at the outset of the land assault.

Sicily remained, and if the allies could take it they could open up the Mediterranean to regular convoys. Moreover, being a fairly small place, it would not require a large garrison. It was the gateway, the front door, to Italy.

JULY 1, 1943

The Husky operation will begin in about a week. It is a very large amphibious operation, with the plan calling for the landing of 150,000 troops in the first echelon.

The Husky operation was determined upon by the combined chiefs of staff during the ANFA [Casablanca] conference in January.[1] My own prior recommendation had been to undertake the Brimstone operation as an easier task and one in which success would contribute directly to success in a later Husky.[2] Moreover, it is from the Brimstone area that the majority of the raids come against our ports along the North African shore, and I believed that success in Brimstone would so improve the situation along our long and exposed line of communications that we could concentrate defensive formations, particularly anti-aircraft units, into eastern Tunisia and later in Husky. The only major objection I had to the Brimstone operation was the difficulty of providing adequate air support for the landing.

The combined chiefs of staff decided against Brimstone in favor of Husky for three reasons: (1) The capture of Husky not only directly threatens Italy but has a more direct effect in facilitating our use of the Mediterranean, particularly through the critical Husky channel. (2) Air support could be more effectively provided for landing. (3) It was believed that the commitments for the defenses of Brimstone might grow larger than the place was worth to us.

In my original recommendations I had also pointed out that the Brimstone operation could be undertaken earlier than Husky because of the smaller forces required in the assault, but, for the reasons given, the combined chiefs of staff directed that we undertake the Husky operation.

During the course of the Tunisian campaign, a small staff of officers began studying and planning Husky; after early February, when it became apparent to all of us that the result of the Tunisian campaign was merely a matter of time, all of us began to turn our attention very directly to Husky. It was with a considerable degree of disappointment that we found we could not possibly do it before early July, because of the necessity of waiting for the arrival of required landing craft and so on.

My initial tactical plan for the capture of Husky provided for a concentrated assault on the eastern and southern portions of the island. The logistic people said this was absolutely impossible to maintain, so we set up a plan that provided an assault by echelon from east to west, involving the Catania area on D-day, the southwest assault on D plus two, and the Palermo assault on D plus five. When General Alexander and General Montgomery studied this plan, they became convinced that the land forces would be too weak at any one point to support themselves against possible counterattack and that we must provide a more concentrated assault. The whole problem was thrown back into the hands of the logistic people, and two factors had come about that convinced the logistic people that something more might be done than was originally contemplated. These factors were the provision of more LCT's [landing craft, tanks], which would be very valuable in maintenance, and the production and arrival here of a number of "ducks," with which it is hoped to supply [our troops] over the beaches rather effectively. The logistic section finally concluded that the concentrated assault in the southeast could probably be maintained and, consequently, we went back to that plan. This plan does have certain weaknesses, particularly in putting all our eggs in one basket and giving the enemy air force and submarines a chance to shoot against a concentrated target. It minimizes our opportunity for surprise but does give us depth of attack and assault.

As studies progressed, it became increasingly apparent that Pantelleria would be extraordinarily valuable to us in giving decent air support to the attack, particularly on the southern side of Husky. The Pantelleria fortress was then considered to be very strong, since it was known that its garrison was something over ten thousand and the nature of the island is such as to make it easy to defend. Nevertheless, I decided in view of its importance, both from the positive and negative angles, that the attempt should be made. I directed the assault to be made somewhere in early June and to be preceded by a most intensive air bombardment. I told the commanders and staffs that I believed the Italian morale would be so shaken by the bombardment we could put on the island that an infantry assault would probably never have to be made. The ground force detailed for the attack was the First British Division, under General Clutterbuck. He was not favorably impressed by the prospects. He made a personal visit to me to lay out the difficulties and feared that he would have a great number of his men slaughtered. Even General Alexander was vastly impressed by the most unfavorable reactions upon the Husky operation, if we should encounter a repulse in Pantelleria.

Because of these fears and doubts, I engaged to make a personal reconaissance of the place by sea two or three days before D-day. My reconnaissance, made in company of Admiral Cunningham, convinced me that the landing would be an easy affair and resistance would be light, and I directed definitely that the plans go ahead as ordered. Actually the place surrendered before the leading assault boats got to the shore, and the defending commander later stated that he did not even know an infantry attack was intended for that day. We captured over eleven thousand troops. (Incidentally, I won sixty-five francs from the prime minister on the basis of one centime per Italian over and above his estimate of five thousand men on the island.)   .

In the meantime, plans for Husky had gone ahead, with the American forces, under General Patton, assigned to the southern side of the island, and the British forces, under General Montgomery, against the east. General Montgomery's force is the Eighth British Army; General Patton's, the American Seventh. General Patton's force comprises in the assault the First, Third, and Forty-fifth

Divisions, with strong elements of the Eighty-second Airborne Division. His immediate follow-up division is the Ninth, which is to be brought in as rapidly as possible. General Montgomery's attack is in even stronger force, because he has the vital task of capturing the Catania airfields and the ports of Augusta and Syracuse. One of the complications of this assault is that at least one thousand tons [of ammunition, fuel, and food] daily, for the American forces, will have to come in through Syracuse and be brought directly across the lines of communication of the British forces.

The command post problem was very serious because of the impossibility of providing necessary naval communications in time from the Bizerte area. Since in the early phases of any amphibious operation the naval commander is in complete charge of the expedition and complete reliance must be placed on naval communications, the rest of the headquarters had to follow wherever the navy could find proper communications. This place is Finance.[3] It is General Montgomery's initial command post also. The admiral will be there for some time. General Alexander, Air Chief Marshal Tedder, and myself will go over just prior to D-day and remain until the first landings have been completed. Events will then have to determine whether I return to the Tunisian area or come all the way back to Algiers. If the fighting is still severe and the immediate problem is to get reinforcements for Montgomery or Patton or both, then my place will probably be Tunisia. If the going is good and the immediate problem is laying on plans for exploitation of initial success, involving formations still in Africa, then my principal duties will be in Algiers.

While I believe we are going to have some rather severe losses at certain of the beaches, I believe that on the whole the landing will go rather well and that we will get our assault formations substantially ashore during D-day. The most critical thing will be the rapid landing of necessary artillery and anti-tank and anti-aircraft equipment, so that security of these assaulting echelons will be provided. Once we have gotten this well arranged, I believe that advances to the first principal objective, which is a line roughly joining Catania and Licata, both inclusive, will be rapidly accomplished. From there, our next effort will be a thrust to the north to cut communications running west from Messina.

In preparation for all this, our air force is conducting a well-considered program of bombing to hold down the enemy air strength and to make his reinforcement and supply of Husky difficult.

The taking of Sicily—Operation Husky—went almost exactly as planned, for the first troops went in on July 10, and with the capture of Messina the island was in Allied hands on August 17. The seizing of Messina, almost a stone's throw across the straits from Italy proper, brought the downfall of Mussolini's government, replaced with a cabinet headed by Marshal Pietro Badoglio.

The appearance of the Badoglio government made clear that the Italians wanted out of the war, or at least to change sides, after all the misadventures since the summer of 1940, but they moved with circumspection; Eisenhower thought they moved with confusion and, to nudge them along to surrender, he allowed

*Montgomery on September 3 to put two divisions across the straits. The move
brought the desired result on September 8.*

*Events after the surrender moved rapidly, as German troops refused to honor
the decision of the Italian government and took up defensive positions, with
reinforcements streaming down the Italian boot from France, Germany, and
other places. On the day after the surrender, Eisenhower sent the British battle
fleet into Taranto, on the high arch of the boot of Italy, to occupy the place; the
Italian fleet had put to sea, to surrender to the Allies, and its bases were wide
open; for the occupation of Taranto, Eisenhower used the British 1st Airborne
Division, which otherwise would have been difficult to deploy at that moment.
More important in terms of future fighting was the sending of three divisions into
Salerno bay, just south of Naples, an obvious place for a jump up the Italian boot,
but an obvious place also to the Germans, who were expecting trouble there.
Salerno—Operation Avalanche—was at the very end of the operating radius for
Allied planes based on Sicilian fields. The Germans had an estimated eighteen
divisions in Italy, and Eisenhower was invading with six. The situation was risky,
and on September 13 the expected counterattack at Salerno began.*

SEPTEMBER 14, 1943

During the last two or three days the Germans have been heavily counterattack-
ing in the Avalanche area, and the situation has arisen which we so earnestly tried
to make the combined chiefs of staff see in advance as a definite possibility. The
essence of this situation is that we have such a painfully slow buildup and the
enemy can constantly bring so much strength against us that so far we have been
unable to push in from the beachhead. On the contrary, our forward troops have
been driven back and, in some instances, we have suffered quite heavy losses and
are in actual danger of a breakthrough. The only things that could have, in
advance, tilted this situation in our favor were more bombers and more landing
craft.

About a month ago the combined chiefs of staff were requested to make
available for a very brief period four additional groups of heavy bombers and some
LSTs [landing ship, tanks] that were then transiting through the Mediterranean
on their way to India. Both requests were disapproved. At that time we had in
the area three additional groups of B-24s (Liberators), which have been sent here
for special operation. We requested authority to keep these until the Avalanche
operation was completed. This request was also disapproved.

In the face of these refusals, doubts were frequently expressed in this headquarters as to the wisdom of going on with Avalanche. I felt that the possible results
were so great that even with the meager allotments in landing craft, particularly
LSTs, and in air force, we should go ahead. I so informed the combined chiefs
of staff.

This decision was solely my own, and if things go wrong there is no one to
blame except myself. It is only fair to say, however, that all three commanders
in chief backed up the idea, and it is also only fair to say that they have striven

in every possible way to make good these deficiencies through redoubled efforts in using what we have. I have no word of complaint concerning any officer or man in the execution of our plans.

I believe that we are going to succeed because I think that our air force will finally disorganize the attacks against the Fifth Army and that very soon Montgomery's advance will have some effect on the enemy near Salerno. Moreover, we have adopted extraordinary measures to rush reinforcements to Clark, and it is clear to me that if he can only hold on a week longer he will be in position to reorganize and resume the offensive.

Among measures that have been adopted since the opening of the operation in order to strengthen our grip on southern Italy and to relieve the pressure on Clark are the following: (1) Admiral Cunningham boldly rushed some cruisers loaded with soldiers into Taranto as quickly as the Italian ships left there, and although he lost one cruiser, which was mined, he has succeeded in putting ashore at Taranto the entire British Airborne Division. (2) Every possible means has been given to Montgomery in order to help him speed up his advance. (3) We have placed parts of the Eighty-second Airborne Division in Clark's area as reinforcements and are continuing to do so according to the schedules he gives us. (4) Landing craft set aside for the bringing up of the service elements of assaulting divisions have been diverted to transport the Third Division to the battle zone. (5) The Thirty-fourth Division, which is loaded in Oran under the assumption that it would be able to go into Naples, will be pushed up into Salerno area and landed over the beaches. This will be an awkward and difficult performance, but it looks like it will be necessary. (6) The Seventy-eighth Division, using the eighteen LSTs that the combined chiefs of staff finally made available to us (after refusing a month ago), will follow the First Parachute Division into Taranto. Unfortunately, when this authority was received on the twelfth, these ships were already fully loaded and considerable time was consumed in unloading them. However, the first eight are free and are proceeding to Sicily to pick up the Seventy-eighth Division. (7) The air force is working at a most intensive speed, both night and day. It is performing magnificently. So are the navies.

NOVEMBER 12, 1943

The factors influencing the decision to attack at Salerno are found in official records including minutes of commanders-in-chief meetings. When the decision was under discussion certain of the commanders felt that it was too bold a move, in view of the increasing German strength in Italy, and believed that the operations then known as Buttress and Goblet should be set up as projects of the first priority. The result of these operations would have been merely to have thrown large forces into the Toe where, due to lack of ports, all landing craft would have been absorbed in maintenance and where delaying action by the enemy would have been easy. Without remaining means for conducting additional amphibious operations farther to the north, we would have had little hope of reaching Naples in many weeks. While admitting that conditions might arise making it necessary to carry out the Goblet or Buttress operations, I felt, all through the summer, and particuarly after the collapse of Italian resistance in Sicily, that we were not justified in pursuing a "nibbling" policy. Salerno was the most northerly point at which we could provide reasonable air cover for our attacking fleet. Therefore, the Fifth Army was directed to prepare plans for attacking in Salerno bay but was required, because of the landing-craft situation, to include in its troop list the forces which had been set up originally for Buttress (toe) and/or Goblet (heel) attacks.

It was realized that the enemy could concentrate rapidly against the Salerno forces, but I insisted upon that attack in the firm conviction that our strong air force and our naval gunfire would enable us to make good the landing.

During the early days of September, the intelligence reports indicated a steadily increasing strength of German defensive power in the Salerno area, and the question was reopened as to the wisdom of making the attack. I adhered to my view because of the reasons stated above, and although we knew the dispositions of almost every single German battalion, I thoroughly believed that success at Salerno would save much time and countless lives in the project of taking Naples, which was necessarily our first major operation. Without the use of the Naples port, our operations could never be anything more than harassing in character. Nothing that has happened since has caused me to change these views.

At noon of the day that the attack was to be launched, I received a message from Rome stating that Badoglio had suddenly decided to cancel previously made arrangements for announcing the armistice that night. I sent him a sharp telegram immediately, which should be included in the diary.[1] That telegram explains exactly what happened. The result was that the Italian fleet started to sea that night. This left the ports of Bari, Brindisi, and Taranto wide open, so an emergency decision was taken to rush troops into Taranto on warships (First British Airborne).

The immediate and tangible results of the armistice were, therefore, the acquisition of the Italian navy, together with some merchant vessels, and the opening up of the heel of Italy to unopposed invasion. This last was possible because there was at that time no German concentration unit in the heel. This caused German rearguards still facing the Eighth Army, coming up the toe, to fall back rapidly and within a very short time our advance elements were on the Foggia line.

In the meantime, the Germans reacted swiftly against our Salerno landings and made heavy attacks against the three divisions plus a little armor that we had landed there in the first waves. Actually, by the time the German counterattack reached its maximum, on the thirteenth and fourteenth, we had gotten in some additional force. The resulting tactical situation was not at all favorable, but on the fourteenth our whole air force, strategical and tactical, concentrated on the battle area and very badly upset the German formations. Our naval gunfire likewise proved effective, and by the evening of the sixteenth (on which day I visited the Fifth Army) the immediate danger was over and we could reorganize preparatory to taking up the advance. The advance of the Eighth Army from the toe unquestionably made the German left flank nervous, and this also had marked effect in bringing the counterattack to a halt. From that time on, the Germans began using the terrain most effectively to delay our advance. Demolitions and mines were their chief weapons, coupled with rearguard actions in all the passes through the very mountainous country.

We realized at once that another strong and rapid amphibious operation in rear of the enemy's west flank would have a most advantageous effect—and the weather was still good enough, could we have provided the means to do it. We immediately started shuttling the Third United States Division into the battle area but we did not have the equipment and the capabilities of staging a divisional assault.

The desirability of such an operation remained the same throughout the ensuing weeks, but conditions, largely due to weather and German reinforcements, changed so much as to make the affair practically impossible. To make a successful division landing, we needed, first, the necessary landing craft, aside from those absolutely essential to unloading in ports and our buildup. We needed next to land the division at a place where beaches were practicable and where it could be supported within a very short time by the advance of land units. Deterioration in weather affected us in three ways. First of these was to make the landing on the beaches more difficult and to make maintenance extremely doubtful. Second, it made the prospect of advance by land forces so slow and tedious that there was almost the certainty that a divisional force would be destroyed before we could reach it. Finally, it rendered the operations of our superior air force very problematical and this factor, which played such an important part in the original decision to attack at Salerno, became of little significance.

As a result of all these things, our only recourse was to keep pounding away at the enemy's rearguards, seeking out weak spots, and pushing forward in an effort to drive the enemy back of Rome as soon as we could. This process is still going on but it is exceedingly slow. The country is unsuitable to the use of tanks and all the fighting has to be done by the infantry supported by artillery. We need more infantry divisions and are doing our utmost to get them into Italy.

Our buildup problem is complicated by several factors. One of these is that we have only five American divisions left to us in the Mediterranean theater, and we can scarcely keep two army corps on the front and make provision for getting a division out of the line occasionally to rest and refit. This is especially true because one of the United States divisions we have left is an armored division. The next thing is that the combined chiefs of staff are particularly anxious for us to get the Fifteenth Air Force located in southern Italy as soon as we possibly can in order to assist in Pointblank.[2] This movement requires an enormous amount of tonnage and my latest estimates from Alexander are that our present backlog of vehicles, including air force, is forty thousand. Although the combined chiefs of staff have authorized us to keep a group of LSTs until December 15, we still will not have our buildup in a satisfactory state by that time. It would be most advantageous if we could keep them an additional month, but apparently this further delay would cut directly into the Overlord plan.[3] I will take it up with the combined chiefs of staff, all of whom are due to go through here very soon. Approval would also retain for us some chance of making an amphibious assault by a reinforced division.

I have made three trips to Italy and am making another one three days from now. Command has become extremely difficult because the air commander feels he must be in Tunis with the bulk of his forces, the naval commander is back in Algiers, and Alexander is in Italy. Every problem that arises involving the three services requires an enormous amount of communication because the holding of commanders-in-chief meetings in the Tunis area is a laborious affair.

DECEMBER 6, 1943

When Secretary Knox visited this theater sometime in October, he brought to me news that I was to be relieved as commander in the Mediterranean in order that General Marshall could have command in England.[1] My assignment, according to the secretary, was to be chief of staff of the army. This is the only word that has ever been spoken to me on this subject by any American official, except that when General Smith was in Washington in early October certain possibilities along this line were discussed with him. A number of British friends, among them Admiral Cunningham and Dickie Mountbatten, have brought me news on the prospective changes, but none of these, of course, has been official.

When important personages began transiting this theater on their way to the Cairo Conference (Sextant), I met most of them, in turn, and gathered the following impressions.[2]

First, I met the prime minister in Malta. He told me that originally it was intended that General Brooke should command in England and the Mediterranean command should remain undisturbed. However, when the Americans, at Quebec, insisted upon American command in England, it became politically necessary (and the truth of this statement is obvious) that the British should have command in the Mediterranean.[3] He said that later proposals of the president's were, however, to the effect that General Marshall should take over strategic direction of the whole European campaign, while General Brooke should actually command in England, and I should remain in command here. This, the prime minister said, he could not accept. There were many sidelights that the prime minister gave to me on the whole proposition. However, these were not particularly important, and at the time of my meeting him, he felt that the original proposal would go through as first approved; namely, that General Marshall would take command of Overlord in England and I would possibly go to Washington. He was quite disappointed when I insisted that under these circumstances I would want to take General Smith with me. He expressed a great desire to have General Smith remain here to assist the new commander. I told him this was one point on which I would not yield, except under directions from the president.

Before my meeting with the prime minister, I had a conversation with Averell Harriman, who was then on his way to Moscow.[4] He said that the president,

Churchill poses in the regalia of Africa,
with the ever-present cigar.

while very reluctant to allow General Marshall to leave Washington, had stated that in the event General Marshall did leave Washington he would insist that I come back to Washington to take over General Marshall's job. The prime minister, in his meeting, told me that there were only two Americans that he would willingly accept in London as commander of Overlord. These were General Marshall and myself. While nothing could be more flattering to me than to have my name coupled with General Marshall's in this fashion by both the president and the prime minister, yet I cannot escape the feeling that the whole matter might have been worked out in such a way as to avoid drastic rearrangement of the Mediterranean command. I think we have made Allied command work here with reasonable efficiency, even though at times it lacks the drive that could be applied were the force entirely homogeneous with respect to nationality.

I have seen quite a bit of Colonel Elliott Roosevelt, who is apparently quite close to the president in family councils. He feels that the president is quite undecided as to what is the best thing to do, especially since the meeting at Teheran, where it is understood that Stalin insisted both upon Overlord in the spring and upon the utmost pressing of the Italian campaign during the winter.

Colonel Roosevelt has had many conferences with his father and has evolved a formula which he hopes his father will accept. He believes that the things actually troubling the president are that (1) General Marshall's great contributions to the cause of the United Nations (which are recognized and acknowledged by all) entitle him to a field command on the theory that a chief of staff will never be remembered in history, while every independent field commander will be given place possibly far out of proportion to this contributions; and (2) there should be a single mind directing the coordination between Overlord and operations in the Mediterranean theater. This means an over-all command for the European theater in some form or other.

Elliott Roosevelt's theory is that General Marshall's place is different from that of any previous chief of staff in the American army and that his position in history is already fixed. He contends, moreover, that the European campaign from England, no matter how important, will be only a phase of the war and that the contemplated change will deprive the president of General Marshall's great abilities during the stages against Japan.

His next point is that the president could secure the needed coordination between Overlord and operations in the Mediterranean theater, which coordination is functionally a responsibility of the combined chiefs of staff, by merely appointing General Marshall as the executive of the combined chiefs of staff during the critical stages of the operation. This plan would not remove General Marshall from his present position, would give him a virtual field command during the most critical stage of the operations, and would secure the rapid coordination envisioned by the president in single command.

Under Colonel Roosevelt's scheme, General Brooke would be the actual field commander in England, while I would remain here.

All the above is important only because it is tied up in the vaster question of operations to be carried out during the next several months.

I was called to Cairo for consultation with the combined chiefs of staff and, in going, insisted that my three commanders in chief go with me so we could present our case as a team. Unfortunately, Alexander could not attend due to illness, but I felt that I knew his ideas so well that even his mind would be represented, indirectly, at the conference.

Briefly, my contention was as follows: The most important land objective in the Mediterranean, from a strategic standpoint, is the Po valley because of the fact that land forces based there are extremely threatening to the German structure in the Balkans, in France, and in the Reich itself. Next, from that position, landing operations either to the east or to the west can be more readily supported. Third, a position in that area brings our air forces closer and closer to the vitals of the German industries.

I pointed out that to attain such a position by early spring would require more assets than are presently in sight and that it was my belief that to provide these assets would delay Overlord from sixty to ninety days. I pointed out also that if a campaign toward taking of the Po valley began to develop favorably, there would at a certain point become available landing craft and forces that could be used for rapid descent upon the Dodecanese and destruction of the German position in the Aegean Sea, but only if Turkey should come into the war. I disclaimed any purpose of discussing the advisability of Turkey's entering the war because I know nothing about it.

The second assumption under which I discussed the Mediterranean operations was that we would use only assets presently in sight and would have to content ourselves on land with a line covering Rome in Italy. Upon attainment of that line, forces would be disposed to carry on active minor operations against the enemy, but the general attitude would from thereafter be defensive, unless there came about a considerable weakening of the German forces. Upon attainment of that line, I said that the Dodecanese again offered an opportunity for gaining considerable advantages at relatively low cost, but provided always that it was considered politically desirable to bring Turkey into the war. Without the Turkish landing fields, I do not see how the Aegean position can be broken cheaply and quickly. A number of questions were brought up with respect to the broad concepts and all of them were answered, apparently to the satisfaction of the combined chiefs of staff. My own commanders in chief contented themselves with giving certain details of requirements for a successful operation in the Aegean.

Since my visit to Cairo, I have had to stay closer to my command post waiting for news as to when the important personages would be coming back through this theater. Necessary arrangements for security, housing, and inspections are laborious, and since this type of decision is apt to be taken very suddenly, I have to stay here waiting for the answers. I have even been afraid to make a very

At dinner during the Cairo Conference. Elliott Roosevelt is facing his father.

necessary visit to Italy because of the fear that I would get stymied there by weather.

Just after writing the above entry, word came of President Roosevelt's return from Teheran. Eisenhower flew to Tunis next day and met FDR's plane that afternoon. The two men were scarcely seated in the automobile when Roosevelt said, "Well, Ike, you are going to command Overlord."

⌜ IV ⌝

VICTORY IN EUROPE

The decision to appoint Eisenhower to the European theater, and to relieve him from command in the Mediterranean, made good sense—although the waging of war is not always a matter of good sense. Eisenhower could have had no sure feeling that he was going to obtain the appointment until in fact he received it. Talking to Colonel Roosevelt was an awkward way for him to find out what was going on at home; it displayed Ike's high uncertainty of his personal future, for otherwise he surely would not have wasted his time in what amounted to military-political gossip.

In analyzing what, according to good sense, was the best solution, it clearly was best to leave General Marshall in Washington, for Marshall knew how to handle President Roosevelt, a formidable and dangerous figure. The president was especially dangerous when he was friendly, for it was then that his amateur urges became pronounced and he was likely to suggest some inappropriate solution to a problem. Roosevelt was very friendly with leaders of the American navy, and he liked the air force generals. This meant that there was constant danger that he would move away from supporting the ground forces represented by Marshall, in favor of some panacea offered by his naval or air commanders. Marshall was just the man to contain the president's amateur urges. On one notable occasion, at a meeting, Roosevelt called Marshall "George," for this was the way the president softened up every high official in American government, civil and military. Marshall froze at the appellation, and Roosevelt never tried it again. Marshall avoided any sort of private friendship with the president and refused to go up to Hyde Park to see Roosevelt, despite numerous and pressing requests that he do so. He later said that the only time he ever went to Hyde Park— where he knew he might get into an awkward situation and find the president *subtracting from his authority in some inconvenient way—was on the occasion of Roosevelt's funeral.*

Marshall was also the man to handle General MacArthur, whose rivalries with navy commanders in the Pacific were public knowledge, and who would have liked to order around the people in the War Department as if, once again, he himself was chief of staff. Marshall very much was a Chaumont man, and at one low point in his army career, in 1933, MacArthur had ordered him away from troops, to a training command for the National Guard in Chicago—a military dead-end, apparently. Marshall had protested the order, and MacArthur confirmed it. As matters turned out, the Chicago assignment represented no malice on the part of MacArthur, but Marshall would have been more than human if he had not seen some malevolence in the act. In any event, Marshall also was a keen observer of human foibles, and easily took MacArthur's measure. So long as Marshall was chief of staff, MacArthur's position in the Far East was in no danger of getting out of hand.

And Eisenhower, a younger man, had all the experience in supervising an Anglo-American staff. Eisenhower's diplomatic talents, which were many, had worked well in combining Britishers and Americans into a single supreme head-quarters in North Africa. The British liked Ike, and Churchill especially found him attractive and was very willing to have him back again in London, where he was a known quantity. Churchill, who liked to give military advice not merely to his own commanders but to American generals, may have sensed that it would be an awkward thing to give advice to General Marshall. Indeed, in 1943 there had been a run-in between Marshall and Churchill, when the latter in a tiresome way was urging that after conclusion of the North African campaign the Anglo-Americans should invade the island of Rhodes—in the eastern Mediterranean, a strategic bastion of no discernible use to anyone. Marshall exploded at the meeting, interrupting the prime minister with the remark that "No American is going to land on that God-damned island!" Churchill probably took Marshall's measure in that remark, and though in his heart of hearts he may well have known that he, the prime minister, had learned nothing about military affairs since the Boer War, it was easier to deal with the affable Eisenhower.

Ike, therefore, was chosen and at once found himself in a welter of advice, in the course of which he was forced once again to fly back to Washington for discussions.

1944

FEBRUARY 7, 1944

In early December the president told me I was to move to England to become the supreme commander, Allied Expeditionary Forces.

The task of laying out the new American theater in Africa and of securing the American commanders I wanted for England was complicated by the fact that

General Marshall went on a trip around the world. Upon his return to Washington (about Christmas) he agreed to my recommendations and then ordered me to the United States for a short visit.

It was a poor time to go—there was much to be done in the way of detailed arrangement applying to old and new staffs, indoctrination of new officers arriving in Africa, and the ever-present necessity of getting to London in a hurry.

But I went.

The problems here had been under study for a long time, but the fatal defect, in my opinion, was that all planning had been done on a basis of a three-division assault. I would not accept this except on a basis of definite order from the combined chiefs of staff. This opinion I expressed to a Brigadier General Chambers when he was in Africa, long before I had any idea that I personally would have the slightest thing to do with this operation. Montgomery came here ahead of me and arrived at exactly the same conclusion. When I came, I put my convictions in a long telegram and sent it to the combined chiefs of staff. That was about January 20 (the telegram is filed in the diary).[1] Today, February 7, the British chiefs of staff and the United States chiefs of staff are still examining the problem.

At the time Anvil-Overlord was planned it was thought that no landing craft would be needed in Italy after the end of January.[2] Now, with Shingle stalemated, there is a need there that cannot be ignored.[3]

We can't close our eyes to that, no matter how much we shout "principle and agreements."

But the whole original Anvil-Overlord assault involved only a total of five-plus divisions in the assault. I think there must be seven-plus. And with Italy requiring

Commander conference in London, January 1944.

an allotment, it looks like Anvil is doomed. I hate this, in spite of my recognition of the fact that Italian fighting will be some compensation for a strong Anvil.

The fighting in the Pacific is absorbing far too much of our limited resources in landing craft during this critical phase of the European war. In my opinion we (the United Nations) have erred in this particular, and the error may prove serious. The forthcoming operation should have every resource the two nations can produce until the moment when the invading force is firmly established on the Continent—say to D plus ninety. But we are fighting two wars at once, which is wrong, so far as I can see from my own limited viewpoint.

Much discussion has taken place concerning our command set-up, including newspaper evaluations of personalities and abilities. Generally speaking, the British columnists (not the chief of staff or the prime minister) try to show that my contributions in the Mediterranean were administrative accomplishments and "friendliness in welding an allied team." They dislike to believe that I had anything particularly to do with campaigns. They don't use the words "initiative" and "boldness" in talking of me, but often do in speaking of Alex and Monty.

The truth is that the bold British commanders in the Mediterranean were Admiral Sir Andrew Cunningham and Tedder. I had peremptorily to order the holding of the forward airfields in the bitter days of January 1943. I had to order the integration of an American corps and its use on the battlelines (if I had not done that, Tunis would have evaded us a much longer time). I had to order the attack on Pantelleria. And, finally, the British ground commanders (but not Sir Andrew and Tedder) wanted to put all our ground forces into the toe of Italy. They didn't like Salerno, but after days of work I got them to accept. On the other hand, no British commander ever held back when once an operation was ordered. We had a happy family, and to all the commanders in chief must go the great share of the operational credit. But it wearies me to be thought of as timid, when I've had to do things that were so risky as to be almost crazy. Oh hum.

MARCH 22, 1944

During the two months since I arrived in this theater, our problems have been divided into two general categories, the first of which applies to the responsibilities of the combined chiefs of staff, and the second to the responsibilities devolving on this headquarters.

In the second category are all such problems as the determination of proper methods of attack, including the use of special weapons, and various expedients for developing satisfactory port facilities. Training, organization, assignment of personnel, and insuring adequacy of supply have all engaged the attention of this and lower staffs. In general, satisfactory progress has been made in all problems of this type.

The matters that have really caused us trouble are those in which only the combined chiefs of staff can make final decisions. The principal ones are the resources to be allocated to Overlord, which matter involves also the possibility

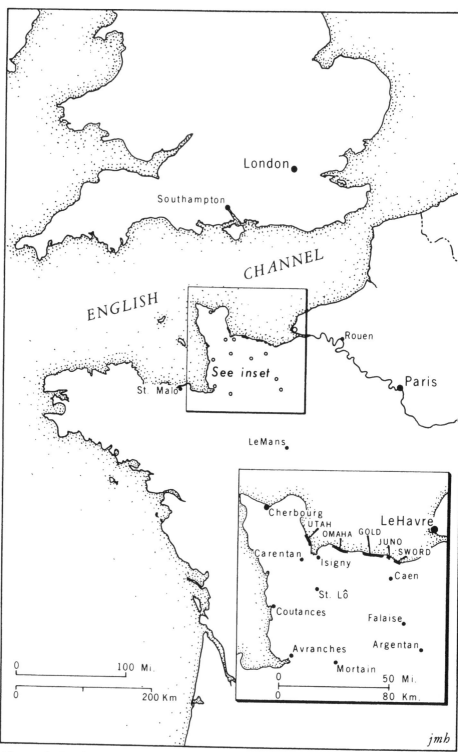

London

Southampton

CHANNEL

ENGLISH

See inset

St. Malo

Rouen

Paris

LeMans

Cherbourg

LeHavre

UTAH
OMAHA GOLD
JUNO
SWORD

Carentan
Isigny

Caen

St. Lô

Coutances

Falaise

Avranches

Argentan

Mortain

0   100 Mi.

0   200 Km

0   50 Mi.

0   80 Km.

jmh

Normandy Beach.

of staging Anvil or abandoning it—at least in its original formal conception. Another of these problems is the organization and command of the air forces, and a third is the arrangements for dealing with political matters, more especially so far as France is concerned.

Resources in which we have disturbing shortages are, first of all, landing craft, and second, possibly, supporting naval gunfire. I am given to understand that the naval ships exist to give us all the naval gunfire support we can possibly use but the extensive minefields on the target coast very stringently limit the possibilities of employment. This question worries us a great deal because there is no doubt that naval gunfire in overwhelming strength will be absolutely necessary. The landing craft situation and, to some extent, the availability of the actual naval vessels for gunfire support are directly tied up in the nature of the operations to be carried out in the Mediterranean in the early summer. It is becoming increasingly apparent that any attempt to do Anvil by our target date and on a basis of a two-division assault and ten-division buildup is out of the question. Our original loading plan, designed to provide us with an efficient five-division assault, called for a great many more of the various types of landing craft than are now available. The only source from which any additional ones can come is the Mediterranean. I have definitely recommended to the combined chiefs of staff that we leave in the Mediterranean only the lift for a one-division ship-to-shore assault. Over and above this there will be in the Mediterranean, of course, a number of landing craft under repair or completely unserviceable. These will, however, be useful in maintaining the appearance of a threat in that area while the one-division lift will provide means for keeping up the tempo of the offensive. The additional twenty-six LSTs [landing ship, tanks] and forty LCIs, large [landing craft, infantry], that will just become available to us will be a Godsend and will provide some margin of safety as well as flexibility in the assault. For two months I have been struggling in every possible way to provide for a real Anvil, but I have come to the conclusion that we are simply striving for the impossible. This whole question is a most involved one, and we have spent much time in trying to get the whole chief-of-staff committee to see the thing as we do.

In the political field, the situation has been no less complicated. I quite agree with both the president and the prime minister that too great a concession to the French National Committee will result only in that body becoming even more arbitrary and highhanded than at present and will cause us acute embarrassment.[1] On the other hand, we are going to need very badly the support of the resistance groups in France, and it is our general opinion that these can be brought into full play only through the agency and leadership of the French committee. The latest directive of the president on this matter, which has not yet been approved by the British side of the house, is that the whole matter be thrown back in my lap and, virtually, that I deal with any French body that seems capable of assisting us.

The necessary conferences and studies in all these matters have greatly limited the ability of higher commanders to inspect troops and to give their attention to vital questions of discipline, morale, and training. All unit commanders, even

Eisenhower, Churchill, and Bradley taking aim—while inspecting armored troops in England prior to the invasion.

down to include regiments, are constantly revising loading plans and their attention is thus also divided.

The air problem has been one requiring a great deal of patience and negotiation. I found, upon coming here, that the British had a great fear that the American idea was to seize all the air in Great Britain and apply it very locally in the preparation of Overlord. It took long and patient explaining to show (1) that we had no great interest in coastal command, which organization would have to continue in its present set-up, although it would be most useful in protecting our ships as we went into the assault; (2) that a discontinuance of Pointblank was farthest from our minds because through Pointblank is about our only means of forcing the German air force to fight, and thus allow us to gain ascendancy over it;[2] and (3) that the big bomber, particularly the command bombing force, was not to be misused on targets for which it is not particularly suited.

After long discussions and negotiation it developed that the British did not trust Leigh Mallory to be the directing head of my air forces.[3] This came as somewhat of a surprise to me since I understood he had been especially selected by the British themselves for this post. I found, on the other hand, that they did trust Tedder, and I immediately announced, through written memorandum, that Tedder would be the directing head of all my air forces, with Leigh Mallory, Spaatz, and Harris operating on a coordinate plane.[4] I definitely proposed that the turning over of Spaatz's and Harris's air forces to me should be made consequent upon the approval by Portal and myself of a general air preparation plan which would take into account all of the objectives of Pointblank so far as they were consistent with our great need for preparing for Overlord. In the messages coming back and forth from Washington, a sudden argument developed over the use of the word "command." This whole matter I had considered settled a week ago, after many weeks of argument. This did not seem important at the time the drafts were first drawn up, but as long as the question was raised I have recommended to General Marshall that a word be adopted that leaves no doubt in anybody's mind of my authority and responsibility for controlling air operations of all three of these forces during the critical period of Overlord.

The actual air preparatory plan is to be the subject of a formal meeting on this coming Saturday, March 25, between Portal, Spaatz, Harris, Leigh Mallory, Tedder, and myself.

If a satisfactory answer is not reached, I am going to take drastic action and inform the combined chiefs of staff that unless the matter is settled at once I will request relief from this command.

(PS: At a chief-of-staff meeting this A.M.—Wednesday, March 22—I was told the word "direction" was acceptable to both sides of the house. Amen!)

APRIL 12, 1944

Today two matters arose which were most disturbing.

Two weeks ago the CAS and I agreed upon a general plan of operations for the air forces, and under that agreement—and the authority of the combined chiefs of staff—it was understood that the CAS [British chief of air staff—that is, Portal] was to direct Harris and Spaatz to report to me for instructions.[1] I had been assured that this was all sorted out when last evening Spaatz told me he was still getting instructions directly from the CAS. In spite of the fact that the instructions he is getting from CAS conform exactly to what we want to do, the fact remains that from the British side of the house the actual amalgamation of the air forces has not yet taken place.

I immediately got in touch with Tedder and Portal. The difficulty is that the original agreement stated that as soon as we had agreed upon a plan of operations, this agreement was to take effect, and it now develops that our plan for bombarding certain transportation centers may involve such a loss of French life that the British cabinet is objecting to part of the plan. Under the strict wording of the agreement, this prevents the CAS from placing the two bomber forces under my command.

I protested bitterly at allowing details of a few targets to interfere with the operation of a whole plan, and the CAS agreed to say to Spaatz that he would get his instructions from Tedder. He also stated that he believed tomorrow night would see final acceptance of the whole proposition so that this matter could be tidied up once and for all, and we would know where we stood. In the meantime, operations are going forward as we desired, but it is disturbing to think that it takes so terribly long in order to get understandings translated into actual directives.

(PS: The matter was arranged next day.)

The second and even more important matter involves differences between the British and the United States chiefs of staff on the Anvil proposition. Because of these differences the United States chiefs of staff have reversed their decision to divert to the Mediterranean landing craft which had been originally intended for the Pacific. This is a very sad blow because during this whole summer we are going to need every item of strength we can possibly get in the European theater.

I have read the various messages passing back and forth between the British and the United States chiefs of staff and I must say that I honestly agree with the position of the United States chiefs of staff—and this in spite of the British contention that by reversing their decision the Americans are not playing fair under the original decision to make Germany the principal target this year. The consequences of our impending operations are so appallingly great that, in spite of any personal views I have, I am determined to do anything within the realm of possibility in order that we may get this additional strength in the European theater this year.

(PS: I sent a special telegram on this subject to G.C. Marshall on April 17, following a conference with the prime minister, General Alexander, and CIGS.)[2]

MAY 22, 1944

In considering the months of fighting by the Fifth Army [the American army in Italy], I am reminded of the attitude of that headquarters a year ago this spring, which illustrates not only the shortsightedness of the average human but the intense personal outlook that most officers have upon even such a critical thing as war. In January, 1943, when we were considering the setting up of the Fifth Army, General Clark was very anxious to have that command instead of his then title of deputy commander in chief. He was warned that the Fifth Army would be a training organization for some months and nothing else, while in his position of deputy he would probably soon get a front-line command. In fact, he was offered one, which was approximately a corps in strength, but the title of army commander was too attractive. Within a month after taking command of the Fifth Army, he and some of his staff began to plague me as to their future. They became very fearful that the war in the Mediterranean would be won and they would never get into it, although I assured them that their troops sooner or later had to get into action. I showed them that such an outcome was inescapable. Nevertheless, they were most unhappy throughout the whole spring, and I had to make special efforts to keep up their morale.

In view of the fact that this army has been in action continuously since last September 9, I suppose these things are forgotten by them, but they are most revealing and somewhat amusing.

In this command, the teamwork in the SHAEF [Supreme Headquarters, Allied Expeditionary Force] staff has been easier to establish than it was in the original Torch staff. On the other hand, complete devotion to the principle of unity of command has been more difficult to establish among these commanders in chief than it was among Cunningham, Tedder, and Alexander, when all three came under my command about February 3 or 4 of 1943. Part of the answer lies in the fact that we were then engaged in desperate battling and everybody could see the sense of and necessity for complete unification. The answer also lies partially in the fact that those three men were of the broadest possible caliber, while two of my present commanders, although extremely able, are somewhat ritualistic in outlook and require a great deal more of inoculation.[1]

One of our most difficult problems here has been the setting up of a completely satisfactory air organization. This comes about because of the widely scattered interests of the air forces and the great strength of units that have been acting in almost an independent way. However, somewhere about April 10, a special arrangement was worked out that gives the supreme commander all the authority necessary to secure full support from all the air forces in England, even though the procedure involved is somewhat more laborious than was the case in the Mediterranean.

In contemplating airborne operations, which I had originally thought would present very little difficulty because of our tremendous preponderance in fighters, we have run into a great deal of difficulty because of the almost universal coverage of the European continent by strong flak. When going into areas where gliders cannot land at night we run into most appalling difficulties and obstacles due to this fire. This is one phase of the operation that still worries me, and I am somewhat concerned that the Eighty-second Airborne Division will have a most sticky time of it. I am going to see whether or not special support by fighter bombers cannot be given them.

Our efforts to arrive at some arrangement, approved by both governments, under which we could actually carry on advanced planning with the French, have proved unavailing. The principal obstacles have been two: first, both governments have been absolutely unwilling to give the French any information whatsoever involving the impending operation; second, neither government is apparently willing to accord the measure of recognition to the De Gaulle committee that the committee itself believes it should have. This creates a friction and bad atmosphere. I believe, however, that once the operation is started I can secure from the French the cooperation that I need.

Recent inspections of troops have shown them to be tough, well trained, and in good fettle. I have visited approximately twenty airfields, some twenty divisions, and four units of the American navy. I believe that all these units are ready to operate effectively. This coming week is crowded with more inspections.

Unity in allied command depends as much upon the comprehension and good judgment of officers in high positions as it does upon blind adherence to a principle. An allied command cannot possibly be handled as would a completely homogeneous one. There always exists the danger that public reaction to a local tactical defeat will be that of blaming a commander of another nationality. It is the duty of the highest commander of an allied formation to make sure that his views, when overridden by an immediate superior, are transmitted by that superior to the supreme commander himself. When everybody sees the necessity for this procedure it can operate without causing any difficulty.

JUNE 3, 1944

Subjects: (a) proper coordination with the French; (b) weather; (c) beach and undersea obstacles; (d) future success of the air in breaking up effectiveness of hostile ground units; and (e) future organization.

The matter of coordination with the French has been highly complicated because of lack of crystallization in ideas involving both the political and military fields. Specifically, the president desires that coordination be effected with the French on the basis of dealing with any group or groups that can effectively fight the Germans. His directive apparently recognizes the influence of the National Committee of Liberation in France but he is unwilling to promise any exclusive dealing with the group since that, he apparently believes, would be tantamount to recognizing the committee as a provisional government of France, set up from the outside.

We have our direct means of communication with the resistance groups of France but all our information leads us to believe that the only authority these resistance groups desire to recognize is that of De Gaulle and his committee. However, since De Gaulle is apparently willing to cooperate only on the basis of our dealing with him exclusively, the whole thing falls into a rather sorry mess. De Gaulle is, of course, now controlling the only French military forces that can take part in this operation. Consequently, from the purely military viewpoint, we must, at least until the time that other French forces might conceivably be organized completely independent of his movement, deal with him alone. He, however, takes the attitude that military and political matters go hand in hand and will not cooperate militarily unless political recognition of some kind is accorded him. We do not seem to be able, in advance of D-day, to straighten the matter at all. I have just learned that De Gaulle has failed to accept the prime minister's invitation to come to England, saying that he would make his decision this afternoon.[1]

The rapid sorting out of all the conflicting ideas is quite necessary if we are to secure the maximum help from the French both inside and outside the country.

The weather in this country is practically unpredictable. For some days our experts have been meeting almost hourly, and I have been holding commander-in-chief meetings once or twice a day to consider the reports and tentative predictions. While at this moment, the morning of June 3, it appears that the weather will not be so bad as to preclude landings and will possibly even permit reasonably effective gunfire support from the navy, the picture from the air viewpoint is not so good.

Probably no one who does not have to bear the specific and direct responsibility of making the final decision as to what to do can understand the intensity of these

Invasion vehicles awaiting shipment at the Southampton docks.

Convoy arriving at Southampton docks for invasion.

burdens. The supreme commander, much more than any of his subordinates, is kept informed of the political issues involved, particularly the anticipated effect of delay upon the Russians. He, likewise, is in close touch with all the advice from his military subordinates and must face the issue even when technical advice as to weather is not unanimous from the several experts. Success or failure might easily hinge upon the effectiveness, for example, of airborne operations. If the weather is suitable for everything else, but unsuitable for airborne operations, the question becomes whether to risk the airborne movement anyway or to defer the whole affair in the hopes of getting weather that is a bit better.

My tentative thought is that the desirability for getting started on the next favorable tide is so great and the uncertainty of the weather is such that we could never anticipate really perfect weather coincident with proper tidal conditions, that we must go unless there is a real and very serious deterioration in the weather.

Since last February the enemy has been consistently busy in placing obstacles of various types on all European beaches suitable for landing operations. Most of these are also mined. Under ordinary circumstances of land attack these would not be particularly serious but because they must be handled quickly and effectively before the major portion of our troops can begin unloading, they present a hazard that is a very considerable one. It is because of their existence that we must land earlier on the tide than we had originally intended. This gives us a chance to go after them while they are still on dry land, because if their bases were under water, they would be practically impossible to handle. If our gun support of the operation and the DD [duplex-drive] tanks during this period are both highly effective, we should be all right.[2]

The underwater obstacles, that is, the sea mines, force us to sweep every foot of water over which we operate, and this adds immeasurably to the difficulties in restricted waters in which we are operating. The combination of undersea and beach obstacles is serious, but we believe we have it whipped.

Because the enemy in great strength is occupying a country that is interlaced with a fine communication system, our attack can be looked upon as reasonable only if our tremendous air force is able to impede his concentrations against us and to help destroy the effectiveness of any of his counterattacks. Weather again comes into this problem, because it is my own belief that with reasonably good weather during the first two or three weeks of the operation our air superiority and domination will see us through to success.

Lately we have been studying earnestly the question of future organization, assuming that we have established a beachhead so firmly that we no longer need fear being kicked into the sea. All British land forces will quickly be in, and I personally doubt that the British will be able to maintain more than fifteen or sixteen divisions in active warfare in this theater. This means that the bulk of the land forces must come from the United States. Logically, also, there should come about eventually the desirability of undertaking offensive operations in fairly distinct zones of advance, with each of the ground groupments supported by its own distinct air force at least so far as fighters and fighter bombers are concerned. When this comes about, every factor of simplicity in organization, national pride, efficiency in administration, etc., indicates the further desirability of having two principal ground commanders—one operating to the northeast, one to the east. (I believe, however, that the British formation will probably have to be reinforced by an American army or at least a corps.) Pending this particular development it will still be necessary to begin the establishment in Europe of an American army group headquarters. I plan to have Bradley command this new headquarters during the transition period, that is, until we are completely established and ready to undertake operations in distinct zones of advance. He will operate during the transition period under Montgomery. Finally, Bradley and Montgomery will each report directly to me.

At that time a certain portion of the so-called "tactical" air force, that is, medium bombers and possibly some of the long-range fighters, will remain under the commander in chief, AEF. This portion of the tactical air force will be available to assist either army group.

I have already issued a tentative directive to plan for future organization of ground and air forces along the lines indicated in this paragraph.

The story of D-day, June 6, 1944, is so well known that it needs no recital in these pages. Suffice to say that one of Churchill's many military ideas miraculously proved to be good, namely, the construction of artificial harbors off the Normandy peninsula, so as to prevent a costly attack upon the well-defended port cities. The Allies attacked along the open coast near the inland towns of Carentan and Caen, and soon the harbors were in place—the American known as Utah and Omaha, and the British called Gold, Juno, and Sword. Meanwhile, paratroopers of the United States Eighty-second and 101 Airborne Divisions landed at St. Mère Église and to the north of Caen to fence off the beach areas long enough to allow the troops a foothold.

Everything went as well as could be expected, and even the weather behaved, until a hurricane on June 19 made it impossible to supply the troops ashore for four days and destroyed Omaha beach, which was littered with sunk or grounded ships—more than three hundred of them.

Other than the hurricane, there were no calamities, and Major General J. Lawton (Lightning Joe) Collins fought his corps into Cherbourg on June 26, opening up the possibility of much easier supply as soon as the wrecked port could be cleared. The buildup continued, until by July 2, just three weeks after D-day, a million men were ashore, with half a million tons of supplies and 171,532 vehicles. By that date a major force had crowded into the narrow beachheads that now had been pushed out into the hedgerow country to the south—ten or fifteen miles, just enough to jam in the men and equipment. The Americans had thirteen divisions, the British eleven, the Canadians one. Casualties by July 2 had not been light but were supportable—about 60,000 for the Allies, with 8,975 men killed. Forty-one thousand Germans were in the prisoner cages.

On July 25 came the breakout, and the race began to roll up German resistance, which soon virtually collapsed. The British under Montgomery pushed south beyond Caen and Caumont, and the spectacular moves were made by the

The American high brass aboard a Dukh, coming ashore at a beachhead,
some days after D-Day.

Normandy Beach.

American First and Third Armies, under Lieutenant Generals Courtney H. Hodges and George Patton, south to Coutances and on to Avranches, where the First Army turned east toward Mortain and the Third fanned out to Fougères, Rennes, and St. Malo.

On August 7 the Germans managed a counterattack at Mortain.

For the supreme Allied commander, making a diary entry on the next day, August 8, the counterattack was one problem. Another was the desire of his British Allies to change his basic strategy by diverting troops scheduled for the invasion of southern France, Operation Anvil, to the Brittany peninsula, below Normandy, so as to take the Brittany ports. The more troops ashore, the more supplies and vehicles needed; the more action against the Germans, the more supplies and vehicles consumed; the need for ports had become pressing. Cherbourg was a mess when Joe Collins's driving divisions took the place, and even the talents of a doughty engineer officer like Lucius D. Clay were not enough to clean up the port in short order. The temptation therefore was to take the ports on the Brittany peninsula, and the idea appealed to the British, despite the fact that the German commander in the little port of St. Malo obviously was going to hold out to the bitter end against Patton's troops—and did so, surrendering on August 17. Brest, fanatically defended with a stiffening of SS troops, held out until September 19, and the harbor and its facilities had been so wrecked by Allied bombing and German demolitions that the allies never made any attempt to use it. Brittany would prove no solution to the port problem, but the British thought they saw a chance there. Considering the speed of the Normandy breakout, they became highly uncertain of the usefulness of Anvil—the invasion of southern France, which was to roll up German resistance by pushing up from the south to join with the Overlord force in the northwest.

AUGUST 6-7, 1944[1]

1. The prime minister and the British chiefs of staff became interested, several days ago, in abandoning Anvil in favor of bringing additional forces into Brittany. A quick study of the proposition showed that (a) there was no assurance that we would have the Brittany ports working during the next several weeks; (b) even when we do get them working, we are counting upon them to support troops already here and scheduled for arrival; (c) if additional troops should be brought in, there is no reason why two or three extra divisions could not come from the United States; (d) to abandon Anvil would, at the best, give us in the first lift only the initial follow-up elements of Anvil, short a great deal of equipment and some personnel. The arrivals in Brittany would, therefore, be piecemeal and slow.

2. Nevertheless, the British felt this was a better proposition than to go on with Anvil.

3. I disagreed. I informed both the United States chiefs of staff and the prime minister of my flat disagreement.

4. This morning, August 8, a message from the United States chiefs of staff

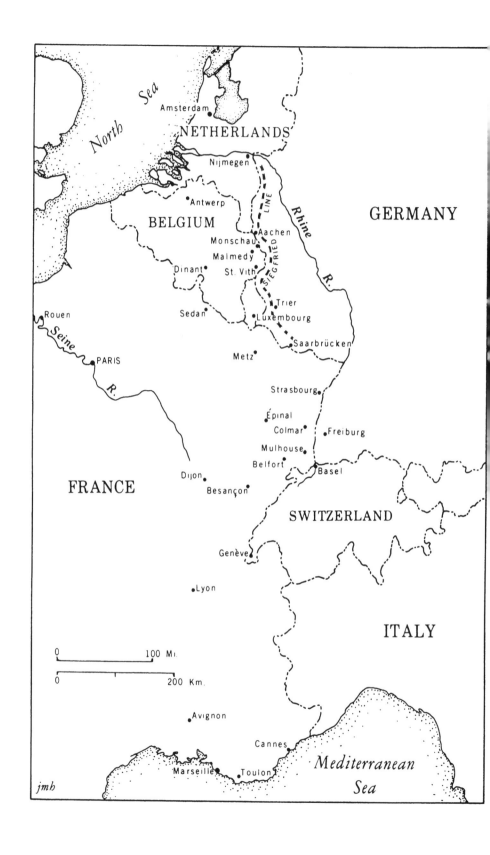

North Sea

NETHERLANDS

Amsterdam

Nijmegen

Antwerp

BELGIUM

Aachen

Monschau

Malmedy

Dinant

St. Vith

GERMANY

Rhine R.

LINE

SIEGFRIED

Trier

Luxembourg

Saarbrücken

Rouen

Sedan

Seine

PARIS

Metz

R.

Strasbourg

Épinal

Colmar

Freiburg

Mulhouse

Belfort

Dijon

Besançon

Basel

FRANCE

SWITZERLAND

Genève

Lyon

ITALY

0   100 Mi.

0   200 Km.

Avignon

Cannes

Marseille

Toulon

Mediterranean Sea

jmh

indicates that I am supported by Washington and that Anvil will go on as planned.

5. *New Subject:* The enemy is apparently holding his present front east of Avranches very determinedly and is even throwing in counterattacks with armor in that region. The attack by the Canadian army this morning south from Caen met the stiffest kind of resistance and has not made much progress. It therefore appears to me that the American right wing on this front should swing in closer in an effort to destroy the enemy by attacking him in the rear. On a visit to Bradley today I found that he had already acted on this idea and had secured Montgomery's agreement to a sharp change in direction toward the northeast instead of continuing directly toward the east, as envisaged in M-517.[2] I believe this will be tactically sound.

6. I am seeing Montgomery tonight to make sure that the attacks on the eastern flank are continued as planned. It appears that our bombing effort this noon was not too effective in front of the Canadians.

The German counterattack at Mortain, begun on August 7, lasted until August 12; meanwhile, the Germans fought fanatically at Caen against the British and Canadians, reducing that town to rubble. Such resistance however was foolish, for it gave Eisenhower and Bradley their chance to encircle the German forces, and by August 14 they had executed an almost classical maneuver by which the Germans found themselves in a gigantic bag, the mouth of which was barely open to the east at the town of Falaise. Realizing what their situation then required, they began to move out as fast as they could, but there were too many troops to get out; the Allies took ten divisions intact when they closed the gap. The delighted Eisenhower two days later visited Falaise, a scene of appalling carnage:

The battlefield at Falaise was unquestionably one of the greatest "killing grounds" of any of the war areas. Roads, highways, and fields were so choked with destroyed equipment and with dead men and animals that passage through the area was extremely difficult. Forty-eight hours after the closing of the gap I was conducted through it on foot, to encounter scenes that could be described only by Dante. It was literally possible to walk for hundreds of yards at a time, stepping on nothing but dead and decaying flesh. (*Crusade,* p. 279)

On August 15 the invasion of southern France began, Anvil, now known as Dragoon, and it proved an easy success. By early September the United States Seventh Army under Lieutenant General Jacob L. Devers had joined with the Third Army above Switzerland, at Epinal, not far from the Rhine.

By the end of August, Eisenhower had thirty-seven divisions in France, with six more United States divisions in reserve in the United Kingdom. There were twenty United States divisions, twelve British, three Canadian, one French, and one Polish. Paris fell on August 25, taken by the French division, a happy choice although an American division was needed to finish off German resistance.

Early in September victory loomed, and not merely victory in France but in

At Bradley's headquarters, August 1944.

Meeting with De Gaulle, August 21, 1944. Churchill once quipped that the greatest cross he had to bear was the cross of Lorraine. Eisenhower found the French awkward allies, both in North Africa and in Europe. During the Battle of the Bulge the French refused to allow the temporary evacuation of a city, to Eisenhower's intense chagrin.

Germany—nothing seemingly could stop the Allied forces, and it appeared possible that they could move into Germany at will, as they already were moving about France at will. Eisenhower began to wonder how he could administer the coup de grace.

September 5, 1944

For some days it has been obvious that our military forces can advance almost at will, subject only to the requirement for maintenance. Resistance has largely melted all along the front. From the beginning of this campaign I have always visualized that as soon as substantial destruction of the enemy forces in France could be accomplished, we should advance rapidly on the Rhine by pushing through the Aachen gap in the north and through the Metz gap in the south. The virtue of this movement is that it takes advantage of all existing lines of communication in the advance toward Germany and brings the southern force on to the Rhine at Coblenz, practically on the flank of the forces that would advance straight eastward through Aachen. Coincidentally, with this advance we should use our airborne forces to seize crossings over the Rhine and be in position to thrust deep into the Ruhr and threaten Berlin.

I see no reason to change this conception. The defeat of the German armies is complete, and the only thing now needed to realize the whole conception is speed. Our rapidity of movement will depend upon maintenance, in which we are now stretched to the limit.

We must use every port and all lines of communication available to us, including Marseilles and the routes running up the Rhône.

Two weeks ago, when General Montgomery insisted upon a whole American army moving to the northeast on his right flank, I told him that he did not need that much strength to destroy the Germans still on his front. With his usual caution he felt it imperative that we make certain of no halt in operations toward Antwerp and Brussels. Because I agreed with him as to the importance of destroying the remaining German forces in that region and of the geographical objectives, including bomb sites, I directed the First Army to advance closely along the boundary of the Twenty-first Army Group.[1] This forced Patton, to the southeast of Paris, to stand still with his main bodies pushing only reconnaissance to the front.

I now deem it important, while supporting the advance on eastward through Belgium, to get Patton moving once again so that we may be fully prepared to carry out the original conception for the final stages of this campaign.

Needless to say, the more rapidly that the Dragoon forces can enter our area, the easier will be this task because the communications will be available not only for supporting Dragoon but for bringing in troops and supplies needed for Bradley's right wing.

The bright hope to end the war early in September came to an end in a most disappointing way—in a supply breakdown, exacerbated by other unexpected factors. Eisenhower found that after all the lightning drives through France, out of the Normandy beachhead, around to the south, up toward Paris, on to the long northeastern border of France with Belgium and Germany and Switzerland— after the excitement of moving forward, the sirens on the tanks blaring, the engines whining, and behind the armor the long lines of infantrymen and the whole paraphernalia of great armies on the move—the supplies gave out. Oil, ammunition, and spare parts for the machinery of twentieth-century warfare could not be carried by men, by quarter-horse-power prime movers, nor by the horses that had dragged most of the equipment of previous armies, even the armies of the First World War. It took machines, and supplying the machines meant possession of ports. Cherbourg was cleared and opened, but it was on the end of a peninsula and not large enough anyway. Brest was a wreck, unusable. Antwerp was taken fairly early in the northern advance but was unusable for a special reason: the Germans gathered their local forces and concentrated them on the island of Walcheren, which controlled the entrance to the estuary of the Scheldt. Capturing their fortifications took until November 9, and two more weeks were necessary to clear the mines down to Antwerp. The first ship came up the channel on November 26. Thereafter, Antwerp became the main supply center for Allied armies, where the ships could anchor along an ancient quay constructed in Napoleonic days. But it was too late to win the war in the year 1944.

Other factors besides blocked Antwerp held up the Allied movement into Germany. One was the crumbling of France's road net under the pounding of Eisenhower's huge vehicles, the tanks, the half-tracks, and the big trucks with trailers, all loaded to capacity and beyond. France's roads were piecrusts, built for the little cars of the 1930s, and could not take the motorized behemoths of war. Another difficulty was the thick weather of northern France, so well remembered by Eisenhower's officers, most of whom were veterans of the First World War. The autumn weather made any outdoor task unpleasant and frequently trouble-some. And in the air age of the 1940s it often prevented the pulverizing attacks by the Allied bombers that had laid down carpets of high explosives that summer of 1944 and broken German resistance at what in other eras would have been strong points. The air age had its limitations, and bad weather was its worst enemy; when Allied airborne divisions went into Arnhem and Nijmegen in the Netherlands, to get a bridgehead above the Scheldt and not merely protect Antwerp but capture launching areas for the V-1 and V-2 bombs and perhaps create a jump-off place for a thrust into the heart of Germany, they not merely met stiff German resistance, but the bad weather prevented the airborne artillery from constricting German movements, and the Arnhem-Nijmegen operation was only a modest success—and for some gallant but surrounded units ("a bridge too far") a failure.

The Allies had fifty-four divisions in France by October 1, but supplying them was more of a problem than in midsummer; the roads broke up, and the weather came down, and with it Eisenhower's hope for victory that year.

All the while the Germans gathered every available division and prepared for *a lightning strike against the overextended and perhaps overconfident Allies, in an unlikely place, the Ardennes forest. The result was the Battle of the Bulge.*

December 23, 1944

Beginning early in November, it was clear that the Germans, after their disastrous defeat of the summer and fall, were succeeding in building up very considerable defensive strength along the Siegfried Line by the use of hurriedly formed Volkssturm divisions.[1] When these first appeared in line, they had very low combat value, but it was felt that unless speedy attack should be made against the Siegfried Line, the relative strength of the opposing forces would gradually become more favorable to the Germans.

It was clearly recognized by all of us that the stretches of the Rhine which we would have to hold prior to making a deep penetration into Germany were the lower portions north of Bonn. It was deemed highly desirable, but not mandatory, that we should be up to the river in the Frankfurt area.

Due to limitations in strength it was not possible for Twenty-first Army Group to join the attacks in the early stages, so the burden fell upon the Twelfth Army Group, supported by the Sixth from the south.

Due to limitations in feasible frontage, Bradley felt that his concentrations on the north had to be moderate in size, although his orders and his intentions were to keep that attack going at full strength regardless of the effect on the attack that he planned for the Third Army. He greatly desired to attack in the Third Army because he believed that in that area the enemy was badly stretched and that we might, with the expenditure of little force, get a breakthrough and rapid exploitation beyond the Siegfried. That would place the entire Saar Valley in our hands.

Ammunition and replacement prospects were cause for worry and in order to support the northern front, the Third Army was given only a very small proportion of incoming ammunition and none of the replacements.

The attacks, as always, were based upon the employment of the ground-air team. While it was realized that France in winter is normally a difficult area for flying, it was still felt that with only average conditions in this regard, our strength would be sufficient to accomplish our purposes.

Actually there ensued the worst period of weather conditions we have yet encountered anywhere in our campaigns. The result was, in the north, that the Roer River, which was expected to be only a relatively minor obstacle, became a major one. Moreover, as the dams on the upper reaches of this river completely filled up, it was realized that the enemy possessed a capability for the practical destruction of any strong Allied force that would cross the Roer. Bombing having failed to knock out these dams, Bradley had to suspend his main attacks in the north while he maneuvered around through very bad country to try to capture the dam sites.

Armor could work only along the roads, and all maneuver became difficult. Because of this pause in the general attack in the north, Bradley was very anxious to continue the Third Army attacks, particularly as initial successes in the Sixth Army Group brought the Seventh Army up close on Patton's right, ready to support him in an effort to breach the Siegfried Line.

During the entire month of November the situation was carefully reviewed daily, and I personally held conferences with Montgomery, with the British chiefs of staff, and many with Bradley, in addition to those with my own staff.

Out of these conferences it became clear that more strength must be shifted to the north and that all incoming formations should go to the support of the First and Ninth Armies. I even attempted to send three new divisions, coming through Marseilles, right on up to the Aachen area, but had to revoke this order when I found that the tails of these divisions would not come in until late January or February.

In the meantime, the operations on the Sixth Army Group front, which had begun so auspiciously, ran into a snag around the Colmar pocket. The German defense there not only absorbed the entire French Army, and so prevented it from covering the Rhine northward to the Siegfried, but held out in addition some sizable American formations from the concentrations farther north.

When the attacks in the Aachen area had to be suspended and those in the south began to slow down, it was noticeable that the German panzer formations started to withdraw from the line, their places being taken by Volkssturm divisions. All intelligence agencies assiduously tried to find out the locations and intentions of these panzer formations but without complete success. We had felt for some time that a counterattack through the Ardennes was a possibility, as we were stretched very thinly here in order to provide troops for attack, and Rundstedt had gradually placed in this quiet sector a larger number (six) of infantry divisions than he required for reasonable security.[2] However, it was not deemed highly probable that the enemy would, in winter, try to use that region in which to stage a counteroffensive on a large scale. Nevertheless, this is exactly what he did.

The attack started on Saturday, December 16. Bradley had just arrived at my headquarters for a conference on replacements when we received word that some penetrations had been effected, with the enemy using tanks.

Sensing that this was something more than a mere local attack, I immediately urged upon Bradley the movement of the Tenth Armored Division from the south and the Seventh Armored Division from the north, both toward the flanks of the attack. I urged him, also, to have army commanders on both flanks alert what divisions they had free, for instant movement toward that region if necessary.

All this he did.

The following morning Bradley went back to his own headquarters to keep a grip on the situation, and during that day and the next, it became clear that the enemy was making an all-out effort to split us and throw our campaign into disorder.

I immediately ordered the cessation of all attacks and the gathering up of every possible reserve to strike the penetration in both flanks. My plan was to hold firmly the shoulders of the penetration, particularly the areas Monschau on the north and Bastogne on the south, prevent enemy penetration west of the Meuse or in the Liège-Namur area, and then to counterattack with Patton's army in the general direction Bastogne-Cologne, this to be followed by an attack by the forces under Montgomery directed as the result and progress of Patton's attack should indicate. Devers was directed to reach out as far as possible to his left, and to make available every single United States division that he could with his own mission merely that of covering vital communications, giving ground if necessary in order to keep his forces intact. (Later this instruction was amplified to direct him to be ready to move back to the general line Belfort-Vosges in order to save the troops in the pocket lying between the Vosges, the Rhine, and the Siegfried Line. The same general instructions were given to Montgomery with respect to the northern flank.)

Except for one or two days during the entire first week of the attack, our air was practically grounded. Fighter bombers did some excellent work in the early part of the week but thereafter both their bombing effect and their reconnaissance were denied to us.

As the week wore on we succeeded in bolstering up the northern shoulder of the penetration, at the same time collecting a United States corps under Collins for use in counterattack. On the south, Patton began a transfer of six divisions to the north of the Moselle. The Twenty-first Army Group likewise collected reserves and placed a corps under Horrocks in the Brussels area. However, the penetration straight westward was still moving, and while on the north it was possible to cover the Meuse bridges rather firmly down as far as Givet, south of that they remained alarmingly weak—even at the end of the week.

The 101st and Eighty-second Airborne Divisions were turned over early in the operation to Twelfth Army Group and joined in the battle. This removed the last theater reserve, and the Eleventh Armored Division was directed to assemble rapidly in the Reims area to protect the center and meet the head-on attack on the Meuse if necessary. This division, having brand-new equipment, is moving very slowly. The Seventeenth Airborne Division was ordered over from England but weather during the week was so bad that today, Saturday, is the first day that offers any prospect of its coming. It will be placed with the Eleventh Armored Division to help secure the line on the Meuse, south of Givet.

During the week, when it became apparent that Bradley's left was badly separated from his right and that his own headquarters, located at Luxembourg, limited his command possibilities to the area south of the penetration, all forces north of the penetration were placed under the operational command of Montgomery. The boundary was generally Givet-Prum, both inclusive to the northern command.

Because of the unsatisfactory situation in the region of Bastogne, where the 101st Airborne Division and other elements were precariously holding out, Bradley felt that he must start Patton attacking to the northward from the Arlon-Luxembourg area no later than Friday, the twenty-second.

He was authorized to begin the attack but with the following definite instructions: he must make absolutely certain of the safety of his right flank in the Trier region, from which a new offensive by the German Seventh Army still threatened; his attack must be by phase lines with all forces held carefully together so as to avoid dispersion and waste in strength before Montgomery can join the attack from the north; also, he has been given every general service engineer regiment, anti-aircraft unit, and other odds and ends that can be made available to help protect the Meuse bridges within his zone; he has been told that above all else at this moment he must protect his right flank and make certain of the Meuse bridges. He definitely feels that Patton's attack, with the present object of joining up with the forces still holding Bastogne, will help in this latter mission because it will threaten the rear of all forces to the westward.

Today the general instructions issued to Bradley repeat all the above. In addition, my own staff is doing everything possible to strengthen the defense of the Meuse bridges south of Givet and to hurry up the arrival in that region of the Eleventh Armored Division. Instructions have been reiterated that the defenses of the Meuse are to be closely coordinated by the Twelfth Army Group.

On Christmas Day the United States Second Armored Division banged in the nose of the German advance, and initiative in the Battle of the Bulge passed back to the Allies. On the very day Eisenhower wrote the above entry, December 23, the bad weather over Bastogne had broken, and that morning the men of the trapped 101st Airborne Division heard the steady roar of planes coming over; 241 C-47s darkening the blue sky, each carrying 1,200 pounds of supplies, while 82 P-47s strafed the Germans in the Bastogne ring with fragmentation bombs, napalm, and machine-gun fire. Patton's tanks broke through to Bastogne on the day after Christmas. The Battle of the Bulge was memory.

The wartime diarist ended his labors with the entry of December 23, and the following months—until May 8 and the German surrender—were a period of incessant movement again, up to the Rhine, the chance gaining of a bridge at Remagen ("Hot dog!" shouted General Bradley as he heard the news over the field phone), and then the end of the Third Reich in a great conflagration of Allied fire, the Anglo-Americans and their Allies coming in from the south and west, the Russians from the east.

When the war ground to a standstill early in May 1945, Eisenhower was commanding the most powerful group of armies the world had ever seen.

⌜ V ⌝

CHIEF OF STAFF

Upon the end of the war in Europe, Eisenhower was a hero, to Europeans as well as Americans, and he was showered with honors. In London on July 12, 1945, white horses drew his open carriage through streets lined by cheering millions to the Guildhall, where he made a remarkably good speech, much commented upon at the time and later. Thereafter came the triumphal visits to Paris (June 14), Washington (June 18), New York (June 19), West Point (June 20), Kansas City (June 21), and Abilene (June 22). The return to Abilene marked almost thirty-four years to the day from the time when, in 1911, he had left the white frame house near the Union Pacific tracks to go to West Point. His mother was still living in that little house and welcomed her son home again.

The dissolution of the Supreme Headquarters, Allied Expeditionary Force and the departure from his command of the various Allied units did not mean any lessening of his military distinctions. After V-E Day he was appointed military governor of Germany as well as commander of American troops in Europe. Upon the retirement of General Marshall from the office of chief of staff, this highest post in the American army went to the man most qualified to receive it.

But then came a large disappointment. The military reward that Eisenhower received for his services in the Second World War, the office of chief of staff, proved a very unattractive job. Probably anything would have been anti-climactic after the victory in Europe. But a special and soon very obvious problem afflicted the army at the end of the Second World War, and Eisenhower as chief of staff found himself in the center of a situation where he could be little more than a spectator; he could not solve the problem. To put the case bluntly, the wartime army was falling apart. The process of collapse was known, somewhat grandilo-quently, as demobilization. As the drafted men went home, the army dwindled not merely in size but élan. The army used what was perhaps the only possible system for demobilization—a point system, according to which the men who had been in service the longest got out first. Points were awarded for months in service, for battle campaigns, for months spent overseas, and (an award that unmarried veterans resented) for possession of a wife, with extra points for children. It was a system of democratic fairness. It also was the very best system the mind of man might have invented to guarantee the total collapse of the great military machine that had defeated Germany and Japan. The most experienced veterans went out first, and as they left, their jobs were passed to the most capable men remaining, and their jobs in turn were passed down the ranks; the game of musical chairs ensured such a constant changing of positions that hardly anyone knew what he was doing. Eisenhower had to preside over this chaos.

The process of demobilization had its maudlin side. Eisenhower had to preside over the hopes and fears of mothers and relatives who were certain that their "boys" were unfairly being confined within the United States Army, and who not merely wrote to him in detail about their problems but sought out the advice of their congressmen, who in turn were not hesitant to remind the United States Army that it was making mistakes if not tragic errors. Dissatisfactions at home produced dissatisfactions in the field, and at the beginning of the year 1946 the morale of troops overseas had so plummeted that riots broke out, in which rowdy soldiers booed their officers and asked only to go home. Discipline was in danger; Eisenhower had to address Congress and explain the policy of releases and promise that any soldier considering himself unjustly retained could write the chief of staff about his plight. For some weeks the first order of business every morning for the principal general of the United States Army was to call for reports from his aides concerning soldiers desiring to leave the service.

As the months passed and the new levies of recruits went to Germany and the Far East, matters improved, but not materially, for the new men were as blasé and careless of military discipline as were the veterans seeking to leave. The result abroad, in terms of the new postwar army, was a sort of ice-cream army, young-sters who battened on the food at the post exchanges, who were too much out of shape to do anything for their country other than show the uniform to a former foreign foe.

A second distasteful for task Eisenhower during his term as chief of staff, after presiding over demobilization, was to preside over interservice discussions about the military budget, so as to get as much of the budget pie for the army as he could. The army was up against the nearly insatiable requirements of the United States Navy, always an expensive service, which at the end of the war had an enormous number of relatively new ships in commission and was not about to take them out of commission, if money could be found to keep them moving. And if the navy was not asking for some piece of an old appropriation or favoring a new levy on the United States treasury, the air force was after it. The United States Army Air Force, as it was known until unification in 1947, was nominally an appendage of the United States Army, but practically speaking it was indepen-dent. Its officers were fairly young men who had risen to high rank in a hurry because of the service's great wartime expansion, and they possessed all of the ambition that their success had generated, and more. For they also faced a technical problem in the postwar era. At the end of the war, their planes had suddenly become obsolescent when just before V-E Day the Germans ushered in the jet age with the big Focke-Wulf fighters. On a bulletin board in Europe in the spring of 1945 some air force wit had scrawled: "Who's afraid of the big Focke-Wulf?" Another wit, more sensible, had answered: "I am." After the war, the air force had to junk its prop planes and retrain its pilots. There also was the need to construct longer-range and very expensive bombers to threaten the new post-1945 enemy, Soviet Russia. The air force needed money and could press its arguments with more convincing contentions than either the navy or the army. The work of protecting the army's budget fell upon Chief of Staff Eisenhower, and he sought to contain his navy and air force colleagues and bring in budget proposals from the joint chiefs that would have united support, rather than allowed the claims of a single service. It was hard work, for until the end of the year 1948, when Eisenhower himself temporarily took the job, there was no chairman of the joint chiefs, and the service representatives often went their separate ways.

Eisenhower's third task as chief of staff was to assist in unification of the armed services, a job that in part meant he had to arrange the independence of the air force and protect both the new third service and his own service, the army, from the revenge of the navy's admirals, most of whom deplored unification. The navy's leadership believed that it could get its way militarily if it could go to Congress and the American people on its own; one of the most defiant of the navy's leaders was its service secretary, James V. Forrestal, until President Truman converted him to unification by making him the first secretary of defense under the Unification Act of 1947. Discussions over what service should have what—whether the navy should have coastal defense, whether the navy was entitled to a separate air force, what the color of each service's uniforms should be, not to mention the cut of the uniforms—these details took Dwight D. Eisenhower's time, to a point where he thought a brisk and determined note asking for retirement might have been his best course in 1945.

In the spring of 1948, during a final leave before retiring as chief of staff, Eisenhower devoted himself to writing a best-seller, Crusade in Europe, a clear-headed account of the winning of the Second World War in the West. The writing was relatively easy. His memory of the events of that time was clear. He had available his headquarters diary and all the other papers relating to his activities during those busy years 1941–1945. And so he undertook the task, which proved interesting and also monetarily rewarding.

The spring of 1948 marked a time when Eisenhower was much in the news for political reasons: he was being mentioned for the presidency that year, curiously by liberals in the Democratic party. A movement began to draft him for the Democratic nomination, led by Representative James Roosevelt of California and helped along by some of the big city bosses such as Mayor William O'Dwyer of New York. The movement died when President Truman insisted on the nomination, which the Philadelphia convention gave Truman without enthusi-

asm. As for the Republican party, Eisenhower's allegiance politically was uncertain in 1948, as he never had voted, and he was at least in that sense available. He made known his unwillingness to accept any nomination; his statement of disinterest sufficed for the Republicans, who that year had a candidate who had run against Franklin D. Roosevelt and who, so the experts said, was going to beat Truman. Governor Thomas E. Dewey took the Republican nomination after a feeble competition from General Douglas MacArthur.

DECEMBER 15, 1945

This job (chief of staff) is as bad as I always thought it would be. I came home from Europe on temporary duty to testify before a congressional committee, expecting to return to wind up my affairs over there, preparatory to coming home for this job. Got sick, couldn't go back, and wound up taking over here on the first.

I'm astounded and appalled at the size and scope of plans the staff sees as necessary to maintain our security position now and in the future.

The cost is terrific. We'll be merely tilting at windmills unless we can develop something more in line with financial possibilities. Of course the number-one problem is demobilization, and due to a bundle of misunderstandings I'll soon have to go before Congress personally and give them the facts of life. They won't like it, but I can't help it. Selective service must be continued for the year, otherwise the thing is chaos. The extension should be indefinite, but no one has the courage to support me in that.

If we can get through one year together we can go to volunteer system. At that time UMT [universal military training] should be ordered, but it will cost one billion a year and, aside from prejudice against it, the cost will hurt. . . .[1]

MAY 26, 1946

I was recalled hastily from a trip because of a feeling that if the government had to go through with its threat of confiscating, or taking over, the railways, I was the one to explain the matter over the radio to the public and to appeal to strikers to stay on the job. Everybody had the jitters, but, in my humble opinion, they worry too much about surface manifestations of something that is of life and death importance instead of about the thing itself.

The important thing is that democracy has arrived at its decade or quarter century of greatest crisis—any global war of the future will be ideological. Our most effective security step is to develop in every country, where there is any chance or opportunity, a democratic form of government to the extent that individualism rather than statism is the underlying concept of government. Russia, completely statist, sees this and is so anxious to spread communism that propaganda, money, agents, and, where countries are close to her borders, even force [is used] to see that communism gets in the saddle. Without using the same methods we should certainly not lose sight of the importance of the objectives.

Although in this country we like to curse John Bull, yet Britain has done far more than we to support countries that want to remain free. Britain is crumbling (has been doing so ever since World War I), yet we gloat rather than get scared.

The underlying, important thing, therefore, is our national lack of understanding that we (our form of government) is under deadly, persistent, and constant attack. To lead others to democracy we must help actively, but more than this we must be an example of the worth of democracy. Industrial power must be achieved, and increased productivity must follow or we are cutting our own throats.

Our strength is a combination of (1) complete devotion to democracy, which means a faith in men as men (essentially religious concept) and practice of free enterprise; to maintain free enterprise we must police but not destroy, either by legislation or by class conflict; (2) industrial and economic strength; (3) moral probity in all dealings; (4) necessary military strength. This could be done at bearable costs if we understood the whole problem, because then we'd do it as a matter of pride and obligation, not on the basis of competing with industry.

All this demands a clear understanding of world issues and what we need to do at home to meet them. In the foreign field we have to select the areas in which we should and can help and then go to work in every conceivable way. If this understanding were universal we'd have no strikes; capital and labor would easily solve their difficulties if both knew their very existence depended upon accord.

NOVEMBER 1, 1946

This year have visited (1) Pacific—Hawaii, Guam, P.I., China, Japan, Korea; (2) South America—Brazil, stopping at Panama and Mexico; and (3) Europe— Germany, Italy, Scotland, and England. Trouble everywhere. So far as we are concerned I feel we're very shortsighted in South America. [Even so] we've got a good chance to win all to our side and to do so long before a crisis arrives. But shortsightedness seems to be as prevalent in government as anywhere else. Personally I think we ought to get out of P.I., lock, stock, and barrel so far as military is concerned, and have so recommended.

NOVEMBER 12, 1946

I have been back from Europe exactly a year. It has been a most difficult period for me, with far more frustrations than progress.

A commander in a theater of war has as his most difficult task the clarifying of his own convictions and conclusions. Once he has sorted out of the conflicting promises and obstacles a simple line of action he can devote himself and his organization to the one job of carrying on the execution of the decision. He runs into strange personalities, weird ideas, glory-seeking, enemy reaction, and all the other incidents of war, but he has a clear-cut path to follow and he can carry on with a free mind and with his full energy. He has to wheedle, demand, cajole, order, follow up, inspect, urge, listen, and talk; the job is always clearly outlined in his own mind, however, so the burdens are lightened.

In Washington the job has not even started when self-conviction has been achieved. On every side are new and strange problems. Navy, state, chief executive, Congress are only a few of the points where a chief of staff has to argue and plead for considerations of his ideas, and in each of these places he encounters a different motivation. Votes, personal popularity, personal hatreds, political and partisan prejudices, ignorance, opposing ideologies . . . [ellipses in original]

When I came back from Europe I found the War Department committed to certain things that seem to me to be outside the realm of logic and of practicality.

Universal military training is costly—no immediate usefulness in emergency except in its peacetime effect in filling up the national guard. (Necessary but costing us problems.)

Oversized national guard. Cost and possibilities of recruitment cause doubt as to practicality of program.

Tremendous reserve. Apparently War Department is committed to a costly program which budget cannot carry.

On top of all this we have problem of planning a permanent regular force, properly officered and recruited from three-year men. Occupation is a headache which demands a given number of men. Without selective service, where do we get them? . . .

A number of well-meaning friends have suggested a political career for me. They seem to listen to my "no" with their tongues in their cheeks.

I've been on an intensive strain since 1938, when I had my last leave save for five days this past summer. I'm suspicious of anyone who believes he could take over the presidency successfully in these days and times.

International reactions are bad enough, but they are insignificant compared to domestic issues. I know nothing of the long, tedious process whereby certain labor leaders have become dictators. Yet all my sympathies are with the workers (my youth was one of such hard work, and my memories of my father's life so clear that I could do nothing else). . . .

The answer is easy in generalization—it is difficult only in practical application, because, although everyone believes in cooperation (the single key) as a principle, no one is ready to abandon immediate advantage or position in practicing cooperation. Moral regeneration, revival of patriotism, clear realization that progress in any great segment is not possible without progress for the whole, all these are necessary.

In a free system laws cannot fully answer the problem; just as written agreements could not satisfactorily meet the requirements of allied command in war. We must produce a healthy economy, raise living standards for all, and preserve individual liberty.

These must be studied: closed-shop, check-off, industry-wide unions, responsible, corporate organization of trade unions (one side). Effective antitrust laws, lockouts, control of raw materials, sound financing—private and government— limiting bureaucratic rule (other side).

Constant information (accurate) available to public is a sine qua non to public decision.

My own guess is that, although government should stay out of this field to utmost extent, all laws affecting above subjects should be evenhanded, with particular emphasis on court action, where necessary. Court orders must be respected.

DECEMBER 2, 1946

In a week I'm to go to a hospital for observation. Luckily the doctors want me outside during the day, so they have picked a Florida hospital. I hope to get back in shape. I'm arthritic, seven pounds overweight, and soft. Have had no real exercise since the shooting stopped in Europe.

The big questions for us today are: How are we to sustain occupational forces with voluntary enlistment at such a low level we cannot meet minimum needs?

How are we to get a reasonable budget approved when the need for national economy is so great? We've cut our estimates, as low as we think we dare, but for all purposes, including expenses of feeding occupied territories, they are still over 9 billion. If we have to cut 2 billions (which seems likely), what to do?

What are we to do about the coal strike if called upon by president to preserve order in the face of cold and privation?

We have no real military formations, no national guard. We'd be really embarrassed if we had to keep even a few thousand men on duty in the coal regions for several months. For the first time I'm becoming discouraged about the prospect of peaceful and semi-permanent settlement of internal economic problems on a sufficiently sound basis to insure the production levels we so badly need. Internal "Munichs" can, in the long run, be as bad as they are in the international field. If we have to break up in a real industrial conflict with "public be damned" the watchword, then our prospects for bringing about world order are slim indeed. If we are not healthy, we can communicate no health to the world.

Admiral Leahy shows his age, especially in conference.

DECEMBER 7, 1946

Taking off for hospital in Florida to see if I can get rid of bursitis-arthritis. Painful but not disabling, at least as yet.

Coal strike still on. Congress (Republican) meets in January.

Press conference this A.M. brought up again the question that is going around so much these days, "What am I going to do about politics?" They don't want to believe a man that insists he will have nothing to do with politics and politicians.

Selective service, universal military training, unification of armed forces, budget, personnel, will all be principal subjects of legislation next session.

FEBRUARY 6, 1947

Lunch with Senator Harry Cain from Washington. He belonged to XVIII Corps (Ridgway) during war. Energetic, logical, friendly. He ought to make a fine senator.

Shoulder and arm much improved from treatment in Florida. Since coming back saw New York specialist, Dr. Barr, at Cornell Medical Center. Says I'm fine.

Ambassador Gardner dropped dead today. He was on his way to the United Kingdom after weeks of partying with Washington friends. Pressure of hospitality probably had something to do with his death.

Congress says our budget will be further cut. Ours now stands at 6.2 billions after original estimates by . . . [illegible] services of 14.3 billions. God knows this security business is costing a staggering amount, and I'm on the side of the congressional purpose of saving money. But if I'm pushed much more, I'll simply have to ask them "how" to do it. We're about at our wits' end. We've really got occupation troops (at minimum allowable), supporting troops, pipelines, airforce of about three-fifths of what I think we need, only reasonable research and development funds, the same for intelligence. Much more of a cut and occupation will fail and then, look out.

Costs are high—labor, materials, everything is out of sight.

We should know the final answer within a few weeks.

MARCH 8, 1947

It is almost two years since VE-Day. By this time I thought that a soldier (unless he deliberately sought public notice) would be forgotten and left alone to do his job, whatever it might be. Certainly I did not anticipate a continuation of the demands that a uniformed man speak so often. Red Cross, USO, veterans organizations, church societies, DAR and other women's associations, state bar, labor and industrial organizations are constantly plaguing one to talk. Some of them are difficult to refuse. I so firmly believe we should all do our part to reawaken in our country a realization of our own blessings and what we have to do to protect them (this protection involving also spreading them) that when any organization that has a similar purpose asks me to appear, I feel a sense of guilt when I decline. However, I turn down the vast majority for three reasons: (1) the demands upon my time are too great; (2) the weight of a soldier's words rapidly diminishes if he uses enough of them; (3) a fair presentation of the whole subject requires consideration of subjects outside the strictly military, and if the military head of the army is not exceedingly careful he will awaken the crazy, distorted, but nevertheless dangerous, misconception that the US Army wants to achieve some position other than that of servant of civil power. . . .

MARCH 29, 1947

Jack Whiteley, a valued British officer in SHAEF [Supreme Headquarters, Allied Expeditionary Force], is here for a visit. Recently Freddie De Guingand and Jimmy Gault and wife have visited in our house.[1]

The burning question of the day is help for Greece and Turkey. . . .

Off on an inspection tomorrow, Bragg, Jackson, Benning, Montgomery, McClellan.

APRIL 1947

After long argument and a good deal of table pounding have gotten staff down to plans and ideas that approach the feasible.

Air: 70-group program. Total air purchases annually by all services, approximately 3,000. Strength, 400,000.

Ground: Occupation forces; service, school, and training forces; 2 1/3 divisions reserves until occupation is completed; base garrisons (total 670,000).

National guard: Eventual target 680,000.

Reserves: Unlimited, except that only ones to be paid are Class A units. These must be limited to units to balance regular and national guard combat forces.

Universal military training: When authorized, to be implemented gradually. Without it, the national guard and organized reserve programs are impossible of attainment. Overhead must be further cut in planning. Whole job must be done for 1.5 billions.

Industrial mobilization, research and development, intelligence, all must be coordinated to eliminate duplication, but to make sure no field is neglected. Thank God unification is surely coming.

MAY 15, 1947

Four years ago we had just completed our first great victory, conquest of North Africa. I predicted the date, almost exactly, at Casablanca in conversation with President Roosevelt and others.

Today some of our problems seem even more serious than strategic problems seemed then.

At home we have rising prices (Packard had to go up yesterday), labor troubles, housing shortages, and tax squabbles. Unless we find a formula which will stabilize the price structure, we are due for most serious times.

Abroad there are so many nations needing our help that the whole job seems appalling, even though it is clear that help to some of them is definitely in our own interest.

Great Britain, France, Italy, Greece, and Turkey are possibly foremost, although Germany and Austria likewise present situations that can grow most serious if we do not take positive and intelligent action. I personally believe that the best thing we could now do would be to post 5 billion to the credit of the secretary of state and tell him to use it to support democratic movements wherever our vital interests indicate. Money should be used to promote possibilities of self-sustaining economies, not merely to prevent immediate starvation.

For the moment Britain's need is not money but it needs food and, far more important, comprehensive assistance in getting its economy in working order. She is our greatest natural friend. We must get her healthy.

France somewhat the same, but more critical because of the Communist strength. Italy even more so. Time, in these two countries, is of the utmost importance. No use to save Greece and Turkey for Communism if these two should go.

All over the world (including South America) the story is the same, though varying in intensity as to time and in critical importance to us. The next two years should establish the pattern; if it is unfavorable to us it will be partly our own fault, but it will be wholly black in its implications for the future.

JULY 24, 1947

After 1½ years of struggle it appears that a so-called unification of the armed services will be directed by law within the next couple of days.

The proposal for such a move aroused the most intensive campaign of special interest that I have seen in Washington. Some services were apparently so unsure of their value to the country that they insisted upon writing into the law a complete set of rules and specifications for their future organization and duties. Such freezing of detail in an age that is witnessing the most rapid and significant scientific advances of all history is silly, even vicious. The writers of such provisions would probably have done the same with respect to horse cavalry, old-fashioned coast defense artillery, and towed field guns. But we'll make it work, and as changes are needed possibly even the supporters of special interests can be made to see the necessity.

A few weeks ago I informed the trustees of Columbia University that, when the president should release me from my duties as chief of staff, I would accept the presidency of that institution. In a way it was a "stampeding" process, except that it had been first mentioned to me more than a year ago. But late this spring a group of the trustees, apparently spearheaded by Mr. Tom Watson, began pressuring me to accept, and at the same time another group wanted me to take the head of the Boy Scouts (a most appealing offer), while a group of Midwesterners said they had a senatorship ready to lay in my lap, without a move except a nod from me. Another group was anxious that I consider a commercial venture, but this type of thing was easy to refuse.

The Columbia board is well aware of my shortcomings in the academic field. I used that as my principal argument against acceptance for many weeks.

My guess is that I'll make the move about next April 1.

A number of scattered people—some friends, some strangers—continue to argue that I should get into the political field, at least to the extent of making myself "available" for a presidential nomination. I have learned that no one will believe a word a man says if that word denies desire for political preference, even though, in other matters, they'd never dream of questioning intent.

SEPTEMBER 16, 1947

I wonder whether I've previously noted down in this book what I've often given, in conversation, as my conviction regarding the progressing world revolution. I believe that democracy has entered its decade (possibly quarter century) of greatest test. If it emerges triumphantly it is my conviction that the system will be safe, will grow and prosper, for many years. But I most earnestly believe that unless those that now live in freedom begin, en masse, to look this world in the face, and begin voluntarily and energetically to meet the issues placed before us, then we are doomed—rather, the system, as we know it, is doomed.

This I have talked, and even preached, since hostilities ended in Europe.

The main issue is dictatorship versus a form of government only by the consent of the governed, observance of a bill of rights versus arbitrary power of a ruler or ruling group. That this issue is with us needs no argument—the existing great exponent of dictatorship has announced its fundamental antagonism to all sorts of capitalism (essential to democracy) and that it will strive to destroy it in the world. Because of Russia's increased power, territory, and world importance as a result of World War II, it is now pushing the issue more determinedly than ever before. Its pronouncements, dating back to Lenin, are more and more guiding its daily operations in Korea, China, the Middle East, Turkey, Greece, Trieste, Germany, Austria, etc. Everywhere the sullen weight of Russia leans against the dike that independent nations have attempted to establish, and boring from within is as flagrantly carried on as is obstructionism in the UN. Russia is definitely out to communize the world—where it cannot gain complete control of territory, as it has in Bulgaria, Poland, Rumania, Yugoslavia, and the Baltic States it promotes starvation, unrest, anarchy, in the certainty that these are breeding grounds for the growth of their damnable philosophy.

Extravagant promise of prosperity to those in want has been a trick of the demagogue throughout history.

Now, if we face a battle to extinction between the two systems (although we declare that we can live with communism if it stays in its own areas and makes no attempt to interfere with us), what are the problems?

To prevent Russian expansion (1) by direct conquest and pressure; (2) by infiltration.

Over the long term to win back areas that Russia has already overrun, and finally to produce a real accord among all nations that will prevent war. This must be preceded by a collapse of dictatorship everywhere, at least of all dictatorships that aggressively seek to dominate others.

(1) This is the problem that can be solved only by the maintenance of adequate American military strength. We must hew to the line of principle and be in position to sustain our positions. Anything less will mean merely a succession of

new Munichs, finally war under conditions least favorable to us.

(2) Our own policy should be announced in simple, positive (not negative) terms, so that all, particularly our own people, can understand it.

A free nation needs independent, friendly nations with which to trade. We need manganese, rubber, lead, zinc, and soon will have real shortages in oil, iron, copper.

Unless broken economies are restored they will almost certainly fall prey to communism, and if the progress of this disease is not checked, we will find ourselves an isolated democracy in a world elsewhere controlled by enemies. The result is clear.

We must restore these broken economies and give freedom a chance to live.

We must be strong, morally, industrially, financially, militarily. Most of all in our common understanding of basic issues and common determination to do those things we need to do to insure the health of American democracy.

Unity is more necessary now than it was in Overlord.

DECEMBER 1, 1947

The world situation grows more tense, although here and there are one or two points of light on a forbidding horizon. Of these encouraging items the most significant is the seeming determination of the new Schuman government in France to grapple directly with the communist effort to paralyze France. The issue could scarcely be put off and luckily he has the support of Herriot, who has patriotism and guts. . . .[1]

Mamie's birthday, November 14, 1947.

DECEMBER 2, 1947

Heard today, through a mutual friend, that my wartime secretary (rather personal aide and receptionist) is in dire straits. A clear case of a fine person going to pieces over the death of a loved one, in this instance the man she was all set to marry. Will do what I can to help, but it would seem hopeless. Too bad, she was loyal and efficient and the favorite of everyone in the organization. Makes one wonder whether any human ever dares become so wrapped up in another that all happiness and desire to live is determined by the actions, desires—or life—of the second. I trust she pulls herself together, but she is Irish and tragic.[1]

DECEMBER 31, 1947

This morning I had time to reflect briefly on the events of the year just past. From a personal viewpoint the following seems most important.

(1) The irritating insistence of certain columnists and commentators that I take a partisan political stand, based upon the erroneous assumption that I would like a high political office. Disavowal of any such intent is not accepted—it has become so traditional for political candidates to be coy that any mere refusal to act affirmatively in such things and flat denial of political ambition are not only discounted, they are taken to be part of the game—so, according to these worthies, I am a candidate until I shall say, "I would not serve as president even if, against my will, I were elected to the office." Of course my refusal to say such a thing is a bit quixotic—no man has ever been nominated or elected who did not want the office and worked for it. But I simply recoil from the thought that any American can say what he will or will not do for his country under circumstances of the unforeseen future.

But I have observed with much relief a lessening of this comment and conjecture in recent weeks, and I believe that Wallace's third party move has completely taken me off the spot. He has increased the confidence of the Republicans that anyone can win for them.

(2) After years of pressure I've tentatively agreed to write a memoir of the war. Doubleday is to be my contact, who deals also with the *New York Herald Tribune*. I cannot go to work aggressively on my notes until I'm out of this job.

(3) In June I agreed to undertake the presidency of Columbia, effective about the summer of 1948. I hope I can do some good, but I don't see why an educator would not have been more suitable in the post. The trustees understand thoroughly two conditions I've laid down. I must convince myself, within a year, that I can be of real service. I must have more leisure and recreation time than my average of the past twenty-five years. If either of these conditions is not met, I'll quit. . . .

Marriage of my son, and news that I may expect a grandchild in April. Wonderful! Mamie and I are delighted. . . .[1]

Press conference before retiring as chief of staff.

With Mrs. Roosevelt, June 1948.

1948

JANUARY 4, 1948

Long ago I determined that, if ever I should publish a war memoir for which I should be paid, I would remember with substantial presents some of the people who served me so faithfully and unselfishly during the war, as members of my immediate personal staff. They include

Arthur Nevins (because he will have to help me in publication), $1,000
Colonel Lee (for his son, D.E. Lee),[1] $1,000
Butcher (he's already profited by his book)
Kay Summersby, whose personal diary has been turned over to me for checking of dates, $1,000
Miss Chick, who devoted so many of her off-duty hours to typing, $1,000
Michael McKeough, $1,000
Sgt. Dopp, . . . [illegible]
Miss Sarafian and Miss Rae, $500 each
Miss Hayes, $500
Sergeant Dry, $500
Sergeant Moaney, $500
Sergeants Hurt and Williams, $250 each
Colonel Gault, a very nice present, value of $500 to $1,000.
If anything should happen to me I would like for Mamie, out of sale of my papers, to carry out this on a 50 percent basis, assuming that she gets $200,000 to $500,000 for total sale.
Also Sergeant Murray and boys in house, $200 each.

JANUARY 15, 1948

The tossing about of my name in the political whirlwind is becoming embarrassing. Much as I've hated to say more than "I don't want a political office," I've decided I must. Too many people are taking the columnists' interpretation of my intentions as fact. How to say anything without violating my own sense of propriety—how to decline something that has not been offered me, how to answer those, like Finder, who honestly believe I have a "duty"—all this cannot be done in the words of Sherman. What a mess! But I've come to the conclusion I must face up to it before February 1. I'm told that in New Hampshire it will be too late, after February 9, to withdraw delegate slates from the primary, and it's criminal to allow people to waste their votes.[1]

COLUMBIA
UNIVERSITY

When his term as chief of staff began to run out, Eisenhower looked around for something to do and settled for the presidency of Columbia University, located in the great metropolis, an old and established institution. Its head for nearly half a century, Nicholas Murray Butler, had resigned, and its trustees were looking for a capable successor with a national reputation. On June 7, 1948, Eisenhower became president of Columbia.

As head of the leading institution of higher learning in the City of New York, Eisenhower did not cut much of a figure. But then Columbia was a place where the faculty was outstanding and the president did not need to cut a figure. Eisenhower did the usual entertaining and entered upon his duties as a fund raiser with dignity and intelligence. He spent a good deal of time in his office, a habit that led one Saturday morning to a confusion wherein a watchman refused to allow him into Low Memorial Library because, the watchman said, he was not the president of the university. The Columbia habit was not to work on Saturdays, and Eisenhower did not resemble his predecessor, Butler.

The ways of Columbia were difficult to discern, and Eisenhower perhaps did not find them altogether to his taste; during his Columbia service he took up painting, discovering that it relaxed him and was entertaining and productive. Most of his paintings he threw away, but some of them survived to become collectors' items.

Living in the nation's largest city, Eisenhower found many requirements upon his time, and his calendar quickly filled up with luncheons, dinners, and meetings. On many of these occasions he made speeches. Then Secretary of Defense Forrestal asked his help—unification was not working, despite the Unification

Act. Forrestal was not in control of the situation and began to behave in erratic ways that presaged his mental breakdown and suicide a few months later. Forrestal knew that Eisenhower was his friend and in an almost pathetic way asked for assistance.

In the tight-budget years after 1945, the military services could only look back on the war years, with their limitless appropriations, and wish that at least in that single respect the war was still on. The need for financial retrenchment was obvious, and no one quarreled with that, but the grand question was just how much the services should obtain (as well, of course, as the constant issue of how much each service should have). It was at this point that the figure of $15 billion came into view. In long retrospect it sounds suspiciously like a round number, and it probably was, though at some point the figure might have had justification. As soon as it appeared, however, it became a kind of ideal figure, and no one could easily get away from it. The Truman administration decided, for better or worse, to force the services within that figure. And after the leaders of the services agreed, albeit with grumbling, the administration began to whittle the figure down toward $14 billion. The inflation of the postwar years cut into the real dollar value of the ceiling. The administration, strongly backed by Congress and the American people (when they thought about the issue), refused to raise the figure to allow for inflation. The figure of $15 billion surely would have been cut well below $14 billion had not the Korean War intervened and begun an era of

Football practice at Columbia.

ever-increasing military budgets that has continued to the present day.
The military was in trouble over the budget, and Eisenhower was perplexed
by the arbitrary nature of the administration's actions. He did not understand the
essentially conservative outlook of the president, who despite advocacy of the
Rooseveltian social programs and promotion of foreign aid programs—including
Point Four, aid to the poor countries around the world—was a fiscal conservative.
The president read the annual budgets closely and through long experience in
government, including his years of service on the Truman Committee to investi-
gate the war effort in 1941–1944, knew all about the way that budgets could go
up and down. The president was friendly to the military and had served in the
First World War. Truman, indeed, had been a reservist since 1905, when he had
reached the age of twenty-one; one of his first irritations upon becoming president
was that the War Department retired him from his status as a reserve colonel.
But he had no special respect for professional military officers and knew their
profligate (he thought) tendencies with dollars. In the postwar years, especially
after this election to the presidency in his own right in 1948, he felt that the
military had to be kept on leash, so far as concerned their budgets. One of his
irritations with Secretary of Defense Forrestal was the secretary's inability to
handle the budget issue, and he soon took a special measure to solve that problem.

DECEMBER 13, 1948

Secretary of National Defense has called me to Washington for quick survey of
difficulties in way of achieving efficiency in coordination of defense services.

Idea is that I am to come here about January 21, 1949, to work as his military
consultant for two to three months to iron out many of these difficulties.

Basic and firm strategic concept is first requirement. Once this is achieved
much else will fall in line.

Final approval of plan must be given by president, and then complete and loyal
adherence to decision must be demanded and obtained.

This means also that responsibility for major tasks as between the services must
be fixed. Previous visits, on an occasional hit-or-miss basis, he no longer considers
satisfactory. The first day here is ended. Conferences with Symington, Vandenberg, et al.; Denfeld; Blandy; McNeil (budget); Gruenther; and Forrestal.[1] Also
others on short basis.

Blandy agrees with me that all services should work out a minimum (disaster
averting) strategic plan coupled with a decent program (arranged in priorities
coordinated among services) for successively higher levels of preparation. Assured
risking minimum to involve a total of $15 billion for all services. What should
each have.

Do same for $10–11–12–13–14–16 billion.

We understand that the old promises of $15 billion annually still hold, but the
fear that performance will fall behind, as it always has in the past, is a deterrent
to real planning.

I've tried very hard to make executive and legislative people understand that no economy and efficiency can be produced in military preparations except on planned and steady basis. Unexpected cuts and new appropriations are alike expensive.

Moreover, when a budget is planned (in good faith) on an X basis, and it is later cut by x/10, the government does not really save 10 percent. Part of the effect is wastage, at least in the military services.

We've never gotten our $15 billion for the year and the deficit has been greater than the mere percentages chiseled off by the Bureau of the Budget and Congress.

DECEMBER 17, 1948

Returned from Washington on fifteenth, in time to go to yule-log lighting in John Hay Hall, then to dinner at Links Club. Bob Woodruff, Mr. Kellogg, Mr. Auchincloss, Mr. Wolff, etc.

In Washington I conferred with Forrestal, Hinton, Gruenther, Leva, Webster in office of navy department, Denfeld, Blandy, Morrison, and assistants, Gardner of the navy, Symington, Vandenberg, Norstad, and others from the air, Mr. Woods of Hoover Commission, Committee on Future Wars, many miscellaneous.[1]

I had no chance to examine details of budget but gathered following:

All defense services believe that they have sacrificed much in attempting a combined budget of $14.4 billion for military purposes.

President will cut this even more.

The services had decided to go along with 14.4 and though none liked it they were going to present a unified front that should have operated to keep the going fairly steady. To this there was the possible exception that secretly the air was counting upon its great public popularity to upset the agreed-upon division and get about six billion with eight to be divided between army and navy.

This would mean one task force for the navy (four carriers and auxiliaries), antisub organization, and continuing the building of one supercarrier (65,000 tons).

Privately, I believe this a better distribution than is now proposed, but I insisted that I not get into the current budget struggle when I go down to consult and advise with Forrestal. All seem to agree fairly well that army should not be cut further.

All have found it easy to run to Congress and public with personal ideas and convictions. We will not have unification until the secretary of defense is made very powerful, power to appoint and fire, among other things.

1949

JANUARY 7, 1949

After much thought I believe there is only one cure for the troubles of the national defense establishment. We must get the three chiefs of staff to agree on "majority rule." If such a rule could be self-imposed, and faithfully adhered to, I believe the joint chiefs of staff would, at one fell swoop, recover all of its lost prestige and regain respect in the public mind.

Several procedural items would then become important: (1) insure full debate of each subject; (2) never reveal vote of any member; (3) any chief of staff has right to present case to secretary; (4) careful analysis of differences prepared for secretary in any subject where three points of view are sustained. Fact, opinion, areas of concurrence, areas of nonconcurrence, conclusions. All this to be done by principal military assistant to secretary of defense. (5) Decisions once reached, all are to carry out faithfully, loyally, enthusiastically. Services the same.

Voluntary adoption of such a plan offers the only hope. In present conditions, law alone will not do it. Everybody understands "evasive action" these days.

But majority rule is only hope.

JANUARY 8, 1949

I believe the president has to show the iron underneath the pretty glove. Some of our seniors are forgetting that they have a commander in chief. They must be reminded of this, in terms of direct, unequivocal language.

If this is not soon done, someday we're going to have a blowup. There are a number of men in Washington who would encourage such a prospect, in the hope of getting a few headlines out of it. And we have some service people who are unwise enough to fall for such a trap. God help us if ever we go before a congressional committee to argue our professional fights as each service struggles to get the lion's share of the money.

The president could stop all this if he'd act now. But if public airing of grievances is continued, some day it will go far beyond the bounds of decency and reason and someone will say, "Who is the boss? The civilians or the military?"

Jim [Forrestal] is looking badly. He has a conscience and a sense of duty. These, coupled with his feeling of urgency and his terrific, almost tragic, disappointment in the failures of professional men to "get together," leads him to certain errors. Among these none is worse than the way he treats himself. He gives his mind no recess, and he works hours that would kill a horse.

Except for my liking, admiration, and respect for his great qualities I'd not go near Washington, even if I had to resign my commission completely. To a certain extent these same feelings apply to H.S.T. [Truman], but he does not see the problems so clearly as does Jim, and he does not suffer so much due to the failure to solve the problems. I like them both.

Part of the mess we are in is due to neglect of our armed forces, dating from the end of hostilities in 1945.

I vividly recall appearing before Congress very early in 1946 (congressional library) and informing them that demobilization was going to be slowed down to a rate that would avoid destruction. During 1946, 1947, and early 1948 I pleaded for a $15 billion budget. We never got it and we're suffering because of it. Now inflation has raised everything so much that even the $15 billion begins to look inadequate. (If we could make up deficits of past years we could still get together a fine force.) Curiously enough, the president has always agreed with me when I've talked to him, but budget director (and later the Congress) have always cut and cut.

JANUARY 14, 1949

The trend toward governmental centralization continues, alarmingly.

In the name of "social security" we are placing more and more responsibility upon the central government, and this means that an ever-growing bureaucracy is taking an ever-greater power over our daily lives. Already the agents of this bureaucracy cover the land—to justify their existence and render those reports that seem to show a "profit" on their operations they nag, irritate, and hound every businessman in the United States.

This morning's paper says that the American Museum of Natural History is nearing bankruptcy, at least that it is now living, after great retrenchment, on deficit spending. Undoubtedly, the final answer will be "federal aid." This is indicative of what is happening to us everywhere. The "tax and tax, spend and spend, cut and cut" formula is working wonderfully for the shortsighted persons who cannot (or do not desire to) see beyond the next election date.

Columbia University is feeling the effects, disastrously. Taxes leave prospective donors to university income so little in the way of spare income that only the most strenuous efforts keep us going at all. So, since this is typical of nearly all the privately endowed universities, we hear more and more, from educators them-selves, of "federal aid for education." It is a dangerous slogan.

In certain limited fields the federal government could properly take action that would have some indirect, beneficial results on privately endowed institutions. Scholarships in some fields could be established. Contractual arrangements for research seem economical and profitable. In a few areas, where the economic situation does not permit even adequate primary and junior high school educa-tion, some help should be given, in the effort to develop reasonably intelligent voters in a democratic system.

But the real hope of the shortsighted is to get federal money to support institutions, free grants of money to use as university authorities may desire.

The proposition is immoral, and its adoption, in this general sense, will lead to statism and, therefore, slavery.

The private university has a most important function. Its thinking, its research, its processes are free—not dominated by politicians seeking reelection. Therefore it sets up and maintains standards that have a direct and beneficial effect on the many state universities. Without these standards of quality, without this example, instruction in state universities will gradually fall under the domination of politicians.

The state university, today, is a valuable, necessary, and very wonderful institution. But let private institutions fall under federal domination and the next step is for all institutions to demand federal help. This means federal control, eventually. And the best way to establish dictatorship is to get control of the educational processes in any country.

This trend must be halted in its tracks.

To help stop it is one of the reasons I've taken on this strange, difficult, and often frustrating task.

Except for a few young and able men here, there seems to be little awareness of what is happening to us, or threatening us. Older men are concerned, but only in financial deficits. They seem to think that if only we can trim, crowd, gouge, and beg our way "into the black," all will be well. Of course this is important, but primarily so in its assurance that we, at least, shall remain free and so continue to exert a great influence in opposing centralization of all controls in the hands of government.

The older trustees, officials, and friends of the university fear a businesslike organization (or so it seems). They move, think, and act slowly and fearfully. They won't see that we are living in a modern age, where leadership must manifest itself in terms of teams and that such teams must be interlocked in purposes and in operation. Financial support for Columbia must come from thousands (the days of the $100 million gift are gone or going fast). And money is the central university problem as of now.

JANUARY 27, 1949

Have just completed a week of struggle in the Pentagon, possibly futilely. The bitterness of the fight between air and navy is so noticeable that it is never absent from any discussion.

Fundamentally the quarrel is—

The air says:

1. The job of operating against an enemy country by bombing belongs to the air, exclusively.

2. The latest type bombers now assure a technical practicability of operating against targets 4,800 miles removed from the base; thus, from several points within our possession, we can easily reach vital Russian targets.

3. These planes fly so high, so rapidly, and by such divers routes that interception will be difficult, so difficult that our losses will be easily supportable.

4. The navy refuses to accept the agreed principle that its primary role is

control of the seas; it is encroaching on the air force job in order to provide an excuse for greater size and power and is doing it by means of the expensive "carrier," especially the supercarrier, which can have no other mission than that of participating in great bombing operations against land targets.

5. The navy is conducting a relentless propaganda campaign, regardless of approved decisions of the joint chiefs of staff, to delude Congress and the people into building up a useless and expensive navy, thereby depriving the air of what it needs.

The navy says:

1. The big bomber can never again operate against a well-prepared, alert defense; the navy (Radford) calls the new bomber a "sitting duck."[1]

2. Because of this, all appropriations for big bombers is sheer and stupid waste.

3. To bomb an enemy successfully the bombing plane must be accompanied by fighters.

4. Only the movable base can provide this support; fixed bases will be knocked out.

5. Ergo, the bombing must be done by navy from huge carriers.

6. Therefore, the navy should have more money, the air force far less.

The fight is personal as well as organizational and, to me, has all the earmarks of a vehicle by which rival personalities are struggling for prestige and power. This does not apply to all concerned, but I am sure that much of its bitterness has its inspiration in some such motives.

It is possible the air is wrong; it may be that the job of intercepting and destroying the big bomber will be so simple as to preclude effective bombing by the long-range, unescorted big planes.

But, if this is so, particularly considering the flexibility that long range provides in choice of route, then I am sure that navy bombers cannot operate effectively either. If the job of interception is so easy, I am sure that the number of escort planes that can be provided from a carrier task force will not be able to protect the bombers. This, if true, and provided the navy is more realistic than the air force, means that the whole theory of air war has to undergo modification. The great expense of the supercarrier will be no more justified than that involved in building huge bombers. (God knows both are expensive, even for the United States.)

I believe we can do something to get ourselves on an even keel. (1) Restore prestige, authority, and exclusive responsibility in strategic matters to joint chiefs of staff by providing a means whereby that body must come to decisions. Majority rule is my suggestion, accompanied by secret vote and absolute adherence to its decisions by each of the three individuals composing it. (2) Make every possible test to determine facts in the "bomber versus interception" quarrel. This should be feasible, with both services cooperating.

Jim F. and I have agreed to try to keep the minds of all centered on the main facts of our present existence: (1) The free world is under threat by the monolithic mass of communistic imperialism. (2) The United States must wake up to prepare a position of strength from which it can speak serenely and confidently. (3) This means it must keep open its access to needed raw materials; stockpiling is designed to carry us over any temporary interruptions. (4) We want allies. (5) We must hold our position of strength without bankrupting ourselves.

FEBRUARY 2, 1949

Have had two days briefing in navy department.

Interesting, and confirms impression that navy now views its main mission as "projection of American air power" against enemy.

Control of seas is not primary and exclusive function in this view.

My idea of majority rule in joint chiefs of staff is out. It will not be accepted. Now I shall (at McNarney's suggestion) attempt to get president to appoint a president of the chiefs of staff and assign him to Forrestal. This may work; but I doubt that it will cure basic evil, which my scheme was intended to do. This evil is the freedom with which each service attacks any decision of the joint chiefs of staff or secretary of defense that it does not like.

But anything would be better than what we have now.

Jim F. is apparently highly discouraged. He exaggerates greatly the possibility that I will materially help in his task of "unifying" the services. He blames himself far too much for the unconscionable situation now existing. He is obviously most unhappy. At one time he accepted unequivocally and supported vigorously the navy "party line," given him by the admirals. Only today he said to me, "In the army there are many that I trust—Bradley, Collins, Gruenther, Wedemeyer, and Lemnitzer and Lutes, to name only a few.[1] In the navy I think of only Sherman and Blandy among the higher ones.[2] Possibly Conolly, also."[3] It must have cost him a lot to come to such a conclusion.

FEBRUARY 4, 1949

Have just concluded several days briefing by navy. They have a number of intelligent, enthusiastic, and well-informed people in their administrative and planning sections. But just as in some other departments, the principal effort seems to be "selling," rather than critical analysis and logical conclusion.

Their maintenance system is the biggest and best.

Their organizational system is superior to anyone else's.

Their carriers can carry on an air war much better than can a land-based air force.

Their planes are faster, cheaper, longer-ranged, etc.

Their personnel systems are the best.

Every vessel they have, active and inactive, is vitally important to security of United States.

The battleship *Missouri* serves a highly useful national purpose.

The marine air force knows more about supporting ground forces than does any other air force.

The navy is not getting enough money.

I've heard the same with respect to other services, but I suppose it is true that many of the enthusiasts in each service believe what they say. The only time you hear anything about the poor taxpayer is when they talk about another service.

Well, something has to snap, and so far as I'm concerned it will have to be the patience of the president and secretary of defense.

They are going to have to get tough—and I mean tough!

FEBRUARY 9, 1949

Long conversation with president this afternoon. I agreed to act as chairman of joint chiefs of staff for a brief (I hope) period pending change in law or formal arrangements for getting "unification" on the rails.

The president agreed: (1) to lay down law to secretaries of service departments and chiefs of staff; (2) to get an undersecretary for Mr. Forrestal; (3) either to get a chairman of chiefs of staff by law or by appointment of McNarney as president of chiefs of staff; (4) to support strongest possible air force; (5) to back Mr. F. and me to hilt in forcing compliance with directives; (6) to cut certain of navy's assumed missions in order to obtain more money for air; and (7) to get some help in modernizing army's equipment.

Talked for an hour. Most satisfactory. The only disturbing thing is that president and Mr. F. apparently assume that I have some miraculous power to make some of these warring elements lie down in peace together.

Van [General Vandenberg] will not agree navy needs any carrier larger than escort type. I feel that in first months of war a few big carriers might be our greatest asset. I want to keep ten in active fleet—about six to eight of which should be always in operation. Van thinks I'm nuts, but I'm convinced I'm right, at least so long as we have them.

FEBRUARY 19, 1949

There is clearly evident a realization on part of members of joint chiefs of staff that they must work efficiently, intensively, and cooperatively if they are to regain and preserve the prestige that properly belongs to them. They see the fallacy of exploiting, each on his own, whatever influence each might have in Congress for the moment, and in this way permit shrewd investigators and analysts to play one service against the other to the detriment of the whole.

I personally and very earnestly believe that $15 billion to $16 billion per year is all that this country need spend for security forces, if it is done every year (with some additional amounts to cover past deficits). I will have no part of any scheme until we've gotten this much and used it efficiently for increasing the total. All know this; consequently, they are ready and eager to begin again from the very bottom the study of our strategic position, in the effort to obtain the best possible layout of defense forces. Unless they make progress in agreeing upon "must" tasks and, therefore, "must" appropriations, around which a desirable peacetime structure can be built, I'll quit and begin criticizing. That will be the only way left to get action, but it could be repugnant, and out of character.

MARCH 19, 1949

The situation grows intolerable. Denfeld apparently wants to do right, but he practically retires from every discussion in favor of Struble, who infuriates everyone with his high, strident voice and apparent inability to see any viewpoint except his own.[1] Moreover, he has that trick in argument of questioning, or seeming to question, the motives of his opponent.

I've had talks with the new secretary, Johnson, who will take over at the end of the month.[2] He seems to admire F. greatly.

Saw the president, who told me that he had some difficulty in convincing Johnson to take job, but finally succeeded.

I explained to Johnson that Bradley wanted no part of job of chairman of chiefs of staff and Johnson says he'll accept McNarney. He (J.) is also going to ask for more civilian help. In spite of all this, J. is insistent that I make no plans to terminate my Washington duties for next six months at least. He says he told president he'd take job only if I'd stay on. Getting a bit crowded.

Recently Marx Leva and I made a special effort to get Jim F. to go on ten days leave. His need for a rest grows very obvious. He's nervous, upset, preoccupied, and unhappy. He promised me he'd think it over. I've waited two weeks and nothing has happened. Talked to him about it again, and he said, "I'll wait now until Louis takes over." That seemed to bring up a thought and he said, "You still think it's all right for me to go; you have confidence that Johnson will do a good job?" I looked at him in some amazement, finding on his face a most worried, even harassed look. I tried my best to reassure him; strangely enough, he gives as his fear a feeling that Johnson may be "too easy," that his effort to play politics will prevent him from being tough. Happily I have no fear on this particular score, so could talk most emphatically.

I wonder whether Johnson will have Forrestal's devoted and extraordinary sense of duty.

For years Eisenhower had suffered from a malady of the digestive system known as ileitis and had not known about it; then, in the early part of 1949, it attacked him with a vengeance, and for some weeks he did not recover. On the evening of March 21 he stretched out in his Washington hotel room and knew he was sick and for days thereafter remained in bed. Transferred to Key West, on the recommendation of President Truman, who had so enjoyed the hospitality of the submarine base there that he had maintained a Little White House in the rambling buildings of the base, Eisenhower at last began to feel better. He did not, however, find out what really was troubling him and undergo an operation, until some years later, in 1956.

One of the advantages of his momentary incapacitation was that he went off cigarettes, permanently. Until that time he had been smoking four packs a day. During his illness he had no solid food and no cigarettes. Eventually his physician, Major General Howard Snyder told him that he could have a few cigarettes a day, but the allotment was so small that he consumed it well before the day was out, and he began to think that, after all, he might as well have no cigarettes as so few. With this logic at work, he gave them up. He perhaps salved his feelings by telling himself that his oratorical duties at Columbia required better care of his throat.

APRIL, 1949, KEY WEST

What so many people fail to realize is that we've not spent $15 billion per year on our forces since 1945. I'm of the opinion that we should shoot for a sum (call it expected expenditures) to make up the total or accumulated deficit and then to level off at $15 billion per year (exclusive of stockpiling, etc.). If we could use that sum intelligently and logically what a difference it could make.

This is first entry since I came South after getting sick on March 21.

JUNE 4, 1949

While in Washington, I had a severe digestive upset this spring, which finally put me to bed on March 21. By the end of a week I was fit to travel and President Truman invited me to use his residential facilities at Key West. I went down there with General Snyder and remained until April 12. On that date he took me to the Augusta National Golf Club where I remained until May 12.

(Later. Interrupted.)

One of our greatest troubles is inability to plan for a given amount of money. Some new authority always intervenes to cut it down in spite of prior commitment by the president himself. Once (in January 1947) he called me on the plane when I was in Coral Gables hospital to tell me he had to go back on a specific promise for $110 million for army equipment (tanks and trucks). That was on advice of Webb, but generally the president does not tell me himself, we just get the bad news.[1] Right now it comes through secretary of defense. We work like the devil on an agreement on a certain sized budget, and then are told to reduce it. We "absorb" everything—rising costs (in the past four years they are bad), increased pay, stockpiling, etc., etc.

Of course the results will not show up until we get into serious trouble. We are repeating our own history of decades, we just don't believe we ever will get into a real jam.

We are many billions short of the sum total we could have had under the $15 billion stable program, but that's the way it goes.

Forrestal had retired in favor of Louis Johnson on March 28, 1949, and after a visit to Florida became so depressed that he went back to Washington, where it was decided that he needed prolonged psychiatric treatment. Admitted to the naval hospital at Bethesda, he was responding well to treatment and by mid-May was looking forward to his discharge in another month or so. Then the restraints were relaxed, a tragic miscalculation, for on the night of May 21–22 he was reading late in his room on the sixteenth floor, from an anthology of poetry, and he copied off a chorus from Sophocles:

> Worn by the waste of time—
> Comfortless, nameless, hopeless save
> In the dark prospect of the yawning grave.

This was not the medicine he needed, and he went to the unguarded kitchen window of his floor and jumped.

JUNE 11, 1949

There is no use trying, after his death, to decide exactly what I thought of Jim Forrestal. But one thing I shall always remember. He was the one man who, in the very midst of the war, always counseled caution and alertness in dealing with the Soviets. He visited me in 1944 and in 1945 and I listened carefully to his thesis—I never had cause to doubt the accuracy of his judgments on this point. He said, "Be courteous and friendly in the effort to develop a satisfactory modus vivendi, but never believe we have changed their basic purpose, which is to destroy representative government."

He insisted they hated us, which I had good reason to believe myself. I still do, but now, everybody does. Moreover, those who were then asleep now are professional patriots and Russian haters.

In his memoriam Eisenhower may have credited Forrestal with too much foresight. There was something of the doctrinaire about Forrestal, or if not that then his was too intense a personality, too willing to take an idea and overanalyze it. Forrestal lacked the power of decision, perhaps because he overanalyzed. But whatever his psyche, he was deeply impressed by the long telegram sent from Moscow by George F. Kennan early in 1946: the telegram in which the later so well-known Soviet specialist analyzed the Russian character in terms of its peculiar combination of ideas and interests, especially its historic roots in Russia's modernization and the country's long heritage of autocracy. Forrestal passed Kennan's essay around to all the government officials he could think of and was largely responsible for the establishment of Kennan back in Washington as a resident expert on the Russians.

Forrestal's death was a great loss, a tragedy—even for a man like Eisenhower, who was accustomed to seeing men die at the height of their powers. It made no difference that Eisenhower knew some of Forrestal's weaknesses. But as the summer of 1949 wore on, he one day received a visitor, the governor of New York, who had recently been defeated in a second bid for the presidency of the United States. Thomas E. Dewey was a man with a mission; that day Dewey came to the house of the president of Columbia University. The general was much surprised by Dewey's proposal.

JULY 7, 1949

Governor Dewey visited my [house] yesterday. He stayed at my house for two hours. He says he is worried about the country's future and that I am the only one who can do anything about it.

The governor says that I am a public possession, that such standing as I have in the affections or respect of our citizenry is likewise public property. All of this, though, must be carefully guarded to use in the service of all the people.

(Although I'm merely repeating someone else's exposition, the mere writing of such things almost makes me dive under the table.)

He feels that New York State is vital to any Republican aspirant to the presidency.

He assumes I am a Republican and would like to be president. (When this last came out I was flabbergasted. I must have had a funny look on my face, because he said, "I know you disclaimed political ambition in a verbose, wordy document, but that was when you were just a soldier.")

This reaffirms a conviction I have formed, which is that no denial of political ambition will ever be believed by a politician, unless the disclaimer is so old he is tottering rapidly to the grave. In this case the refusal would not be a denial of ambition, merely an expression of regret.

The governor then gave me the reasons he believed that only I (if I should carefully preserve my assets) can save this country from going to hades in the handbasket of paternalism, socialism, dictatorship. He knows that I consider our greatest danger the unawareness of our majorities, while aggregated minorities work their hands into our pockets and their seats to the places of the mighty. So he dwelt at length on the preservation of freedom, my favorite subject.

The governor next outlined a political career for me, starting very soon: (1) declare my Republicanism; (2) run for governor of New York State and be elected; (3) accept nomination for presidency, but always keep fairly still as to my specific views.

His basic reasoning is as follows:

All middle-class citizens of education have a common belief that tendencies toward centralization and paternalism must be halted and reversed. No one who voices these views can be elected. He quotes efforts of Hoover, Landon, Willkie, himself.

Consequently, we must look around for someone of great popularity and who has not frittered away his political assets by taking positive stands against national planning, etc., etc.

Elect such a man to presidency, after which he must lead it back to safe channels and paths.

As indicated, the talk was long. I wish I could merely say what Sherman said. But how can I know today what the situation of this country will be four years from now, and whether I'll believe I could do something about it better than most others could. It all seems unreal and forced to me, but I'm not egotistical enough to give any kind of an irrevocable, arbitrary answer at this moment.

So I said, "I shall never want to enter politics. I shall never willingly seek a vote. I shall always try to do my duty to the United States but I do not believe that anything can ever convince me that I have a duty to seek political office." The sad thing is that even as I said this I know that to him I meant, "Why surely, provided I ever become convinced I can win."

He is as likable as he has always been in private conversation. It seems that in public he has no appeal but he is a rather persuasive talker on a tête-à-tête basis. But in this conversation he attacked a subject on which I've listened to a lot of eloquence. Gad, how I wish that both parties had the courage to go out for militant advocacy to the middle of the road and choose some issues outside of the nation's economy on which to fight out elections. Then, my answer now would be as easy as it was before I came back from Europe, for instance, when I answered President Truman in Berlin just four years ago, now.[1]

Oh yes! Governor said, unless I do something, by 1950, of political significance (elected to governorship) I'm through. When I grinned and said, "You've given me the best of reasons for doing nothing," he replied, "Not if you want to preserve democracy."

Incidentally he, the governor, offered me the senatorship from New York State, but advised against my taking it. His reasons are far too long to set down here, but fundamentally they are: Get elected governor and New York State is yours without necessity of taking unequivocal stand on national issues. This will not be true in Washington.

He refused to take final answer of no on governor business. I am to let him know in fall.

JULY 17, 1949

Louis Johnson wants me to come to Washington as chairman of joint chiefs of staff, permanently, or at least, indefinitely. It is queer, but people in political life consider that anyone not in Washington is a lost soul, lost to ambition, to public regard, to any public usefulness.

Of course I'll not do it—there are more able men available for that job than possibly any other in government. But he'll think I'm running out on him.

SEPTEMBER 27, 1949

A stranger than fiction thing took place this summer. An emissary from Mr. Fitzpatrick (described to me as Democratic boss of this state) came to Denver to offer Democratic nomination for senator.[1] (See couple of pages back, describing conversation with Governor Dewey last summer. Emissary was George Allen and I said, "No.")

Of course I assured him of my appreciation, but I reiterated that "Nothing has occurred to change my convictions from those I made public on the general subject of my participation in politics in 1948."[2]

However, I was interested to hear George's explanation of why Mr. Fitzpatrick should consider me a Democrat. The answer of Mr. Fitz to George's question on this matter was, "A man of his convictions cannot be a Republican."

Yet no one has condemned paternalism, yielding to pressure groups, raiding the federal treasury in favor of any class, etc., etc., more than I have. The answer is that political bosses don't care what a man thinks—they just want to know whether he is probably a man who can get votes (by honest expression of his views or by trickery).

Mrs. Clare Boothe Luce came to see me this morning.[3] She wanted nothing, except to discuss in a general way the future of the country and the opportunities of the Republican party to affect that future favorably. Incidentally, the pressures on her to reenter politics are considerable, but she is resisting them, at least until she can see some evidence of effective leadership and teamwork in her party. She does not want to be merely a "voice in the wilderness," and, considering the distasteful features of political life, who can blame her.

She seemed to me pessimistic, or downhearted, but was willing to go back into harness if she could have some inspiration and some indication that she would not be "fighting windmills."

I came into her calculations (or analysis) only to the extent that she believes I may turn out to be one who could provide the leadership she believes to be mandatory.

General failure means to her: increasing use of federal subsidies; growth of paternalism; weakening of community responsibility and individual rights; gradual and steady growth of federal influence and power until we will far surpass the United Kingdom in this regard. Along with this, loss of industrial leadership through loss of incentive and initiative. Finally, weakening of the individual and worsening economic conditions will bring: dictatorship.

She was very earnest. Her only advice to me was to keep on speaking out on points of my own beliefs in government, etc. If people want to accept them (majority) then I may find myself in a box (that is, I may not be able, eventually, to resist the demands that could be placed upon me to enter politics). If these views are not accepted, nothing is hurt and my conscience is clear.

She suggested, however, that in the first case I might still be able to avoid personal involvement in political struggles because in the next couple of years we might find and advertise some younger man—one who could provide the inspiration that the Republican party has lacked for twenty years. "Except for Vandenberg, who came to front after he was too old."[4]

In my files is a recent note from Senator Vandenberg. I've put down something of my conversation with Governor Dewey. Then this meeting with Mrs. Luce.

Many others (but of far lesser prominence) have talked to me along the same lines.

The situation is far different in all these minds from what it was in 1948. Then, all Republicans thought they'd win easily.

So, no "leaders" wanted me or bothered me. All the "Republican" pressure on me was truly from the grass roots, because the bosses wanted the top man to be one they could control.

The "Democratic" pressures came from the bosses, all except Harry S. Truman and his personal crowd. They were desperate, and I was a possible port in a storm. Now—everything is reversed!

But, my own convictions are the same as they were from 1943 to 1948. What I dread is the faint possibility that circumstances and people could combine in some way to convince me I have a duty in politics. But I do not believe it, and if I should ever, in the future, decide affirmatively on this point it will be because I've become oversold by friends.

Well, nothing to do now but continue to fight for what I believe in, which is decentralization of both responsibility and authority in government.

OCTOBER 14, 1949

Fifty-nine today.

The bitter fight still goes on in Washington, with the navy cursing the other services. The whole performance is humiliating—I've seriously considered resigning my commission, so that I could say what I pleased, publicly.

Walter Sammis (one of our trustees) conveys to me an invitation from the Philadelphia Union League Club to address them on November 22. I refused on basis of partisanship—I stick to my determination not to appear with a definitely Republican or Democratic party.

OCTOBER 21, 1949

Some of the other services have now been cursing the navy. I've presented my theory, which is, stop looking backward and cursing mistakes and those who've made them.

NOVEMBER 2, 1949

For days I've hoped for a chance to note in this book a brief record of some of the things happening to me. Meeting here with a Christian Arab, Mr. El-Bandak. His story of the plight of 130,000 Christians in Palestine is a pitiful one, but what makes this notation logical at this point is his rather naïve conviction that I can do something decisive about it. What I've been wanting to argue out with myself is the question so often posed to me, "What are you going to do about an alarming situation which only you can correct?"

Must go home. Will try to finish tomorrow.

NOVEMBER 3, 1949

Yesterday Sherman was appointed chief of naval operations. Day before yesterday the new United States of Indonesia was launched as an independent state. I wish luck to both—they'll need it.[1]

Personal political problems, which I thought had been solved forever by my several public statements in 1948 (to say nothing of similar utterances covering the period 1944–1948), are now plaguing me again.

Among individuals of some prominence who have either flatly stated or hinted broadly that I am to be a political figure in 1952 are (aside from those already named somewhere in this book): Sam Pryor, Connecticut; Mr. Scott, congressman (former Republican national chairman); Mr. Calhoun, McAfee, Forgan, all businessmen from St. Louis, Chicago, New York, and, I suppose, a dozen others, some of whom visit me on "other" business and then switch to political possibilities. For example, Allan Kline, head of one of our great farm organizations.

The approach varies, as do some of the details of argument. But it all ends up as follows: (1) The Republicans have no leader who can inspire a following; (2) no one, not now widely known, could be built up into a position of leadership by 1952; (3) if the Democrats are elected again, in 1952, the country is through as a nation of competitive enterprise, socialization is sure to engulf us; (4) people trust me; (5) I can be nominated and elected; (6) I can save the nation.

Now, if any one of these several steps can be disproved then some, at least, admit I have no bounded duty to become the Republican candidate. But, without exception, my visitors lay these arguments down as facts and then look at me for the answer.

Another side of this—some of these people state or imply that they are beginning to start the ball rolling over this country to sweep me into office without the formality of awaiting my consent. On the other hand, a message sent me by a very strong manufacturers association (not the National Association of Manufacturers) was to the effect that I had soon to let them know that, in the event of nomination, I'd be "willing." The emissary's (or alleged emissary) argument was that this gang was ready to spend five million dollars, and they weren't going to do that if there was any later chance of my declining. So I told the man to say "Nuts." In fact the thing smacks of the same ineptitude that has characterized a lot of American business leadership over the past forty years.

I am not, now or in the future, going willingly into politics. If ever I do so it will be as the result of a series of circumstances that crush all my arguments, that there appears to me to be such compelling reasons to enter the political field that refusal to do so would always thereafter mean to me that I'd failed to do my duty.

I must say that, as of this moment, my imagination cannot conjure up any picture of emergency, disaster, or danger that would point irrevocably to me as the sole savior of the United States. Put that way, the thing sounds silly.

But the pressure continues, and I'd pay a good bit, this instant, for a simple, honest, and convincing answer that would not require me to go through all this, step by step, with so many visitors.

But I cannot say to anyone that I would not do my best to perform a duty. I do not admit that the type of activity urged upon me can likely become something I shall recognize as a duty, but the trouble comes when my callers will not use any other word. At least they've become smart enough to avoid the insinuation that I'd like it.

NOVEMBER 25, 1949

For many days I've hoped to note down here a few thoughts. Not long ago (afternoon of November 18, I think) I had another long talk with Governor Dewey. He remains of the opinion that I must soon enter politics or, as he says, be totally incapable of helping the country when it will need help most. He is most fearful (as are thousands of others, including myself in varying degree) that we, as a nation, will fail to see the dangers into which we are drifting and, as a consequence, will approve governmental actions from which there can be no retreat. He insists that my voice in opposition to such drifts will be absolutely ineffectual unless I should occupy a political platform. He wants me to run for governor of New York in 1950. I said no, but he wants to talk about it once more.

Since his sincerity cannot be questioned (he certainly has nothing to gain by my running for state office) the whole matter cannot be lightly dismissed. It takes time, patience, and effort to let him see that I'm as convinced of the rectitude and logic of my course as he is of his.

Anyway, I promised to see him, together with a couple of his trusted advisers, merely to let some others give their opinions on the matter.

After all these years of nagging at me, pro and con, Democratic and Republican, I still: (1) do not want any political office, even if it could be handed to me without effort on my part; (2) believe that I can be more influential (over the long term) in promoting respect for American institutions by following my present course than by entering politics; (3) sense no obligation, of any kind, to run for office; (4) do not believe I am failing in performance of duty to country merely because someone else says it is my duty to become a political figure; (5) do not agree that someone else of the same general convictions as those in which I believe cannot be built up into the kind of public figure that he should be by the time of convention in 1952; (6) do not consider it appropriate for me to be making constant announcements about political ambitions; I have none, and I've said so.

Every day this question comes before me in some way or other. Personal letters, visitors, requests for addresses, etc., etc. I'm worn out trying to explain myself. Dewey, Clare Luce, Kline (Farm Bureau), Calhoun (St. Louis), and three others, Bedell Smith (talking for a group he describes as "big" industrialists), Lucius Clay (from Jimmy Byrnes), and Roy Cullen (Houston) are a few who have actually visited me to talk politics. Many others have written (names are in files). In addition I've had volunteer offers of help from many, many people—some of them among my best friends. Pete Jones, Bill Burnham, Bill Robinson, etc.

1950

Sometimes a new year means little either for the life of an indvidual or the history of a nation, but the year 1950 marked both an important change in Eisenhower's life and a profound shift in the focus of American national effort. The Korean War, opening in June, would cost the lives of 33,629 American young men, a very large sacrifice, but in addition to snuffing out all those young lives it militarized American foreign policy in a way that would have been unbelievable in the previous half decade—the years from 1945 to 1950 when the army, navy, and air force were squabbling over a few hundred millions of appropriations. After the Korean War began, the idea of a defense budget totaling $15 billion vanished from the American scene, never to be mentioned again. Each year of the Korean conflict was to see the military budget run to about forty-two billions, and after the emergency passed in 1953 the budgetary calculations were lowered only for a short time. Soon after came the pressures of inflation and of new military technologies and the need to purchase post-Second World War models of the older technologies; all of these factors pushed the defense budget ever upward, until by 1960 expenditures were about forty-two billions; by 1981 the figure had tripled.

Along with the Korean War came national uncertainty and querulousness of a sort that reappeared twenty years later at the height of the Vietnam War, for in each of these limited wars the old soldiers and ultra-patriots were enraged by the country's inability to force its enemies to unconditional surrender. Along with the frustration came accusation and ill will that focused frequently on individuals. Talk of treason was in the air, leading Republican politicos in 1950–1953 to speak of twenty years of treason.

Eisenhower found himself assailed by these new forces, although he did not share the partisan criticism of the Democrats. He remained carefully above politics, uncertain of his political allegiance, although ever more a focus of Republican solicitation. Toward the end of the year he received a call to military duty from Washington, which took him to Europe. He asked for and received a leave of absence from Columbia, but it was in fact the end of his activities as a university president, for after the military duty another kind of duty would beckon.

C. JANUARY 1, 1950

This begins my attempt to keep some notes of my own in a form that I can later read. I do not like to dictate them, while my penmanship, in spite of my earnest efforts, quickly degenerates into a hopeless scrawl that, within a matter of days, is entirely meaningless to me. So I take advantage of this extraordinary present from IBM (Tom Watson) to begin my own training on the typewriter and to kill two birds by practicing on notes that I should like to remember.[1]

All through the notes that I have made since the war's end runs the strain of annoyance, or irritation, of my seeming inability to draw completely clear of public suspicion that I seek some political office, without baldly and arbitrarily making certain statements that I believe no American has the right to make. Those notes are scattered over periods of months and are characterized chiefly by their irregularity and haphazard composition. They have ordinarily been dashed off in crowded minutes, with little time to insure exactness of expression or even to check on the thought expressed. Nevertheless, I know, without referring to the little black book in which they are to be found, that my statement as to their reflection of a worrisome personal problem is absolutely correct.

To describe accurately the position in which I now find myself will take far more time than I can devote to this laborious business today. However I can make a start and perhaps I can find the opportunity during the coming week to put down the essentials of the situation. Admittedly the doing so promises no return to anybody—least of all me. No, here I think I'm wrong. I believe my effort, if successful, will tend to clarify my mind to some degree and thus give me greater confidence that I am not straying from what I believe to be principle in any of my statements, conversations, or decisions affecting any part of this confusing problem.

First, the personal angle.

I do not want a political career; I do not want to be publicly associated with any political party, although I fervently believe in the two-party system and further believe that, normally, a citizen is by no means performing his civic duty unless he participates in all applicable activities of his party, to include participation in precinct caucuses.

Consequently, it seems necessary to give reasons for regarding my own as an exceptional rather than a normal case.

My basic purpose is to try, however feebly, to return to the country some portion of the debt I owe to her. My family, my brothers and I, are examples of what this country with its system of individual rights and freedoms, its boundless resources, and its opportunities for all who want to work can do for its citizens —regardless of lack of wealth, political influence, or special educational advantage. Nowhere else on earth has this type of material, intellectual, and spiritual opportunity been so persistently and so successfully extended to all. Regardless of all faults that can be searched out in the operation of the American system, I believe without reservation that in its fundamental purposes and in its basic structure it is so far superior to any government elsewhere established by men, that my greatest possible opportunity for service is to be found in supporting, in renewing public respect for, and in encouraging greater thinking about these fundamentals. Since I believe that all Americans, even though they do so unconsciously or subconsciously, actually support these basic tenets of Americanism, it follows that in the field in which I should work (that is, the bringing of these basic tenets to our conscious attention) there is no difference between the two great parties. Therefore I belong to neither. Their function is to bring before the people the chance to choose between two different methods in the application of the principles to specific problems and to allow the people to choose between two specific slates of candidates. It seems to me that there are cogent reasons why I should eschew this partisan field of citizenship effort.

In the first place, I shall never lose my direct and intimate interest in the legitimate aspirations and the welfare of our veterans of World War II. They, I hope, have confidence that I shall try to discharge toward them every obvious obligation—and they comprise both Democrats and Republicans. Whatever name or reputation I have, they made for me—I cannot conceive of their believing that I was showing proper appreciation of this fact if I should join a political party. (At least I am sure that those of the opposite party would look at me with a jaundiced eye.)

In the second place, I have been a soldier—necessarily without political affiliation—all my life. I should like to be of some help from time to time in that type of governmental problem for which I have been educated. That classification is military. If my counsel is ever desired in that kind of question, I should like to be available no matter what political party might happen to be in power at the moment. In other words, I should like to remain just what I've always been, a military officer instantly responsive to civil government, regardless of its political complexion.

In the third place, I accepted, after long urging, the presidency of Columbia in the belief that in this post and with the help of these great faculties I could do more than anywhere else to further the cause to which I am devoted, the reawakening of intense interest in the basis of the American system. Having assumed the responsibilities of this post I do not believe it appropriate for me to proclaim a loyalty to a particular political party. We have here men and women of all parties—our alumni and supporters, upon whom we are dependent for our existence, likewise come from all parties. My joining a specific party would certainly antagonize some. In my conviction, even partial adherence to a specific party or any partial entry into the political field would demand from me an instant resignation from Columbia. But here (in Columbia) is the place I think I can do the most good for all—even if that most is a rather pitiful amount.

I believe that the army of the United States is this country's most devoted, most efficient, and best-informed body of its size now existing. The army upholds the Constitution, our basic governmental document and the foundation of the system that places the civil power of government in the master's position over the military. The good army officer has always been particularly careful to remain loyal to this concept—both in deed and thought and, beyond this, in appearance. Many people regard a soldier's entry into politics as an effort to overturn this concept. Such a thought springs from prejudice and woeful ignorance, but it is idle to claim it does not exist. Consequently many individuals in the army would fear that my entry into the political field was showing a disregard of the possible consequences to the army's reputation—they might even feel that I was "letting the army down." This, by itself, might be of only minor consequence. But the possibility of false interpretation on the part of the public—inspired by political partisans to whom no dirty trick is unknown—could be very serious to the welfare of the army, which, I repeat, is the finest organization in government—any government.

There is an angle to this same subject that is important, though little noticed. It is the danger—once we become accustomed to thinking of our military leaders as potential political leaders—that their selection (which is done by the party in power at the time of selection) will certainly be based as much upon political considerations as upon their demonstrated military capacity. Such a grave occurrence in time of war could defeat the nation. That this line of reasoning is not baseless is demonstrated by the history of France throughout the nineteenth and early twentieth centuries.

As between the so-called concept of the welfare state and the operation of a system of competitive enterprise there is no doubt where I stand. I am not on any fence. In the same way I am not on any fence with respect to my attitude toward a possible nomination to political office. I want none of it and believe that to change my attitude would be bad both for me and for what I hope I can do in the line of public service. People will believe me when I say that I'm against the handout state but nevertheless a military liberal. They will not believe me when I say I am not interested in a political office—even the presidency. We are just not capable, in this country, of conceiving of a man who does not want to be president. Too many men running for political office have said just that, so the response is, "Oh yeah!" Well, the obvious course is to say nothing and to continue to preach what I believe, regardless of criticism by the columnists.

In the back of this book are two memos, written by my two best friends in New York [unfortunately the memos are no longer in the original diary]. Neither is a politician—one is a banker, the other a newspaperman. They take opposite sides in arguing the question "Should General E. now associate himself definitely with the Republican party and participate in the ensuing struggles between the two parties, specifically in the congressional elections of the coming fall?" Why they happened to decide to write and give me their thoughts on this question, I do not know. But I am keeping them because each summarizes, fairly accurately, the arguments brought to me by many others—some on one side, some on another. Eberstadt, Byrnes, Dewey, Hoover, Sprague, Brownell among the more widely known politicians, and dozens of people on the business and industrial side, have talked to me on the same subject—but the answer remains the same.[2]

JANUARY 4, 1950

Today the New York *Sun* ceases to exist as a separate paper. It has been bought up by the Scripps-Howard chain. The one point that makes the incident of some significance is the explanation given by the ex-publisher of the *Sun* for its demise. His printed statement is pasted on this page [reprinted as extract below]— particularly because of his contention that labor leaders have become so unreasonable in their demands that they are defeating their own ends, i.e., by forcing small industry into bankruptcy they are creating conditions in which the workingman cannot fail to suffer.

THOMAS W. DEWART: With profound regret we announce to our readers and staff that with today's editions The New York Sun will cease to exist as a separate journalistic force. Its name and good-will have been sold to The New York World-Telegram, a Scripps-Howard newspaper. We of The Sun urge our readers to give to the new "World-Telegram and The Sun" the same loyal support which they and their predecessors for generations have given to us. It is the hope and desire of everybody concerned that this association will give to America's largest city the best and strongest afternoon newspaper in the United States.

Mounting costs of production, unaccompanied by commensurate increases in advertising revenues, have made some such course inevitable. Chief among the rising costs have been those of labor and newsprint. Our working force is almost wholly organized and our relations with the workers have always been friendly and cordial. But the simple truth is that union demands have become too great for us to meet in the face of serious losses in income. In this time of rising costs we are compelled to protect the interest of our bondholders, most of whom are our employes. The fact is, and we say it without bitterness or recrimination, that the demands of the unions have wrought here in New York—what they are working elsewhere throughout the nation—an unprecedented and increasing number of casualties among newspapers which once were great and strong. Despite continued warnings of the economic consequences, various unions have forced, and are continuing to force, higher wages, until, in the newspaper business as a whole, these have risen beyond reason. In the ten-year period from 1939 to and including 1949, the average advance in individual pay of The Sun's employes was 80.1 per cent. In the same period, the price of newsprint rose from $48 a ton to $100 a ton. Prices of all other supplies increased in corresponding ratios.

Recently advertising revenues of The Sun and The World-Telegram have not kept pace with mounting production costs. Both papers have long appealed to a literate and intelligent public. Between them they have divided approximately 650,000 circulation—enough to assure the economic stability of one newspaper, but not enough for two in this metropolitan area.

The World-Telegram is a member of a nation-wide newspaper organization. Its management naturally desired to strengthen its position in the nation's greatest city. Accordingly, it made an offer for the name and good-will of The Sun, which has been accepted with great regret. The sale was completed last night.

Thus it becomes our sad duty to announce the end of the great journalistic venture which began with the first issue of The Sun on Sept. 3, 1833.

Without undue immodesty it may be said that in its more than 116 years The Sun achieved world-wide fame. Its roster of brilliant writers has never been excelled. Throughout its career it has supported constitutional government, sound money, reasonable protection for American industry, economy in public expenditures, preservation of the rights and responsibilities of the several states, free enterprise, good citizenship, equality before the law, and has upheld all the finer American traditions. It has opposed indecency and rascality, public and private. It has fought Populism, Socialism, Communism, governmental extravagance, the encroachments of bureaucracy and that form of governmental paternalism which eats into the marrow of private initiative and industry. With respect to all these things, we may proudly and truthfully say that we have fought a good fight and held unswervingly to the true faith.

Our deepest appreciation goes to the men and women whose ability and loyalty have made the paper a great power, not only in this city, but throughout the nation. We extend to our readers and loyal advertisers our heart-felt thanks and assurance that in the "World-Telegram and The Sun" they will find the characteristics which they have liked best in The Sun.

To the "World-Telegram and The Sun" we extend our best wishes and our heartiest goodwill.

Another important reason for noting here the passing of the *Sun* is found in that paragraph of the final editorial of explanation that states what the paper stood for during its existence. These are the things in which I believe. If a paper that has preached these things cannot secure enough support to operate success- fully, the question is "Are these principles, as guides to American action, now to go into the discard?" If they are, I am wasting a lot of energy—but I'll go down fighting. The cartoon below appeared in the final issue of the *Sun*.

FEBRUARY 7, 1950

General Snyder and I have decided that it is not possible for me to remain in New York and at the same time resist sufficiently the demands upon my time so that I can maintain a schedule indefinitely. Moreover we have found that whenever I return from a vacation it is only a matter of a very few weeks until I am showing again the effects of strain, long hours, and tension. Reservation of a day or half-day each week (aside from Sundays) fails because of my giving way to some insistent demand for a conference, meeting, luncheon, or similar chore. So now we are to try something different: we are reserving one full week out of each two months, to be completely blacked out of my calendar. Preferably I am to leave the city during the "no work" week, but if not then I am to lock the front door of my house. This ought to work, but only today I have broken into the March week to accommodate the meeting of the Boy Scouts national execu- tive council. That's the way it goes. (And it is only February 7, 1950.)

MARCH 22, 1950

I give up on the typewriter. I've turned over my new electric machine to one of the secretaries. Am too awkward and too old to learn.

Last week Mamie and I spent five days, with George and Mary Allen, at the Sea View Club at Atlantic City. I'm convinced that the only way I can maintain a reasonable average of activity is to go away from this city at least as often as once every two months.

Monday I had Harvey Mudd, Mr. Krout, Mr. Lovejoy, and John Dunning for lunch to see the idea of an engineering center.[1]

That evening I spent (5:00 – 10:00) at the Council on Foreign Relations, following an hour's meeting of the board of the Metropolitan Museum.

Tuesday I went out to Newark, to address an alumni meeting. Today I spent the morning in the college—lunch at faculty club—at 4:30 I go to a meeting of the committee to support medical education, tonight to some d--- dinner. I believe the name is Sibleys. A few nights ago I went to a dinner for the Garretts (ambassador to Ireland) given by Mrs. Garrett's sister—duke and duchess of Windsor also guests. We were out very late.

Tomorrow night I lecture (1 hour) on peace. The donor of the money to support a yearly lecture on the subject wishes that I deliver the first one.

Many men have appeared at my office or at my home to volunteer their services if and when I decide I have responsibilities in the political field: Governor D, Russell Sprague, Brownell, Sam Pryor (Connecticut, Panam), Arthur Gardner (2211 Thirtieth Street, NW, Washington, Decatur 8455, an associate of mine in World War I), Dave Calhoun (St. Louis), Bill Robinson, Pete Jones (in special way), Ed Clark, Jimmy Byrnes, Mrs. Luce, dozens whose names appear in correspondence file, Lucius Clay, Russ Forgan, Wes McAfee (president Union Electric), Eberstadt, Hoover (in house of former).

The last thing that an office seeker seems to think of is just plain honesty. If he can be devious, he thinks he is smart; he'd rather be evasive than direct. He wants to give pat answers—he will never, for a second, admit that the true course, usually, is a middle one, between extremes. He hasn't the guts to be "middle of the road." He's afraid of attacks and "me too" from both sides.

My speech in St. Louis on September 3 to lawyers was on this point.

UNDATED

Another kind of typewriter!

I am quite sure that some of the nervous tension that the doctor (and others) seem frequently to detect in me——(as far as I got).[1]

APRIL 5, 1950

Barnard trustee meeting tonight.[1]

There is probably no more complicated business in the world than that of picking a new dean within a university. Faculties, including the retiring dean, feel an almost religious fervor in insisting upon acceptance of their particular views. These are as varied as there are individuals involved, and every man's opinion is voiced in terms of urgency. The result is complete confusion, and I cannot see why universities have followed such a custom. But I'll be d--- glad when we have a new dean of engineering and the fuss, fury, and hysteria die down.

Some of my Republican connections in Kansas have broadly hinted or openly stated that I should declare my association with them. They know of course that I believe we must have a Republican victory in 1952; from this they do a lot of arguing that, in my opinion, fails to look very far into the future.

APRIL 27, 1950

Lately a couple of "Gallup Polls" have put me back into the political gossip columns, although there never has been a complete cessation of loose talk about me as a presidential possibility.

A few evenings ago Gallup reported running me against President Truman. Bad business. But nothing to do about it. I hope the president is too philosophical to take real note of the 60-to-30 report against him.

Public speaking gets to be more and more of a burden. I can limit, very well, the appearances before big audiences—prepared speeches, etc. But every luncheon and dinner, some even that appear to be social only, seems certain to bring around the moment where a host declares, "I'm sure General Eisenhower will be kind enough, etc." How I hate it. Sometimes I think I'm trapped by my liking for people.

Am going to try my first New York golf this P.M.

APRIL 29, 1950

Some time ago I listed in these notes the names of men who have been urging me to go into politics. I've tried to put down the names only of those who seem to be in position to cause some ripple of interest, who seem to have convictions on the matter and therefore deserve the courtesy of a hearing. None has changed my mind an iota—probably Mr. Hoover has shaken me more than anyone else —and strangely enough he did not urge me to do anything. He simply talked from the assumption that duty might compel me to do something I would not choose to do.

A man named Simmons, from Houston, and one named Wanke from Fort Collins, Colorado, have recently started embarrassing movements, but I think we've got them stopped. The most studied document I've received on the subject is from Graeme Howard, a most conscientious (sometimes I think humorless) individual who has an important job with the Ford Motor Company. He concludes that I must (1) announce Republican affiliations now; (2) speak, this summer, in favor of outstanding senatorial and congressional candidates (Republican, of course); and (3) thereafter merely await the inevitable nomination.

All this or else I'm failing to do my duty to this nation and, finally, I will come to realize I have so failed—and will die an embittered and disappointed man.

All very pretty, but I still don't believe it.

The international situation deteriorates even though we see, occasionally, favorable editorials. I wonder how long the few remaining areas in the Southwest Pacific can hold out.

Our leadership is too intermittent; communism is on the job every minute of every day of the 365. Our VIP's are concerned only when there is a crisis—Iran, Greece, Trieste, Berlin, etc., etc. As to China, we wrote a white paper to show how right we were.[1] God, such stupidity. When we liberated those areas of

Europe in World War II where resistance movements were strong, we learned to be careful to prevent later lawless action by the former guerrillas. (MacA. and the Philippine Islands did not learn this.) What do our bosses think that the Chinese commies are now going to do? I believe Asia is lost with Japan, the Philippine Islands, Netherlands East Indies, and even Australia under threat. India itself is not safe.

MAY 2, 1950

Yesterday my mother would have been eighty-eight years old, had she lived.[1]

In a recent issue of *Life* Magazine was a most flattering story by Quentin Reynolds. It was written about me and my activities at Columbia. This week another article came out, this time in *Harpers*, which castigated me, on the ground that here the students and faculties hate me, and I return the sentiment with interest.

If I could solve the money problem of the university* I would not only regard this as almost an ideal place, but I'd have great opportunity and time for personal study. But it's the nagging money problem that keeps me going always, including nights. And so I get tired out.

Recently I wrote a letter to Mrs. Cecil Killion, a member of the university staff who is retiring after long service. In her reply she used a sentence, "Columbia has been a more interesting and colorful place since you became its head." The remark is interesting only by way of showing that not all the oldtimers resent the effort to bring Columbia and the world into closer, cooperative effort.

JUNE 30, 1950

Calendar says Friday but it feels like I've lost a day.

On Wednesday I went to Washington. First Walter Reed Hospital, then a number of friends in Pentagon.[1] Haislip, Collins, Matt Ridgway, Al Gruenther. (Couldn't see Brad, he was sick.)[2]

I went in expecting to find them all in a dither of effort, engaged in the positive business of getting the troops, supplies, etc., that will be needed to settle the Korean mess.[3] They seemed indecisive, which was natural in view of the indecisiveness of political statements. I have no business talking about the basic political decision (to support or not to support South Korea). It happens that I believe we'll have a dozen Koreas soon if we don't take a firm stand, but it was not on that basis that I talked to my friends. My whole contention was that an appeal to force cannot, by its nature, be a partial one. This appeal, having been made, for God's sake, get ready! Do everything possible under the law to get us going. Remember, in a fight we (our side) can never be too strong. I urged action in a dozen directions and left a memo for Brad. We must study every angle to be

*I hear we may avoid an operating deficit this year, but at the cost of deferring truly needed maintenance.

prepared for whatever may happen, even if it finally came to the use of an A-bomb (which God forbid).

By early July 1950 the Korean War, begun on June 25, had hardly stabilized, despite the appearance of order and plan in the administration's reaction to the outbreak of the conflict. The truth was, and Eisenhower knew this, that after the decisions of June 25–30 by which President Truman extended American involvement to land, sea, and air and arranged to have the support of the United Nations Security Council (the Russian envoy momentarily was boycotting the council meetings, angered over the refusal of the United Nations to give China's council seat to the Communist Chinese instead of the Nationalist envoy from Taiwan, so it was possible to avoid a Russian veto), General MacArthur in Japan had very few forces that he could immediately send to Korea. A scratch group named for its commander, Task Force Smith—a few hundred men—was flown over within a few days and went to the front, on the theory that if American uniforms appeared they would give pause to the attacking North Koreans. But the attackers who possessed tanks and planes (the South Koreans did not) were coming rapidly down the peninsula, and South Korean forces were disintegrating. Militarily Korea was a mess, with a very real danger that all resistance would be wiped up before MacArthur could get any large ground units into action.

JULY 6, 1950

Yesterday I was in Washington. Went before a senate subcommittee in the morning; lunch with the president; visit with Averell Harriman, and, later, with Mr. Finletter, Mr. McCone, General Norstad, and Averell.[1] Saw Louis Johnson for a moment.

The subcommittee hearing was on American propaganda. Our people assume that the world knows something about us, our system of government, our international policies, our economic system, etc. Actually we know very little about others, but they know far less about us, and it is essential in the world struggle that the world know something about our good intentions, latent strength, respect for rights of others.

Since our opponent has to depend on lies, and we can tell the truth, the advantage would seem to be all with us. But the truth must be nailed, bannerlike to a staff, and we must do that by convincing the whole world that our announced intentions of peace are the truth.

Lunch: both George Marshall and I told the president that his decision of a week ago must be earnestly supported.[2] Speed and strength, both are needed. We encountered good intentions but I'm not so sure that we met full comprehension.

Later, in talking to others named above (except Johnson), was encouraged to believe that he, the president, would be getting the same advice from his other advisers as he did from GCM and me.

Johnson complacently said, "I've given MacArthur all he asked for," and I had the impression that merely saying "approved" meant, to the secretary, that all was well. As [I] inquired as to the time element, he said, "Pretty good." God, how I hope!

But there seems no disposition to begin serious mobilizing. I think that it is possible that military advisers are too complacent when talking to HST.

By the end of July matters in Korea began to go a little better, for the North Korean attack ran out of steam when it came up against resistance from the Americans and the remaining South Koreans in the neighborhood of the port of Pusan, at the tip of the peninsula. Here the forces of the United Nations—the UN not merely had supported the American intervention but also had organized a joint command—managed to form a defensive perimeter. Lieutenant General Walton H. Walker, one of Eisenhower's European commanders, whom he much respected ("top-flight corps C.G., fighter, cool," he had written on February 1, 1945), was in command of the Eighth Army in Korea. Early in September, with the reluctant consent of the joint chiefs, MacArthur engineered a brilliant landing at the port of Inchon, high up on Korea's west side; at the same time the Eighth Army broke out of Pusan, catching the extended and overconfident North Koreans in a pincer. Soon the United Nations forces were rolling up the North Koreans, shoving the scattered remnants of their troops across the thirty-eighth parallel, and without much thought—this was a crucial decision—following them in an effort to unify Korea under one government—as the United Nations general assembly had sought to do in 1948.

Trouble was to come from this decision to destroy a communist satellite. The Chinese communists had warned against such a move, and the United Nations forces had failed to take the warning seriously. That trouble lay in the future, and meanwhile the president of Columbia University turned his attention back to politics.

OCTOBER 13, 1950

Haven't written in this since going on my summer vacation.

Today Governor D called me (I suppose from Albany) saying that if questioned he is going to announce his hope that I would accept a Republican draft in 1952. There seemed to be no doubletalking about the matter. I merely said I'd say, "No comment."

Even though matters were going well in Korea, the administration was highly uncertain whether the attack of North Korea upon South Korea, obviously sanctioned by the Soviet Union, was simply an attempt to roll up South Korea, where only a few American military advisers had remained to help train the South Korean forces, or an effort to delay the planning for a Japanese peace treaty (which was well underway), or perhaps—most likely—a diversionary effort: a clever stratagem to concentrate the bulk of American ready divisions and naval and air power in and around a remote peninsula of Asia, while the real Soviet attack would come against Western Europe. The North Atlantic Treaty had been signed in April 1949, but not much had been done to improve the defenses of Western Europe. The divisions of the NATO Allies were weak in manpower and equipment, and even the United States Army divisions, as MacArthur's unpreparedness in Japan had shown, were hardly in a state of readiness. President Truman therefore sent word that he wanted to see Eisenhower.

OCTOBER 28, 1950

On Monday, October 23, I arrived at the Blackstone Hotel in Chicago to find there a message asking me to call the president. I placed the call immediately and was informed by the president that he should like to have me come to Washington for a conversation, to talk in general terms about an assignment for me involving a command for the Atlantic Pact defensive forces. He stated that if I would get in touch with him upon coming to Washington (where I am now) on the weekend of the twenty-eighth, he would try to make time available for a talk and that, so far as he was concerned, this would be completely satisfactory.

I was scheduled for a press conference in Chicago and while nothing was suggested by any of the press representatives at that conference which would betray any knowledge on their part of the president's telephone call, I was confronted immediately after the conference by a question from Earl Wilson indicating an accurate knowledge of the incident. I requested that he make no mention of his knowledge because of the embarrassment I would experience during the ensuing week. This he agreed to do, but it appears that some little knowledge did leak out and I was intermittently questioned by other press representatives in the cities I visited—St. Louis, Indianapolis, Cincinnati, Charleston, West Virginia.

I arrived in Washington by a military plane about midnight on Friday, the twenty-seventh.

This morning, the twenty-eighth, I visited General Collins, Secretary of the Army Pace, and the president; also had a talk with General Gruenther.

The situation seems to be about as follows: The American chiefs of staff are convinced that the commander in chief for the Atlantic Pact forces should be named immediately. Originally, it was apparently the conception that the commander should not be named until there were actually large forces to command; that during the formative period a chief of staff, heading a large planning, logistic, and administrative group, could do the work. The opinion finally prevailed that if a commander's prestige was going to do any good in this problem, it would be best used during the most critical period of all, namely, while we are trying to get each of the nations involved to put forth maximum effort in producing, training, and maintaining defensive forces.

It now appears that all of the chiefs of staff group of the Atlantic union (the group of which General Bradley is chairman) have concurred in this conclusion, and I am informed that they unanimously desire that the commander should be an American and specifically myself.

From the moment that this possibility was first mentioned, many months ago,

I have steadfastly stood by one statement. This statement is that I am a soldier and am ready to respond to whatever orders my superiors in the defense forces and the president, as commander in chief, may care to issue to me. The president is particularly anxious that the matter be not placed upon a cut-and-dried, "order and obey" basis. He apparently wants to be able to announce that if I should take such an assignment, I am responding to a "request."

There is, however, one major obstacle at this moment to completing the details which would make the assignment effective and public. This is the fact that there are a number of controversial subjects lying in front of the council of defense ministers, and it appears to be the desire of the American and British staffs to handle all of these questions as a bundle—they do not want to agree merely to those points in which other nations offer no objection, and by doing so leave unsolved those parts of the plan to which other nations may object.*

Specifically, the most controversial subject of all appears to be that of rearming Western Germany. America and Britain want to proceed with a partial rearmament and thus throw the Germans into the whole defensive structure. The French have objected to any consideration whatsoever of such a scheme, although later it appears that they have advanced a theory involving a complicated form of partial German rearmament and hodgepodge organization that they feel might be approved by popular French opinion.[1]

In this general argument I appreciate the French position and sympathize with it. However, I am definitely of the opinion that the French leaders should realize that the safety of Western Europe demands German participation on a vigorous scale and should get busy on the job of educating public opinion in France to accept this proposition—subject, of course, to clear evidence that the Germans cannot regain a position from which they could threaten the safety and security of France. Because of this belief, I am of the further opinion that the Americans and British are correct in refusing to agree to a plan that would necessarily remain largely a paper one and would give more opportunity for debate than for action. They should hold out for a sensible solution for this vital problem before agreeing to accept on behalf of America responsibility for command.

I scarcely expect to see this situation clearly and unequivocally resolved. Rather, I suspect that the French may make certain promises and engagements that will at least partially justify a favorable decision on the part of the Americans and British, and that possibly the command will be set up with very great areas of indecision and doubt with respect to the Western German question. If nothing at all is done in the way of resolving these difficulties and I am still asked to command, I would have very great doubts as to the wisdom of my consenting to accept the position. It might be better to make an issue of the matter, even though my own attitude might be very seriously misunderstood in this country or abroad. If, however, there is developed any chance whatsoever that this vital

*In late February (1951) Jack Slessor (chief of staff, air, Britain) came to my office in Paris. He said this idea belonged to American chiefs of staff only; that British were confronted with a package, which they did not like.

point can be settled logically, as before indicated, it seems to me that I have no choice in the matter whatsoever.[2]

As of this moment, I would estimate that the chances are about nine out of ten that I will be back in uniform in a short time.

All this will occasion a very great deal of adjustment in my personal life. Mamie's heart condition deteriorates a bit year by year and I hate to contemplate the extra burden thrown upon her by attempting to set up housekeeping in Europe, particularly when she would also be worried about the condition of her father and mother back in Denver. Actually this phase of the whole business would be the only one that would give me any great private concern.[3] As for myself, I do not think it is particularly important where I am working as long as I feel I am doing the best I can in what I definitely believe to be a world crisis. It will, of course, be a wrench to give up the work I am so earnestly working on at Columbia, but there are some fine young men there that can carry on, and I am sure that my friends all over the country who have promised to help will not let them down merely because I have to go away temporarily. As to the period of time in which I might be involved in such an affair, I do not see how a hard and fast estimate can be made. I firmly believe that my own maximum possibilities for service—based upon my alleged prestige in Europe—will begin to diminish very soon after the organizational phases of the proposition begin to show results. We must remember that the whole scheme may be one that will have to remain in effect for ten, fifteen, or twenty years.† Consequently, it seems to me that it would be important for me to throw in at an early date some acceptable and reasonably young commander to take over and carry on the work for a reasonable length of time. While I realize that I might be able to carry on for five or six years, I think it is bad practice to allow such developments to fall into the hands of older men. Particularly, I would not want to see the habit started of assigning successive commanders who had almost reached the end of their usefulness as soldiers.

At this moment, there is no telling when decision on these matters will be reached.

NOVEMBER 6, 1950

Today I start on a trip to Chicago, Dallas, Texas Agricultural and Mechanical College, Houston, Oklahoma City, Chicago, home. I travel in interests of American Assembly, a project on which I've been working almost two years, but under various names. Its purpose is explained in a memo I'm attaching to this book.[1] It has appealed mightily to businessmen, and support, both moral and material, has been fine. Right now we're working on the money for original capital (though

---

†February 1, 1951: My own belief is that, in the element of time, the United States should establish clear limits and should inform Europe of these estimates. This applies to the length of time we should maintain sizeable American forces in Europe. [Editor's note: An interesting commentary when at the present writing, 1981, NATO is celebrating its thirty-second birthday.]

I personally never ask for a dollar) and through my explanations to selected groups we've tagged, already, well over one hundred thousand. Roy Cullen, $25,000 [on March 1951 Eisenhower turned back in his diary to this November 6, 1950, entry to make this parenthetical comment: "reneged; so far as I know, he has never paid this."]; Mr. Greenway, $25,000; Mr. Olin, $25,000; Bob Woodruff, $10,-000; Boots Adams of Phillips Oil, $50,000; Pete Jones, $10,000; Metcalf (foundation), $10,000; Tom Watson, $35,000; Bob Kleberg, $10,000. In thousands are just a few of the larger contributors. So I'm encouraged. Philip Young, in direct charge of the project, is a splendid leader.

The Allied conference adjourned in Washington without reaching a conclusion on the German problem.[2] So far as I'm concerned I shall go ahead on my current tasks and let the future (particularly the military future) take care of itself.

A couple of weeks ago Mr. Dewey announced that if elected governor of New York this year he would try to get the New York Republican delegation to urge me as Republican candidate for president in 1952. The storm broke out again, within the past few days it has subsided publicly, but in private conversation it never dies.

Have urged universal military service of two years duration, without pay for all eighteen-year-olds. Jim Conant is in general agreement. Marshall does not agree, ditto Lovett.[3] While sometimes I wonder whether I do not exaggerate in my own mind the seriousness of the world situation, I likewise am not certain that some of our officeholders are not either complacent or too slow to trust the American people with the bald facts of the world situation. Some of these officials think we can buy security; solvency and security can scarcely be separated, yet I hear talk of $55 billion a year for several years.[4] Tragic.

In Washington I feel that there is some hysteria, certainly one does not gain a lot of confidence when it is hinted that he will probably have to undertake a very serious and prolonged assignment in Europe in order to preserve American security and can obtain no satisfactory answers to such questions as how many divisions, groups, and ships are involved in America's planned building programs. Vagueness seems to be no crime or fault—the answer is "In Europe Eisenhower can solve all the problems." Sweet, but valuable only as an opiate. Goddamit, is there no desire to know where we are going? If Forrestal had only had the stamina to equal his honesty and sense. And poor HST, a fine man who, in the middle of a stormy lake, knows nothing of swimming. Yet a lot of drowning people are forced to look to him as a lifeguard. If his wisdom could only equal his good intent.

Marshall, the best public servant of the lot, obviously wants to quit.[5] (I don't blame him—he has no children.)

Late in November the Chinese struck hard at MacArthur's forces in Korea. The troops were overextended, and the United Nations commander in Tokyo had split his forces by allowing the Eighth Army under Walker to move north of the thirty-second parallel on the western side of the peninsula and the X Corps under Lieutenant General Edward Almond to go north on the eastern side.

Walker and Almond communicated with each other through Tokyo. Early in November the Chinese had made known their presence and then mysteriously faded away, but when they struck on November 26, with a clangor of bugles, in great force, estimated by MacArthur to be between two and three hundred thousand, the United Nations troops soon were in headlong retreat.

NOVEMBER 29, 1950

Once in a while I reach for this particular book to make a notation. Just why, I do not know, for I so rarely write down anything of the day's happenings that my other book will never be filled, if I should live another thirty years.*

Last eve I went to dinner with Mr. Clarence Dillon. Guests (among others) Mr. Langley, Lord Brand, Mr. Leffingwell, Mr. Rockefeller (J.D., Jr.), Mr. Brady, Mr. Dillon (Jr.), Mr. Millbank, Mr. Schiff.[1] The dinner was arranged to give me an opportunity to describe the American Assembly, thus paving the way for associates to go after these men for financial support for the Assembly program.

Actually everyone was in such a blue funk over the tragic news from Korea that there was no hope of turning conversational interest into any other channel. So, in response to my host's suggestion that I chat for a while to the others, I took the Korean debacle and tried to show some of the additional problems it imposed upon us as citizens. This led to the conclusion that in most cases we didn't have the facts, the truth, on these problems. And so, finally, I ended up arguing for the American Assembly idea.

DECEMBER 5, 1950

My evening schedule for this date is typical of my current life. Invited to three dinners, all of which I thought I should accept and (as it turns out after enough talking between my aide-de-camp and prospective hosts) I'm going to all three. By arrangement I go to the first for cocktails, the second to chat a while, and finally make the third, supposedly, just as the party is to go to the dinner table. What a mess! The first is an engineering smoker; the second a veteran organization honoring my old friend Amon Carter; and the third (the one I personally accepted a long time back), a dinner honoring my friend Dave Calhoun.[1] Both Amon and Dave have been active in helping the American Assembly.

The Korean situation is tragic, although I still believe that MacA. can stabilize the situation if he comes back far enough to stretch the hostile lines and expose their communications to incessant air attack.

What have we been doing here in the Zone of the Interior [the United States] for five months? Something is terribly wrong. I feel that my hunch of last July

*Editor's note: Somewhat confusedly Eisenhower was using two diary books. The one in which he wrote the present entry was a printed book and he crossed out the date of March 29. His other book was a looseleaf notebook; he had begun to use it because he was attempting to type his entries, and when that effort failed he continued to use it, writing by hand.

6 was right, but I was wrong when I supposed that both the defense departments and the White House would heed the fine advice I gave on preparation.

DECEMBER 16, 1950

I'm halfway to Europe.[1]

On yesterday morning had a talk with Ferdinand Eberstadt at Herbert Hoover's. The latter's theory is "arm to the teeth and stay home."

Talked a long time with Averell Harriman. Whole idea was a long-range policy in foreign affairs. See two memos in back of book.[2]

⌐ VII ⌐

NATO

Eisenhower's departure to become supreme commander of Allied forces in
Europe, under authority of the North Atlantic Treaty Organization established
in 1949, brought the return to active duty that he not so much had feared as
anticipated; in the belief that he was only on a temporary mission, he asked for
and received a leave from Columbia University. But with the return to duty came
increasing public prominence and, in 1952, the call to political duty.

President Truman had asked Eisenhower to return to military duty because of
the high uncertainty that reigned in Washington and in other Allied capitals as
to the intentions of the Soviet Union in beginning the Korean War. When that
conflict had broken out on the other side of the globe, the guess that attracted
the most adherents in administration circles in Washington, as mentioned, was
that the Soviet Union had egged on its satellite North Korea into an attack on
South Korea so as to draw American military strength from Japan and from
anywhere else and to concentrate American power in a remote peninsula in Asia,
whereupon the Russians would open an all-out attack on Western Europe. The
Soviets had exploded their first nuclear test device in August 1949, and they
seemed capable of taking Western Europe whenever they wanted. NATO forces
were weak. Some observers said that all the Russians needed to get to the Channel
was shoes.

Knowing that something had to be done in Europe, Truman had called upon
Eisenhower, whose duty was to galvanize the European Allies and get some troops
lined up against the Russians so that any Soviet exploratory moves by the divisions
in East Germany would come up against a plate-glass window, a trip wire, and
their intentions would become clear. Eisenhower's task also was to see if he could
match the Soviets man for man, which would come after construction of the
window or trip wire.

The treaty arrangements, the legal foundations, were all in place. The United States three years earlier, in 1948, had begun negotiating with the wartime allies to see what could be constructed out of both the Treaty of Dunkirk (1947) between Britain and France and the inclusion of not merely London and Paris but also the Benelux countries in the Brussels Pact (1948). From this base of five nations American negotiators brought in three northern tier nations—Denmark, Norway, and Iceland—and added Britain's principal dominion, Canada, and the two southern nations, Italy and Portugal. The North Atlantic Treaty was signed in Washington on April 4, 1949. Later the signatories were to invite Greece and Turkey (1952) and West Germany (1955).

It was one thing to form an alliance and declare that from it had sprung an organization named NATO and quite another to put flesh on the bones. The latter task was Eisenhower's in 1951. The European nations had benefitted hugely from the Korean War, as their factories received war orders or orders generated either by war orders or by the diversion of American production to war orders; the Korean War boom, in addition to the huge infusion of funds into Western Europe that had come with the Marshall Plan beginning in 1948, pushed the economies of the western part of the Continent into a "take-off" of consumer-oriented economic growth that enabled some of the Western European nations, such as West Germany and France, to approximate the standard of living of the United States in the 1970s and 1980s. The European nations in the year 1951 could not look that far into the future; for them the Korean War was a long distance away, thousands of miles to the east; all they could see was another effort by the United States to push them around, perhaps to take from them the fragile new livelihood that the Americans had created through the Marshall Plan by involving them in a Third World War. They vowed to resist any effort to push them into a premature rearmament.

For Eisenhower the memory of the great days of the Second World War was still close, and the need for European rearmament seemed obvious; he chose to overlook the difficulties.

1951

Left New York City at 4:00 P.M. for Washington, from which latter place I shall take off on a preliminary trip to Europe. The trip is "preliminary" in the sense that it is exploratory in preparation for my new assignment as supreme commander of Allied forces in Europe.

Yesterday (rather day before) I was visited by Senator Duff, Senator Ed Clark, Mr. Forgan, a Mr. Benton, and Russel Davenport.[1] The purpose was to talk over our foreign problems and try to develop a "positive" approach to the obvious problems. During the conversation I happened to speak in derogatory terms of "war profits," and Mr. Benton followed this up persistently, saying that if such things were to be said, our mobilization plan would be killed. While he had obviously misunderstood me (my conception of war profits is the making of money out of national disaster) yet the significant thing was that he kept talking about the "appeal" and the "reception" rather than the plan I laid out. Later, thinking this over, it struck me that he was thinking "political" effects, possibly in connection with a possible political future for me.

This irritated me, so much so that I felt it necessary to repeat again what I've so often said before. So my last chore in New York was to telephone Ed Clark. (I kept Schulz in room not because I don't trust EC, but because I wanted a check on what I said.)[2] I told him that it was important that he (and all his associates) understand that I had not changed my mind about politics. I still say as I've always said, "I hope always to do my duty to my country; but I cannot even conceive of circumstances as of this moment that could convince me I had a duty to enter politics." God knows I should not be compelled to reiterate my attitude toward "duty." My going to Europe should, I think, prove that I'm determined to meet every requirement of duty.

Back from tour of NATO countries, January 31, 1951.

Anyway, I told him that if Benton is assuming that I'm going to enter politics he'd better be disabused in a heck of a hurry or, some day, he'd get a rude shock.

JANUARY 3, 1951

So far as my new job is concerned, the "staff mind" is working in typical channels in Washington. Instead of everybody concerning himself with the substance of the problem (national attitudes, industrial capacities, military programs, and present strength) the principal subject of discussion is the one so dear to the hearts of academic soldiers and sailors, "command systems." Principally this stems from the primary failure to see that command in allied ventures implies and imposes a great national responsibility upon the nation assuming it, since staffs think of command in terms of kudos and glory (arising out of the erroneous thinking that such command is comparable to that exercised by the individual over his own service).

Anyway there has already been discussed in some detail the various applicable "systems of command" within my over-all organization and each country's staffs have been encouraged to give their attention to these matters and fix their own conclusions. The result will be trouble, and I warned Al Gruenther (who is to be my chief of staff) to keep still about it. He probably thinks I'm a bit nuts, but I've been through it before. We are going to find (as always) that our system will make everyone a bit angry, but now we've given them the right to advise and suggest, so we are going to make them believe we've violated their considered opinions instead of their casually expressed comments.

In 1944 the British and Monty situation was not unlike this one.

FEBRUARY 1951

Many months ago I decided to transfer to this book (instead of my little blank one [the printed diary book]) the notes I occasionally make upon current happenings. I forgot the reason except that of a faint hope of using a typewriter in a loose-leaf book. I gave that up, but will now try to dictate occasionally.

MARCH 2, 1951

I have now been in Paris for about ten days occupying a temporary headquarters in the Astoria Hotel. The problems to date have centered far more on the annoying and frustrating details that impede the effort to get ready to work rather than any important subject connected with the arming and training of European forces.

Yesterday I went to see the British chiefs of staff. We had lunch at Claridge's and I immediately returned to this city. The general talk was about plans and schemes for organizing for the defense of Western Europe, with one eye on the possibilities of doing something to alleviate the bitterness of British popular reaction to the recent announcement of Fechteler as the supreme commander in the North Atlantic.[1] I personally believe we can do something by emphasizing the importance of the Mediterranean area command and announcing some British naval officer as the commander. (This command would not include control over the American naval forces given me for protection of my right flank, nor would it interfere in any way with my scheme of command for the protection of Western Europe.)

Admiral Sherman is coming to see me tomorrow with Admiral Carney.[2] I hope that we shall reach such clear understandings of what we are trying to do that I can push right ahead in forming up the various sub-sectors of this command, making announcements as to commanders, and thereafter getting on with the real job that we have. General Juin, whom I want for command of ground forces in the center, will not return to Paris for some days. I understand that I will have some difficulty with him because he will insist upon taking actual operational control of supporting air forces. But he does not see that such an organization will give both the American and British air forces the excuse to hold back on allocation of air units to this command. They will claim that the "ground" viewpoint is manifesting itself and that the air cannot afford to make sizeable allocations in an area where the air "will not be so used as to realize its maximum capabilities."

Of course, all this kind of talk is largely balderdash, but each of the services has its own little fetishes and prejudices and insists upon living by them. In our own way, we service people are not completely free of the kind of thing that motivates the ordinary or smalltime politician—this is the inability to shake loose from considerations of a short-term self-aggrandizement or advancement in favor of long-term, eventual good for all of us. (In spite of this statement, I still believe that the uniformed services produce a higher average of concern for the public good and selfless devotion to sheer duty than do any other professions or industrial or labor organizations.)

Right now, France is without a government. The one headed by Mr. Plevin has fallen, and we do not know when one can be successfully organized to take its place. Britain is torn apart by savage resentment against the government for consenting to Fechteler's appointment in the Atlantic. The source of this, of course, is England's traditional concern with the sea and the sea lanes that connect it to all other parts of its empire. Moreover, national prestige and glory have been damaged. This is the type of thing that should be foreseen by so-called statesmen and political leaders, but, instead, they just blunder along and leave the results of their errors for someone else to clean up. Too often, these poor victims are the men in uniform.

I am collecting a most able staff. I am particularly impressed with Schuyler and Anderson, two Americans. In addition, a little personal group I have made up of Gault, McCann, and Carroll are most unusual.[3] De Havilland, a Britisher on the council of national representatives, seems likewise to be a very capable person. Among the French officers I have not formed any real conclusions; but among the government officials who have just lost their places I liked Plevin, Schuman, and Moch very much indeed.[4]

On Wednesday (February 28, 1951) General Clay appeared before the senate joint committee and ably and persuasively advocated the wisdom of placing no present limit on American military aid to Europe. He was so much more effective and convincing in his approach than Marshall, Bradley, or any of the others that I cannot escape the fervent wish that he were our secretary of defense. So far as newspaper reports could convey the impression he made upon senators, it was profound.

MARCH 3, 1951

Admiral Sherman comes to see me today: March 3, Saturday.

Some days ago I read a remarkable paper on Soviets, by an Admiral Stevens. I think I'll put it in back of this book because, with minor exceptions, it represents my beliefs, exactly. But he states the thing clearly.[1]

MARCH 5, 1951

Don't think I'll write in this any more unless matter is purely personal or involves some of this political denial.

And one good thing about this dismaying and unattractive assignment is that I should be finally and fully removed from the personal political ambitions of others, which are reflected, often, in their presentations to me.

One of the men I've admired extravagantly is Herbert Hoover. I am forced to believe he's getting senile. God knows I'd personally like to get out of Europe and I'd like to see the United States able to sit at home and ignore the rest of the world. What a pleasing prospect, until you look at ultimate consequences, destruction.

MARCH 13, 1951

Each day we get a cabled summary of news from the United States. In general our summary concerns subjects connected only with SHAPE [Supreme Headquarters, Allied Powers in Europe] or some military subject, sometimes merely with me as an individual.

One phase of the reports now coming in reminds me that I never seem to catch up with the true intensity of American interest in any and all men who may be considered, even remotely, as presidential possibilities. I thought my coming to Europe would tend to still the gossip about me. Not only am I out of the States, I'm on a uniformed duty. But the nagging, speculation, and suspecting grows worse.

Today I received a cartoon from Detroit *Free Press* dated March 5.

Drew Pearson reports Senator McCarthy is digging up alleged dirt with which to smear me if I run for president.

Pegler hints darkly that by character and ability I'm something of a scoundrel and moron.

And so on.

Now, I realize that these curious people have a full right to their own convictions, and a right to talk about them. But it would seem to be the role of decency to avoid heaping poisonous criticism on the head of anyone who is doing only one thing, working like a dog just to preserve their right to say whatever they choose. At least they might wait until I by some word or token imply that I want a political career.

Actually my name is more often mentioned in dispatches as a possible president than it is as a slave, with one of the most irksome jobs ever designed by man.

MARCH 17, 1951

General de Lattre is to be here in a few minutes (at 8:45 A.M.) to see me reference his request for reinforcement for Indochina: the French have a knotty problem on that one—the campaign out there is a draining sore in their side. Yet if they quit and Indochina falls to Commies, it is easily possible that the entire Southeast Asia and Indonesia will go, soon to be followed by India. That prospect makes the whole problem one of interest to us all. I'd favor heavy reinforcement to get the thing over at once; but I'm convinced that no military victory is possible in that kind of theater. Even if Indochina were completely cleared of Communists, right across the border is China with inexhaustible manpower. Well, we'll see what General de Lattre has to say, but I know he'll want me to make a recommendation to the French government; this I shall not do (unless, of course, asked by the government itself).

Day before yesterday we sent in a particularly complete organizational system, including selectees for principal command assignments. If promptly approved it should do something to help European morale.

APRIL 9, 1951

Today I go to Germany to inspect some troops in each of the occupational (Western) zones. I shall be gone until a week from today.

The senate voted to send four divisions to Europe—if more are needed, it is the "sense of the Senate" that Congress should be consulted.

Curiously enough, in spite of the fact that I believe this particular action to be awkward, if not damaging to the course for which we are spending so much, I agree with the basic thought expressed by the Senate. If American public opinion does not support adequate reinforcement of Europe pending the development of adequate European force, and to inspire such development, then it is absurd for the president to send here a single soldier. I've tried to get everybody to see that a union of minds and hearts is the indispensable formula for success —if this union is not established then we must seek some alternative to collective security for the free world. Any alternative promises little more than tragic failure; this, it seems to me, is the basic truth that we at home, and Europe especially, must understand, now.

Yet with all the free world in an uproar because people believe that MacA. is trespassing on purely civilian functions, it becomes difficult for anyone in uniform (and especially me as the commander in Europe) to preach this truth unendingly. Every personal enemy and every communist would find some way of making capital out of the circumstance. So far as the personal part is concerned, I don't care one whit, but such people would not hesitate at damaging the NATO concept in order to attain their ends.

Had a nice note from Harold Stassen. Recently I exchanged notes with Governor Dewey (on basis of a columnist's report that he and I were deadly enemies). Bill Benton is coming to see me soon.

Jim Wise came to see me today. Reminded me to write a note to Bill Donovan regarding Columbia University. This I'll do as soon as possible. Maybe I have time before my next engagement.

APRIL 17, 1951

I have just returned from an inspection trip of Allied units in Germany. The trip was really more one of a country visit than an inspection, but I did contact small units at their daily training—ceremonies were forbidden.

On Wednesday last, while visiting in the French zone, a reporter told me that MacArthur had been relieved by order of the president from his duties in Japan. I naturally refused to comment and shall continue to do so.

The MacArthur issue, one has to suspect, was so ancient a problem to Eisenhower that its continuation over so many years had worn out his ability to think about it; long ago he had known of MacArthur's difficult behavior—the personal quirks, the ability to antagonize—and the Truman-MacArthur quarrel could not have surprised him. To be sure, silence was his only possible public stance.

APRIL 23, 1951

Had to stop. Since writing above I've been very busy both in the office and traveling. Tomorrow I go to Italy for two days, to be followed almost at once by a trip to Holland, Belgium, Norway, and Denmark.

Admiral Lemmonies (French) has joined us as a naval deputy. While the need for such an assistant is not so obvious as in some of the other cases, yet his presence assures that France's maritime interests (which are, of course, considerable) will not be neglected by this headquarters.

He (Admiral L.) has given me a preliminary memo of his views. They conform almost exactly to the principles I urged upon the interested staffs last January. (Use naval power on flanks.)

It is difficult to assess the mental attitude of Europe. Gruenther and I had lunch today with French chiefs of staff. They seem fatalistic, if not apathetic.

More the same day.

Iran. Numbers of people (today an American oilman) have been saying that the position of the West, specifically Britain, is deteriorating rapidly in Iran. They say the situation is getting far worse than most realize.

Lord knows what we'd do without Iranian oil.

My talks with British friends indicate that that country is alive to the danger, but no one yet has told me the real trouble. My American friend merely said that we'd better get busy and give the Iranians an acceptable contract, "or else."

In Iran the British had drifted into trouble by refusing to make a more generous contract for Iranian oil. The Anglo-Iranian Oil Company had driven such a sharp contract that it was unacceptable to Iran's rising nationalists. The position of the shah in this British-Iranian imbroglio of the early 1950s was ambiguous, for he too was a nationalist but he was very young and thus far in his career had not shown himself to be a strong character. The prime minister, Dr. Mohammed Mossadegh, a rich landowner and ardent nationalist, took over the oil company; British technicians walked off their jobs, and there was talk of drastic measures. In the end, Mossadegh lost his job; the shah reasserted a weak control; and the Iranian situation rocked along for another generation before it exploded.

APRIL 27, 1951

Have just completed an inspection trip to conventional forces in North Italy. Spirit is high in that section—the morale of the troops I saw was surprisingly good. These units included, however, both Alpine and Bersaglieri formations, traditionally elite groupments in the Italian forces.

General Marras seems most capable. He is the chairman of their joint chiefs of staff. The general in charge of the air force is also (to all appearances) a most efficient leader. General Castiglione, who is to be named by Marras to command the ground forces in our "southern flank" organization, seems thoughtful and almost scholarly. I don't know whether he can produce the necessary "punch."

Cappa (army chief of staff) is fairly old and I assume will soon retire. He is fat but appears energetic.

The armament of the Italian forces is a bewildering assortment of obsolete and cast-off equipment from several nations—United States, United Kingdom, and Italy. Training ammunition is meager, even though I was told that Italy makes fine ammunition and would be happy to make its own if the United States would let it have the necessary specifications.

I hope we can give Italy a few T-26 tanks, at least. Thus each armored formation could have a tiny core of fairly well-armored and armed vehicles. A few Shermans are all they have in anything larger than the T-24 (light) tank.

In the United States the "great debate," which is nothing more than a heterogeneous collection of personal, partisan, and private quarrels, still rages. For most it has now been simplified (oversimplified I mean) into a Truman-MacArthur struggle.[1] How tragic that, at this critical stage in world history, we should be torn apart by human selfishness. We should, by all means, continue to debate seriously the various means and methods open to us for waging effective war against communism. There is much room for instructive discussion and argument, but we have not a minute to waste, nor any right to weaken ourselves, in the wicked business of attempting to satisfy personal ambition.

As far as I know, every senior officer in this headquarters would like to be somewhere else. Every man here is serving because of an overpowering sense of duty and of urgency in human affairs. It is too bad that they have to combat daily the pessimism and discouragement born of a realization that in London, Washington, and Paris, unworthy men either guide our destinies or are fighting bitter battles in the hope of getting an opportunity to guide our destinies.

If ever we needed moral and intellectual integrity, now is that time. I thank God (and I mean it) for the few who still hold the respect of the masses. For my family and for America, the only real passions of my life, I shall continue to work as effectively and optimistically as I have the strength to do. But I desperately wish that there could be now established in places of influence in the free world new, young, and virile civil and military leaders devoted only to their respective countries, to decency, and to security.

MAY 15, 1951

Bradley, with a party, is coming to Europe on June 2. Collins and wife will be here before that. Each will stay two to three days.

We are having a stream of American visitors. Publishers, industrialists, professors, etc. I give time to all and am astonished at the lack of knowledge of basic facts on the part of many who are supposed to be educated.

Today I intended to get out for exercise, golfing with a lot of war friends and with Mr. Hilton and Joe Binns (Waldorf-Astoria).[1] Rain intervened. Possibly Saturday will be OK.

Just read an article by Bertrand Russell, philosopher. Very good indeed as a mode or code of living today.

MAY 30, 1951 (DECORATION DAY IN THE UNITED STATES)

Another Decoration Day finds us still adding to the number of graves that will be decorated in future years. Men are stupid.

MacArthur seems to have retired into the Waldorf Towers, from which stronghold he issues statements and occasionally emerges to see a baseball game. The first he does through Whitney—who, I think, is one of the Old Chief's mistakes.[1]

I cannot much blame MacA.—I get the impression that he is in a state of "watchful waiting." For what, I wouldn't know, but I do know that in his position I'd be after the bass of Wisconsin, the trout of Wyoming, or vacationing on the beach. Recently I wrote to him—had a nice reply. While I'm determined to stay aloof from all the current snarling and fighting in the United States, I'm most of all determined never to get into the "personality" kind of argument. In that respect the military men (especially including MacA.) have been exemplary.

Messages reaching me since the MacA. fight began are even more insistent than previously that I am going to get involved in 1952 politics. In the back of this book I've placed a couple of samples.[2]

JUNE 4, 1951

Dinner last evening with Paul Hoffman, Henry Ford, and Mr. Paul Helms (of California). Paul has just published a book, *We Can Win the Peace*. He is determined I'll have to get into politics and he is sad—he knows how I feel about it and agrees with me. I'd like to see him in politics—I'd resign to work for him.

JUNE 5, 1951

Lawrence Whiting (Chicago) and Clare Francis both came to see me today. The same story on the political side. One thing is certain. The average United States citizen is confused, if not fearful and afraid. Otherwise there'd be no feeling that I should get into the political field. The feeling is, of course, not so widespread as my informants would have me believe (a human generalizes quickly from a few incidents) but even its meager existence is disappointing.

After some months in Europe, Eisenhower began to believe that a United States of Europe might be the solution to the petty jurisdictions that confronted reformers of the ways of the Continent. The business of cooperation so necessary to the proper functioning of NATO involved so much diplomacy, and his time was so taken with the diplomatic discussion, that this conclusion was almost natural; perhaps he was looking for a way out. Whether he realized how ancient was this dream of European unity is hard to say, or likewise whether he understood how some visionaries of the 1920s, such as Count Coudenhove-Kalergi, whose experience went back to the Austro-Hungarian empire, had tried without success to propagandize for a United States of Europe. It is possible that he sensed how the economic revival of Europe, because of the Marshall Plan and the Korean War boom, was making the ancient rivalries of Europe and Europeans ever more attractive, for economic prosperity gave time to think about such matters. Maybe at the time he was writing, June 1951, the last possible chance for unifying the Continent was disappearing in the tides of postwar prosperity, which were beginning to roll. The subject was intriguing.

JUNE 11, 1951

I am coming to believe that Europe's security problem is never going to be solved satisfactorily until there exists a United States of Europe, to include all countries now in NATO: West Germany and (I think) Sweden, Spain, and Jugoslavia, with Greece definitely in if Jugoslavia is (if necessary, the United Kingdom could be omitted).

It seems scarcely necessary to enumerate the problems that arise out of or are exaggerated by the division of West Europe into so many sovereign nations. Norway is short of manpower, Italy 'way over. Italy has excess productive capacity in vehicles and plants. Many others have none at all. France and Germany (the key powers of the region) are on opposite sides in many problems because of French hatred for the Boche as well as the fear of a restored Western Germany. Each nation watches its neighbor to see that the neighbor's contribution to the common security is at least equal to the first nation's ratio, and none is ever so convinced.

As SHAPE I have no ministries to take over ministerial functions in finance, construction, policy, etc., etc. The weak, inarticulated mechanism that tries to serve as the NATO overhead is futile.

I think that the real and bitter problems of today would instantly come within the limits of capabilities in solving them, if we had this single government.

Moreover, I believe inspired leaders could put it across. But everyone is too cautious, too fearful, too lazy, and too ambitious (personally).

So many advantages would flow from such a union that it is a tragedy for the whole human race that it is not done at once.

American help, which could soon be radically reduced both in amount and duration, would quickly render such an organization immune to attack. With this are problems solved—all harder ones would soon disappear. I could write a volume on the subject.

Local governments would not necessarily be identical. It would be necessary that each adopt and observe a simple "bill of rights." Socialist Sweden could live alongside a capitalist Germany, but the elimination of trade barriers and all economic and political restraint on free movements.

JUNE 14, 1951

John and Barbie with David and Ann, and Min, arrived yesterday.[1] Weather, fine.

Mr. Foster of ECA was here today.[2] He paints a sorry picture of Washington —the mere fact of presidential support almost certain to defeat any bill before Congress. Taft, Wherry, et al. (and especially Kem and McCarthy) are disciples of hate—hate and curse anything that belongs to the administration.[3] Heaven knows there is plenty for which to criticize the administration legitimately and decently and strongly, but what they are doing is apt to make HST an "underdog" and backfire on them. How we need some brains (on both sides) and some selflessness.

There seems to be a bad shortage of machine tools. When we get over this emergency I am going to take as one element of my personal ambitions, that of preaching of the need for machine tools as part of military preparation until some d--- administration will take the necessary measures. I've heard the same story time after time and it seems to me we should learn.

Also in stocking raw materials. I thought I worked on this one in 1946, 1947, 1948. But when this emergency lets up I'm really going to town.

JUNE 25, 1951

On Saturday night, the twenty-third, we received word that Pupah (John Sheldon Doud, Mamie's father) had died. He has been in precarious health for many years —when I met him in 1915 he had a blood pressure of 240 and weighed that many pounds, but, as always in such case, the finality of death came as a shock. Min (Mamie's mother) was visiting us at the time and so I sent her, Mamie, John, and Dr. Snyder off to Denver. They left here at midnight, Saturday. This morning we received news that the party had arrived safely. . . .[1]

Mr. Potofsky came to see me.[2]

Opposes any thought of dealing with Spain—quite bitter about it.

Insists that for every advantage we would obtain we could lose so many friends as to suffer a net loss. There is a definite chance he is completely right, particularly if our efforts to deal with Spain place another early drain on our scarce items and raw materials. All these erstwhile enemies and near-enemies want the "world" and sometimes they are close to arrogant in saying what they will not give as quid pro quo. Our lesson with Russia from 1941 to 1946 ought to be remembered.

The German problem—the need to get West Germany into NATO, so as to add German divisions to those of the NATO Allies—was Eisenhower's most acute difficulty as supreme commander in 1951–1952. The Allies were, of course, reluctant to move on this issue. Only a relatively short time had elapsed since the end of hostilities in 1945; they could not forget Nazi Germany's immense military power and immense capacity for evil; the turnaround in Allied friendships (hostility toward the Russians, friendliness with the Germans) was coming too quickly. Everything was moving in the direction of bringing the Germans into NATO, for the Marshall Plan had revived West Germany's economy; the next step after economics was politics (on its way through formation of a West German government in 1949); the third step would obviously be military. But how to take it?

JULY 2, 1951

Tomorrow I go to London to keep three dates, made long before I took this job: (1) memorial service at St. Paul's for twenty-eight thousand American dead of World War II who lost their lives while serving in Britain; (2) dinner of English Speaking Union; and (3) dinner with Winston Churchill, Pug Ismay, Cunningham, Portal (Brookie is out of country).

More and more political stuff these days.

I'm saying "nuts," because they urge me to "get into the fight."

The German problem grows acute. The Western Allies are not too imaginative in coming forward with ideas that will safeguard West Europe (allaying fears of Germany) and will at the same time get Germany wholeheartedly on our side in the struggle against communism. If I believed in taking time out to "regret" I could write several pages on some of the things Clay and I warned against in late

NATO   [197]

1945, and how we were told to mind our own business.[1] Chief of all our worries was that the world would come to be divided East vs. West and that our policies then in vogue would succeed in putting Germany in the other side, at least in making her ineffective on our side. As of this moment we ought to be showing Germany how definitely her national interests will be served by sticking and working with us.

JULY 10, 1951

On Sunday morning I was visited by Charlie White, president of Republic Steel. His principal reason for looking me up was to say that he had just completed a close examination into the coal and steel industry in Britain. He is convinced that Britain is again going downhill economically and that the real reason is that they are not producing enough coal. He believes that labor is not performing efficiently and that management is not providing the incentives that will get labor to develop. He feels that since the government has completely nationalized these industries, political leaders must participate in the problem and get busy, or slow disaster will overtake Britain. He feels that coal production must increase in Britain to the point where that country can again export coal.

This whole conversation was so interesting that I asked Mr. White to meet with representatives from my headquarters and possibly the Economic Co-operation Administration headquarters. To this he enthusiastically agreed, because he thinks that with pressures exerted from the right directions, Britain can save herself.

Mr. White then launched into a description of conditions, present and future, within the United States, as he sees them.

His first hypothesis is that in the next election there must be a Republican victory and that government has fallen so low in the minds of most Americans, that it can exert no leadership and has no prestige. This condition, he believes, influences adversely our position abroad. He thinks that the Republicans have been very stupid and have again and again allowed internal fights and personal struggles for nomination to be the cause of Republican defeat in general elections. He desperately hopes that such a fight may be avoided this time. At this point he brings in a prophecy concerning the business cycle in the United States. He says that in spite of the rearmament program, we are due for a recession, although probably not a full-scale depression, in the United States. He is certain that this will occur as the rearmament program tapers off. In support of this he quotes figures concerning the annual output of passenger cars and refrigerators as being far in excess of the annual consumption rate in the United States. He says this observation applies to many other items. (While he gave approximate figures in several items, it seems unnecessary to repeat them here.) As a result of this situation, he believes that the man elected president of the United States at this coming election cannot possibly be reelected in 1956. His next argument is that the Republicans must have two acceptable candidates to offer the public, one to win in 1952 and restore "sound business practices" to the United States, and the second to win the election in 1956.

He says that he speaks for no one except himself. He has worked out his plan by himself. This plan is that Mr. Taft should be elected in 1952, that I should support him, and that I should accept the post of secretary of defense in the cabinet. (He apparently does not know that it is against the law for a soldier to fill that particular post and that General Marshall is filling it now only by virtue of a special dispensation from Congress.) The scheme would be for Mr. Taft to agree in advance that he would not seek reelection and that I should be promised this by the Republican leaders.

I told Charlie White that, of course, I was flattered that he should think of me in these terms, but so far as I was concerned (1) I now have a job of transcendent importance to the United States. Because it is a military post, I do not find it possible to participate in American partisan politics. (2) I have always insisted that I would never be connected in any way with politics, even after I could finally lay aside my uniform, except in such exceptional circumstances where a duty was clearly indicated. In this case, I do not see any call to duty.

Mr. White left after repeating that the idea was solely his and not to be repeated to anyone else.*

JULY 13, 1951

Mr. Paul Miller of Gannett newspapers thinks I'll soon have to say whether I'm a Republican or Democrat. I think he agrees now with my contention that a soldier has to keep his mouth shut on such matters.

AUGUST 6, 1951

Paul Hoffman, John Cowles, Paul Helms (California) came to see me.[1]

They recognize that I have an important duty in this post.

They believe that I have (rather, will have) a more important duty, to accept Republican nomination.

They wanted to talk about the business of making it possible (at what they call the "proper" time) for the Republican party to place this duty upon me. They see of course that the requirements of the military post I now occupy are such that I must keep my mouth closed on all partisan matters. The problem that they discuss at great length is the procedure of shifting from a military post to that of a receptive candidate for the presidency next spring.

I've told them, as I tell all, that I'll certainly always try to do my duty to the country, when I know what that duty is. As of now I have a duty; I cannot yet even describe the circumstances that would be conclusive in convincing me that my duty had changed to that of assuming a role in the political field. But I stuck

---

*Mr. White came back to lunch at my office on Thursday, July 12. He has become convinced that American businessmen can do much to wake up European businessmen to the need for strong leadership in support of the common security. He is going to work at it.

to one thing; if I have to help to prove that I have such a mission then the factor of duty becomes rather slim.

SEPTEMBER 25, 1951

For the first time in years I've seen a "political poll" (as usual, conducted by Gallup) that puts me well down the list in the order of preference among Republicans. It is comforting—maybe the pressure will ease up. I hear that the Democrats still rate me high, but that causes me no concern. I could never imagine feeling any compelling duty in connection with a Democratic movement of any kind.

OCTOBER 4, 1951

The temptation grows to issue a short, definite statement saying no (in almost arbitrary language) to all the arguments that seek to convince me that I should accept (if offered) the Republican nomination for the presidency. Some go so far as to say I should so state publicly, now. Others even that I should start seeking and scheming for the nomination. All this last is rot—I will never seek any nomination. But as to the first the difficulty arises in the mere attempt to be honest. If I wanted to be president I'd resign today and start traveling the United States about January 1. But the personal belief that I could do a good job would have to be so strong as to make me feel justified in leaving this onerous and strenuous post of duty. That is impossible. The only way I could leave this duty is to believe that a great section of the United States want me to undertake a higher one. This could be a real draft, something that all agree cannot happen. In this I take real comfort because it will at least eliminate the necessity of my making any personal decision as to my own suitability. I scarcely mean that, because no one is really suitable; I think I mean that I will never have to decide whether or not I'd make a relatively good president. In the meantime, I can give my best to this task and hope that my silence will help politicians to consider the relative suitability of those that do want the nomination.

Of course, because of the remote, very remote, possibility that persons may, in spite of my silence, succeed in producing a grassroots draft, I have to think more about the subject than is involved merely in a negative attitude. When people like Paul Hoffman, Governors Dewey and Stassen, Senators Duff, Carlson, Lodge, etc., great friends like Clay, Clark, Roberts, etc., etc., and others like Craig (American Legion commander of last year) all begin to assert that I have a duty, it is not easy to just say NO.[1] I hear that a petition is circulating in Abilene to get a 90 percent demand from my hometown. I don't know what the whole state would say but I do know that ex-Governor Woodring (Democrat) and ex-Senator Darby (Republican) both believe I should run. No more of this—I'll just have to rock along. But I'm growing concerned about one thing: the degree to which all this might hurt the job of establishing a collective, cooperative apparently gave sympathetic consideration to my views regarding the reducing of Economic Co-operation Administration money) but when I do become convinced that the constant newspaper and other speculation is hurting our national effort then I'm going to do something. My replies (written or verbal) to everyone always include a paragraph substantially as follows:

"The job I am on requires the support of the vast body of Americans. These Americans have the right to believe that their agent is serving all of them and is not seeking to advance the fortune of any group as compared to another. For me to admit while in this post, or to imply, a partisan political loyalty would properly be resented by thinking Americans and would be doing a disservice to our country, for it would interfere with accomplishment of the job assigned to me. The successful outcome of this venture is too vital to our nation's welfare to permit any semblance of partisan allegiance by me."

OCTOBER 5, 1951

Letters from John Cowles and Lucius Clay are purely political. I'm amused to note that even good friends finally fall prey to the idea that anyone would want to be president. Not me.

OCTOBER 10, 1951

The NATO meeting at Ottawa set up a new committee, appropriately nicknamed the "wise men" because the purpose is to solve the problems that the existing civil machinery has failed to solve. The several nations have promised to provide given amounts of military force on a specified time schedule. This so-called "plan" does not contemplate a scale of effort that will meet the "requirements" for the defense of Europe as estimated by a combination of several military bodies. Yet already we've found that these schedules will not be met— the effort is too big, say the politicians, if we are to avoid economic collapse. Since economic collapse in Europe would spell defeat of the NATO concept, it would appear we have a case of the immovable object and the irresistible force.

The big factor omitted from this kind of talk is morale. Civilian leaders talk about the state of morale in a given country as if it were a sort of uncontrollable event or phenomenon, like a thunderstorm or a cold winter. The soldier leader looks on morale as one of the great factors (the greatest) in all his problems, but also as one about which he can and must do something.

The "wise men" must learn this lesson. Materialistic factors are important, but much more is involved here. Each should start, in his own country, a crusade to explain the purpose of NATO—the protection of a free way of life. The threats to freedom should be identified. The obstacles to providing defense against those threats should be clearly defined. The hopelessness of alternative solutions should be impressed upon us, proved by the facts of the case.

The self-interest of each nation in the success of the whole should be demonstrated. On this basis of understanding of facts, on this sense of values, we should develop the highest possible head of steam (morale). The job is just that, because, in total assets—raw materials, men, intellectual capacity of peoples, productiveness, scientific skill, appeal of a cause—we are immeasurably stronger than the iron curtain countries.

I hope the wise men will see this. Certainly I'm going now to try to make them see it. (I'm scheduled for half an hour talk before them.)

OCTOBER 15, 1951

The authorities in Washington are slowly but necessarily coming to the point where they tell some of the truth about America's production program. I begged officials (when they were asking me to come over to this job) to know exactly what we were doing. I suppose they thought I was merely hopeful of ducking what we all know was a thorny assignment—at least they merely looked annoyed when I asked whether we were certain we knew the depth of the responsibilities we were assuming and knew that we could discharge them. Oh hell, now we cry, delay, delay, delay!

Since the 1880s, when the United States Navy revived after years of neglect and decay, the bulk of American military expenditure had gone into the navy, and Eisenhower had come of age and joined the army at a time when, just before American entrance into the First World War, the navy was clearly trying to be queen of the seas and certainly was the queen of the American military budget. In the interwar years the navy ate up more budget by far than did the army. During the Second World War the expenditures of all services were easy to get through Congress and there was no argument, but after the war the problem of maintaining the huge American postwar navy again arose in all of its complexity. Eisenhower in Europe saw the forces of America's NATO Allies almost bereft of military equipment except for hand-me-downs from the war, and he had the impression, which was as good as truth, that the Russian forces were reequipping. When he paid a visit to the Sixth Fleet in the Mediterranean and again beheld all the expensive naval hardware, he was inclined to think the time had come to spend money more systematically.

OCTOBER 18, 1951

Just back from a trip to the Mediterranean Sea, where I visited the Sixth Fleet for three days. The more I look at present-day armaments, of all kinds, including the most advanced (so-called), the more I'm convinced that we should institute a basic study at home to examine into the economics of national security.

On a panel designated for the purpose I'd ask the following to serve: six leading manufacturing industrialists (working executives, not figureheads), six bankers, six lawyers, six doctors and public health officials, six Red Cross officials (and professors in social services), six labor leaders, six (working) shop superintendents and foremen, six public utility executives (railroads, telephones, etc.), six labor representatives from same industries, six experts from each fighting service, six governmental representatives.

(My plan would be to have at least two of each group of six meeting continually.)

I think we should go clear back to methods of damaging the enemy in any possible war of the foreseeable future.

Then let us examine ways and means of inflicting that damage. The most economical and efficient methods should be evolved. We might find out just where in the world the several kinds of tactical organizations would be most efficient and thus we might begin to get a clear idea of real efficiency in peacetime organization. I personally think we are pursuing certain programs merely because they sound efficient; we are afraid not to do them. Yet they are expensive and are driving us (along with a lot of political expenditures) straight toward inflation of an uncontrollable character. Wouldn't the monster in the Kremlin rejoice to see us admit insolvency.

Our heavy tank program, hydrogen bomb, B-36, very heavy carrier, and similar programs should all be dissected from the standpoint of comparative purposes, special and unique capabilities, inescapable need, duplicatory effort, luxury. In the same way the whole organization of the army, navy (including marines), air, should be ruthlessly pulled apart and examined in order to get down to the country's requirements.

We should reexamine our whole philosophy of defense, in its foreign and domestic aspects, and do what is intelligent for democracies to do. Industrial mobilization could save our nation (if properly planned for) when our whole peacetime military strength might cost us ten times as much and largely fail in a [illegible]. In 1941 our peacetime navy took a terrible blow on the first day of the war, but the navy built after the war started did a great job in both oceans, particularly against Japan, where it really, with air force help, won the war. And this does not ignore the work of the great divisions that won and held the bases from which air attacks were made.

If we don't have the objective, industry-government-professional examination that will show us where and how to proceed in this armament business, we will go broke and still have inefficient defenses. We can have security without paying the price of national bankruptcy, if we will put brains in the balance. We cannot afford prejudice, preconceived notions, fallacies, duplications, luxuries, fancied political advantage, etc., etc. Our country is at stake. Many will give her lip service; few will give her self-sacrifice, sweat, and brains.

In the autumn of 1951 politics in the United States began to become pressing, for Eisenhower's Republican friends told him that Senator Taft could take the nomination if Eisenhower sat back and waited for a draft. Taft wanted the presidency and was after it. He possessed almost no personal magnetism—he had as much warmth as an iceberg—and the predictions of Eisenhower's friends that Taft if nominated would lose the election were as true as any predictions could be, short of being verified by history. In the autumn of 1951 it was clear to most

*Republican leaders that Eisenhower would accept a draft—his various statements
always spoke of the possibility of assuming a duty, a political duty. Naturally he
did not want to get out and push for the nomination, to thrust the duty on
himself. And yet if he sat back, Taft might win and take the party down the road
to defeat, just like all of the ill-starred Republican candidates beginning in 1932.
President Truman, a skilled politician if there ever was one, believed Taft would
be a pushover for any Democrat, and ardently hoped the Republicans would be
stupid enough to nominate him. For all thinking Republicans the prospect of a
Taft candidacy was horrifying.*

OCTOBER 29, 1951

Today I was visited by several individuals who brought up the political struggle
in the United States. Chief among these were Mr. Weir, head of the National
Steel Company, and Mr. Harold Talbott, who, as I understand it, has been
associated with Republican politics for some years.

In general the argument of both men was the same. It is about as follows:

1. In the absence of some serious opposition, Mr. Taft is going to capture the
Republican nomination for president before the convention itself meets. In other
words, when the convention convenes, there will be so many delegates pledged
to him that opposition will be useless.

2. Mr. Taft can get in an election the solid vote of the oldline Republicans,
but no others. Specifically, Mr. Talbott said he could get no votes from anybody
under thirty years of age. The further statement was made that in our country
today are 40 percent Democrats, 31 percent Republicans, and 28 percent independents. This last figure was completely astonishing to me and I doubt its
accuracy.

3. The proof is clear, according to these gentlemen, that Taft cannot be elected
president of the United States. Fundamentally, they believe that Taft's lack of
appeal is the belief in the United States that he represents a reactionary type of
thinking, and especially that he represents a reactionary wing of the Republican
party.

4. Mr. Truman, they believe, would beat Mr. Taft very easily. Mr. Weir said
that any other Democrat could likewise beat Mr. Taft.

5. Four years more of Democratic, uninterrupted, government in our country
will put us so far on the road to socialism that there will be no return to a free
enterprise. They firmly believe that we would follow the example of Britain until
we became fully socialized, which means, of course, fully regimented.

6. The only way to halt this chain of events and to give the United States a
breathing space is for me to make a proper move within a reasonable time
(although neither man stated the exact time) to allow all elements of Republican
party, other than the supporters of Taft, to nominate me as president. They think
that I would be easily elected because of what they call my appeal among
independents and also among certain sections of the Democratic party.

These representations happen to coincide with four letters that I received today from people at home (one of them completely unknown to me), outlining the same argument. The whole business is merely repetitive and, except for the utter seriousness with which it is presented, it grows very monotonous. It is certainly burdensome.

In reply, I said to these men as I have said before:

1. I do not want to be president of the United States, and I want no other political office or political connection of any kind.

2. I am now on a job in which success is of the most tremendous importance to the future of the United States.

3. One of the great factors in producing success in this job is support from the bulk of the American population. Consequently, I have no right to announce any partisan leanings of any kind, because to do so would jeopardize the great project on which the United States is spending so much money and on which her future so clearly depends.

4. I entered upon this post only from a sense of duty—I certainly had to sacrifice much in the way of personal convenience, advantage, and congenial constructive work when I left New York. I will never leave this post for any other kind of governmental task except in response to a clear call to duty. I will not be a participant in any movement that attempts to secure for me a nomination because I believe that the presidency is something that should never be sought, just as I believe, of course, that it could never be refused. What future circumstances could convince me that I had a duty to enter the political arena, I am not prepared to say. I simply do not know what they could be. I merely admit that, as of now, I would consider the nomination of which they speak, if accomplished without any direct or indirect assistance or connivance on my part, to place upon me a transcendent duty.

5. Because of these convictions, if ever I should decide that I have a political duty to perform, it would be incumbent upon me instantly to submit my resignation to the president.

It is difficult indeed to maintain the attitude I tried to explain to my visitors. It would be much easier to simply have done with the whole business by arbitrarily declining to give it any thought whatsoever. Possibly I shall do this yet. As of now, I see nothing to do but to keep my mouth shut.

OCTOBER 30, 1951

Mr. Colby Chester came in this morning to repeat the same argument. He also brought to me a letter from a Texas mother.

NOVEMBER 9, 1951

Senator Benton visited me to show that I have no true spiritual and intellectual affinity with the Republicans. His arguments have been made to me before, but he had a hard time when I asked him about some of the Democratic stalwarts, McKellar et al.[1] He merely insisted that there are more ignorant, venal, repulsive individuals in positions of influence in the Republican party than in the Democratic.

Tom Campbell came in the afternoon. He doesn't care what party I'm in—prefers Republican liberals—but says United States demands me in politics.

NOVEMBER 10, 1951

This morning Congressman Javits (my district in New York) tells me that I must lead, instruct, and exhort on basic issues in America. Because we traditionally think of a president as our only real leader there is much talk of me for presidency. (He is one working in this direction.) But what the United States really wants of me, he says, is to give the country my convictions, opinions, and information, particularly in the field of foreign affairs.

NOVEMBER 16, 1951

Paul Hoffman and "Tex" Moore (chairman of the board, Time, Inc.) came to see me four or five days ago. The purpose was (as always) to convince me I must get into the political business. I replied (as always) that any word of mine on this subject before I was relieved from current responsibilities would be flatly negative. Since such a relief doesn't seem logical (except in response to some command situation), I again urged that the progressive Republicans get behind someone else and work. To my mind Lodge, Hoffman, Driscoll, or, possibly, Governor Petersen of Nebraska could be built up if the necessary work would be done.[1] I'd be delighted to see any of them occupy the president's chair. The trouble is that the practical politician just dismisses such an idea with, "It can't be done." And yet we can sell Crazy Crystals, Hauser's book, and Pepsi-Cola![2]

(Incidentally my real choice for president, by virtue of character, understanding, administrative ability, and personality, is my youngest brother, Milton.)

Today Mr. Bradford, vice-president of United Press, came in with the same story.

General Bradley called this A.M. He was accompanied by Vice-Admiral Davis. They wanted to discuss the Rome meeting of NATO. They fear that the question of incorporating Greece and Turkey into a NATO military command may be brought up and wanted to discuss possibilities with me. The real complication arises out of the insistence of both countries that they must be in SHAPE—they will not, initially at least, agree to their incorporation into a Mideast command, to be headed by a British supremo. Last month I told Bradley that the Mideast command was certain to be a "can of worms." Many returning travelers have told me that the Greeks and Turks have a curious belief that under this headquarters they'd be safe—in a Mideast command they'd be in a dangerous situation. I am afraid there was not much skill used in making the approach to the Greeks and Turks; they are seemingly determined to oppose the simple and easy solution to the organizational question. The October meetings between standing group and those two nations got nowhere.

NOVEMBER 24, 1951

Jean Monnet came to see me. He cannot go to the Rome meetings and is anxious that I stress the need for European amalgamation in political as well as the earlier steps involved in Schuman Plan and European army.[1] Since I believe implicitly in the idea, I shall do so, even if some of the politicos present resent my intrusion into their field. America has spent billions in ECA and is spending more billions in MDAP [Military Defense Assistance Plan], and much of it will be sheer waste unless Europe coalesces.[2] Denmark, Holland, Belgium, Luxembourg, France, Italy, and Western Germany should form one federated state. To help this America could afford to spend a lot, because we'd get something successful, strong, sturdy.

But the politicos throw up their hands in fright and hopelessness. I doubt that even America could get many of them to fight courageously for this vitally essential development. (I made a speech last February 3 in London on the subject.)

Day before yesterday I completed a trip to welcome the Canadian brigade and the Twenty-eighth and Forty-third United States Divisions to Europe. The men of all units seem to me exceptional: possibly my advancing age makes all young men look intelligent, spirited, strong.

Today nine congressmen came to see me. Subject: "Expenditures in the Executive Departments." I'm to be questioned about centralized procurement agencies—on the basis of past experience, not on my present job. I have enough to do; I grow weary having to give attention to someone else's task. The committee could learn more by having an organization of efficiency engineers and staying right in Washington than it can by globe trotting for a solid year.

DECEMBER 11, 1951

A day or so ago I received a comforting letter from Cabot Lodge, who has been selected by a number of Republican politicians, of the progressive wing, as their leader in the effort to nominate me for the presidency. He says that the project is hopeless without my active preconvention cooperation. That settles the whole matter. As to the path of duty in the possible case of an honest Republican draft I could have (do have) honest doubts. But there is no slightest doubt in my mind as to the impropriety, almost the illegality, of any preconvention activity as long as I'm on this job. So, since I cannot in good conscience quit here, my reaction is "Hurrah." I've just prepared a letter to Cabot saying that he and his friends must stop the whole thing, now.

The Rome meetings were, in many ways, highly valuable and, certainly, interesting. Because there was no startling development to hand to the press the reports have been of a pessimistic and cynical tenor. In spite of difficulties (and Lord knows they are big) there is no cause to despair.

DECEMBER 15, 1951

Governor Stassen came to see me. He is trying to get the Republican nomination but calculates his chances as very low. But he feels that by trying he keeps the party from surrendering to the reactionaries. He is still asserting that if I will enter the race before "it becomes too late" he will immediately announce himself as my lieutenant. The nice thing about his visit was that he asked me nothing— he, as he said, merely reported developments, and restated his position, frequently given to me during the many months since 1948. In any event, I said nothing except that "Do as you please. I'm busy at my duties. I shall never, in advance of a convention, indicate a political intention."*

From every side, in Europe, I get complaints reference Britain's attitude toward a European army.

DECEMBER 21, 1951

Two or three days ago the prime minister of Great Britain made a visit to SHAPE. He was accompanied by the British ambassador to France and by Anthony Eden, the foreign secretary.

Our talk largely centered around the concept of a European army. General Gruenther has made a rather extensive summary of the conversation, but it is easy to see that the plans presently under discussion on the Continent do not conform with the ideas Mr. Churchill has had in mind. Consequently, he is very lukewarm —it is better to say he is instinctively opposed—toward them. However, since we here agree with him that the attempt to make Great Britain a participant in the European army project would only slow the matter up, it is clear that his personal opinions have no real significance except as they affect the warmth of his political and moral support.

It is quite true that Europe really needs the morale and support of Great Britain; several of the continental countries have become accustomed to look to Britain for this kind of leadership. We had a very warm discussion on the whole matter, and, while I most certainly did not convince him, I am sure that he realizes he must do something in the way of giving us the kind of support we ask. He is quite ready to admit that, in the long run, a politically unified Western Europe is essential to the welfare and security of the free world. He is likewise ready to admit that we should try to make the formation of a European army one of the steppingstones toward such a political union. But he balks at the idea of

*(December 21, 1951) With reference to the Stassen visit, I intended to summarize the account he gave to me. He has done that himself in the form of a note which I have just received. It is contained in my correspondence files under his name.

attempting to set up a single ministry to deal with the administrative and other ministerial problems of a European army and will go no further, in his own convictions, than to propose and support some kind of a coalition force. In other words, he wants to go back to exactly the thing we had in World War II and merely multiply the number of participating nations (and most certainly multiplying the difficulties).

Frankly, I believe that, subconsciously, my great friend is trying to relive the days of his greatest glory. He has taken upon his own shoulders, as he did in World War II, the dual position of prime minister and of defense minister. He is struggling hard to bring about a recognition of specially close ties between America and Britain and is soon to depart for the United States in furtherance of this purpose. I am back in Europe in a status that is not too greatly different, in his mind, from that which I held with respect to him in World War II. To my mind, he simply will not think in terms of today but rather only those of the war years. (Yet it is a curious fact that, in spite of his insistence that men must wear their own national uniforms, wave their own national flags, sing their own national hymns, and serve under their own national officers, it is still true that in the late summer of 1942 he offered to put British soldiers in American uniforms in order to facilitate their entry into North Africa. For that one moment, he saw a special need and, therefore, acted in accordance with that need.)

My regretful opinion is that the prime minister no longer absorbs new ideas; exhortation and appeals to the emotions and sentiment still have some effect on him—exposition does not.

1952

The new year that was to see such a change in Eisenhower's personal fortunes dawned for him like many other new years, with humdrum responsibilities occupying his time and threatening to occupy his mind. The conversation with Churchill had been depressing, for how could he deal with so formidable a personality as the great man of British politics, the man who had taken a stand against Hitler when such a stand was not popular, and whom time had justified? Churchill now loomed as the greatest statesman in all of British history—greater than Cromwell by far, greater than his ancestor Marlborough, greater than Wellington, who was only a great captain, greater than Disraeli and Gladstone, not to mention the leaders of the early twentieth century. And Churchill had to be preached to, not reasoned with. When so many Americans were preaching to Eisenhower he had had his fill of emotion and appeal, and anyway it was almost impossible to talk to a man who was likely to go to sleep in the middle of some exposition.

The preceding year had turned in problems of this kind, and the pressing upon him of political issues, essentially his candidacy. He had plenty of experience in the rough and tumble of military politics and hardly desired to begin a new experience freighted with personal attacks and maneuvers and perplexing activities. If the Republicans really wanted him, he reasoned, they could come and get him.

But, then, Lodge was pushing, and the result was an outright, open, public announcement of candidacy.

JANUARY 10, 1952

On the seventh, due to a series of incidents, I decided to issue a short statement of my convictions concerning any possible connection between me and the current political contest in the United States. My position is that I'm doing a duty—I shall not leave it except if called to a more important duty. I would so consider a nomination by the Republican party.

The immediate cause of my statement was an announcement by Senator Lodge on Sunday the sixth that he intended to enter my name in the New Hampshire primaries. In answer to questions he said I'd be a candidate for the Republican nomination. Time and again I've told anyone who'd listen that I will not seek a nomination. I don't give a d--- how impossible a "draft" may be. I'm willing to go part way in trying to recognize a "duty," but I do not have to seek one, and I will not.

So, my statement made these things clear, and if there is any more misunderstanding I don't see how it can be charged to me.

JANUARY 22, 1952

This morning's paper states that the president's budget, just submitted to Congress, amounts to something over $85 billion with a contemplated deficit for the year of $14 billion. Only in two of the years of World War II has an American budget equalled this figure—it is a record for peacetime. Of the budget, the paper states that approximately $65 billion is to be applied to military preparedness, including help for our allies.

I have not been a party to any of the military estimates included in the budget. I know that the men who have made the studies are capable, honest, and patriotic. Yet I know something of the methods of making such estimates, and I am well acquainted with some of the countries in which the size of national budgets has stifled initiative and caused great difficulties otherwise.

I am very greatly afraid that certain basic truths are being forgotten or ignored in our public life of today. The first of these is that a democracy undertakes military preparedness only on a defensive, which means a long-term, basis. We do not attempt to build up to a D-day because, having no intention of our own to attack, we must devise and follow a system that we can carry as long as there appears to be a threat in the world capable of endangering our national safety.

As far back as 1945 and even earlier, I began discussing these subjects with the president, members of Congress, businessmen, personal friends, and others. I talked with Jim Forrestal more than with anyone else about these things because of his very great honesty of purpose and his dedication to public service. Moreover, he was so personally concerned by the dangers that our nation was incurring that he wanted to talk about these things. Some of my associates in the service and in other governmental or civil positions have been equal to Jim Forrestal in selflessness, but few have had his insatiable desire to learn and then to apply his knowledge for the public good. So we explored and searched together to see if we could define an appropriate course in language clear enough to be specific and yet general enough to be applicable over a period of time.

Almost everything that we came to think important could be classed as obvious fact, some so obvious as to be trite. Nevertheless, one of the facts we agreed upon is that, more and more, we seem to be in need of education in the obvious, whereas too many so-called educators take great delight in pushing us farther and farther into the obscure.

We felt that it is necessary to recognize that the purpose of America is to defend a way of life rather than merely to defend property, territory, homes, or lives. As a consequence of this purpose, everything done to develop a defense against external threat, except under conditions readily recognizable as emergency, must be weighed and gauged in the light of probable long-term, internal, effect. For example, we can and do adopt in time of war restrictive practices that, if applied in time of peace, would constitute serious damage to the system of government set up by our Constitution. Censorship, price controls, allocation of materials and commodities, and the like are necessary in a great war. In time of peace, certain of these controls could possibly be applied in unusual and serious circumstances, but only in the event that there are some specific self-limiting provisions included so that shrewd politicians cannot, through the manufacture of continuous emergency, do permanent damage to our system.

This need for avoiding damage to our system markedly influenced Jim [Forrestal] and me as we approached the development of estimates as to military requirements. No argument is needed to show that excessive expenditures for nonproductive items could, in the long run, destroy the American economy. National bankruptcy would necessitate a type of control or confiscation of property that would be in utter contradiction to the assurances and safeguards of our Constitution. At the other extreme, the traditional tendency in our country in time of peace has been to neglect the armed forces to the extent of folly. Even subsequent to World War II, with everybody, including ourselves, hoping for some kind of modus vivendi with the Russians, this traditional tendency had to be combatted. From 1945 to the day of his death, Jim Forrestal devoted his most earnest efforts to this horn of the dilemma, because American thinking seemed to be again afflicted with complacency and disbelief, while he never once wavered from his profound conviction that communism was our great threat—that communistic Russia would never relax its pressure against us as long as we were exponents of free government.

In the very early days of 1947, when Jim was secretary of the navy and I was chief of staff (Bob Patterson was secretary of war) and we had preliminary talks on this subject, we came to the general conclusion that if we would be provident and prudent in the salvaging and preserving of materials left over from World War II, and our money would suffer no depreciation, we should be able to produce a minimum defensive structure, reasonably appropriate to our needs, with a yearly expenditure for all services of $15 billion (exclusive of stockpiling and other expenses of that type).

In several conversations, the president seemed to agree to this general calculation but expressed the hope that our relations with Russia could be steadily developed to the point where this sum could be substantially reduced. Of course, all of us agreed with the hope, but Jim himself believed that we should be prepared to carry a load of this magnitude for a good many years.

The reason that we felt it so important to make some estimate of this kind is that one of the most expensive practices in the maintenance of military force is unevenness in the scale of preparedness and in yearly appropriation. Peaks in one year or a series of years, followed by unwise reductions in a period when economy is the sole watchword, tend to demand extraordinary expenditures with no return. Consequently, we very greatly hoped to produce a plan and budget that would be, in effect, an element of bipartisan policy and which would be as free as possible of the defects and costs brought about by yearly cuts or increases, usually due to impulses or aberrations of the moment.

In the 1945 days of our association—really before we became firm friends—Jim Forrestal and I differed seriously on one subject. This was the proposal for unifying the three services. He had visited me, twice, during 1944, while I was still commanding at SHAEF. Although he was primarily concerned, at that time, in other subjects, we mentioned this one casually. I thought he believed in unification, but I was obviously mistaken. Of course, neither of us failed to see the need for close coordination between the services and unified control both of operational and of budgetary planning. Our difference involved the best methods to accomplish this. At first, he was afraid that the scheme that I supported would glorify the military at the expense of civilian control. I tried to prove to him that the opposite was true. He favored "committee" as opposed to "single" civilian authority. (In this connection, it is interesting to note that almost the last recommendation that Jim Forrestal ever submitted, in 1949, pleaded for a higher degree of centralization of authority in the defense department.)

Our $15 billion goal was never realized in any year. Every kind of attack was made upon our estimates and all sorts of chiseling took place. Incidentally, all of us were aware of the habit of bureaucrats to ask for greater appropriations than they reasonably expected to get. This had been the practice of many, on the theory that, since Congress was bound to cut appropriations in order to show that it was "economy minded," the only recourse was to pad original estimates to the extreme limit of possible justification. Following the war, the men with whom I worked (and this includes all that I can now remember) decided that we would refuse to follow with this practice. We would ask for what we believed to be the minimum needed and then stand honestly and firmly behind our estimates and conclusions when we were called before appropriate congressional committees. (I since have sadly concluded that we were a bit naive.)*

The chiseling and cutting of estimates was accompanied and made worse by a steadily depreciating value of the dollar. Thus, in the fiscal years 1947, 1948, 1949, and 1950, the defense fabric continued to shrink at an alarming extent— and this in spite of frequent protestations—on the part of responsible officials.

I personally left the office of chief of staff in February 1948, but already the situation was drifting to the point that I tried to bring certain of my convictions to the attention of the public rather than merely to couch them in terms of recommendations to governmental superiors. For example, in a book I published in 1948 [*Crusade in Europe*], I warned of the dangers of deficiency in military strength although, of course, I did not believe it appropriate or proper for me to recite the many instances where the recommendations of my associates and myself had been rejected or disregarded. It is interesting to speculate where we would now find ourselves had it not been for the communistic invasion of South Korea and the consequent awakening of the whole free world to the warnings that people like Jim Forrestal had been expressing time and time again in previous years.

Now I am afraid that we are risking damage from the other horn of the dilemma—that is, the danger of internal deterioration through the annual expenditure of unconscionable sums on a program of indefinite duration, extending far into the future. This is a subject which I am bound, in my present position, practically to ignore. It has great political significance at home and I have already publicly stated that, if the Republicans decide to place a political mandate upon me, I would not attempt to evade it. Therefore, if I should, while on this critical military duty in SHAPE, attempt to express my convictions about the matter, I would at the very least destroy my usefulness to the country in this program in which it is embarked. However, the only justification for the imposition of an expenditure program that foresees a minimum $14 billion deficit is an immediate prospect of war—an emergency which removes all normal limitations upon maximum financial, industrial, and military effort. We are not told that this budget is for the emergency of a single year; therefore, our people can only assume that we plan to continue the practice on the same scale.

I am astonished that an administration including, after all, many men of conservative and cautious tendencies could have approved or at least concurred in such a budget. Men like Symington, Lovett, Sawyer, Finletter, and Kimball certainly must see the terrific dangers of such a program, unless it is stated to be specifically of an emergency character and definitely limited in a way to show that it is so contemplated and regarded.[1]

In this case, there is newspaper speculation to the effect that these budgets will continue to rise at least until 1954 and then possibly to "level off." If this is true (and I cannot believe for a moment that it is), then we are headed for worse than trouble. The effect will be disastrous.

---

*Forrestal, Patterson, Royall, Spaatz, Handy, Nimitz, Sherman, Norstad plus others. Also I submitted to J.F. (at his request) a final memo, covering this among a variety of subjects.

I realize, of course, that if the Russians should commit the great blunder of venturing upon global war, or even if we should stumble into such a tragic situation, then the people now urging expenditures of this type in the name of security will be hailed in history as men of vision, foresight, and great wisdom. But I know that those men have no better access to secret or otherwise valuable information than I have. There is no greater probability of war today than there was two years ago; and no one can say for certain that there is any greater probability of deliberately provoked war at the end of this year or of next than there is now. We can say only that properly balanced strength will promote the probability of avoiding war. In this sense, we need the strength soon—but it must be balanced between moral power, economic power, and purely military power.

Reasonable men have no recourse except to plan on the basis of stable, relatively assured income and outgo. To do otherwise is adventure far beyond the point of reason. Not only do I believe that military expenditures themselves should be cut, but I believe that the government today should take the lead in establishing rigid measures of economy and efficiency in all its activities so as to accomplish at a very minimum some ten to twenty percent savings in all these other activities.

Only two or three years ago the president told me very solemnly that an aggregate national budget of more than $42 billion would quickly spell unconscionable inflation in the United States. Today we talk about $85 billion and apparently mean it to be indefinitely prolonged into the future.

In considering this subject, of course it is necessary to make allowances for ample support of the war in Korea. No one has ever given me even a vague estimate as to what that war is costing, although I have asked a number of supposedly responsible officials. Possibly many of them are just as uninformed as I am. Cutting of appropriations does not apply to the conduct of that war, which should, of course, be supported earnestly. (Incidentally, I might remark that I am one of those who believes that we did the right thing in defying and opposing the communist advance into Southern Korea. While it is manifestly an awkward place in which to fight, and there seems to be no satisfactory conclusion to the struggle, yet it is my own opinion that, had we allowed the South Korean republic, which was sponsored by the free nations, to go under, we would have by this time been kicked out of Southeast Asia completely, and it would be touch and go as to whether India would still be outside the iron curtain. If we had lost those areas, I do not know exactly how we would obtain some of the raw materials we now import from those regions.)

If we do not, as American citizens, weigh this situation and reach a reasonable answer in this year's appropriations, we will be so committed to a possibly unwise military program that either we will begin to go far more rapidly down the inflation road or we will again have to accomplish a sudden and expensive contraction in that program. In this latter case, much of this year's appropriations would have, of course, gone down the drain.

JANUARY 29, 1952

Two friends I highly respect, George Sloan and George Whitney, have both told me I have a duty, a responsibility, to state my views on "the important issues of the day." I've written letters to both, arguing the point. I'll enclose a copy of one in this book.

NATO is going schizophrenic. On the one hand it develops encouragingly, on the other it is very ill.

Understanding and morale increase. Europe is much closer than ever before to establishing the kind of union among the free countries of this region that safety and prosperity demand. But the economic position is bleak; our Congress will soon have to be told that there is no chance of material progress equalling initial promises. This is true even in the United States. The result?

FEBRUARY 11, 1952

Jacquelin Cochran is here with a tape and picture record of the "Eisenhower Rally" at Madison Square Garden on the ninth.[1] I am to see the whole business this evening; undoubtedly some publicity will be generated out of my mere viewing it. I can't help it; the performance at the Garden is not only something to make an American genuinely proud—it is something to increase his humility, his sense of his own unworthiness to fulfill the spoken and unspoken desires and aspirations of so many thousands of humans.

Our times are tumultuous—people are returning to instinct, emotion, and sentiment. Responsibility is becoming again something real, not just an election record.

FEBRUARY 12, 1952

The picture brought by Miss Cochran was very elaborate and long. Viewing it finally developed into a real emotional experience for Mamie and me. I've not been so upset in years. Clearly to be seen is the mass longing of America for some kind of reasonable solution for her nagging, persistent, and almost terrifying problems. It's a real experience to realize that one could become a symbol for many thousands of the hope they have.

Harry Luce came to see me.[1] He is stimulating.

The meeting of the NATO council in Lisbon in February 1952 turned out to be a happy event, in that the ministers present opted for a program that was the largest ever attempted by the NATO powers. The hope at Lisbon, expressed in the form of a program for member nations, was that the powers would deploy a total of a hundred divisions; of this figure fifty would be for immediate service, and the others subject to mobilization. As events turned out, a round hundred

*With Secretary of Defense Lovett, President Truman,
and Army Secretary Frank Pace, shortly before
retirement, 1952.*

*was a large figure, for NATO never generated much more than half this figure,
with only twenty-five on the line for the outbreak of any conflict. The ministers
momentarily thought that more could be available, and to Eisenhower it must
have been exhilarating to see this kind of hope, after all the months during
which he had listened to pessimism and the complexities of unresolved problems.*

February 28, 1952

The Lisbon meeting of NATO ministers has terminated. Its results were all that
I could have expected, even more. If the sober calculations on which our plans
are now based can be governing in all countries, this coming year I should
estimate that within a short time this job can fairly be considered as "on the
rails."

Political people at home urge me to ask now for relief. That strikes me as next
to insane. Possibly my work here is not so important as is the work devolving upon

the president of the United States, but to my mind it is more important than seeking the presidency. But if they will let me alone it is possible that I can soon (several months) turn the job over to another.

Monday I go to Turkey and Greece. More headaches and problems.

⌐ VIII ⌐

THE FIRST
ADMINISTRATION

The Lisbon meeting of the NATO council marked the high point of hope by
the NATO Allies for a very large military force in Western Europe, and never
again did the figure mentioned at Lisbon achieve even the remotest possibility
of acceptance. It was perhaps fitting that this high point of hope was the time
when Eisenhower left the organization and went back to the United States and
the political campaign.

Shortly before the Lisbon meeting the call came, or one might perhaps better
say that the call came when Eisenhower announced formally that he was a
Republican. By that time his military friends such as Lucius Clay and delegations
of influential Republicans had taken his opinions on this and that. It must have
appeared as if half the party leadership had made the pilgrimage to SHAPE to
be, as the general would have put it, briefed, so they could go home and debrief
to all the Republican faithful who relied on people who had made the Hadj.
Meanwhile the old stalwarts of the party were beginning to rally around Eisenhower, even if some of the regulars chose to remain with the former front-runner,
Senator Taft, down to the bitter end in the convention that summer when
Eisenhower won on the first ballot.

The Eisenhower diary has nothing to say about the hectic talks in New York
that spring, the fight at the convention in July over the seating of delegates, and
the arduous campaigns in the autumn as the Eisenhower train went across the
country and exhibited the Republican candidate. The wizards of press relations
got to work, and Eisenhower was put on television to carry the message to the
faithful and to convert as many of the heathen as chose to have their hearts
softened. The television spot broadcasts were not complicated. As Eisenhower

stared unblinkingly into the camera a voice might come in with a sepulchral question, "Mr. Eisenhower, can you bring taxes down?" In answer the candidate blinked, smiled, moistened his lips, and said, perhaps reading from the sheet behind the camera, "Yes. We will work to cut billions in Washington spending and bring your taxes down." Viewers then heard a Republican refrain, music, or a printed message appeared, after which the program returned to its prize fights or quiz shows.

Equally important as the spot commercials, and maybe more important, were the huge billboard signs that showed a grinning Eisenhower looking out at viewers and holding up two fingers in a Churchillian V for victory. What with such a message the legend of the poster was superfluous, though a caption usually read, "Vote for Ike in November," or "Vote Republican."

Against this sort of competition, from a man whose face and name was familiar to all Americans, the Democratic candidate Governor Adlai E. Stevenson of Illinois never had a chance.

Back in New York City after the campaign and voting, Eisenhower awaited the trip to Washington for the ceremony of January 20 and filled out his time by seeing people, talking about jobs, and writing in his diary in anticipation of history yet to be made.

1953

JANUARY 5, 1953

Talks with Senators Butler, Watkins, Cordon and Knowland on subject of governorship of Hawaii.[1] Matter of building a good, sound, and progressive party that can win elections when statehood comes.

Officials of National Educational Association called to show seriousness of situation, present and future.

Charles Hook, Jr., to be deputy postmaster general.

Going to visit Winston at Baruch apartment at 5:00.

The four senators named above favor Sam King over a man named Crossley. The real fact is that no one should be appointed to political office if he is a seeker after it.

We can afford to have only those people in high political offices who cannot afford to take them. Patronage is almost a wicked word—by itself it could well-nigh defeat democracy.

JANUARY 5, 1953 (PART TWO)

The process of selecting a proper governor for Hawaii has brought to me my first personal example of the traditional kind of political appointment. In prior cases it has been my job to try to discover, in the United States, the individual that

The convention triumph, July 11, 1952. L. to r., Henry Cabot Lodge, Jr., Patricia Nixon, Senator Bricker, Mrs. Eisenhower, Senator Nixon, Speaker Joe Martin of the House of Representatives, the candidate.

Election night.

I consider best fitted for the discharge of a particular set of duties—after that my next chore was to make certain that I could get that individual for the job. (We have been remarkably successful in this regard. I had none of my choices even attempt to decline a cabinet post; so far as I know, the cabinet designees have had few declinations in their search for their principal assistants.)

In the case of the governor of Hawaii, there are two principal candidates who are themselves seeking the job. Each has developed a "pressure group" to support his claims. Such an approach to a public service position violates every instinct I have. To seek such a post is, to me, clear evidence of unsuitability. I feel that anyone who can, without great personal sacrifice, come to Washington to accept an important governmental post is not fit to hold that post. This, of course, is not true in some of the more technical and professional positions, and it is unfair to assume that everyone should share my feelings in the matter when high positions are involved. But just the same, my respect and admiration for any individual who turns out to be a seeker after a political post diminishes almost to the vanishing point.

Some days ago Mr. Brownell and I tentatively decided that a man named Crossley was the best suited for the job and so informed him.[1] Since then I have learned that quite a number of other individuals (including such diverse types as four senior Republican senators and Charlie Willis) believe that to ignore the claims of Samuel King will practically destroy the Republican party in Hawaii.[2]

With Churchill and Bernard Baruch, January 5, 1953.

My experience in this case has generated in me the profound hope that I will be compelled to have little to do, during the next four years, with the distribution of federal patronage. Having been fairly successful in late years in learning to keep a rigid check on my temper, I do not want to encounter complete defeat at this late date.

As president-elect of the United States, Eisenhower immediately was on the receiving end of all kinds of pressures, domestic and foreign, and one of the first individuals to make a beeline for the new source of American political authority was the wily prime minister of Great Britain, Churchill, who grasped at an excuse to come to the United Statest to visit his old friend Bernard Baruch, conveniently living in New York City not far from Morningside Heights, where Eisenhower still was in residence. Churchill had come back into power in 1951, defeating the Laborites under Clement Attlee, and rather than passing power to his younger confederate of many years, Anthony Eden, he decided to hang onto it. He loved power, and like all old men he believed he had much to contribute in the way of experience. Not least, he perhaps calculated, was his closeness to General Eisenhower, who in 1951 was moving toward the presidency. In early January 1953, Churchill was ready to get to work on the erstwhile major general whom he first had met in the dark summer of 1942 when Eisenhower had come to England in hope of organizing an Anglo-American army.

Already, of course, the Churchill government had gotten into a maladroit argument with the wily nationalist prime minister of Iran, Dr. Mossadegh. Old "Mossy" was quite up to taking on the prime minister of Great Britain—and probably enjoyed the experience. The Iranians under Mossadegh had national-ized the British oil company, which they had every right to do, and the British had sent home their oil workers, thinking that the refineries would collapse. But the Iranians refused to give in, and relations between London and Teheran reached the breaking point; the Americans had proposed good offices, with no good result.

Basically the problem was one of British prestige. The Second World War had revealed grave weaknesses, economic and military and even (in the war's origins) political, and the British had been pushed around too much in the immediate postwar years; almost any action by a former colonial nation was bound to irritate. At one point Churchill was making a speech in the Commons about the manner in which the British lion was being poked at and shoved. He mentioned a long list of offending little nations, cleverly describing their mean actions with the same letters as their names. When he got to Guatemala his amused listeners leaned forward expectantly, thinking he couldn't find a decent verb to describe Guatemalan improprieties. There was a pause as the orator thought hard, and out it came: "Girded by Guatemala!", he shouted.

The Guatemalas of this world were getting Churchill's goat.

JANUARY 6, 1953

Mr. Churchill is as charming and interesting as ever, but he is quite definitely showing the effects of the passing years. He has fixed in his mind a certain international relationship he is trying to establish—possibly it would be better to say an atmosphere he is trying to create. This is that Britain and the British Commonwealth are not to be treated just as other nations would be treated by the United States in our complicated foreign problems. On the contrary, he most earnestly hopes and intends that those countries shall enjoy a relationship which he thinks will recognize the special place of partnership they occupied with us during World War II. In certain cases he would like to make this connection a matter of public knowledge—in others he apparently would be satisfied with a clear understanding between us, even if these had to be reached secretly.

Of course, in specific instances we would be damaging our own interests if we should fail to reach prior understandings with the British; for example, in most of our Asiatic problems. However, even in these cases, we will certainly be far better advised to treat, publicly, every country as a sovereign equal. To do otherwise would arouse resentment and damage the understandings we are trying to promote.

I assured him that I am quite ready to communicate with him personally, on our old basis of intimate friendship, where discussion between us would help advance our common interests. But I made it clear to him that when official agreement or understanding must be reached, it must be done through those channels that will establish proper records for the future and that will make certain of the proper domestic collaborations that our form of government requires.

He is unquestionably influenced by old prejudices or instinctive reaction. I tried to point out to him the great importance to the free world of bringing about a more effective cooperation among Western European nations. I pointed out that neither his country nor mine could afford to see Western continental Europe completely pass under communist domination, either through military action or through subversion and internal decay. To such a thought he reacts with a rather grudging approval but wants to turn instantly to the prospect of American-British partnership. With respect to the concept of European unity, he will say "I have already approved that." But he does not respond with any enthusiasm to an insistent assertion that the United States cannot see any great profit in supporting Western Europe economically and militarily unless that region will, through economic and political cohesion, help develop its own maximum power.

Both Foster Dulles and I have pointed out to him that until Europe makes a success of the European Army and the Schuman Plan, we can have little confidence of its future.[1] One of the stumbling blocks to such success is Europe's feeling that Britain is not greatly concerned and will not help them politically, economically, and otherwise. It is almost frustrating to attempt to make Winston see how important it is to the welfare of all three regions—Europe, Britain, and the United States—to exert British leadership in bringing about this development.

He talks very animatedly about certain other international problems, especially Egypt and its future. But so far as I can see, he has developed an almost childlike faith that all of the answers are to be found merely in British-American partnership.

In this connection, I pointed out to him that the recent British proposal to Iran, which was forwarded to Iran as a joint Truman-Churchill proposition, would have been far more effective if sent purely as a British proposal. Better than this, he should have sought, on a confidential basis, our good offices to get the matter proposed as a Persian proposition. All that he did was to get Mossadegh to accuse us of being a partner of the British in "browbeating a weak nation."[2]

Winston is trying to relive the days of World War II.

In those days he had the enjoyable feeling that he and our president were sitting on some rather Olympian platform with respect to the rest of the world and directing world affairs from that point of vantage. Even if this picture were an accurate one of those days, it would have no application to the present. But it was only partially true, even then, as many of us who, in various corners of the world, had to work out the solutions for nasty local problems are well aware.

In the present international complexities, any hope of establishing such a relationship is completely fatuous. Nationalism is on the march and world communism is taking advantage of that spirit of nationalism to cause dissension in the free world. Moscow leads many misguided people to believe that they can count on communist help to achieve and sustain nationalistic ambitions. Actually what is going on is that the communists are hoping to take advantage of the confusion resulting from destruction of existing relationships and in the difficulties and uncertainties of disrupted trade, security, and understandings—to further the aims of world revolution and the Kremlin's domination of all people.

In some instances immediate independence would result in suffering for people and even anarchy.

In this situation the two strongest Western powers must not appear before the world as a combination of forces to compel adherence to the status quo.

The free world's hope of defeating the communist aims does not include objecting to national aspirations. We must show the wickedness of purpose in the communist promises and convince dependent peoples that their only hope of maintaining independence, once attained, is through cooperation with the free world. On the one side lies slavery, preceded possibly by a momentary independence, as in the case of Czechoslovakia. On the other side lies possibly a slower and more orderly progress toward independence but with the certainty that it will then be healthy and sound.

All this we must prove by our deeds as well as our words. Consequently there is great danger in the two most powerful free nations banding together to present their case in a "take it or leave it" fashion. It will be far better for us to proceed independently toward the solution of knotty problems but to agree on fundamental factors and proposals before we make public our separate suggestions. In this way we will create confidence and even if occasionally there is a lack of uniformity in the detailed methods we suggest, this will be an advantage rather than the contrary.

Winston does not by any means propose to resort to power politics and to disregard legitimate aspirations among weaker peoples. But he does take the rather old-fashioned, paternalistic approach that since we, with our experience and power, will be required to support and carry the heavy burdens of decent international plans, as well as to aid infant nations towards self-dependence, other nations should recognize the wisdom of our suggestions and follow them.

This is true—in the abstract. But we cannot expect that it will be accepted unless we convince others by persuasion and example. Long and patient negotiations, understanding, and equality of treatment will have to be used.

Much as I hold Winston in my personal affection and much as I admire him for his past accomplishments and leadership, I wish that he would turn over leadership of the British Conservative party to younger men. He could perform a very great function by coming forward with his inspiring voice only when critical circumstances so demanded. I am very much afraid that he will never voluntarily adopt this kind of semiactive role. (For myself I am determined that whatever the cause of my own retirement from public life, I will never stay around in active position so long that age itself will make me a deterrent to rather than an agent of reasonable action.)

JANUARY 7, 1953

Mr. John Williams spent a considerable time with me—staying for lunch, with other guests including Señor Monteros of Mexico and Senator Lodge.[1] Williams, I consider, is a wise and devoted citizen.

I shall rely heavily on his advice in the fields of fiscal policy, economic outlook, elimination of artificial price controls, etc.

At 5:00 P.M. I go to final visit with Winston Churchill.

JANUARY 8, 1953

One year ago, yesterday, I publicly stated—in Paris, France—that I was a Republican. Plenty has happened to me as a result.

JANUARY 15, 1953

United States problems, caused by potential enemies and by others over whom we have no control are, of course, serious and even critical. But the pity is that these are aggravated, or time and money for their solution is lessened, by intense local differences that frequently reflect only narrow-mindedness, prejudice, or selfishness. Wildcat strikes, segregation in Washington, bitterness of the CIO because Durkin made the mistake of picking another AFL man as his principal assistant.[1]

JANUARY 16, 1953

For some weeks I have been devoting harried moments to preparation of my inaugural address—to be delivered next Tuesday. I want to make it a high-level talk. By this I mean I want to appeal to the speculative question of free men more than I want to discuss the material aspects of the current world situation. But how to do it without becoming too sermonlike—how to give it specific application and concrete substance has somewhat defied me. My assistant has been no help—he is more enamored with words than with ideas. I don't care much about the words if I can convey the ideas accurately. I want to warn the free world that the American well can run dry, but I don't want to discourage any. Above all, I don't want to give the Soviets the idea they have us on the run. I want to tell the American people that, internationally, we are entering a new phase, but I don't want to be using the inaugural address to castigate and indict the administrations of the past twenty years. It's a job.

The inauguration of January 20, 1953, went off without difficulty, and Dwight D. Eisenhower became president of the United States. But because he had been for so long in the public eye and had not merely seen but been a part of the highest decisions of government during that period, the elevation to the presidency was almost an anticlimax. When Eisenhower, a few days after Pearl Harbor, had flown to Washington to assist General Marshall, he at first had been only another brigadier general in the War Department. Then his obvious talents brought him more authority until Marshall in the spring of 1942 chose him to command in England, obviously the top foreign job for any American military man—MacArthur was far away in Australia with hardly any troops and the prospect of getting very few in the following months; Admiral Chester W. Nimitz was trying to refloat the sunken ships of the Pearl Harbor fleet. Doing well in the North African campaign, the general reached the military heights; Eisenhower's star thereafter remained at the zenith. The cables and telegrams came and went, and he communicated at top levels and frequently visited the seats of power.

Eisenhower moved into the White House with a feeling that it was no strange place. How totally unlike the experience of his predecessor, Truman, who on the morning of April 13, 1945, was observed trying out the presidential chair in an awkward way, owlishly looking across the huge empty desk, and moving his eyes uncertainly around the oval room. When Eisenhower sat down in the chair behind the desk, he felt at home.

JANUARY 21, 1953

My first day at the president's desk. Plenty of worries and difficult problems. But such has been my portion for a long time—the result is that this just seems (today) like a continuation of all I've been doing since July 1941—even before that.

FEBRUARY 1, 1953

Mamie and I joined a Presbyterian church.[1] We were scarcely home before the fact was being publicized, by the pastor, to the hilt. I had been promised, by him, that there was to be no publicity. I feel like changing at once to another church of the same denomination. I shall if he breaks out again.

FEBRUARY 2, 1953

Today I give my first "state of the union" talk before a joint session of the Congress. I feel it a mistake for a new administration to be talking so soon after inauguration; basic principles, expounded in an inaugural talk, are one thing, but to begin talking concretely about a great array of specific problems is quite another.[1] Time for study, exploration, and analysis is necessary. But, the Republicans have been so long out of power they want, and probably need, a pronouncement from their president as a starting point. This I shall try to give.

I hope, and pray, that it does not contain blunders that we will later regret.

FEBRUARY 7, 1953

Early experiences with the Congress have led me to some strange and unexpected conclusions. Surface indications to date are that the individuals from whom I had expected the greatest amount of opposition and with whom I would find cooperation to be difficult have shown a contrary attitude. Senator Taft has been the model of cheerful and effective cooperation—so have Senators Bridges, Capehart, Dirksen, and others of this general group.[1] In the house Joe Martin, Charlie Halleck, and John Tabor have been most helpful, and while these men have not been classed in the public mind as the extreme conservatives, neither have they been known as members of the more liberal wing of the party.[2] At the same time, I have found in the Senate that some of my best friends have either been extremely sensitive or have become rather temperamental. Frank Carlson so dislikes a particular individual that I want to give an important post in government to that I have to withhold the name of one of the men who could do one of our toughest jobs in admirable fashion.[3] Saltonstall has been very fearful and ineffective in handling cases of men who have to dispose of large amounts of stock in order to qualify for office.[4] While in every case the men I have named have been quite willing to comply with the provisions of the law (and I am referring to interpretations given by some eminent men such as John W. Davis) I have found that some of our senatorial friends are so politically fearful that they carry the meaning and intent of the law far beyond anything that could be considered reasonable.[5]

The result is that sooner or later we will be unable to get anybody to take jobs in Washington except business failures, college professors, and New Deal lawyers.

All of these would jump at the chance to get a job that a successful businessman has to sacrifice very much to take. Reasonable sacrifices are, of course, to be expected; in fact the government can scarcely afford to allow anyone to occupy an important post unless he did have to sacrifice very materially in order to take it. But it is the carrying of the practice to the extreme that will eventually damage us badly, unless we get some logical breaks in the Senate in the handling of these cases.

All my early cabinet meetings have revealed the existence of a spirit of team-work and of friendship that augurs well for the future. Everybody is working hard and doing it with a will. At the moment my two slight worries involve Weeks of commerce and Durkin of labor.[6] The former seems so completely conservative in his views that at times he seems to be illogical. I hope that I am mistaken or if not, that he will soon become a little bit more aware of the world as it is today.

Mr. Durkin seems to me to carry a bit of a chip on his shoulder. Whenever he presents anything in the cabinet meetings, it is with an attitude that seems to be just a bit jeering. Again I hope I am mistaken.

Naturally, in both cases I shall do the best I can in personal conversations to eliminate what I think I see in the two of them. It is the kind of problem I have often had before, and I am by no means discouraged. It is merely that I want this team to function better than any I have ever had around me before. All other members of the cabinet, including Lodge, Stassen, Dodge, and Mrs. Hobby, are performing exactly as I expected and I am delighted with them.[7]

The White House and executive staff is rounding into shape rapidly, and I believe is going to function exceedingly well. Most of the members are individuals who have been together for a long time, and it should be a much easier task for them to develop a real team than it is for the cabinet.

In certain positions of government it has been difficult to find the right people to take over the responsibilities. Arthur Flemming, president of Ohio Wesleyan University, is the only man I know that could fulfill the responsibilities devolving upon the chairman of the Civil Service Commission—at least the responsibilities that I intend to place on that officer. Yet there are a few people on the Hill that have a curious notion that Arthur Flemming is a bit of a New Dealer. Actually I find him a very distinct middle-of-the-roader—as well as a brilliant and devoted man. But I have had to come to the conclusion that I cannot use him except in posts where no Senate confirmation is required. I had the same experience in my hope of sending Val Peterson to India as ambassador, when one senator defeated the idea. This difficulty springs from the fact that the Republicans have been so long in opposition to the executive, Republican senators are having a hard time getting through their heads that they now belong to a team that includes rather than opposes the White House. Senator Taft has grasped this fact more quickly and more definitely than have any of the others and I repeat that—to date—he has been a model teammate.

FEBRUARY 9, 1953

This morning we had our regular Monday morning meeting with the Senate and House leadership. The principal subject for discussion was the proposed legislative program.

A tentative schedule was suggested by Senator Taft, who took the state of the union speech as his basis and worked up a detailed program that he thought would best suit the calendar of the Congress. The subjects agreed upon as "must" legislation were: (1) Reorganization Bill—already passed. (2) Appropriations bills to reach the Senate not later than May 15. (3) Hawaiian Statehood Bill. (4) Taft-Hartley amendments. (5) Limited extension of controls, allocations, etc., dealing with materials required for defense program and critical defense areas. (6) Legislation related to submerged lands. (7) Extension of Reciprocal Trade Act. (8) Custom Simplification Bill. (9) Extension of old age and survivors insurance, to cover groups presently excluded. (10) Extension of bill for temporary aid to schools in critical areas. (11) Adding of two commissioners for the District of Columbia.

This list, of course, is not an exclusive list but does lay before the Republicans of both houses a general outline that will be helpful.

A subject that is coming up soon for decision involves the Reciprocal Trade Agreement with other nations. In our present law is a so-called "escape" clause, which provides that under certain conditions the Federal Trade Commission may recommend an increase in our tariffs and, upon the approval of the president, such increase can go instantly into effect.

The case presently to be decided involves briar pipes—just plain smoking pipes. It is inconsequential insofar as the volume of imports is concerned and the number of people engaged in the business of making pipes here in the United States. However, it is a very important case from the standpoint of establishing attitude and future policy, and I am informed by the secretary of commerce that the whole world—as well as the American Congress—will be watching the decision.

So far as fulfilling the conditions for the application of the escape clause, this particular case is clear-cut. On the other hand, our whole policy of collective security among the nations of the free world depends on an ability of these other nations to make a living. This means that they must have the ability to export, and since the United States consists of by far the greatest single market in the world, it means that we must be quite ready and willing to import items where these do not seriously damage our economy.

Specifically, the kind of items that we should like to import are those where a great deal of hand labor is involved and where these items are not essential to the workers in our economy, particularly in time of war. This type of essential item we would far rather make here at home. (I am not discussing here the essential raw materials that we need from abroad. In this category we need especially those items in which our own production is inadequate.)

Consequently, the question at issue is to decide between the letter and intent of the law on the one hand, and the clear damage that will be done to some of our allies by such compliance.

The law provides also that certain officials, among whom I think are the secretary of state, the secretary of defense, the secretary of labor, and the director of mutual security, must all advise the president as to their convictions in such a matter, and I have a suspicion that without exception they will recommend that the tariff remain at the 50 to 75 percent rate that now exists. To avoid the increase would manifestly be to the best interests of the United States as a whole.

However, the entire Reciprocal Trade Law expires in a very short time and we have to depend upon a Congress—part of which is not sympathetic to reciprocal agreements—to reenact it. Consequently, to decline to grant the increase, when the case is so clear-cut as to comply with legal conditions, would probably provoke the Congress and might result in a failure to reenact the law.

On the other hand, approval would hurt the morale of our allies far more than it will hurt them economically.

Again, we come up against the whole question of the ability of a free government to continue functioning in spite of pressures from groups inside the body politic, where these pressures are created by immediate self-interest. Numbers of our writers of today believe, indeed strongly urge, that free government can continue to exist only as the central authority—in our case, the federal government—assumes a stronger and stronger role in directing the economic processes of the country. By exercising a stronger authority over the economy, these writers mean bureaucratic rather than purely legislative control. In this way they would hope to get away from the group influence, to which an elected official is so sensitive, while at the same time they would preserve the general forms of free government and individual liberty through the dependence of the bureaucrats upon the Congress for appropriations.

Thinking of this kind leads to a greater and greater dependence upon the so-called "regulation" commissions, most of them having a combination of legislative, executive, and judicial functions.

The Congress has at times referred to some of these commissions as an "extension of Congress." This would be an accurate description if their functions were limited to legislative action and their decisions always subject to approval by the executive. This is not the case, and I would not be surprised that a very strong argument could be made against the functioning of some of them, on constitutional grounds. In any event, to the degree that we depend more and more upon the regulatory commission, we are departing from the system laid down in our Constitution, a system that groups all functions into three categories and keeps these mutually independent of each other. Since America has always believed that this functional dispersion of power is equally important with the geographical dispersion accomplished by the reservation of all powers to the states and to the people, except where such power is especially granted to the central authority by the Constitution, it follows that to the degree that we depend upon the regulatory commission, we are threatening the individual liberties and the entire system of free government that they established.

Of course, we well understand that whereas in the early days of our republic the "liberal" was any individual who pled for less government in our daily lives, we have come to the point in the past thirty or forty years where the present-day liberal is the man who demands more and more government in our lives, claiming that only in this way can the mass of the individuals be protected against the greed and lust of the predatory few. Individuals of this school shout their undying hatred of the "practitioners of special privilege," but the fact is that the only special privilege that could possibly exist under the systems that they advocate would be the high-ranking bureaucrats of Washington.

Admittedly, masses of people have suffered under the injustices inflicted by people controlling means of production, not only in our civilization but in past ones. However, individual fortunes come and go; shirt-sleeves to shirt-sleeves in three generations is almost an accepted characteristic of modern civilization. But once an all-powerful and self-perpetuating government has fastened itself onto the people, then exploitation of the masses will revert again to the kind practiced by the Hitlers and Napoleons of the past—and indeed, as it is practiced by Stalin today.

All of this, of course, is not provoked by a mere instance of the "briar pipe" case, but that case is indicative of what goes on in a democracy. It points up the need for the people to be constantly on the job of reminding all of us what these trends—or the accumulation of a sufficient number of these instances—can eventually mean. If we do this seriously and persistently enough, we should be all right.

FEBRUARY 13, 1953

Yesterday, the twelfth, I had luncheon with our retiring ambassador to Great Britain, my good friend Walter Gifford. He wanted to give me several suggestions and some of them I think to be rather valuable.

First, he expressed the complete conviction that Winston Churchill is no longer a real power in the Conservative party—certainly not its real leader. He is more tolerated than obeyed. Walter says there is no question of Winston's personal popularity as a Britisher, but it is well understood in all circles that he has grown sufficiently old that he is really stretching—if he has not outlived— his usefulness.[1]

This fact creates a very awkward situation because his cabinet has to bear both the burdens of government and the additional one of pretending that Winston is the boss.

Again I am reminded of how hard it is for older men to retire and accept the inevitable verdict of passing years. I have watched this over my life, and I continue to pray that I, in my turn, will not fall victim to the same human failing. So far I have not wavered as I tried earnestly to step down and out when I came back from Europe in 1945, believing that the experiences of the immediately preceding years may have taken a much greater toll out of me than I even suspected. Next, when I left the office of chief of staff I again tried to keep out of active work, but finally succumbed to the arguments of the trustees of Columbia University. Incidentally, I thoroughly enjoyed that work as quickly as I got over the initial feeling of strangeness. Having settled there and having already informed the trustees that at the age of sixty-five I would insist upon getting out, I had the NATO position thrust upon me and I had to go back to . . . and twice I suggested to individual trustees of Columbia that they find some way of putting me on the inactive list and not counting upon my returning there for duty after the NATO tour should be over.[2]

Of course, after being there less than a year, the pressures from political figures became so great that again I was persuaded that I had a duty to turn to another task, that of offering myself as a political leader to unseat the New Deal - Fair Deal bureaucracy in Washington.

So here I am—and the reason for reciting the record to date is that if I do finally succumb to the same kind of thing that now seems to rule my great friend Winston, I will at least have a record that for a period I had somewhat better sense.

The next thing that Walter wanted to tell me about yesterday was the confusion that reigned in London for a time created by the unfortunate manner of naming his successor.

About a year ago I visited London and during the course of my visit there Walter told me that as soon as a new administration came into Washington, he was determined to retire as ambassador to Great Britain. With this knowledge, I of course was interested in the task of selecting a completely acceptable and useful successor. We started this job shortly after the election in early November and it was not long before we determined that, all things considered, Winthrop Aldrich would be our best bet. This selection was made on the most confidential basis, but to our consternation it was soon public knowledge in New York City —and indeed, throughout the nation.

Foster Dulles considered this situation so embarrassing that he felt he would have to make a prompt public announcement of the fact that we intended to nominate Winthrop Aldrich when the new administration should take over. I agreed, but did put in my word of caution that Walter Gifford would have to be protected in every possible way. I was very greatly concerned that he should not be embarrassed, not only because he is an able American citizen and had done a good job in London, but because he was also my good friend. Having said this, I promptly dropped the matter from my mind.

Actually, it turned out that Walter received from Foster Dulles a letter one morning informing him that a change would probably be made (something that Walter, of course, already knew since he had himself made the decision), and that afternoon Foster called Walter to inform him that the announcement of his successor would have to be made promptly because of unfortunate leaks here at home.

Walter acted promptly to put a proper appearance on this kind of emergency action and had a story published in the *New York Times* to the effect that he was going to retire promptly on January 20. The next thing that happened was the immediate announcement from the United States of the intended appointment of Winthrop Aldrich. This upset the British government very badly—and I must say most understandably. As Anthony Eden pointed out in his informal protest to Walter Gifford, this meant that Britain was being subjected to pretty rough treatment when there was no effort made to get the usual "agreement." He said that with this precedent, any small nation could pursue the same tactics, and if Britain should protest, they could argue that since the United States had done this and Britain had accepted it, no real objection could be made.

To guard against any such development as this, I am going to advise Anthony, when I see him next month, to lay the blame for this whole unfortunate occurrence squarely on me. He will have the logical explanation that my lack of formal experience in the political world was the reason for the blunder. Actually, I was the one who cautioned against anything like this happening, but manifestly I can take the blame without hurting anything or anybody; whereas if the secretary of state would have to shoulder it, his position would be badly damaged.

Walter apparently moved earnestly to repair the damage done, and it will probably be quickly forgotten. However, it left a very deep resentment in him, and I must say I don't blame him. On the other hand, it is quite clear that Foster intended no insult or discourtesy. On the contrary, he has a great admiration, just as I do, for both Walter and our British friends. He simply was thrown off balance by a leak that should never have occurred, and he apparently decided that it would be a greater affront to the British if they read about our intended action in the newspaper than if they received notice, rather abruptly, through our ambassador. However, the final mistake made was that when Foster telephoned to Gifford—apparently on the afternoon of November 29—he failed to ask the ambassador, as a personal favor, to notify the British government of the whole unfortunate occurrence and to say that the "agreement" would be sought as soon as possible and that our intended appointment would be subject to the receipt of such "agreement."

Gifford pointed out that the real importance of this occurrence was a feeling on the part of the British, at that time, that the new administration intended to be pretty rough with them and with our other allies. They are, of course, very sensitive indeed and are watchful for every affront to their dignity and rights. Beyond this, they feel that they should have something of a special position with us because of our close partnership during World War II.

This, I think, is only logical because it is quite clear that unless the English-speaking peoples of the world can live relatively close together and can set something of a model for the necessary cooperation among free peoples then we are truly in for desperate trouble. However, no such special relationship can be maintained or even suggested, publicly. In public relationship all nations are sovereign and equal. This means that on the personal and informal basis we must find a way of agreeing with our British friends on broad objectives and purposes. Thereafter, each must pursue its own detailed methods of achieving these purposes. Some hurt feelings will occasionally be inevitable—but as long as our hearts are in the right places and both sides are reasonably intelligent, we should be able to work for the common aim of a free and secure world based upon common sense among nations and decent respect for each other. . . .[3]

Walter Gifford's final recommendation to me was to promote Julius Holmes to ambassador and assign him to a fairly important post.[4] I assured him I already had this in mind but believed that Aldrich would need Holmes in London for a few months. After that we would find a proper post for him, because he is a most able and devoted career man. Moreover, there is nothing New Dealish about him.

APRIL 1, 1953

The happenings of the past few weeks emphasize again how difficult it is for a party that has been in the minority for twenty years to take up the burdens of responsibility for the operation of the government. We have had a number of misunderstandings, to say nothing of blunders. Sometimes these have been either my own fault or the fault of some other part of the Executive Department. More frequently, I think, they result from the readiness of political legislators to fly into print at every possible opportunity. I repeat, this is especially true because of the fact that for so long a time the Republican party has been opposed to, and often a deadly enemy of, the individual in the White House.

One of the difficulties that is now more of a carry-over than a new incident is occasioned by the so-called Bricker amendment. Senator Bricker wants to amend the Constitution to limit the power of the president in making international agreements. Likewise, he wants to limit the position of an approved treaty as "the supreme law of the land." By and large I think the logic of the case is all against Senator Bricker, but he has gotten almost psychopathic on the subject, and a great many lawyers have taken his side of the case. This fact does not impress me very much. Lawyers are trained to take either side of any case and make the most intelligent and impassioned defense of their adopted viewpoint. This tends to create a practice of submerging conviction in favor of plausible argument.

I realize that there are very few lawyers whose standing and position have been such that they could afford to take only cases that completely agree with their own political and philosophical convictions. This, however, does not affect the observation I have just made, and I truly believe that that observation is at least partially correct. In any event, such lawyers as John W. Davis, General Mitchell, Foster Dulles, and Herbert Brownell are of the opinion that the effect of the amendment would be to damage the United States materially in its efforts to lead the world in support of the free way of life.[1] These are not only able lawyers, they are also experienced in government. This is important.

Senator McCarthy is, of course, so anxious for the headlines that he is prepared to go to any extremes in order to secure some mention of his name in the public press. His actions create trouble on the Hill with members of the party; they irritate, frustrate, and infuriate members of the Executive Department. I really believe that nothing will be so effective in combating his particular kind of troublemaking as to ignore him. This he cannot stand.

Throughout these weeks, with the difficulties of which the above two are random examples, there has been a growing strength in the friendly relations between the Republican leaders of both Houses and the Executive Department. I think it is scarcely too much to say that Senator Taft and I are becoming right good friends. This applies, also, to the mass of Republican senators, who in general will follow Taft's lead. In the contest on Bohlen's confirmation, eleven Republican senators voted against us.[2] There were only two or three who surprised me by their actions; the others are the most stubborn and essentially small-minded examples of the extreme isolationist group in the party. I was surprised by the vote of Bricker and Goldwater.[3] These two seemed to me a little bit more intelligent than the others, who sought to defend their position with the most specious kind of excuse and the most misleading kind of argument.

In spite of all this, Taft held the mass of Republicans squarely in line, and the Democrats, with the exception of two only, voted solidly with us.

Of course, if this kind of thing were often repeated, it would give some weight to an argument that was presented to me only yesterday. It was that I should set quietly about the formation of a new party. The method would be to make a personal appeal to every member of the House and Senate; to every governor, and to every national committeeman whose general political philosophy and purpose seem to belong to that school known as "the middle way." It may come about that this will be forced upon us, but the difficulties are vast, and if we can possibly bring about a great solidarity among Republicans, if we can get them more deeply committed to teamwork and party responsibility, this will be much the better way.

In the House I do not anticipate a great deal of difficulty, but in the Senate the record of the past few weeks is encouraging only insofar as the majority of Republicans is concerned. However, if we can win away from the McCarthy-Malone axis about five or six of their members, the splinter group will be reduced to impotence.[4]

On such a basis, I think we should be able to build a splendid progressive record, including substantial balancing of the 1954 budget, greater achievements in our whole security program, a stronger position in Asia, real progress in the NATO concept, and possibly a real prospect of lowering taxes by the end of the 1954 fiscal year. If we can have the solidarity that will accomplish these things then the chances for the Republicans retaining control of the House and Senate (which involves the vital chairmanship of committees) shall be really bright.

If that comes about, the only remaining great problem will be the date of my announcement that I am through with politics.

MAY 1, 1953

Yesterday was one of the worst days I have experienced since January 20, the major part of the wear and tear coming through a meeting of the legislative leaders. Luckily there were one or two features of the meeting that provided reason for a subsequent chuckle. All in all, therefore, the day's end was not quite as bad as some of the moments in its middle.

The difficulty arose at the weekly meeting of the executive departments and the leaders of the Republican party in the Congress. The purpose of the meeting was to bring about some kind of rough agreement as to the general character and extent of the changes that would be recommended by the administration in the Truman budget, submitted to the Congress at the end of last year.

After three months of sweat and study, the executive departments had come up with recommendations that the requests for new money be cut by something like $8 billion. Moreover, the expenditure program for the fiscal year 1954, although largely frozen by commitments and contracts made long ago, was cut and figured until it had been reduced by $4 billion.

This whole program was explained in the light of the desire of the administration to avoid any weakening of our defensive posture in the world; in fact, in the light of the need for increasing the presently available strength, particularly in the air forces.

Most of those present seemed to have a clear appreciation of the agony of work and scheming that had gone into the business of making this kind of a cut, and it was carefully explained that future experience ought to bring about even greater opportunities for savings. Quite naturally, when we have achieved the defensive buildup that is considered the minimum necessary, savings should be much greater, even if we have to continue in the conduct of the more or less "cold war."

In spite of the apparent satisfaction of most of those present, Senator Taft broke out in a violent objection to everything that had been done. He used adjectives in describing the disappointment he felt that were anything but complimentary. He accused the security council of merely adopting the Truman strategy and, by a process of nicking here and chipping there, built up savings which he classed as "puny."[1] He predicted that acceptance by the Congress of any such program would insure the decisive defeat of the Republican party in 1954. He said that not only could he not support the program, but that he would have to go on public record as fighting and opposing it.

I think that everybody present was astonished at the demagogic nature of his tirade, because not once did he mention the security of the United States or the need for strength either at home or among our allies. He simply wanted expenditures reduced, regardless. Of course, the individuals who had been working so hard on this program, the secretary of the treasury, the director of the budget, the director for mutual security, and the acting secretary of defense, were all astounded, and it was obvious that they felt they had been badly let down—that they had had a right to expect great understanding and cooperation—particularly in view of the fact that they had never failed to keep the leaders as well informed concerning their progress as was possible in the circumstances.[2]

The ludicrous part of the affair came about when several of my close friends around the table saw that my temper was getting a little out of hand at the demagogic proceeding, and of course they did not want any breach to be brought about that would be completely unbridgeable. So George Humphrey and Joe Dodge in turn jumped into the conversation as quickly as there was the slightest chance to interrupt and held the floor until I had cooled down somewhat. After that I simply laid out the general basis of our global strategy, its inescapable requirements in terms of vital areas, the obvious truth that protection cost a mint of money, and defended the individuals on the security council who had worked so long and so earnestly to bring about the projected savings—a process that of course had to encounter and accept calculated risks at more than one point. By the time that the senator had seen the reaction to his own talk and heard the general comment about the table, he was, to a very considerable amount, backing up; before the meeting was over he had the appearance of being a jolly good fellow who had merely expressed himself emphatically.

Nevertheless, even assuming that he now accepts our position in complete detail (which I do not expect), he still has lost a great bit of his leadership position in front of his associates who were here with him. I do not see how he can possibly expect over the long run to expect to influence people when he has no more control over his temper than seemed apparent at the meeting; likewise, I do not see how he can maintain any reputation for considered judgment when he attempts to discuss weighty, serious, and even critical matters in such an ill-tempered and violent fashion.

Of course I am pleased that I did not add any fuel to the flames, even though it is possible that I might have done so except for the quick intervention of my devoted friends. If this thing ever has to be dragged out into the open, we at least have the right to stand firmly upon the platform of taking no unnecessary chances with our country's safety, but at the same time doing everything we can to protect its solvency and its economic health.

Before the day was over, my friends dropped in to chat with me about the occurrence and to express the opinion that the whole incident cleared the air and enhanced the prestige of the administration, because of the quite obvious acceptance by all the others present of the honesty and efficiency of our work. However, I still maintain that it does not create any confidence in the reliability and effectiveness of our leadership in one of the important houses of Congress.

MAY 14, 1953

During the first four months of this administration's existence, there have gradually come forward a number of men who are establishing themselves as very competent, capable, and dedicated public servants. Since nothing is static in human affairs, I could not possibly say that my present opinion of these individuals will remain the same through the four-year term (assuming even that all of us live and keep our health). However, it may be interesting, when the time comes for me to make up my own mind as to the identity of a logical successor, for me to look back on these notes and find in them impressions I have formed after four months of intimate association with these personalities.

First, the older group—of roughly my age or, in some cases, even a little older:

John Foster Dulles, secretary of state

I still think of him, as I always have, as an intensive student of foreign affairs. He is well-informed and, in this subject at least, is deserving, I think, of his reputation as a "wise" man. Moreover, he is a dedicated and tireless individual —he passionately believes in the United States, in the dignity of man, and in moral values.

He is not particularly persuasive in presentation and, at times, seems to have a curious lack of understanding as to how his words and manner may affect another personality. Personally, I like and admire him; my only doubts concerning him lie in the general field of personality, not in his capacity as a student of foreign affairs.

George Humphrey, secretary of the treasury

He is a sound business type, possessed of a splendid personality, and truly interested in the welfare of the United States and of all the people that compose it. He is almost a direct opposite of the caricatured businessman that so often appears in the columns of the "liberal" press. He is persuasive in his presentations and usually has his facts well in hand. He is an acceptable figure in every conference and always adds something to its deliberations.

Charles Wilson, secretary of defense

In his field, he is a really competent man. He is careful and positive, and I have no slightest doubt that, assisted by the team of civilian and military men he has selected, he will produce the maximum of security for this country at minimum or near minimum cost. If he fails, it will be because of his inability to sell himself and his programs to Congress. In this connection, if he will only make greater use of Roger Kyes (his principal assistant, and selected by him personally) as the man to represent the Defense Department before Congress, I should say he will be making a very wise move. Kyes, also a good business executive, is likewise persuasive in conference and presentation. Already he has achieved a real standing with the various members of the Congress. On the other hand, Mr. Wilson is prone to lecture, rather than to answer, when asked a specific question. This not only annoys many members of Congress, but it gives them unlooked for opportunities to discover flaws in reasoning and argument.

It is the one direction in which I feel that Charlie Wilson has a definite weakness. And, while I frequently advised him to delegate to Kyes and others maximum responsibility in this field of legislative work, I am still doubtful as to the final outcome.

The three above-named men are all of my age or slightly older. They are, nevertheless, very active members of the administration and I invariably seek their advice and counsel in all affairs of great moment whether or not the subject directly affects the activities of their particular departments.

Another group of people, somewhat younger, are likewise important in the administration. The ones that come instantly to mind are:

My brother, Milton Eisenhower: president, Penn State College
Henry Cabot Lodge: American representative to the United Nations
Herbert Brownell: attorney general
Harold Stassen: director for Mutual Security
Joseph Dodge: director of the budget
Oveta Hobby: secretary of Health, Education, and Welfare
Sherman Adams: head of the White House staff
Charles Halleck: Republican leader in the House of Representatives
Richard Nixon: vice-president
Senator William Knowland, of California
Robert Stevens: secretary of the army
Robert Anderson: secretary of the navy
Robert Cutler: my administrative assistant and director of the National Security Council
C.D. Jackson: my administrative assistant for psychological warfare activities
Dr. Arthur Flemming: director of defense mobilization
Philip Young: chairman of the Civil Service Commission

To this list, I could add a great many others. But most of them are individuals who, by reason of their very specialized assignments, do not figure prominently in councils and decisions of really broad scope—for example, Jerry Persons and his group of assistants, Dr. Hauge, and Tom Stephens.[1]

Of the list I have just named, I should remark as a general impression that none of them has really disappointed me; on the contrary, they have performed both individually and as a group beyond my original expectations. At this minute, I am not going to attempt to set down my opinion of the qualifications and personalities of each. It would take far too long. However, in a few cases, I do want to make some record of my current impressions.

So far as my brother *Milton* is concerned, I am, of course, a prejudiced witness. However, I have no hesitancy in saying I believe him to be the most knowledgeable and widely informed of all the people with whom I deal. He is a great character and personality, a humanitarian, and a truly capable organizer and leader. So far as I am concerned, he is at this moment the most highly qualified man in the United States to be president. This most emphatically makes no exception of me. . . .[2]

I would not, of course, offer to Milton—and he would not accept—any position in the government. He does, however, consult frequently with various members of the government and is my most intimate general adviser. He has been of invaluable assistance in helping develop our reorganizational plans and has consented to make a visit as my personal representative to South America, to take place during his vacation period this coming summer.

Next to Milton in general all-round capability (and I am speaking of capabilities now with particular reference to governmental service), I would place *Henry Cabot Lodge.* He is well-educated, widely experienced, quick, shrewd, and possessed of a fine personality. He has long been in politics and is therefore apt to form judgments somewhat more colored by political considerations than would an individual whose background is more like Milton's. However, he is, by instinct and upbringing, an honorable man—and remains so even in political argument and discussion. He is doing a particularly good job in the United Nations, where his quickness of wit and his great ability and extemporaneous debate serve us very well indeed.

He has been quite unpopular with certain sections of the Republican party—especially the so-called reactionary wing. There is no question, however, that he represents the general stream of American thinking far better than does an individual such as Senator Malone or any other of that particular school.

Herb Brownell. Here is a man with long experience in politics, especially in the conduct of political campaigns. It would be natural to suppose that he would become hardboiled, and that the code by which he lives could scarcely be classified as one of high moral quality. The contrary seems to be true—certainly he has never suggested or proposed to me any action which could be considered in the slightest degree dishonest or unethical. His reputation with others seems to match my own high opinion of his capabilities as a lawyer, his qualities as a leader, and his character as a man. I am devoted to him and am perfectly confident that he would make an outstanding president of the United States.

Charlie Halleck. This man is a different type. He is a Phi Beta Kappa, which means at least that he is highly intelligent and mentally adept. He has had a reputation as being a ruthless politician, but I find him not only considerate and kind but a real team player. He does believe in discipline in an organization, and he has no patience whatsoever with the individuals that "stray off the reservation" when it comes to a matter of Republican regularity. He is charming company and, so far as I can determine, of exemplary tactfulness. Perhaps my opinion can be best expressed by merely stating the fact that he was high on my list of acceptable vice-presidents when my opinion was asked last July. And, since that time, he has steadily grown in my estimation.

Arthur Flemming and *Philip Young.* These two individuals are highly knowledgeable concerning governmental function and organization. Both are very well educated, Flemming now being the president of Ohio Wesleyan, on leave—while Phil Young has just served several years as the dean of the business school of Columbia University. I consider both to be invaluable in the administration and respect highly the counsel and advice I get from them. They both seem to possess executive ability in an extraordinary degree and, all in all, it is difficult indeed to class anybody above them except in the single quality of broad experience. (Both are relatively young men.)

For the moment, I shall not attempt to go further in my descriptions of the individuals I have named herein, since the mere fact that I have named them implies correctly that I have for them real admiration and respect.

Over and beyond this list, there are others in business or in state governments who rank highly in my estimation. At some later date, I shall attempt to list a few.

JUNE 1, 1953

Some days ago Senator Taft told me he was not feeling well. Shortly afterwards he went to the hospital (Walter Reed) and later went on to Ohio, where he entered another hospital. I understand that there are grave doubts among the doctors as to the exact nature of his trouble. There is currently some fear that he is really very sick, possibly even indefinitely incapacitated. On the other hand, there is a possibility that he merely has some kind of acute glandular disorder and will soon be able to take up his normal duties.

From the personal viewpoint, an indefinite incapacitation on his part would be quite a blow to me. Over the past several months Senator Taft and I have gradually developed a curious sort of personal friendship. It is not any Damon and Pythias sort of thing that insures compatibility of intellectual viewpoint, nor even, for that matter, complete courtesy in the public discussion of political questions. On the other hand, we have reached a very amicable and definite understanding as to the methods of handling common problems and, to date, he has never failed to attack vigorously any particular chore that I ask him to undertake within the Senate.

On the partisan political side, his loss would be little short of calamitous—because it would probably mean loss of Republican control of the Senate. The governor of his state is a Democrat and would be expected to appoint a Democratic senator. With Senator Morse voting with the Democrats, this would give to them a majority, and of course we would lose the chairmanships.[1]

On the broader horizon of the country's welfare, I am not certain how I would calculate the effect of Senator Taft's disappearance from political activity. In most domestic matters he and I stand firmly together. The real point of difference between us is that he wants to cut taxes immediately, believing that this is possible if we arbitrarily reduce the security establishment by about $10 billion. And he believes that in no other way can the Republicans be returned to the control of the Congress in 1954. I personally agree with none of this. I believe that the American public wants security ahead of tax reduction and that while we can save prodigious sums in the defense department without materially hurting our security, we cannot safely, this year, knock out enough to warrant an immediate tax reduction. To do it without a tax reduction would, of course, produce another deficit of extraordinary size, force us to seek an increase in the legal debt limit, and would be most inflationary in its effect.

But I do believe that we can make sufficient reductions this year to show the American people that we are doing a sensible and sane and efficient job, and win an election next year on a record of economy, efficiency, and effective security. With consistent attention to these matters, I believe that we can cut government expenditures far enough to justify real tax reductions for the fiscal year 1955. All this, of course, assumes that we go ahead with the elimination of the excess profits

In or out of office, Eisenhower loved to fish, ride, and generally live the life of out-of-doors. Here he could put his mind on what counted—the fish, the horse, the scenery.

tax and the emergency rise in personal income taxes, on next January 1.

In the foreign field, Senator Taft never disagrees with me when we discuss such affairs academically or theoretically. He believes in the theory of cooperative security and mutual aid. However, when we take up each individual problem or case, he easily loses his temper and makes extravagant statements. He always does this when he starts making a public speech—he seems to work himself into a storm of resentment and irritation.

The result of all this is that our allies fear him and all he influences. They think he gives McCarthy ideas and McCarthy, with his readiness to go to the extremes in calling names and making false accusations, simply terrifies the ordinary European statesman. Incidentally, I very recently read part of a German broadcast, in which the German Von Cub stated in effect "McCarthy makes it so easy to hate Americans that it is necessary that all of us who understand America's decent motives and basic friendliness should speak up in behalf of the things she is doing in our own countries."

The implication from all this is that Senator Taft and I will never completely really agree on policies affecting either the domestic or the foreign scene. Moreover, we will never be sufficiently close that we are impelled by mutual friendship to seek ways and means to minimize any evidence of apparent opposition, no matter how much we might differ in basic belief.

In many ways he has cooperated so well as to excite my admiration and certainly far exceeded the expectations I held last December. On the other hand, he is so impulsive, and at times so irascible that he can scarcely be classed as a skillful statesman. His best friends explain his irascibility as frankness, and his blind prejudices as outspokenness. His worst enemies call him stupid and a political schemer. He is certainly not this last. But he is likewise far from being a Dick Nixon, who is not only bright, quick, and energetic—but loyal and cooperative.

JULY 2, 1953

Daily I am impressed by the shortsightedness bordering upon tragic stupidity of many who fancy themselves to be the greatest believers in and supporters of capitalism (or a free competitive economy), but who blindly support measures and conditions that cannot fail in the long run to destroy any free economic system.

Lenin held, of course, that capitalism contains within itself what he calls "contradictions" which not only make certain of its inadequacy as a basis of government, but which he claimed are certain to bring about revolution of the proletariat.

The first of these contradictions he called the capital-labor contradiction. He claimed that there were no restraints upon the power of the capitalists—the great corporations and the syndicates—to confront the masses with the choice between the extremes of abject acceptance of a condition of slavery on one hand or bloody revolution on the other.

The second contradiction in the capitalistic system he described as the inevitable conflict between separate groups of capitalists each struggling for the sources of raw materials and other means of production. In essence, of course, this meant capitalistic wars between capitalistic states for the domination of the world's surface.

His third contradiction was the inherent conflict, as he argued, between the advanced, industrialized nations of the world and the dependent masses of backward peoples. He saw in the unequal advances made by peoples in industrialization only opportunity for exploitation by the stronger and more advanced. This he regarded as inhuman, brutal, cruel, and another factor certain to cause world revolution.

Any material contemplation of the points raised by Lenin could easily show that his intentions had plausibility only when considered in terms of extremism. All human experience tends to show that human progress, where advanced numbers of people and intricate relationships are concerned, is possible only as extremes are avoided and solutions to problems are found in a great middle way that has regard for the requirements, desires, and aspirations of the vast majority. Consequently, the inevitability of the results of the so-called contradictions in capitalism is open to question. In fact, we flatly deny that they have to become so serious as to cause the destruction of a competitive form of enterprise and a free government based upon it.

Of course, in an exhaustive study of some of the communist writings, the kind of reasoning sketchily illustrated by the examples given above leads them to their fundamental conclusion that free systems of government cannot possibly exist in the world. Conflicts among pressure groups—in short, the intimate selfishness of men—are cited by the communists as evidence that man is really incapable of self-government.

Indeed, in Lenin's arguments it is interesting to note that he flatly rejected the theory of some of the early communists, those represented in the second internationale, that a majority of citizens in any country would necessarily be converted to communism before the communistic theory could be successfully applied in that country. He scorned such a doctrine and insisted that any circumstance or accident that gave a group of devoted communists an opportunity to seize positions of power was really all that was necessary. Thereafter, the communistic theory in its entire scope would and should be quickly applied to the entire country.

Of course, there have been happenings in history that would seemingly give a certain validity to some of these communistic arguments. But I believe that, no matter what were the true basic causes of deterioration of democratic systems established among the citizens of ancient Athens and Rome, it is safe to say that the principal contradiction in the whole system comes about because of the inability of men to forego immediate gain for a long-time good. I believe that the educational process has convinced the vast majority of Americans, for example, that the true interests of labor and capital within our society follow courses that are far more nearly parallel than conflicting. I believe that capitalistic—that is to say, self-governing—nations have long ago foreseen that any kind of war is too high a price to pay for the hope of a piece of additional territory. I believe, also, that, in the high average of cases, industrialized countries approach the problem of relationships with backward areas on the basis of mutual benefit and advancement.

But when it comes to the making of decisions as between the immediate and selfish interest of a nation, a group, or an individual on the one hand, and on the other the long-term good of the world, the nation, or the individual, we do not yet have a sufficient number of people who are ready to make the immediate sacrifice in favor of a long-term investment.

Specifically, our country has depended for decades on a system of tariffs designed originally to protect infant industries and, in latter days, to protect an American industry against cheap labor to be found abroad. This doctrine was undoubtedly a good one to follow as long as we were a debtor nation; since we had to acquire currencies of foreign countries in order to pay for the imports we bought, it was to our interest to keep them of the lowest possible aggregate value. Otherwise, all our gold reserves would have been gradually draining away, and with disastrous consequences on our own economy.

As the years and two World Wars passed across the stage, America became the greatest creditor nation the world has ever known. No longer is it to the interest of America to keep imports down and exports up just to preserve the financial soundness of our whole system. In certain instances, it is possible that particular industries should be protected because of their importance to us in the event of war. For example, I suppose that there is no substitute for a small but competent watch industry in our country because, in time of war, the skills and facilities of such an industry would be available for the making of fine instruments of all kinds. Similar arguments can be made in the case of certain other industries. But, by and large, the case for lowered American tariffs is so generally valid that to see so many so-called enlightened people opposing such a trend leads me almost to repeat again the sentence with which I opened this memorandum.

Industries, big and little—sheep growers, pipe makers, silk scarf manufacturers, miners of tungsten, and so on, and so on—all these people are so concerned for their own particular immediate market and prosperity that they utterly fail to see that the United States cannot continue to live in a world where it must, for the disposal of its products, export vast portions of its industrial and agricultural products unless it also imports a sufficiently great amount of foreign products to allow countries to pay for the surpluses they receive from us.

Along with this main proposition go a number of corollaries. An important one springs out of the continuous struggle going on in the world between the communistic theory and free systems of government. Since communism is aggressive, it reaches out to absorb every area in which can be detected the slightest discontent or other form of weakness. Where men and women and their children suffer the pains of hunger and exposure, communism quickly makes great headway. Consequently, unless the free world espouses and sustains, under the leadership of America, a system of world trade that will allow backward people to make a

decent living—even if only a minimum one measured by American standards—
then in the long run we must fall prey to the communistic attack.

Another item in this particular phase of the situation is the American complete
dependence upon other areas for certain types of materials such as tin, cobalt,
uranium, manganese, natural rubber and, increasingly, crude oil. There are countless others. Unless the areas in which these materials are found are under the
control of people who are friendly to us and who want to trade with us, then again
we are bound in the long run to suffer the most disastrous and doleful consequences.

The general conclusion of these meandering thoughts is that leadership must
find a way to bring men and nations to a point where they will give to the
long-term promise the same value that they give to immediate and individual
gains. If we could produce clear and dispassionate thinking in this regard, if we
could get today the questions of world trade and world cooperation studied and
settled on the basis of the long-term good of all, we could laugh at all the other
so-called "contradictions" in our system, and we could be so secure against the
communist menace that it would gradually dry up and wither away.

As it is, the danger is very real and very great that even the so-called enlightened areas of Western Europe, Britain, United States, and the other English-
speaking peoples will, by stubborn adherence to the purpose of achieving maximum immediate gain, actually commit suicide.

In this situation, we find a reason to say that, even if the free government were
not originally based upon some form of deeply felt religious faith then men should
attempt to devise a religion that stresses the qualities of unselfishness, cooperation, and equality of men.

In the facets of our resources—material, scientific, human, and spiritual—
there is ample assurance not only of security but of continued advance for all the
free world in living standards if only we have sense enough to learn to cooperate
for the long-term benefit of all of us.

JULY 23, 1953

Eight o'clock Senator Everett Dirksen came to breakfast—I asked him to be the
"verbal leader" of the middle-of-the-road philosophy (my philosophy) in the
Senate. Regardless of the formal leadership, he would be the man to take on all
attackers, the champion who would put on the armor and get on the white horse
and take on the fight.

JULY 24, 1953

Numerous conferences and conversations of recent days brought out a few points
interesting enough to make brief notations concerning them.

On Monday night, the twentieth, I had the fourth of a series of biweekly stag
dinners. At this particular dinner the guests got to talking about gold standards,
the value to the United States of the gold now buried at Fort Knox, and the value

of the raw materials of many kinds now included in our stockpiles as a war reserve. As always, a small minority favored "return to a gold standard." When these people were pressed, they had no clear idea as to the method by which this should be done; indeed, they had no real idea of what they were talking about. It developed that what was really the unanimous hope was the achieving of a long-term stability in our dollar. This was expressed in terms of insurance policies. Mr. Schaefer (J. Earl Schaefer, vice-president Boeing Airplane Company, Wichita, Kansas) expressed the opinion that unless people could believe that insurance policies would be paid off in roughly the same kind of dollars as were put into them, we would finally find our investment needs far greater than the capital to fill them.

In any event, it was finally agreed that if all the gold at Fort Knox should sink into a bottomless pit—and no one ever learned of this fact—the disappearance would not have the slightest effect on any of us, so long as we did not have to ship out gold to pay for the excess of imports over exports. As of today, this seems to be a possibility only for the remote future. Consequently, the conclusion—that is of today—is that we don't need the gold except psychologically. If people knew it was gone, there would be a panic.

On the other hand, the materials in our stockpiles represent insurance against disaster. They have a definite and concrete value to our economy. The obvious question is "Why is there not a better backing for a currency than gold?" Such questions as these were pursued the entire evening. As usual, everybody went away carrying with him the opinion with which he came.

A few days ago (Monday, July 20) I had luncheon with Governor Byrnes of South Carolina, my great friend, a man in whose company I always find a great deal for enjoyment.[1]

He came to talk to me about the possibility of a supreme court ruling that would abolish segregation in public schools of the country.[2] He is very fearful of the consequences in the South. He did not dwell long upon the possibility of riots, resultant ill feeling, and the like. He merely expressed very seriously the opinion that a number of states would immediately cease support for public schools.

During the course of this conversation, the governor brought out several times that the South no longer finds any great problem in dealing with adult Negroes. They are frightened at putting the children together.

The governor was obviously afraid that I would be carried away by the hope of capturing the Negro vote in this country, and as a consequence take a stand on the question that would forever defeat any possibility of developing a real Republican or "opposition" party in the South. I told him that while I was not going to give in advance my attitude toward a supreme court opinion that I had not even seen and so could not know in what terms it would be couched, that my convictions would not be formed by political expediency. He is well aware of my belief that improvement in race relations is one of those things that will be healthy and sound only if it starts locally. I do not believe that prejudices, even palpably unjustified prejudices, will succumb to compulsion. Consequently, I believe that federal law imposed upon our states in such a way as to bring about

Golf with the vice-president. In everything he did, Eisenhower liked to excel. He was an excellent golfer.

a conflict of the police powers of the states and of the nation, would set back the cause of progress in race relations for a long, long time.

On a later date (July 21, 1953) former President Herbert Hoover, with a group of others, had lunch with me. We discussed the formulation of a new governmental commission, the real purpose of which would be to make a study of federal functions and organization, and in doing so, to expand the work and findings of the Hoover Commission of some four years ago. For my selections to the new commission, I have chosen Mr. Hoover, Mr. James Farley, Attorney General Brownell, and the director of defense mobilization, Mr. Arthur Flemming. Mr. Hoover is delighted with the opportunity to get back into the middle of this big problem. However, I was a bit nonplused to find that the only individuals he wanted on the commission were those whom he knew to share his general convictions—convictions that many of our people would consider a trifle on the motheaten side. As quickly as I found this out, I tried to make my other three appointments from among individuals whom I knew to be reasonably liberal or what I call middle-of-the-road in their approach to today's problems.

The Bricker amendment to the Constitution is being pushed by the senator from Ohio as his one hope of achieving at least a faint immortality in American history. The purpose of the Bricker amendment is to assure the American people that no provision of a treaty may override, internationally, any portion of the United States Constitution. Beyond this, it provides that no part of a treaty that affects the domestic affairs of the United States can become the law of the land until proper legislation is enacted by Congress. Now up to this point there is no quarrel about the matter at all. A number of us believe that an amendment to the above effect is completely unnecessary because we hold the present Constitution is perfectly clear on this point. Because we do so believe, we are quite willing to have an amendment specifically restating the proposition. But Senator Bricker wants to add (at the insistence of a certain fearful section of the American Bar Association) a provision to the second of the above purposes by saying that the congressional law passed for the implementation of a treaty would be invalid unless it would have been completely valid in the total absence of a treaty. This I cannot accept and none of my advisers will accept. To do so would completely wreck the traditional and prescribed balance between the executive and the legislative branch in the making of treaties.

Senator Knowland has introduced a substitute amendment containing only the parts of the Bricker amendment of which the administration approves.

It is almost hopeless to write about the Korea-Rhee situation.[3] Both the communists and the South Korean government have raised so many difficulties in the prosecution of the negotiations intended to end the fighting that it raises in my mind a serious question as to whether or not the United Nations will ever again go into an area to protect the inhabitants against communist attack. It has been a long and bitter experience, and I am certain in my own mind that except for the fact that evacuation of South Korea would badly expose Japan, the majority of the United Nations now fighting there would have long since attempted to pull out.

It is impossible to attempt here to recite the long list of items in which Rhee has been completely uncooperative, even recalcitrant. It is sufficient to say that the United Nations went into Korea only to repel aggression, not to reunite Korea by force. The armistice was intended to stop the fighting after the United Nations had proven its ability to stop such aggression and was intended also to mark the beginning of political discussions which would hope to reunite Korea and accomplish the evacuation of that country by both the Chinese and the Allied troops.

There has been so much backing and filling, indecision, doubt, and frustration engendered by both Rhee and the communists that I am doubtful that an armistice even if achieved will have any great meaning. Certainly we must be extremely wary and watchful of both sides. Of course the fact remains that the probable enemy is the communists, but Rhee has been such an unsatisfactory ally that it is difficult indeed to avoid excoriating him in the strongest of terms.

I have mentioned above the commission on government reorganization and functions, authorized by the Congress. I personally doubt the need for its organization, because of the simultaneous authorization of another commission which will have to do with the division of functions, duties, and responsibilities between the federal government and the several states.

It seems to me that this second commission, in order to reach its answers, will have to cover almost the identical ground that the organizational committee will. Essential functions of the federal government can be specified and segregated only in the light of what it is proper for states to do. Nevertheless, and in spite of the fact that these views were carefully explained to congressional leaders, two or three individuals on the Hill were so determined to have a new "Hoover" commission that I had to accept the Hoover Commission in order to achieve the other one, from which I expect much.

A third commission is to study the whole problem of foreign trade. Here again, if we succeed in getting a thorough study and unbiased analysis, we should have a very sound background for the programs that we shall have to present to Congress during the coming months. Pressure groups always want to establish new tariffs—I believe that an increased volume of trade, with decreasing obstacles of all kinds, is absolutely essential to the future of the free world. Undoubtedly, at numerous places in this notebook, I have discussed the reasons for this. But this does not mean that the job of getting our people (particularly the ivory fringe of the Republican party) to examine this matter dispassionately and intelligently and with the hope of serving the enlightened self-interest of the United States, is an easy one.

JULY 31, 1953

Recently I have had a few experiences that illustrate the peculiar kind of disappointment that comes to me these days and, I suppose, has come to everyone who has ever occupied this office.

During the election campaign of last year and the prenomination activities extending back over two or three years, a man named Eugene Pulliam, of Indiana, has been one of the men who persistently urged me to seek the presidency. He is a newspaper publisher with papers in Indiana and Arizona, possibly elsewhere. He was one of those who always insisted that his convictions as to my duty in this regard were based upon completely selfless factors—he was "interested only in the good of the country." A number of times he repeated, "I want nothing and you cannot possibly do anything for me." . . .[1]

I have taken the trouble to look up the activities and responsibilities of the federal communications commission and have concluded that while no great technical proficiency in the field of communications is mandatory, yet the qualities of good judgment, sound common sense, and, above all, a reputation for complete integrity and devotion to the public service should be sought in any candidate for this position.

In this case Len Hall reports that the man is not "too bad."[2] By this he means that nothing in the record would lead to the belief that the man is venal or would be a definite menace to the government. On the other hand, there is nothing to show that he would be a credit to the administration or that he would be an effective public servant. . . .[3]

I do not mean to say that I can claim to be shocked by this attitude—I have been around enough to know that there are many people who believe this attitude to be characteristic of every politician. Nevertheless, it does grow a bit wearisome to have recommendations based upon this kind of thinking come in from people who in their personal conversations with me protest their complete dedication to the public service, their devotion to the single objective of America's health and welfare, and their complete disinterestedness in the patronage of politics.

A case of a slightly different kind involves the success that the motion picture lobby has had in seeking the approval of Congress to its contention that all taxes on admission tickets should be removed. Our excise taxes are onerous, heavy, and, in many cases, not only unjust but positively stupid. For example, in the matter of excise taxes on whiskey, it has become quite clear that the taxes are so high as to reduce the revenue derived—and bootlegging on a large scale has thereby been encouraged. It was reported to me only recently that bootlegging is as prevalent as it was in the height of the prohibition days. This means not only that we are losing the revenue we should be getting; we are also building up a new rank of racketeers and vastly increasing the costs of law enforcement and crime detection and prevention.

Nevertheless, this administration in its efforts to provide a decent, well-thought-out tax program had first to face the stark and ugly fact that there was going to be a serious deficit in this financing, substantially greater than was publicly predicted by the outgoing administration. This meant that while we were making the study and developing a plan for tax reform that we would have to have the maximum revenue. Therefore to begin the process of eliminating certain of the excise taxes could not fail to start a general rush in this direction, and the result would be a terrific loss of revenue, which we could not afford.

As a consequence, we decided to hold the line during this session of the Congress, and by next January to have ready for presentation a tax program which would take into consideration the condition of the different businesses, their prospects, their necessities, and so on.

It is true that the motion picture industry has gone through a very hard time because of the competition of television, as well as other influences. Nevertheless, the American public is still keenly aware of the fact that much of the cost of motion pictures has gone into extravagant and almost senseless competition, and the salaries of the so-called "stars" whose qualifications were normally nothing more (in the case of the women) than platinum hair and shapely legs, or men with good profiles and vibrating voices.

I have personally met a number of these people; those with whom it is a pleasure to talk informally constitute a very small portion of the whole. I think one out of ten would be an exaggeration. Yet these people have been reported constantly in the public prints as having incomes of a half a million a year, or at least in the hundreds of thousands; fabulous salaries of directors, producers, and so on have likewise been publicized. The movies ran the old-fashioned vaudeville practically off the stage; they enjoyed for many years practically a monopoly in popular indoor entertainment. Both the legitimate theater, and the opera and the concert companies were hard put to it to stay in business. With this monopoly they indulged in the kind of publicity and salary binges that I have just mentioned and grew careless indeed in the kind of pictures that they produced.

Now they have all awakened to the fact that they are strictly up against it. If a citizen has to be bored to death, it is cheaper and more comfortable to sit at home and look at television than it is to go outside and pay a dollar for a ticket.

I personally do not believe that the cure for all this is to be found in singling out the movie industry for special privilege in the tax field. Even if my reactions as just recorded are somewhat on the harsh side—and indeed I think they are —the fact remains that the movie industry not only sought relief, they insisted upon total elimination of the excise taxes as applied to their industry.

Congress promptly agreed. In fact the members almost seemed to be in a great rush to get aboard the bandwagon, and I suppose this can be traced to the influence of local and smalltown movie houses in political campaigns.

In view of the similar appeals that I have had from the fur trade, the jewelry industry, the cosmetic people, and so on and so on, I think that the movie industry—in spite of the very eloquent appeal made to me yesterday by Mr. Bob Livingstone, Lincoln, Nebraska, vice-president of National Theater Owners of America; Mr. Robert Coyne, New York City, director, Council of Motion Picture Association of America; Colonel H.A. Cole, of Dallas, director, Council of Motion Picture Association of America; and Mr. Pat McGee, Denver, director, Council of Motion Picture Association of America—has overreached itself so far as to make it almost necessary to veto the bill that congress passed in this regard.

Like everybody else, I believe that entertainment and recreation at a price within the reach of every citizen is an absolute necessity for our people. I would like to be a party to improving the quality of the movie industry. And I realize that if we persist in a level of taxation that forces the closing of countless of the theaters we now have in the land, any reform or improvement will be difficult to achieve because of the lack of revenues. I think that already the revenue of the movie industry has fallen from something like $1.5 billion to about $1 billion. Here I am merely quoting the figure given me yesterday by one of my visitors.

Nevertheless, the tax is not wholly to blame. The action of the Congress in removing the industry completely from the burdens inherent in the excise tax program is, in my opinion, unwise and unjustified. My conclusion is that in this case the hope of immediate gain on the part of the theater owners and others led them too far. I think that had they been content with getting the tax cut in half, I would have been glad to go along with them. Even if they had gotten it reduced by two thirds, I think I would have approved the bill. As it is, I do not yet see how I can possibly approve the bill without feeling that I am completely unfair both to the government and to every other entertainment and luxury industry in the country.

Incidentally, I am reminded of a visit to my office by Ben Fairless. He came in several weeks ago. The call was merely a personal one, but as president of United States Steel, he mentioned the question of the excise profits tax, which I was then attempting to have extended by the congress. He said, "The extension of the tax will cost our company eighty million dollars. We think you ought to insist upon extension. You cannot possibly favor one group in the country at the expense of another—and we are willing to bear our share until you find a more equitable way of dealing with the matter that the excess profits tax was supposed to cover. Everybody agrees that it is a vicious and stupid form of taxation, but in the light of the circumstances, you should continue it until next January." The point of registering his statement—in almost his exact words—is that he is a representative of the class that the so-called liberal is always calling "thief," "robber," "economic tory," and all of the other names that imply venality and utter selfishness.

Of course, all of us are selfish. The instinct of self-preservation leads us into shortsightedness, and self-centered actions, often at the expense of our fellows, are all around us. But the very least that we should attempt to do, it seems to me, is to think of our long-term good as well as of our immediate gain. One thing that the long-term good of each of us demands is the fiscal, economic, industrial, and agricultural soundness of America. There is no future prosperity for any except as the whole shall prosper. So what I am probably trying to say concerning my reactions to the above incidents is that at least Ben Fairless exhibited a more intelligent kind of selfishness than did the politicians seeking special favors for an individual or an industry demanding a completely privileged position for itself.

End of tirade!

AUGUST 1, 1953

Senator Taft's death came so quickly after his first knowledge of any illness that I think it astonished even those of us who had some reasonably early warning of the nature of the illness.

He came to see me in Augusta, where I was staying at the Augusta National Golf Club, on April 19, and spent the night with me. At the conclusion of a golf game on April 20 he remarked to me that his hip hurt him a little bit—that he had noticed some pain in the region of his hip for a couple of weeks. He said that he thought he possibly should see a doctor.

On May 20 he went to Walter Reed Hospital for preliminary examination; and on May 27 General Snyder told me that he had certain alarming symptoms of cancer.

On June 10 I was in Minnesota when I received word that the senator had made public announcement that he would have to give up his leadership duties in the Senate.

On June 19, I attended a conference in Mr. Shanley's office attended also, among others, by Senator Taft, Secretary Durkin, Mr. Shanley, and Congressman McConnell.[1] It was the first time I had seen Senator Taft using crutches and I thought he looked fairly badly.

On June 24 he attended a legislative breakfast and on June 25, a legislative luncheon at the White House.

On June 29, a meeting of legislative leaders was held in the cabinet room, which Senator Taft attended. Thereafter he came to my office for a short conference. He looked fine, with good color, and was very jovial. He was particularly delighted with his physical improvement, saying that although he had lost twenty-five pounds since he first became ill, he had, in the week just preceding my meeting with him, gained four pounds. He was quite sure he was well on the road to recovery.

On July 4 Senator Taft went to New York, and on July 8 an exploratory operation was performed. General Snyder had told me some time before that he was going to have such an operation and he thought the senator had delayed it unnecessarily and unwisely.

On July 21 I called him on the telephone. He was feeling well and said that within one week he was going to leave the hospital and come back to Washington. We discussed a number of matters, including the appointment as assistant secretary of labor of a man named Siciliano.[2]

On July 31 he died, never having left the hospital.

AUGUST 19, 1953

Some months ago John Wisdom undertook the formation of a committee of Southerners with the object of devising ways and means for strengthening the Republican party in the Southern states.[1] There was a great deal of difficulty experienced in the attempt to form and operate such a committee, and finally it was suggested that the trouble lay in the fact that the committee had a certain "official" atmosphere when it should properly be an informal grouping of Republican leaders in that section. There has been possibly some truth in this contention since Mr. Wisdom was actually attempting to function in his capacity as a member of the executive committee of the Republican national committee.

Now, I understand, all have agreed that the committee should be organized quickly but on an informal basis.

This morning I called the national chairman (Len Hall) to tell him of my intense personal interest in the objectives of this committee. I have little concern as to whether the committee is formal, informal, or anything else—I am simply interested in finding out from intelligent and experienced people what should be our next and succeeding moves in that region.

Chairman Hall is to see Mr. Wisdom tomorrow and will try to get this whole matter straightened out and the whole project on the rails.

AUGUST 19, 1953 (PART TWO)

Several days ago in Denver the attorney general explained to me the general nature of the responsibility placed upon his department, by the Supreme Court, for rendering to that body a brief on the above subject. It appears that the Supreme Court desires both a memorandum of fact as well as an opinion concerning the intent of the Fourteenth Amendment.

It seems to me that the rendering of "opinion" by the attorney general on this kind of question would constitute an invasion of the duties, responsibilities, and authority of the supreme court. As I understand it, the courts were established by the Constitution to interpret the laws; the responsibility of the Executive Department is to execute them.

This morning I telephoned to the attorney general to present this view to him. He promised to have the idea carefully examined—because it seems to me that in this instance the Supreme Court has been guided by some motive that is not strictly functional. The Court cannot possibly abdicate; consequently it cannot delegate its responsibility, and it would be futile for the attorney general to attempt to sit as a court and reach a conclusion as to the true meaning of the Fourteenth Amendment.

The attorney general will, regardless of his conclusions as to the question I raise, render to the Supreme Court at the proper time a complete resume of fact and historical record.

OCTOBER 14, 1953

Discussion with Charlie Wilson regarding: (1) Advisability of ceasing all base development in Morocco and making the Spanish bases alternative to the final two that we had intended to build in the Moroccan area. I believe the Spanish area will be militarily and politically stronger than those in Morocco. (2) On question of his, I told him that I believed he should be very careful in establishing a precedent of providing unexpurgated secret reports to other officials of government, including the Congress. These reports are almost invariably based upon a variety of facts and factors, some of them lying completely outside the realm of interest of the person wanting to see them. We have so much trouble in leaks —explained and unexplained—that I know of no way to conduct ourselves except to be exceedingly careful in following the rule "Secret information only to those who must have it in order to carry on their duties." In the case of reports submitted to us by experts we enlist on a voluntary basis, each one gives us his frank views on the implied understanding that his opinions will not be revealed. (3) Wilson states that an order has been issued by the State Department (without reference to the secretary of defense) to the effect that General Handy in Europe should immediately stop delivering military aid supplies to Jugoslavia. I told him to discuss the matter with Secretary Dulles. I had not previously heard of it.

OCTOBER 24, 1953

Ernest Weir came in to see me this morning. He stated that in his opinion Pennsylvania would be lost to the Republicans unless (1) I should demand that the four leaders (the two United States senators, Mason Owlett and Governor Fine)[1] all agree on a compromise candidate for governor and support that candidate without reservation; (2) I do this in person and fairly promptly. Mr. Weir states that Len Hall will be helpless in making these warring factions come together at all, but he believes that the three, other than Senator Duff, would be rather amenable to such a suggestion—but that Senator Duff will never get into this kind of arrangement unless I make it a personal request.

The man that Ernest Weir puts forward as a possible compromise candidate is Dick Simpson, currently a congressman from Pennsylvania.

He said that in his opinion Len Hall should arrange for a meeting in Washington of the four men above-mentioned and that then Len Hall should bring them into my office so that I could express this conviction and this desire.

Ernest Weir looks on the foreign situation much as I do. He believes that we must develop some kind of a workable arrangement in the world for reducing tension or we are lost. Moreover, and vitally important, he believes that mutually profitable trade must be the basis of mutual cooperation in the world. He is working rather actively in promoting these ideas, and I have advised him to coordinate with the State Department in order that his efforts will not only follow the basic lines I had advocated by the administration, but will take into consideration the tactical situation that so often dictates the timing of these efforts.

Finally, Ernest Weir commented at some length on the lack of competent leaders (I think he really meant popular leaders) among the several segments of the Republican party. He thought that our National Committee and its chairman were not making themselves sufficiently felt in public. He thinks this criticism applies equally to the Senate and to the House of Representatives.

By implication he left me with the idea that, in his opinion, I must personally do more to urge Republican support of a middle-of-the-road philosophy. While he did not mention any names, he did more or less deprecate the idea that anyone else or any group of others were in sight to take over this job.

He admitted that it was a rather sorry state of affairs if this entire load had to be carried by the president but said, "There it is."

OCTOBER 26, 1953

Mr. Cole came to see me about public housing and slum clearance.[1] He stated he was going to try to get along on about $80 million in 1955. I think the 1954 program is about $85 million. Here we have a program that I would rather increase a little bit, so far as authorizations are concerned, even if we did not obligate it all during the year. My idea would be that we may want to do a job in the low-cost housing and slum-clearance field—that is the kind of thing that would be very valuable in helping prevent unemployment if any such contingency should appear to be imminent.

In the year 1953 the State Department was under Republican management for the first time in a generation, and some of the lower-level appointees proved unfortunate choices—none more so than R.W. Scott McLeod, an erstwhile member of the FBI, office assistant to Senator Bridges of New Hampshire, who came into the department as security officer. He took his duties seriously and stirred up the members of the foreign service and the department employees by giving the impression that they were all liberals and pinkos and therefore in danger of losing their jobs. Scotty McLeod in 1957 was accredited to Ireland as American ambassador, and in that dumping ground for professional Irish-Americans he was forgotten; he died in 1961. For a while he was loose in the State Department, and one of his acts of insouciance was to hold for five weeks a letter sent to the department by the head of the Socialist party in America, Norman Thomas, and then to send a smart-aleck reply. Infuriated, Thomas went to the top.

OCTOBER 27, 1953

Norman Thomas came to my office to voice several objections concerning some contacts with the State Department. His story is about as follows:

I (a) Last spring he heard a rumor to the effect that the State Department was classifying socialists practically as communists; he said that statements had been made to the effect that no socialist would be employed by the State Department, and any then in the employ of the State Department would be discharged when located.

(b) Mr. Thomas wrote a letter to the State Department about this report.

(c) He received no reply for five weeks, at the end of which period he received a letter from Mr. McLeod.

(d) Concerning this reply he had two or three bitter criticisms. I think the first was that a man of his standing should receive an answer signed by the "security officer" of the department. (While this objection was not put in this bald language, this meaning seemed implicit in what he had to say.)

He also said that the security officer presumed to establish State Department "policy" as applying to the civil service. Mr. Thomas considered this completely unwarranted and objectionable.

He thought the McLeod letter was vague in many respects, but he was particularly resentful of the implication that the writer of the letter made no real distinction between a socialist and a communist.

Finally, the fact that Mr. Thomas had to wait five weeks for an answer brought forth the rather sarcastic observation that "This administration has obviously made no progress in its announced intention of giving the country a 'businesslike' government."

II. Mr. Thomas has been traveling abroad and states that he took occasion to check in with people in our foreign service and other civil positions and to discuss with foreigners many of the things that attracted his attention. With respect to this trip, he states

(a) The morale of our foreign service has never been so low as it was a couple of months back when he was in Europe.

(b) Everyone seems to be upset by the absence of clearly stated criteria for determining who shall stay in the service and who shall be discharged.

(c) Our foreign friends feel that we have been making a ridiculous show of ourselves in giving a splendid example of both futility and stupidity in the way we have been managing our people abroad.

(d) There are far too many individuals in all of our headquarters and offices abroad. The need for discharging or transferring many of these people makes it doubly important, Mr. Thomas thinks, for stating very clearly the rules and regulations under which this is to be accomplished.

Mr. Thomas's recommendations and suggestions were not too definite, but he did believe it necessary that individuals in positions of recognized authority (the president and various cabinet heads) should state clearly that we will not: (1) remove anyone from civil service positions for political reasons, except where these positions are clearly "policy forming." The definition of a policy-forming position should likewise be clearly stated; he believes that "policy" positions must be occupied by choices of the administration; (2) discriminate against any person in an operational or administrative position because of his belief in some form of socialized government; (3) confuse socialism with its constant enemy, communism; (4) destroy civil service.

Mr. Thomas stated that he was appearing in the interests of civil service, not of the Socialist party. He says that, as far as he knows, there are very few so-called socialists working in government positions. Moreover, the name socialist covers such a wide range of political thinking and of viewpoint that a so-called rightist-socialist is as much a middle-of-the-roader as is a liberal-conservative.

In a discussion at the White House of November 1953, Eisenhower and his lieutenants in the cabinet canvassed the possibility of reducing the military budget, which one might have thought could have been cut drastically, perhaps back toward the $15 billion annual budget of pre-Korea days—Korea was over, and new weapons were available, presumably the H-bomb and low-yield battle-field nuclear weapons. Still, the task was not easy, for the Eisenhower administration hardly knew what to expect militarily. The conversation began and ended in confusion.

NOVEMBER 11, 1953

I have just had a meeting (4:00 to 6:00 P.M.) with Secretary Dulles, Secretary Humphrey, and Secretary Wilson. Problem: how to provide necessary security and still reduce the defense budget for 1955.

Statement by Secretary Dulles: He believes that we should begin to withdraw ground troops from Korea. This for the reason that we should show confidence in our air and naval strength and should avoid ground deployments in Asia. (If this were done, we could afford substantial reduction in army active strength.) Dulles stated that a week or more ago General Hull recommended that we initiate, now, the withdrawal of American ground troops from Korea. (No one else at the conference knew anything about this recommendation.)

It was agreed that (1) in view of the above and the conviction that some of our service and support units in Europe could be somewhat skeletonized, the army's recommendation for 1,500,000 individuals in 1955 would not, in the absence of some marked change in the international situation, be approved; (2) the dependence that we are placing on new weapons would justify completely some reduction in conventional forces—that is, both ground troops and certain parts of the navy.

In any event, the conclusion of the conference was that we should move toward a reduction in personnel in the armed services, especially army and possibly navy. This may mean, very soon, some reduction of the actual numbers of divisions in Korea. In Europe and in the United States it was felt that we should, in all services, effect some savings in number of individuals, especially in overhead and supporting units. The reduction of divisions in Europe should be constantly studied, but the State Department is to explore matter with Allies.

The Oppenheimer case, the suspicion that the wartime head of the Los Alamos laboratory for the assembling of nuclear weapons, the scientist J. Robert Oppenheimer, might have been a communist agent, was to plague the Eisenhower administration during a period of several years, and it broke early in December 1953. Critics outside the administration were wrought up, for they believed Oppenheimer unfairly accused. To the satisfaction of no one the whole issue was aired in a series of hearings by the Atomic Energy Commission in 1954. The testimony was published in a huge volume, that year. In the hearings it appeared that Oppenheimer in the 1930s and 1940s had had contact with communists and thus had opportunity to pass sensitive information. No one ever proved that he passed anything. In his last years he received the Fermi award of the United States government, a prize of $50,000 given annually to individuals, not necessarily American, for excellence in the area of science. Oppenheimer meanwhile became head of the Institute for Advanced Study at Princeton, which he administered with impeccable good judgment.

Still, when the case, as it was called, initially broke, there was consternation in the White House. In September 1945 the defection of a Russian code clerk from the Soviet embassy in Ottawa had revealed a large Soviet spy network in the United States. The confession of a British subject, once a German citizen, the brilliant nuclear physicist Klaus Fuchs, in 1950, meant that the wartime nuclear bomb project had been penetrated at its highest levels. Fuchs's disclosures led to the arrest of several American citizens—Harry Gold and David Greenglass, Julius and Ethel Rosenberg, and others—and the Rosenbergs were tried and convicted of treason and executed at Sing Sing on June 19, 1953, the first Americans ever executed for such a crime in time of peace. These cases, preceding the Oppenheimer case, had created a feeling of intense wariness among American officials.

DECEMBER 2, 1953

In a telephone call Charlie Wilson states that he has a report from the FBI that carries the gravest implications that Dr. Robert Oppenheimer is a security risk of the worst kind. In fact, some of the accusers seem to go so far as to accuse him of having been an actual agent of the communists. Mr. Wilson says that the atomic energy commission and one or two others in spots where contacts have been made with Dr. Oppenheimer have received similar reports.

He thought that one report had been dispatched to me, but I have not seen it.

When I first came to this office some one individual (I cannot now recall who it was) stated that in his opinion Dr. Oppenheimer was not to be trusted. Whoever it was—and I think it was probably Admiral Strauss—later told me that he had reason to revise his opinion.[1] At the same time, all of my other inquiries merely brought out that Dr. Oppenheimer had long been under observation because of the fact that a brother and sister-in-law (or was it his wife?) had been definitely connected with the communist movement some years back.

In any event Charlie Wilson says that this new report brings forward very grave charges, some of them new in character. I instructed him to inform the attorney general at once. The attorney general will examine the evidence to determine whether or not an indictment should be sought.

From what Mr. Wilson could tell me over the phone, I very much doubt that they will have this kind of evidence; but in the meantime I shall notify each individual with whom Dr. Oppenheimer has in the past had close contacts that until this whole matter is settled, these contacts should cease completely and at once.

The sad fact is that if this charge is true, we have a man who has been right in the middle of our whole atomic development from the very earliest days that it began. I am told that even when General Groves came to the Manhattan District Project, he found Dr. Oppenheimer already on the job. Dr. Oppenheimer was, of course, one of the men who has strongly urged the giving of more atomic information to the world.

Tomorrow morning before the security council meeting, I intend to call into my office the secretary of state, the secretary of the treasury, the secretary of defense, General Cutler, and Allen Dulles and inform them that until this matter is definitely settled all access to sensitive information is to be denied to Dr. Oppenheimer.[2] If there is some one spot where he has an official or semiofficial connection, it is possible that the head of that department or office will have to notify Dr. Oppenheimer of the seriousness of these new charges, and that, while no unsubstantiated charges will be made against him, until this affair is settled, we are forced to sever all connections with him and must ask him to return to us forthwith any information now in his hands that has had its origin in the United States government.

I am not certain as to the exact status of the individuals that served on these voluntary or advisory commissions, but it is possible, of course, that he has a complete file of the most sensitive kind of information.

DECEMBER 3, 1953

This morning I notified the secretary of state, the secretary of defense, the director of ODM [office of defense mobilization], the chairman of the atomic energy commission, and the director of the CIA that a complete bar would be immediately erected between this individual and any information of a sensitive or classified character.

I directed a memorandum to the attorney general instructing him to procure from the director of the FBI an entire file in the case of Dr. Oppenheimer and to make of it a thorough study. I assured him that I did not intend in any way to prejudge the case, but I did want a thorough and prompt recommendation from him as to what further action should be taken.

The investigation shows that the only connection Dr. Oppenheimer now has with the government is in the capacity of a member of the advisory committee for the office of defense mobilization. The director, Arthur Flemming, was consequently instructed to inform the director of the advisory committee (Dr. DuBridge) that the "Q" clearance of Dr. Oppenheimer had been suspended pending investigation and that as a result of that, Dr. Oppenheimer could not attend any further meetings of the committee. He also was further instructed that Dr. DuBridge was to be asked to keep this information secret, and Flemming himself is to inform Dr. Oppenheimer of this situation when the latter returns from Europe.

In the brief time I had to run over the so-called "new" charges, they consist of nothing more than the receipt of a letter from a man named Borden, who now as a private citizen has a post on the advisory committee of the joint atomic energy commission of the Congress. This letter presents little new evidence but merely asserts that the writer has made a long, exhaustive, and careful analysis of all of the accumulated evidence on Dr. Oppenheimer's beliefs and associations, reaching back to 1931, and on the basis of this new evaluation, felt that as a matter of duty he had to present his conclusions to the director of the FBI.

It is reported to me that this same information, or at least the vast bulk of it, has been constantly reviewed and reexamined over a number of years and that the over-all conclusion has always been that there is no evidence that implies disloyalty on the part of Dr. Oppenheimer. However, this does not mean that he might not be a security risk.

Actually, of course, the truth is that no matter now what could or should be done, if this man is really a disloyal citizen, then the damage he can do now as compared to what he has done in the past is like comparing a grain of sand to an ocean beach. It would not be a case of merely locking the stable door after the horse is gone; it would be more like trying to find a door for a burned-down stable.

DECEMBER 10, 1953

I am going to ask George Humphrey to invite Jim Duff to come to his office at an early date. Jim Duff proposes to discuss some of the political advantages to be gained through judicious filling of some vacancies (created by our reductions in personnel) by good, imaginative workers. He is referring especially to filling positions in the field—not to Washington. He thinks that we are very apt to defeat ourselves in trying to save billions for the government by being too chintzy or stingy in some personnel matters.

He is looking for no patronage himself and is not interested. He just thinks we are being a little bit unrealistic in certain instances.

One reason for taking this up with George Humphrey is not only that George controls the purse strings, but because he believes his criticisms apply to such things as the various mints and the customs office.

I am to speak to George about this when he comes to see me this afternoon.

The phrase "atoms for peace" entered the lexicon of international affairs with a speech by Eisenhower before the United Nations on December 8, 1953, and in this address he proposed that part of the nuclear stockpiles of the world be donated to an international "bank of fissionable materials." The result in future years was American lending of scientific know-how and of some fissionable materials to countries seeking to establish experimental reactors or reactors for generating electricity.

DECEMBER 10, 1953 (PART TWO)

On the eighth of December I delivered my second major speech in the field of foreign relations, this time before the United Nations. The first one was delivered on April 16 last before the American Society of Newspaper Editors.

There has been much speculation on what I was trying to do in a talk that dealt principally with the field of atomic energy and atomic warfare and made definite proposals for international action in promoting the peaceful use of atomic science and materials.

The reasons were several. Of these, the first and principal one was exactly as stated—to make a clear effort to get the Soviet Union working with us in some phase of this whole atomic field that would have only peace and the good of mankind as a goal. If we were successful in getting even the tiniest of starts, it was believed that gradually this kind of talk and negotiation might expand into something broader—that at least a faint possibility existed that Russia's concern, bordering upon fright, of the certain results of atomic warfare might lead her, in her own self-interests, to participate in this kind of joint humanitarian effort. Another important objective was to call to the attention of the small nations of the world that they likewise had an interest in the uses to which the world would put its limited available supply of raw material, out of which the atomic bomb is made.

Too many of these small nations have looked upon this matter as one of concern only to the USSR and to the United States—except, of course, as some of them felt that they would be certain targets in the event of atomic warfare breaking out.

The hope of the talk was to awaken in these small nations an understanding that there were steadily opening up new and promising opportunities for using these materials and these skills to the benefit rather than to the destruction of men. Thus it was hoped to help build up a world opinion for turning attention toward these constructive purposes.

Another reason was that even in the event that the USSR would cooperate in such a plan for "propaganda purposes" that the United States could unquestionably afford to reduce its atomic stockpile by two or three times the amounts that the Russians might contribute to the United Nations agency, and still improve our relative position in the cold war and even in the event of the outbreak of war.

Another important reason was to give the population of our country the feeling —the certain knowledge—that they had not poured their substance into this whole development with the sole purpose and possibility of its being used for destruction. This effort also gave the opportunity to tell America and the world a very considerable story about the size and strength of our atomic capabilities, but to do it in such a way as to make this presentation an argument for peaceful negotiation rather than to present it in an atmosphere of truculence, defiance, and threat.

Underlying all of this, of course, is the clear conviction that as of now the world is racing toward catastrophe—that something must be done to put a brake on this movement. Certainly there is none so foolish as to think that the brake can be composed only of words and protestations, however eloquent or sincere. But ideas expressed in words must certainly have a function in getting people here and elsewhere thinking along these lines and helping to devise ways and means by which the possible disaster of the future can be avoided.

DECEMBER 11, 1953

Howard Cullman wanted to talk to me about the possibility of a dock strike— and what he called the false impression concerning cigarettes and their effect on lung cancer created by three doctors who wrote a story in *Readers Digest*.[1]

In the first instance, he was sure that we should be preparing for the possibility of such a strike, not that he was particularly certain it was going to happen, but because he thought that even a moment's inaction on the matter would have the gravest consequence, particularly to the Republican party. (I wrote a note to the secretary of labor to ask about the facts in the dock strike.)

With regard to the report that lung cancer is created by cigarette smoking, Howard Cullman was very vehement in declaring that he was not in the business of trying to kill people off by selling cigarettes, and if he believed this report to be true he would stop instantly.

He said that the cigarette industry had expended a terrific amount of money in research to determine the physical effects of smoking—I believe he mentioned the sum of $50 million. In any event, he said that they have had scientists working on the problem for a long time and that they were unable so far to trace any possible relationship between smoking and lung cancer. He felt that the public health service could get in touch with all of the legitimate research laboratories in the country and merely make known to the public the results so far obtained.

He pointed out that the federal government at this moment is getting about $1.6 billion tax revenue out of cigarettes, which is about ten times the profits made by the tobacco companies themselves. He thought, therefore, that we should have some slight interest in getting the truth of the matter before the public, because of this moment sales have fallen off markedly and even cigarette stocks themselves are falling in price.

I gave Mrs. Hobby this story and told her I had dismissed it from my mind.

DECEMBER 11, 1953 (PART TWO)

Governor Dewey wanted to speak to me about the Niagara power development, the Long Island Railway, his reasons for declining to head the Canadian-American defense board, his intentions concerning his own political career, and one or two items of minor importance.

For me the important one was his attitude on the Niagara River power development. In this particular case the Congress reserved to itself (instead of permitting action by the federal power commission) the power to decide the ways and means of developing the Niagara River water power.

In New York State the governor said there is a law that the water power belongs to the state itself, and that if the federal government attempts to give the right to development to private power companies, it will be in direct contravention of New York State law. This he thought would be a major political mistake.

Beyond this he pointed out that in the TVA region, in the Columbia River valley, and in the Colorado River valley power has been made available to local residents without the additional costs of taxes to be paid to the federal government, which must always be done when the development is by private power companies. If, therefore, this particular development were turned over to private power development, the particular area would be seriously discriminated against in favor of these other regions which have cheap power.

He told me also that he would probably be in opposition to every paper in New York State in the matter of the Long Island Railway. He is frankly opposed to state ownership and operation, but he says the Long Island Railway is flat broke and badly in debt. The public, of course, wants subsidized transportation and does not want to pay the costs of operation. This whole thing means a fairly nasty political problem, but he says he is going to hold out for a fair and just solution to the problem.

DECEMBER 11, 1953 (PART THREE)

Roy Roberts gave me some advice on the Taft-Hartley Law that was identical with that presented by George Humphrey yesterday afternoon.[1] Their common advice was that under no circumstances should I recommend detailed amendments to the Taft-Hartley Act, except only in the particular areas in which I promised amendments during the campaign.

In all other points Mr. Roberts urged that I confine my efforts to attempting to define the limits within which I could accept the law and would not find it necessary to disprove it. As I understand him, what he really wants me to argue for is the approach to the law—the general philosophy to be observed—but that this could be done somewhat more definitively than would be possible in a mere statement of principle. For example, as I understand his attitude, the subject involving closed, union, or open shop could be handled about as follows: "I am personally opposed to the principle of the closed shop and would not find it possible to approve a federal bill containing such a provision. At the same time I believe in free trade unionism based upon voluntary action and believe unions to be an absolutely essential factor of modern industrial life in order that men who work may be assured of fair wages, proper working conditions, and other benefits that flow to them as a body. The present law recognizes and authorizes the so-called union shop but makes provision that in those states where there exists the so-called 'right-to-work' clause, the federal authority shall not attempt to override the state's decision in this matter. In a very complex and controversial situation I believe that the present law is about as accurate a representation of fairness to both sides as can be devised. The Congress seems here called upon to decide between the rights of the individual, or of the minority, as opposed to the majority. I am prepared to accept any decision of the Congress that reflects an apparent regard for both sides of this argument."

Mr. Roberts also expressed a great desire to see the Republican party secure young, dynamic candidates for their entire slate of national, state, and local offices. He said we have a lot of inertia to overcome in this regard, but we must do it if we are going to win.

DECEMBER 14, 1953

The national security training commission. The national security training commission submitted a report advocating immediate initiation of universal military training. They asked also that I include a short paragraph in my state of the union message on the subject.

The office of defense mobilization is supposed to render me an independent report on this subject. It is not yet received, but when it is some decision on this matter will have to be reached and possibly announced.

DECEMBER 17–19, 1953

Impressions of three-day conference.

Amount of caution, approaching fright, that seems to govern the action of most politicians.

Because most have been elected often (or they wouldn't be chairmen of committees in an organization where promotion depends exclusively upon senior-

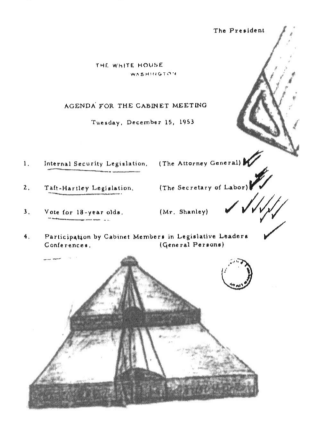

Cabinet meeting, December 15, 1953. According to Eisenhower's long-time associate Kevin McCann, "He was no actor at cabinet meetings. . . . There he followed the counsel of a bronze plaque that once adorned his desk: 'You ain't learnin' nothin' when you're talkin'.' . . . For most of the session he was hunched over the agenda sheet, viciously checking off, when finished, the topics that inflamed his temper, tiredly checking off those that bored him. He never missed a word, but continually was doodling. On the agenda sheet margins or on blank pieces of paper he drew faces, animals, flowers, tableware—tea cups on saucers were favorites." Defiance (Ohio) Crescent-News, October 14, 1980.

ity) this impression creates the uneasy conclusion that slippery refusal to face an issue is the secret of "good politics"—which means, getting elected! Charles Halleck, Ed Rees, Dewey Short, Nixon, Bridges, Wiley.[1]

1954

If during the entire period from, say, the year 1931 down to the present writing (1981)—a half century of American life—one were to choose a time when for a short moment American domestic and international affairs seemed in order, it might well have been the beginning of the year 1954. Never before, nor after, was there such a time. The year 1931 marked the first year when the Great Depression began to affect people everywhere, not merely in the United States but abroad, and after the depression settled down upon the world it deranged the economics and politics of Europe and Asia and brought the Second World War. In the immediate years after the great victory of 1945 the economic affairs of the United States were in an uneasy state, as the country sought to adjust to peacetime. There was concern that there would be another depression—for after every war in American history, great and small, there had been a depression. In foreign relations the feelings of peace that were so strong in 1945 soon slipped away, and people began to talk about a cold war. In 1950 the cold war turned hot, and the conflict in a remote peninsula of Asia did not end until the summer of 1953; no one could be sure it was over until some months had elapsed and the armistice of Panmunjom gave evidence of holding.

At the beginning of the new year, 1954, everything looked bright. The president had seen too many expectations turn to ashes—he himself was uncertain, but he took things as they came and hoped that the aura of success surrounding his presidency after its initial year would last for three more years, at least.

JANUARY 12, 1954

Duties of a president.

10:00 A.M. Greet advertising council
12:30 P.M. Present three medals of honor—with fifty guests present
2:30 P.M. Present award to Captain Rickenbacker (twenty guests)
9:00 P.M. Reception (1,500)

JANUARY 18, 1954

In two more days I complete my first year as president. As I look back on my hopes of a year ago, I have mixed feelings. In some instances progress has been greater, associations more agreeable, and problems really easier than I had anticipated. In many other instances, the exact reverse has been true.

It would be difficult in a hurriedly written memorandum accurately to classify as satisfying or disappointing all of the incidents of the past year, or the personalities with whom I have dealt. However, since events and personalities are rarely disassociated one from the other, it would perhaps be easier to talk about personalities—individually and collectively—and in so doing speak both of the gratifying and the discouraging parts of my year's experience.

First, to be completely personal in the sense that the vertical pronoun implies. When Mamie and I came to the White House, we probably had a fairly good understanding of what living in it would be. The prominent military positions I had occupied for some years had given me some experience that definitely, even though faintly, resembles that through which a president is compelled to live. This was especially true when I was abroad commanding at SHAEF in World War II and later as commander at SHAPE. In both those positions, I led a fairly lonely life, the first time living only with my aides, and the second time with Mamie at Marnes-la-Coquette. We could not visit in restaurants, theaters, or other public places with the same freedom that is enjoyed by the ordinary citizen; problems of security, of protocol, and of autographing were always with us. The finding of time necessary for health and recreation was always difficult.

We knew all of these difficulties would be multiplied in White House existence, but at least we were psychologically prepared for them.

The other side of this particular picture is that after discharging normal hospitality and entertainment obligations, the president and his lady have the privilege of inviting anyone to the White House and have accommodations there to take care of quite a number of people. Since most people like to visit the place at least once, it is normally easy to call upon old friends to come in and share a bit of personal life with the occupants.

So much for that.

The members of the cabinet and heads of principal supporting agencies were selected before the inauguration. The only one of my selectees of last year who proved to be a disappointment to me was Secretary Durkin.[1] He could never free himself of the feeling that he was placed in the cabinet to be a "trade unionist." He referred to his conferences here as "collective bargaining." I liked him personally and did my best to get him to adopt an attitude of serving the entire people, and to do so with his rich background and experience in the whole labor movement. This he could not do, and so I suppose it was inevitable that finally he should become unhappy and leave. His replacement, Mr. Mitchell, measures up, in my opinion, to the caliber of the other members of the cabinet.

As for the cabinet as now constituted, I cannot think of a single position that I could strengthen by removal of the present incumbent and appointing another. I trust this will be so for the next three years, but, of course, in human affairs of this kind one sometimes is compelled to change his mind.

By no means do I mean to imply that anyone of my associates is perfect in his job—any more than I deem myself to be perfectly suited to my own. I merely mean to say that I have had a good many years of experience in selecting people for positions of heavy responsibility, and I think that the results so far achieved by this cabinet and by other close associates justify my conviction that we have an extraordinarily good combination of personalities.

This group has played a big part in legislative accomplishments of the past year. The list of those accomplishments is rather long and in many respects very gratifying. The record has been given in numbers of talks; I mentioned them specifically in a television talk only a couple of weeks ago. For the record, I list below—taken from that talk—what I consider the major achievements of the last year.

1. The fighting and the casualties in Korea have come to an end.

2. Our own defenses and those of the free world have been strengthened against communist aggression.

3. The highest security standards are being insisted upon for those employed in government service.

4. Requests for new appropriations have been reduced by $13 billion.

5. Tax reductions which go into effect this month have been made financially feasible by substantial reductions in expenditures.

6. Strangling controls on our economy have been removed.

7. The fantastic paradox of farm prices, on a toboggan slide, while living costs soared skyward, has ceased.

8. The cheapening of inflation of every dollar you earn, every savings account and insurance policy you own, and every pension payment you receive has been halted.

9. The proper working relationship between the executive and legislative branches of the federal government has been made effective.

10. Emergency immigration legislation has been enacted.

11. A strong and consistent policy has been developed toward gaining and retaining the initiative in foreign affairs.

12. A plan to harness atomic energy to the peaceful service of mankind and to help end the climate of suspicion and fear that excites nations to war, has been proposed to the world.

Above and beyond those achievements, everybody has worked tirelessly to have a program ready for submission to the Congress when it convenes this month. I outlined that program in my state of the union speech on January 7, and special parts of it have been amplified in almost daily messages sent to the congress. All in all, I deem it to be a program that is sound and progressive, and I believe that a large part of it will be enacted by the Congress.

Beyond all this, I think that the individuals in the cabinet and in other important offices like each other. At least, I can detect no sign of mutual dislike among the group. I know that I like them all; I like to be with them; I like to converse with them; and I like their attitude toward their duty and toward governmental service. All together, therefore, my experiences with the cabinet members have been gratifying officially and most satisfying personally.

It could not be expected, of course, that my relationship with legislative leaders would be on quite as satisfying a plane as those with the cabinet. In the latter case, I was personally responsible for the selections and naturally chose no one whose political philosophy I found to be diametrically opposed to my own, and certainly I chose no one whose personality I thought would clash with those of his associates. On the other hand, legislative leaders, being elected in their own right, feel a certain independence in thought and in indulging their own particular theories of government. Particularly in late years the ties of party allegiance have been weakened. Occasionally, during the year, differences with members of my own party were even more pronounced and deepseated than with some of the others.

Having said this, it is, however, only fair also to say that relationships with these people have been on the whole better than I anticipated. Before I announced publicly (January 1952) that I adhered to a Republican philosophy (which admittedly may have been my own interpretation of Republican philosophy), I was quite well aware of some of the deepseated differences that would separate me, in the event of a successful election, from some of the House and Senate leaders.

Others were aware of these deepseated differences. In the years between 1946 and 1952, whenever I was approached by Democrats urging that I declare political allegiance to that party, one of their arguments was that I would be further separated in political philosophy from such people as Senators Jenner, McCarthy, Millikin, Bridges, Langer, and others than I would from the Democratic leaders.[2]

Of all the legislative leaders with whom I thought, in advance, that I would have constant trouble, there was none with whom incessant difficulty seemed more probable than with Senator Taft. While Senator Taft was, as I saw him, far more personal in his attitude toward politics than I could ever be, yet in his case the exact reverse came about.

For many weeks before he died last July, I considered him my ablest associate on the Hill, and indeed one of the stalwarts of the administration. His loyalty was given as a matter of intellectual agreement and, as he once told me, in the spirit of fair play and in his conviction that we were in general trying to travel the same road. I found him to be far less reactionary than I had judged him to be from a reading of his speeches and public statements. In some things, I found him extraordinarily "leftish." This applied specifically to his attitude toward old-age pensions. He told me that he believed every individual in the United States, upon reaching the age of sixty-five, should automatically go on a minimum pension basis, paid by the federal government. He wanted us to proceed more rapidly than we actually did in revising military planning and policy and resulting organization; nevertheless, his actual recommendations closely paralleled the conclusions that we reached as a body. The difference is that we feel we have statistical analyses for sound conclusions on which to base our program, whereas he wanted to do it because it was "different" from what "that man Truman advocated."

In actual practice, whenever differences developed between the White House and some of our Republican senators on matters of importance, we could count on Senator Taft to assert his great influence to bring them into line.

After his death, no one of real strength has shown up on the Senate side.

Knowland means to be helpful and loyal, but he is cumbersome. He does not have the sharp mind and the great experience that Taft did. Consequently, he does not command the respect in the senate that Senator Taft enjoyed. Senator Dirksen seems radically to have changed his attitude toward international affairs and is now seemingly disposed to go along with the administration as its supporter and lieutenant. If this continues, he may well soon become the most effective man, from our standpoint, in the Senate. Senator Bridges, Senator Millikin, Senator Saltonstall, and other experienced legislators are men of good will toward the administration, but they are not natural leaders—and their theory of legislation is by "trading" and therefore modifying and placating. They do not seem to realize when there arrives that moment at which soft speaking should be abandoned and a fight to the end undertaken. Any man who hopes to exercise leadership must be ready to meet this requirement face to face when it arises; unless he is ready to fight when necessary, people will finally begin to ignore him.

In the House, the situation is considerably different. People there are more organizational-minded and seemingly look with some scorn on the "individualistic" attitude of the average senator. We have two splendid men in Joe Martin and especially in our majority leader, Charlie Halleck. He is smart, capable, and courageous. On top of this, he is a team player and is a loyal one. A number of the committee chairmen are far below his standard, but so great are his powers of persuasion that it is rarely indeed that he cannot produce for us a good showing on any proposition that is important to us.

One third of the Senate and all of the Congress will be up for election this fall.

Right now it seems to me that the Republicans are going through an anxious period. They are watching the public to see how it reacts to the program that has been sought by the administration and whether, through that program, my personal popularity will suffer a decline in the country. By and large, they will soon have to make the choice to support or to defy that program—which means to support or to defy me.

This is a tough one for some of them because the program cannot please everybody, and no attempt was made to have it do so. But the entire administration is devoted to the task of selling this program to the people in general—we hope that we shall be sufficiently successful so that these hopeful congressmen and senators will see that their bread is buttered on the administration side.

Another group to be considered is the press corps, in which I include not only representatives of the newspapers, but of television, radio, and newsreels. The members of this group are far from being as important as they themselves consider, but, on the other hand, they have a sufficient importance—and particularly in the eyes of the average Washington officeholder—to insure that much government time is consumed in courting favor with them and in dressing up ideas and programs so that they look as saleable as possible. (For example, I am right now scheduled to go to a cocktail party—something I have not attended in twenty years—for the Washington press corps and given by the senatorial committee on elections. I am to drop in for the purpose, I suppose, of showing that I am not too high-hat to do so.)

On the whole, the press group violates the old adage, "Always take your job seriously, never yourself." This old saw they largely apply in reverse. As a result, they have little sense of humor and, because of this, they deal in negative criticism rather than in any attempt toward constructive helpfulness.

I once heard that human minds are divided into three great classes, depending upon the kind of subject in which the greatest intellectual interest is taken. The essayist contended that the highest type of mind was concerned with philosophies and ideas and their application to the problems of life. He thought the second class of mind was concerned with the physical things about us, the products of our industry, the natural resources of the country, the machines we use, the food that we eat, and so on. The third class he thought was concerned primarily with personalities. This kind of mind is the one, he said, that enjoys gossip.

If this kind of thing has any semblance of truth in it, I would say that it does not speak well for the average writer of the press. They love to deal in personalities; in their minds, personalities make stories.

I suspect that most of these men took up writing as a career for a peculiar purpose. Everybody loves distinction. If a writer can achieve a by-line in the paper for which he writes, he gets a certain thrill out of seeing his name in black type at the head of his own column every day. Beyond this, everybody likes the feeling of authority. There is a quality that has been described as authorial omnipotence. When the author succeeds in having his words published, there is normally no chance for refutation by anyone. Consequently, the author feels that his word is authoritative and that, as a result, he has a great influence on world events. (At least both words come from a common root.)

If any or all of these things are true, it could account for the extraordinary amount of distortion and gross error that characterizes so much of what appears in the newspapers. For more than twelve years, I have been, in one capacity or another, at spots in the world that have been considered newsworthy. Consequently, I have seen, when they occurred, the actual incidents reported, or I have clearly understood the motives of the individuals written about. Rarely is such writing accurate.

I have had opportunities in the busy years to read only a few newspapers, so I do not generalize too far. In the papers that I have read, it seems to me that the *Herald Tribune* of New York observes higher standards in this regard than do most others. From what I have seen of the Philadelphia *Bulletin*, it has very high standards too—and there are undoubtedly others in the country. But the *Herald Tribune* is one that I have had the opportunity to watch closely.

Other papers—the *New York Times*, the Chicago *Tribune*, and many others —have larger and more widespread reporting staffs, have bigger circulations, and in many ways are more elaborate and better done newspapers than is the *Herald Tribune*. But in this one basic qualification—the degree of accurate reporting— these others do not, in my opinion, approach the *Herald Tribune*.

As there are differences in papers in this regard, I think there are, of course, differences in individuals. I have known some people whom I consider very great reporters. Some I have known only slightly, some almost intimately. In Washington today, I think certain ones observe the very highest standards of fairness, accuracy, and objectivity. Among them are Drummond, Krock, Arrowsmith, Clark, Lucey, Darby, and a chap named Donovan. Others who seem to me to be very good are Merriman Smith, Leviero, and one or two more.

In past years, I have known such people as Virgil Pinkley, Charlie Wertenbaker, Thor Smith, Wes Gallagher, Drew Middleton, and a few others who I always felt were unimpeachably honest and straightforward. The fact remains, however, that today I believe the newspaper profession and the public it serves are getting a very poor return in accurate reporting out of the very great amount of money that they must devote to meeting, in the aggregate, the costs of the Washington corps.

Most Washington officials learn enough eventually that they stop reading articles about themselves and their departments, whether favorable or unfavorable.

I think I might recite a story that I heard yesterday from my minister, Dr. Elson:

"Some years back, a prominent Bostonian felt that he had been maligned by a writer in a local newspaper. He was angry and determined to avenge himself against the offender. To determine what action to take, he went to see his friend, Dr. Edward Everett, and told him of the circumstances.

"He ended his account with a question, really several questions. He asked, 'Should I call the man out? Should I sue him? Should I sue the newspaper? Just exactly what is the best way to go about the matter?'

"After some thought, Dr. Everett answered, 'Do nothing. Ignore him.'

"He went on, 'This paper is not very widely read. Of those that read it, half will not read this story. Of those that read the story, half will not understand what this man is driving at. Of those that understand it, half will not believe it. Of those that believe it, half will be people whose opinion means nothing whatsoever to you. So why worry?' "

Scarcely could I end this particular memorandum without saying something of my personal staff. Yesterday someone brought to me an article by a man who criticized my staff severely (me also, of course). His castigation of the staff was that it was completely undistinguished and lacking both color and wisdom. Moreover, he said that it was nothing but an assembly here in Washington of the various characters who had traveled my campaign train with me in 1952. In a sense, this last may be true. But I wonder if the writer thought that I should have selected for traveling on my campaign train people whom I despised and for whom I had no respect intellectually or otherwise.

Actually the staff (and I have been used to, for many years, really brilliant staff work) has performed magnificently. Sherman Adams has grown into the job that he has, and in a very definite sense has created it as he went along.[3] Honesty, directness, and efficiency have begun to win him friends among people who initially were prone to curse him because he had no time for flattery or cajolery, or even pleasantries over the telephone. Supporting him is a group composed of Persons, Shanley, Hauge, Stephens, Hagerty, Cutler, and Jackson.[4]

Each of these men is an extremely capable individual, apt, loyal, and energetic. Immediately supporting them is another layer of such people as Martin, Morgan, Harlow, Minnich, and so on.[5]

Going even further, I have, so far, heard not a single complaint as to misconduct, disloyalty, or any other kind of indiscretion or offense on the part of any of the people that we brought to the White House with us last January. On the contrary, I have heard them consistently praised and complimented by legislators and by a vast army of friends throughout the country.

(So again I must ignore the conclusions of a critical writer.)

During the year we lost Emmet Hughes, who was very capable in assisting me in all the chores having to do with reports, letters, and public talks.[6] Soon we are to lose C.D. Jackson, who has been my personal adviser in the field of psychological warfare.

A real tragedy has been the sickness of General Carroll.[7] Liked and respected by every member of the staff, he was responsible for establishing a secretariat, which the White House had never had and which was badly needed. Now he is in the hospital with a heart attack and will probably be away from duty for a matter of several months. But no matter how long I have to wait, I shall still have a place for him.

JANUARY 27, 1954

This group came in to assure me that Republicans in Pennsylvania are absolutely consolidated, solidified, and are going to support Mr. Wood for governor without alibi or excuse.[1]

WEEK OF FEBRUARY 7, 1954

"Man's right to knowledge and the free use thereof."

An intriguing phrase—it rings in the ears almost as if we could hear Patrick Henry's immortal call to liberty or death. Merely to claim this resounding slogan as our own gives us a feeling of superiority over the demagogues, the jingoes, the tyrants who thrive in the ignorance of others and employ curtains of iron or of oratory to deepen and prolong that ignorance. We thrill ourselves by our own insistence on academic freedom—the teacher's right to knowledge and his privilege of imparting his own interpretations thereof. We point with pride to American schools from primary to graduate level and, comparing them to institutions of learning in Prague, Budapest, and Moscow, we emphasize the extent and scope of our freedoms and the enrichment of human life deriving therefrom.

We are proud of our guarantees of freedom in thought and speech and worship. Of such value are all these things to us that, unconsciously, we are guilty of one of the greatest errors that ignorance can make—we assume that our standard of values is shared by all other humans in the world.

We are not sufficiently informed.
Probably have more need for education than any other.
Twenty-one POWs chose communism.[1]
Farm problems.
Foreign problems.

Not long after Eisenhower set out his situation in the presidency as of the beginning of the apparently halcyon year 1954, a small cloud appeared on the horizon. The president would not have to deal with the cloud, as it slowly increased in size, nor would his immediate successor Kennedy, but it would wreck the presidency of Kennedy's successor. The issue of Indochina went back to the Second World War and well before, probably back to the latter nineteenth century when the French began their ill-fated venture in Indochina. As the years passed the French settlers shamelessly exploited their opportunities in the faraway province, and this heritage then came into trouble when nationalism began to stir in the Far East in the years during and after the First World War. By the time of the Second World War the nationalist movement was strong, and its hopes rose during the Japanese occupation, especially toward the end, when the hardpressed Japanese military conceded many privileges to the native Vietnamese.

War began in 1946 when the returning French failed to recognize the regime established by Ho Chi Minh in Hanoi, and fighting had gone on until by early 1954 the French were close to defeat. The French army was losing lieutenants and captains, graduates of St. Cyr, by the hundreds, and native troops and mercenaries of the foreign legion by the thousands. By early 1954 the war was not yet lost. But the French defenders had chosen an out-of-the-way place, Dienbienphu, ringed about by hills—a stupid place for defense, thought the American observers of French strategy in Indochina—and intended to make a stand, showing the insurgents that men devoted to the glory of France could repulse the attacks of any ragamuffins of the Far East.

If the choice of a position to defend to the death was a piece of foolishness, this stupidity was not yet clear, and meanwhile the Americans had begun to take interest in Indochina. The Korean War had made its defense seem a part of the larger communist issue in the Far East. During the negotiations in Europe over bringing the Germans into NATO, the French were constantly pushing their American opposites for more help in Indochina, not merely financial but military. To the disgust of the Americans, the French price in Indochina for good behavior in Europe always seemed to be rising. Truman's secretary of state, Acheson, had considered it blackmail. There was not much that he or his successor, Dulles, could do, other than pay up. Early in February 1954 one of the payments was coming due.

FEBRUARY 8, 1954

I telephoned to the secretary of defense to tell him of Chairman Saltonstall's anxiety about the plan for sending two hundred technicians into Indochina.[1] Chairman Saltonstall says that the opposition in the Senate Committee is so great that it may affect appropriations for the area. He believes this opposition would diminish if there were an unequivocal statement on the part of the administration that the technicians will be removed from Indochina by June 15, regardless of French capacity to meet the requirement.

I instructed Mr. Wilson to devise the necessary plan, even if it meant the hiring of technicians under the aid program to replace the air force technicians in Indochina.

Mr. Wilson said that he had one or two other ideas to explore but that he would communicate with Senator Saltonstall as soon as practicable to give him the assurances he seeks.

FEBRUARY 10, 1954

Ambassador Kemper (Brazil) called on me and said that strangely enough the small farmers who raise coffee in Brazil are not getting the benefit of the present high prices in coffee and have been led to believe (by their own particular brand of demagoguery) that the operations of a bunch of speculators in New York are tending to price their product out of the market and without any benefit at all to them.[1]

The report merely provokes the observation that here we have a unique phenomenon—that the people of two countries are each being convinced that the wickedness of the public in the other country is responsible for economic disorder in their own.

Incidentally, he told me that in view of the prices coffee is bringing in Brazil (around seventy cents) that a considerable part of the present prices in America must be due to some kind of speculative activity. He thinks the federal trade commission will uncover some definite facts on this.

FEBRUARY 10, 1954 (PART TWO)

Letter was delivered from President Rhee this morning to the State Department and is of such a tone that the State Department is refusing to receive it and to pass it on to me. However, they will have a photostatic copy made of it. That copy I want to see—then it will become a part of my unofficial records.[1]

FEBRUARY 15, 1954

In dealing with the personnel problem both at home and abroad, we might make things easier for ourselves by a greater reduction in authorized strength, at least on the basis of trying it out. If at the end of the year we were forced to build up greater strength, we could do it on the basis of our own choosing.

Information given to the Congress by the executive departments. Frequently there are incidents of some friction between committees of Congress and one of the executive departments involving a refusal on the part of the latter to provide information requested by the committee. Such refusals, of course, are always based on the security factor.

It has been suggested that much of this friction might be avoided if we could evolve a general policy and have it approved at one of our meetings with legislative leaders. The policy would be generous in terms and intent but would provide also a set of criteria for determining whether or not security was involved.

In the matter of filling positions in the Executive Department, I think that we have gotten rather careful in assuring advance approval by the affected members of Congress. I believe that this is a habit that should be observed in almost every subject we study and every project we undertake.

When any idea of any kind is first advanced, someone should have the job of saying "How is Congress or any member thereof affected by this proposal?" The answer to this question should determine the amount of preliminary work that should be done with the Congress in order to eliminate misunderstandings and friction.

FEBRUARY 26, 1954

The Bricker amendment, while it has been rendered largely innocuous, may pass with the so-called George provision in it and this, which deals with executive agreements, I may have to oppose unless its language is greatly modified.[1]

The wetbacks are causing difficulties in our relations with Mexico.

McCarthy is grabbing the headlines and making the people believe that he is driving the administration out of Washington.

Finally, a number of bills have been introduced in the Senate, some with the support of a Republican or two, to provide for school buildings throughout the country.

This is another method by which to embarrass the administration which believes in maximum decentralization. The job is to determine those localities that really cannot afford proper education facilities for the population and to help those out with federal funds. The proposals now before the Senate are really an all-out grab under the still plausible theory that anything you get from the federal government is for free.

MARCH 5, 1954

Discussion was to effect that Senator Dirksen would try to influence Republican members on McCarthy committee to observe proper procedures.[1] Have written memorandum to attorney general to get in touch with Senator Dirksen on the matter of closing out our alien property operations. I told Streeter Flynn I would like to see him in the Senate.[2] I advised Senator Dirksen to make date with Tom Stephens to bring Senator Langer in to breakfast some morning soon. I told Senator Dirksen that the White House was neutral in Republican primaries, including that one in New Jersey.[3] I told the senator that I knew that a number of Republicans were advocating Carbaugh, but that no final decision had been reached.[4] Already accomplished. President will call Bedell Smith. I will talk to Jack McCloy about this matter. Have called Secretary Kyes on this matter and he is contacting Senator Williams.[5]

APRIL 3, 1954

The power of the bomb is not of itself a threat to us or to others. The danger arises from the existence.

In the winter of 1953–1954 a mild recession had afflicted the economy—not enough to worry a great deal about but enough to think about. The cause probably was multiple rather than single, although in general the complexities presumably were linked to the end of the Korean War, which meant an end of war orders and of rises in income linked to them. In April 1953, Secretary of the Treasury Humphrey had brought out an issue of thirty-year 3.25 percent bonds that, according to some interpretation, mopped up money that otherwise might have gone into stocks and mortgages and supported the economy. Chairman William McChesney Martin of the federal reserve lowered interest rates and loosened the money supply, and by the spring of 1954 things were well in hand. Some concern remained, and Eisenhower wanted more loosening.

APRIL 8, 1954

David McDonald (president of the United Steelworkers of America) brought to me a summary of his views on the current economic conditions, together with recommendations for governmental action to head off a depression.

My own opinion of Mr. McDonald is very high. I have used him on two or three confidential studies here in the White House, and have found him to be completely trustworthy and a man of great judgment and common sense.

He had two of his assistants with him in the interview—I had Dr. Arthur Burns and Sherman Adams.[1] The document is filed under David McDonald and cross-referenced to economic conditions, 1954.

Dave recommends a number of "immediate action" projects, each of which would require the expenditure of a great deal of money. Some of his recommendations, particularly in public works, in expanded social security programs, and so on, would constitute nothing more than increasing activity along lines that the administration has already recommended. Others, such as those involving personal tax exemptions, would be in opposition to present administration policy.

I directed Dr. Burns to take his recommendations under instant study and to call together the committee that I believe we call the "Committee for Economic Growth." On it are representatives from every interested department of government. After they have looked over the McDonald plan, I directed that they bring Dave McDonald to a conference and have a roundtable discussion in which each of his proposals is thoroughly examined.

In the meantime, I talked to the secretary of the treasury in order to develop real pressure on the Federal Reserve Board for loosening credit still further. This is a project strongly supported by Dr. Burns, who believes that bankers have always acted "too late and with too little" in the face of approaching recession. Secretary Humphrey agreed with me and promised to put the utmost pressure on Chairman Martin of the Federal Reserve Board in order to get a greater money supply throughout the country.

At the last cabinet meeting Dr. Burns reported on the economic situation and reflected much more emphatically than ever before a conviction that we should begin to "do something." I am filing a copy of his suggestions with this memorandum.[2]

During the week to come I am going to push study and analysis of all the important factors in this problem. I have the feeling that we are about at that place which the aviator would call the "point of no return." From here on I believe it will become clear that we are going one way or the other, and I am convinced that the dangers of doing nothing are far greater than those of doing too much. By which I mean that everything the government can now do to increase the spending power of the country, both by the individual and the government, will, at least until there is a decided upturn in economic activity, be a good thing.

Only the future will determine whether or not this is a fairly accurate estimate or merely the expression of ignorance.

Cabinet meeting, April 12, 1954.

By the last week of April 1954 the situation at Dienbienphu had deteriorated markedly, for at the outset of the siege by the forces of the North Vietnamese the attackers had seized the surrounding hills and emplaced artillery upon them so that it was possible to fire pointblank down on the defenders. Supply to the approximately ten thousand-man garrison was reduced to an airstrip, but artillery fire became so hot that incoming planes frequently were destroyed before they could unload and get out. The North Vietnamese tunneled under the French fortifications, and although the French blew up tunnels whenever they could find them, entombing hundreds and on one occasion perhaps as many as twenty-five hundred men, more troops always were at hand and gradually the attackers worked their way forward, taking strongpoints as they moved.

Secretary of State Dulles at this time had two negotiations going. The one was at a conference in Geneva, called nominally to discuss Korean problems, actually to look into the possibility of some sort of settlement between the French and the North Vietnamese. This kind of a conference was a deep embarrassment to Dulles, who had not found it possible to refuse to attend and maybe even feared not being present or not having a representative, for in that case some result might be reached that would not be attractive. But at the same time as surrender was in the air at Geneva, the secretary was seeking to bring together an anticommunist coalition in Southeast Asia, composed partly of Western nations and partly of local nations, that would be on the order of the North Atlantic Treaty of 1949.

APRIL 27, 1954

The situation at Dienbienphu looks a bit brighter than it has for the last ten days. Apparently there has been some resupply of ammunition and of food, but so far as I know, the difficult problem of the care of the wounded has not been alleviated.

There has likewise been some evidence of a resurgence of French courage and determination. We just received a request for some perforated steel plate for two airfields and for some additional supplies of POL (petroleum, oil, lubricants). They want also a few experts in the laying of steel plate. In addition, they want a small quantity of earthmoving machines.

I have directed expeditious evaluation of our resources and of our legal authority also to comply with the requests at once. The undersecretary of state is following this up and will let me know the result.

Latest reports from Foster Dulles indicate that the British have taken a very definite stand against any collective conversations looking toward the development of an anticommunist coalition in Southeast Asia. Moreover, Eden [Foreign Secretary Anthony Eden] has apparently gone to the Geneva Conference under strict instructions to press earnestly for a "cease-fire" in Indochina, possibly with complete indifference to the complex decisions that the French and the Vietnamese will have to make. The only reason that we can visualize for such action is that the British are afraid that if the fighting continues we—and possibly other countries—might become involved and so tend to increase the danger, in the British opinion, of starting World War III.

The attitude of Britain in this respect is bitterly resented by Australia and New Zealand. It is entirely possible that these two countries will approach the United States separately to request that in company with them—and possibly with the Philippines, Thailand, France, and Indochina—we form a coalition to the complete exclusion of the British. This would be a very tough one for us, but I think that I would go along with the idea because I believe that the British government is showing a woeful unawareness of the risks we run in that region.

At this juncture the McCarthy issue again came into view, because the Wisconsin senator had taken on the Peress case. Investigating the staff at Fort Monmouth, New Jersey, McCarthy had discovered Major Irving Peress, an army dentist, whom he accused of communist sympathies. Peress invoked the Fifth Amendment in testifying before the permanent investigations subcommittee of the Senate Committee on Government Operations. Then the army gave Peress an honorable discharge at Camp Kilmer, and McCarthy called up the camp commandant, Brigadier General Ralph Zwicker, who possessed a fine combat record, and badgered him unmercifully, at one point insinuating that Zwicker did not have "the brains of a five-year-old child." Secretary of the Army Robert T. Stevens defended Zwicker and forbade the general to testify again before the committee. Then Stevens abjectly backed down.

To onlookers the president's position in all this seemed curiously disinterested, for the honor of the army was involved, and in retrospect it still seems curious. The only conclusion one can draw is that Eisenhower found the Wisconsin senator's behavior so distasteful that he refused to read about his investigations in the newspapers or watch the televised hearings.

MAY 11, 1954

Secretary Wilson called me to ask me about a report that the Mundt Investigating Subcommittee had requested the army to provide to the committee the names of all military personnel who had any connection with the so-called Peress case.[1] Later questioning developed that he was not certain whether Senator McCarthy had asked for this information or whether the committee as a whole had done so.

The purpose of Mr. Wilson's call was to seek my advice as to the wisdom of giving this kind of information to the committee. It appears that Secretary Stevens had already tentatively agreed to provide the information but that General Ridgway violently objected on the ground that to give away this kind of information and to establish a practice of subjecting officers to cross-examination and virtual persecution by congressional committees would practically destroy discipline in the army.[2]

I disagree with this rather extreme view taken by General Ridgway, and I feel that this particular case has to be handled strictly on its merits. Of these I know nothing. I have not followed the hearings either in the press or by television or radio; I have no knowledge whatsoever of the connection between the so-called Peress case and the charges that have been apparently flung back and forth between McCarthy and the army.

My own belief is that the army would be well advised to provide every possible bit of information in this case where the security of the country and efficient administration will permit. They must not be in the position of appearing to "cover up."

Two or three days after Secretary Stevens had the famous "secret" meeting with the Republican members of this committee, he came to my office. On that occasion I gave him one piece of advice, which to my mind is still sound. I told him, "Admit that the handling of the Peress case was bungled in the army. Tell the entire truth in connection with the affair and hold back no information unless the security of the country might be involved in some way. Along with these two things stand upon your rights; demand the treatment that should be accorded to an American in a responsible position, and if you are not accorded this kind of courtesy and respectful treatment, do not attend the hearings until you are guaranteed this kind of treatment."

Public reaction to Secretary Stevens's behavior was so bad that the army secretary had to back down. McCarthy, tasting blood, meanwhile had gone after the army for failing to give a commission to one of his subcommittee consultants, the scion of the theater chain, Private G. David Schine, who had entered the army in November 1953. The army sought to defend itself, and McCarthy charged blackmail—that Stevens had tried to shake the subcommittee off its trail by urging investigators to go after the navy and the air force. Televised hearings began on April 22 and lasted for thirty-six days. McCarthy eventually dragged in the name of an innocent member of the law firm of the army's counsel, the urbane Joseph N. Welch of Boston. Welch turned on McCarthy and demolished him, before television. The following December the senate voted to condemn McCarthy for conduct unbecoming a senator.

MAY 24, 1954

The lightest day for appointments that I can remember.

JUNE 15, 1954

I communicated with the secretary of state on the desire of Representative Frances Bolton [Ohio] to be our ambassador to Iraq. I have promised to communicate directly with Mrs. Bolton when we have reached some conclusion.

JUNE 18, 1954

At luncheon, Mr. Hoover told me that he had received from Mr. Adenauer an invitation to visit Germany. I told him that my first reaction was favorable—that I could see no possible objection on the part of the administration to such a visit. However, on this matter I would want, I told him, to consult with the secretary of state and would let him know the result.

I pointed out that American travelers were constantly covering the world on governmental and in private capacities and that I had on several occasions sent individuals as my personal representatives in different regions. However, it was my understanding, I told him, that he was to go purely in his private capacity and because, as he remarked, he was representative of a certain phase of our national life.

Upon returning from lunch, I discussed the matter with Foster Dulles over the phone and then telephoned to Mr. Hoover to tell him that we saw no objection to his acceptance.

He merely remarked that he would let me know in a day or two what he thought the "set-up" should be. This remark I do not understand, but I assume he wants authority to tell Mr. Adenauer that he discussed the matter with me before accepting.

The year that had started out so well was fraying by midsummer, and Eisenhower may have told himself that such was the way with American domestic politics, or the world, or both. In the spring of 1954 there was the McCarthy problem to turn off expectations at home and Dienbienphu to blot out any triumph abroad. Perhaps the experience recalled to him, although he may not have read about it, the various experiences of an earlier president, John Quincy Adams, who in an enormous diary was accustomed to relate some triumph or other and then to tell, time after time, how the occasion of the moment was so marvelous that surely some dastardly event would emerge to wreck it. Old puritan that he was, Adams was susceptible to this sort of speculation, and sure enough, something always came along.

By the summer, McCarthy was on the skids—though one could not be sure. Dienbienphu, however, did not go away, and the place fell to the North Vietnamese communists on May 7, 1954, the day before the Geneva Conference held its first plenary session on Indochina. Thereafter the communists waited out a favorable solution. Undersecretary of State Bedell Smith explained their tactics well. "They have a big fish on the hook," he reported to Dulles on May 20, "and intend to play it out." The operation took time but by early July the French premier of the moment, Pierre Mendes-France, was ready to give up and jump into the net. He had given himself a deadline of four weeks, July 20, to end the war or resign.

JULY 10, 1954

I had a long conversation with Foster Dulles, who agrees in principle and is going to see how we can implement the idea. I requested Dulles to make certain that both Mendes-France and Eden understand the reason for our reluctance to come back to the Geneva Conference. We do not want to have an apparent parting of the ways among us occur in the spotlight of the Geneva Conference.

Helen Eakin Eisenhower, wife of Milton, died on July 10, and the president and Mamie went up to State College, Pennsylvania, for the funeral.

JULY 13, 1954

A group of federal associates, Mamie and I, went to Helen's funeral at State College. Went by plane (Constellation) to Martinsburg (thirty-five minutes). Then by car to State College (one hour and ten minutes). Four P.M.—back in office.

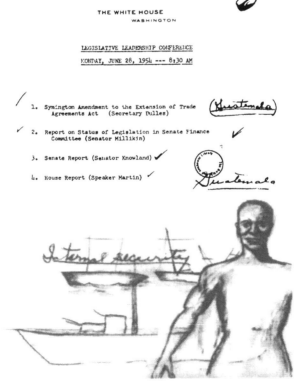

Legislative leadership conference, June 28, 1954, 8:30 A.M.

The First Indochina War, between France and the North Vietnamese, came to an end on July 21, when Mendes-France jumped into the net—and then backdated his performance to July 20 so as to accord with his own deadline. The French and North Vietnamese signed an agreement to divide Vietnam at the eighteenth parallel and to hold all-Vietnamese elections within two years. The agreement provided for repatriation of any Vietnamese who desired to move from one section of Vietnam to the other, north to south or vice versa. All sorts of troubles were to come from this loose arrangement for peace in Vietnam. The French thoughtfully handed this time bomb to the Americans, who thoughtlessly picked it up.

Secretary of State Dulles managed to cover the defeat at the Geneva Conference by concluding the Southeast Asia Treaty, signed at Manila on September 8—the third anniversary of the signing of the Japanese peace treaty. Also signing were representatives of Britain, France, Australia, New Zealand, the Philippines, Pakistan, and Thailand. Dulles would have preferred to have the Manila treaty known by the acronym MANPACT, for Manila Pact, but the analogy with the North Atlantic Treaty proved irresistible, even to inclusion of the final "O" that was euphonically necessary.

But in the autumn of 1954, five days before the signing of the treaty, trouble occurred in connection with Nationalist Chinese-occupied islands—the Tachen, Quemoy, and Matsu island groups—between Taiwan and the mainland. These island groups are much closer to the mainland than to Taiwan; the two Quemoys lie about five miles off the mainland and about 105 miles west of Taiwan. The

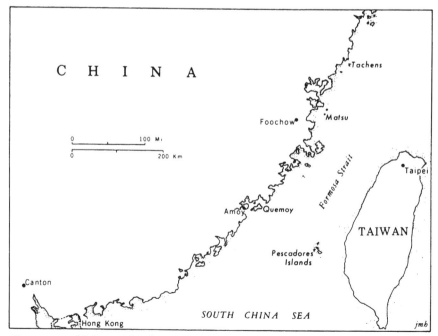

Quemoy and Matsu island groups.

Quemoys and Matsus command the approaches to important harbors, Foochow and Amoy, in the Fukien province of mainland China. On September 3, 1954, the mainland Chinese began shelling some of the Tachen Islands, which lie to the north of the Matsus, with coastal batteries. The Nationalists replied with their own artillery and with announcements of a fight to the finish.

OCTOBER 5, 1954

Discussion this morning on phone with secretary of state. Since New Zealand is the nation that is to bring the resolution into the United Nations, we would be guilty of bad faith if we attempted, in advance, to discuss this matter with anyone who might allow it to leak to the public. Consequently, I advised the secretary of state to be prepared to support the New Zealand position (of asking the United Nations to forbid Chinese attacks on the offshore islands) and, just before the meeting came up, to notify Senator Knowland of our position.

OCTOBER 22, 1954

I gave the Doolittle report on the CIA to Allen Dulles this morning, with instructions to show it to no one else, but he is to report back to me about the several conclusions and recommendations of the report.[1]

OCTOBER 26, 1954

General Stanislaw Maczek just called on me, leaving with me a memorandum dealing with the Polish veterans who fought on our side during World War II and are now in exile.

I promised him that his ideas would be placed before the appropriate authorities. Since one had to do with intelligence, I telephoned to Mr. Allen Dulles, asking him to contact General Maczek at the Raleigh Hotel.

NOVEMBER 9, 1954

The matter of maintenance of mobilization base was subject of the conference between Secretary Anderson of defense, Humphrey of treasury, Brownell of justice, and one or two others.[1]

It was agreed to get on to the matter urgently in order to widen the mobilization base.

NOVEMBER 16, 1954

At the moment, one hundred and fifty bishops of the Catholic church are holding an annual meeting in Washington. The attached is a draft of a resolution which a group of these bishops intended to introduce on the floor to seek its approval by the assembly.[1] Before doing so they brought it to Cardinal Spellman, who

Some of Ike's contemporaries thought that he painted by numbers, but he was far better than that. Here he confronts a favorite subject—his grandchildren and their mother, Barbara Jean.

Camp David, July 1, August 1, 1954. Dwight David Eisenhower and Dwight David Eisenhower II.

At Camp David in August 1954 the Eisenhowers relaxed. The president and his wife with son John and wife Barbara and children. David Eisenhower, for whom, along with the president's father, the retreat was renamed, is being held by his grandmother.

emphatically objected to any such procedure, saying that he thought the matter was sufficiently serious that he should bring it to my attention. He also said that he assured the bishops that their concern was unjustified so far as this administration and I personally were concerned.

At the same time, this paper does show the acute sensitiveness of particular groups in the United States in this matter of what they consider to be proper and equitable representation on all important governmental bodies, especially the Supreme Court.

Eisenhower's former military comrade, General Lucius D. Clay, was a persuasive man whether as a military leader or a member of the Republican party, and in the latter guise he came to see the president to inquire about Eisenhower's candidacy for a second term. The president had not declared himself, nor did he yield to the arguments of Clay, but the man who had helped revive the economics and politics of Western Germany planted an idea that later would come to bloom. Clay argued that Eisenhower's presence in the White House was essential to any reconstruction of the Republican party into a moderate, forward-looking organization. This idea—that the Republican party should be a progressive organization—was dear to Eisenhower's heart and indeed lay at the center of his political opinions.

NOVEMBER 20, 1954

A drive to force from me a commitment that I will be a candidate for the presidency in 1956 has suddenly developed into a full-blown campaign. For some time, even extending back for some months before the 1954 elections, I have had numerous hints, inquiries, suggestions, and obdurations, all designed to get me to express myself definitely and favorably on this point.

Clay approached the matter circumspectly and even in roundabout fashion, but when he once got on to the real purpose of his visit, he pursued his usual tactics—aimed at overpowering all opposition and at settling the matter without further question.

Incidentally, the Clay approach was interesting; it was on the question of my health. There is a feeling, he said, among my friends that General Snyder, being seventy-three or seventy-four years old, is really not capable of providing the medical care and advice that a president of the United States should have. After making certain suggestions as to what I should do in this matter, it came out that he was interested not only in my health at the moment and for the next two years, but on beyond that date.

The next step in the proposition is that the Republican party must be completely reformed and revitalized into an "Eisenhower Republican party." While I do not like this name, nevertheless the idea he has is correct. The Republican party must be known as a progressive organization or it is sunk. I believe this so emphatically that I think that far from appeasing or reasoning with the dyed-in-the-wool reactionary fringe, we should completely ignore it and when necessary, repudiate it. I refer to the kind of person and thinking that is represented by Robert Wood, Fred Hartley, several of our old generals, two of whom are my classmates, Malone, McCarthy, and Bertie McCormick.[1] The political strength that these people could generate in the United States could not elect a man who was committed to giving away twenty-dollar gold pieces to every citizen in the United States for each day of the calendar year. But entirely aside from their political significance is the fact that their thinking is completely uncoordinated with the times in which we live. With them labor is merely an item in their cost sheets, and labor is guilty of effrontery when it questions the wisdom or authenticity of any statement of management or of financiers. They are isolationists who believe that the United States alone could live and prosper in a world gone communist—in which belief they are the most ignorant people now living in the United States. (Possibly I should have taken in more territory.)

Clay says that he belongs to a group, many of whom were involved in the successful effort to get me nominated in July of 1952, whose present purpose is to do several things: (1) bring about this rejuvenation of the Republican party, beginning both at the top and at the grassroots level; (2) find and provide the money to keep this kind of effort on the rails; (3) watch closely the reform in the Republican party so as to make certain that in every area we have fine, young precinct, county, and state chairmen and the same kind of candidates for public office. In doing this particular work, they would serve as sort of an advisory committee for Len Hall. Likewise, they would try to work effectively in stirring up interest at the grassroots level so that the entire organization would be highly effective and in each case would be in the hands of these forward-looking, dynamic people of whom I speak. (4) undertake to provide a better publicity program in support of the "Eisenhower" program; and (5) elect me as president in 1956.

Now, of course, anyone who is so interested as I am in establishing moderate government in this nation cannot possibly object to the nonpersonal parts of this program. Since the men who are associated with Clay both in and out of government are committed to opposing the efforts both of the reactionaries on the one side and the ADAs (represented by Senators Douglas and Humphrey, Brannan, Carroll, Truman, Stevenson, and Mitchell), it is clear that their efforts would be directed exactly along the lines in which I firmly believe.[2] In fact, I think that unless the population of the United States is given an opportunity to embrace this kind of government, that eventually we are going to lose much of the individual liberty, initiative and rights that we now enjoy.

I tried to make Clay see that what we must all do is to work for this kind of idea, principle, or doctrine. Admittedly it was probably easier to personalize such an effort and therefore to use my name as an adjective in describing it. But I pointed out that if we focused the whole effort on me as an individual then it would follow that in the event of my disability or death, the whole effort would collapse. This, I pointed out, was absurd. The idea is far bigger than any one individual.

Here is where we parted company.

Clay said, "I am ready to work for you at whatever sacrifice to myself because I believe in you. I am not ready to work for anybody else that you can name." I argued and reiterated again that this was not "working for any individual." If anyone wanted to work for me in a personal sense, they would work for my opportunity to go golfing, shooting, fishing, and loafing, until there overcomes me the urge once more to go to work. Against this kind of argument, he insisted that he did not mean working for me in the personal sense; but he also insisted that he and his friends needed now the assurance that I would not "pull the rug out from under them." This is exactly the phrase they used on me in 1951, and I well know how such a foot in the door can be expanded until someone has taken possession of your whole house.

This whole group has always played upon my sense of duty. All that an individual has to say to me is "the good of the country" and even where I am involved in things that I dislike and even resent, I probably yield far too easily to generalizations instead of demanding proof of their assertions.

I pointed this out to him and insisted that while I hoped that I would always make every decision based on what I believed to be for the good of the country, yet I carefully warned him that his idea of what is good for the country and my idea—at least so far as it involved my personal participation—could differ widely indeed.

There seems little reason for me to set down here again all of the considerations that in a normal case would argue against my running again for the presidency. I think I have put them in letters to friends, which are probably of record in my files. But a few of them, stated without any attempt at argument, are: (1) age, and the greater likelihood that a man of seventy will break down under a load than a man of fifty; (2) the need for younger men in positions of the highest responsibility so as to symbolize the youth, vigor, and virility of the Republican party; (3) the growing severity and complexity of problems that rest upon the president for solution; (4) the old political truism that presidents lose much of their political effectiveness the instant that they announce they will not again be candidates for office. (This is important because of the constitutional amendment that now prohibits more than two terms to any president. Consequently from the first day of a second term, a president's own party would presumably be more interested in trying to name their next candidate than in carrying out their particular program.) Incidentally, I have never been convinced that the president can lose his influence as easily as this, but since it is sort of an accepted conviction in American political life, it becomes important in this argument.

All this we went over time and again, but Clay was not convinced. On the other hand, he had to be satisfied with my simple statement that when the time came I would decide on what I thought was best for the country, and the mere fact that my decision might not agree with theirs could not be fairly taken as any evidence that I was "running out" on my friends or playing false with anybody.

I don't think that this completely satisfied him, but he would be even less satisfied if I just flatly gave him my convictions as of this moment, which would be wholly adverse. However, I think I am still fair enough to say that I think certain types of emergencies could alter what now appears to be fixed decisions.

1955

Nineteen-fifty-five was the year of the Geneva Summit Conference, the first meeting of the world's major statesmen since the Potsdam Conference a decade before; to outside observers, it appeared as a sure sign that the world was cooling down and that the cold war, announced by Churchill, Stalin, and Truman in 1946 and 1947, was coming to an end. But if one were to look to a quieting of international politics the better occasion would have been a year earlier, in 1954. By 1955 control of the Soviet Union was passing into the hands of Nikita Khrushchev, even though the titular head of the Soviet state was Nikolai Bulganin, who together with Khrushchev appeared at Geneva and who sat proudly for his picture out on the lawn of the former palace of the League of Nations together with the other world leaders—Eisenhower, Edgar Faure of France, and Anthony Eden of Britain (by this time Churchill had retired in favor of Eden). Khrushchev desired to move his country away from the medieval behavior that had marked Stalin's dictatorship, but he was a patriot and wanted to keep the Soviet Union at least abreast of the United States—and if opportunity offered he would push ahead. The hiatus in Soviet leadership that had followed the death of the old dictator in March 1953 now ended, and the quietness of the Geneva scene did not mean that the world was a quiet place.

At home the year was minus the circus performances of Senator McCarthy, who gave up his public activities in favor of alcohol, which would bring him to his death in virtual obscurity—though still in the senate—in 1957. Everything else on the domestic scene was in order, and in that respect it was a good year.

JANUARY 10, 1955[1]

In connection with the memorandum of secretary of state dated January 7, 1955, regarding communications from Mendes-France: The secretary of state and I agreed that there must be no mention of a four-power talk until the ratification procedures on the Paris agreements have been completed in Europe.

JANUARY 10, 1955 (PART TWO)

Morning papers carry Senator Knowland's "nondraft" statement.[1] In his case there seems to be no final answer to the question "How stupid can you get?"

Why he has to talk about such things I wouldn't know—unless he's determined to destroy the Republican party.

If I feel, in 1956, that there is no patriotic compulsion on me to run (war or imminent war), I shall not do so. But it will be my decision and no action of the Republican party will have the slightest effect.

JANUARY 11, 1955

Appointed ex-Senator Robert Hendrickson as ambassador to New Zealand. Adequate—but no more!

JANUARY 17, 1955

Bob Woodruff spent Saturday evening and most of Sunday with Senator George.[1] Bob believes that Senator George will oppose the Bricker amendment, making the Dixon-Yates matter a party issue and will cooperate freely and fully in all matters of foreign relations.[2] Senator George is anxious to see a start in Hartwell (Clark Hill) Dam, a power project in Georgia. He called me Friday evening on matter.

JANUARY 17, 1955 (PART TWO)

The attorney general came to see me this morning. He took up several cases of judgeships, as follows:

1. In Texas an appointment is to be made as district judge. Since we have no Republican senator from that state, Jack Porter, the national committeeman, is taking it upon himself to make recommendations. The difficulty is that he is apparently attempting to relegate to himself the power of appointment.

I have repeatedly told the attorney general that I would appoint no one to a federal judgeship unless the individual was enthusiastically recommended by the American Bar Association. Moreover, in each case there must be an FBI report, which must establish the fact that the man has nothing in his record which could be brought up to diminish his effectiveness as a United States judge.

In the Texas case, Porter has recommended one man whose wife, it is alleged, was very effective in helping carry Texas for the Republicans in 1952. I can think of no more futile kind of argument for advancing in such a case as this.

I told the attorney general to tell Jack Porter what my standards are in these cases and to tell him frankly that I am not going to appoint . . . who, the bar association says, is a very mediocre individual.[1] He would be neither a distinguished judge nor particularly representative of his community.

2. In Mississippi there is a vacancy in the circuit court of appeals. A man named . . . has been recommended to me very highly by some dear friends of mine in Denver. These friends recommended . . . not only as a distinguished citizen, but as a man who was a "great supporter of yours in 1952." The attorney general's investigation indicates that this man is a smooth and fluent talker but not distinguished as a lawyer. Moreover, a man named Prentice, who is the head of the "Eisenhower" movement in Mississippi, believes that . . . appointment would be a poor one. They have another man who fits my standards completely, and

I told the attorney general to recommend this individual officially. (In this case, again, Porter will be angry because apparently he thinks this judge should come from Texas instead of Mississippi.)

3. Strangely enough, however, a man who is recommended highly by Prentice is not only a Republican (in Mississippi) but is also recommended by both Democratic senators from that state. Since I consider Senator Stennis a very fine type of individual, this is a very great item in the other man's favor.

4. In Florida there are two men under consideration, one of whom has been recommended by my good friend Jimmy Byrnes. However, that man is not recommended highly by the American Bar Association, and so I told the attorney general to recommend the other one.

5. In Wisconsin Senator Wiley is recommending a man named . . . who has otherwise no special qualifications. I, of course, have been pleased by the fact that Senator Wiley normally supports the main features of the administration's legislative program, but I must say that he does recommend the oddest individuals for appointment of almost anyone I know. He has an assistant . . . whose standing among people who know him is very low indeed. Yet a year or so ago Senator Wiley practically threatened to divide the Republican party unless I should appoint . . . to some high office. This fellow . . . in Wisconsin seems to be another case of the same kind. Moreover, again, Wiley will not name three or four people and allow me to pick the best man. He insists that this particular individual be appointed.

I told the attorney general to notify Senator Wiley that I would never appoint the man on the basis of reports made to me. The senator can either submit the names of two or three people that he thinks will be good, or we will select a man on our own. If it comes down to a final show of strength, the senator would have a hard time explaining in Wisconsin why he had personally objected, on the floor of the Senate, to the confirmation of any individual considered highly qualified by the American Bar Association and the outstanding individual of the region.

6. In New York there is another case of conflicting claims of New York and Vermont. This involves a vacancy and another prospective vacancy on the circuit court of appeals. Normally, New York should have three of these, because 90 percent of the cases originate from that state. The other two states included in the same jurisdiction are Connecticut and Vermont—normally each has one.

One of the vacancies involves the Vermont position. Because one of the New York judges has moved to Connecticut, the court is somewhat hampered, and the attorney general's office felt we should take the Vermont vacancy and give it to New York. I do not agree and I told the attorney general to find a suitable individual in Vermont.

An added difficulty in this particular case is that the man initially recommended by Senators Aiken and Flanders seems to be rather a nonentity. The American Bar Association is having a terrible time trying to get a real line on him.

Questions involving the CAB [Civil Aeronautics Bureau]. I am told by the attorney general that he has received many complaints from American aviation companies directed against the length of time that decisions of the CAB lie in the White House waiting my final action. This is news to me. I have not spoken to Governor Adams about it, but I did direct the attorney general to stop to see Governor Adams and volunteer his services in making personal recommendations to me on this type of decision. There is no member of my staff qualified—as I see it—to make any independent and worthwhile analyses of these questions. In each case, of course, the secretary of commerce submits his comments because the law requires that the reports come to me through that department. However, to make certain that there is no particular bias in this matter that may influence action in such matters, I think it well that a trained legal staff examine the recommendations not only for their legal sufficiency, but for the ethics and equities that may be involved.

In any event, it is manifestly unconscionable to hold these decisions here for a long time. (I have been told that some of them have been here six months.)

If the attorney general can help eliminate this roadblock, we should at least be observing the old adage, "Indecision carried far enough is worse than a bad decision."

JANUARY 26, 1955

Breakfast with a group (twenty?) of Republican women. The more I see of women in politics the more I am convinced that, on the average, they reflect a far more idealistic attitude toward political activity than do men. It's refreshing to visit with them.

FEBRUARY 7, 1955

Talked to General Clay on telephone: (1) about committee to publicize and support the roadbuilding program [program for interstate highways]. (2) about the seemingly unwise efforts of General Motors to accelerate production at this moment.

The first time Lucius comes down he is to call me, and I promised to see him even if I have to break some other appointment.

FEBRUARY 15, 1955

Senator George was interested in securing approval of application of Eastern Airlines for a certificate of route between New Orleans and Mexico City. Some eight years ago this was approved and later disapproved. Senator George's private thought is that the permit was revoked because of President Truman's acute dislike for Eddie Rickenbacker of Eastern.

All the facts in this case seem to justify completely the granting of the license. The State Department has handled it solely in the interest—at least this is my impression—of securing agreements with the Mexican government covering a whole network of routes rather than dealing with it on a piecemeal basis.

I promised Senator George and a number of others who came with him that I would give the matter immediate and sympathetic study.

I then discussed with Senator George the Clark Hill Dam and the Hartwell project. He understands that it is local political factors in Georgia that are holding up any real prospect of early approval of the Hartwell Dam. The REA [Rural Electrification Administration] cooperatives in Georgia are insisting that they have a right to go at any distance from their own locations and exercise priorities over power sales by federal projects, even where this compels them immediately to turn around and sell to a private buyer.

To this argument I shall never agree, and unless the REA recedes from its position we cannot, at this moment, even use the power we are already generating at Clark Hill. Consequently, the upriver Hartwell Dam would be nearly useless.

In any event, it would be a very highly costly project and only by using it in complete coordination with the Clark Hill Dam could its ratio of cost-benefit be made favorable.

FEBRUARY 19, 1955

Two important points in connection with my weekly conference with Arthur Burns: (1) He is carefully watching developments in the building field and is holding conferences with government officials who have responsibilities affecting this activity. There has been a very extraordinary—even distressing—increase in the number of mortgages of 100 percent character with no down payment. There are various indirect things which Burns thinks may be done gradually to correct this and without changing specific regulations. He will keep me in touch. (2) The other subject has to deal with governmental procurement during the remainder of this calendar year. At my direction, he is to keep in touch with the principal procurers of governmental supplies so that our buying to the largest extent possible counteracts anticipated declines in private activities.

Secretary of Defense Wilson, known as Engine Charlie because of his former presidency of General Motors, was voluble in front of reporters and not too thoughtful of the results of offhand statements. His most famous remark was harmless enough, for he had said that what was good for the country was good for General Motors; but he failed to reckon with the ability of enemies to twist that remark. On another occasion he said that people out of work should go to where there was work. "I've got a.lot of sympathy for people where a sudden change catches 'em," said he, "but I've always liked bird dogs better than kennel-fed dogs myself. You know, one who'll get out and hunt for food rather than sit on his fanny and yell." Anyone with work or out of work thus immediately could feel like a dog. But Engine Charlie's remarks also touched matters of foreign policy.

MARCH 12, 1955

On March 10, 1955, after the security council meeting, I had the secretary of defense into my office to caution him as to the casual statements he was constantly making in press conferences and elsewhere—which sometimes cause very definite embarrassment to the administration. These normally involve subjects touching upon foreign relations.

The latest two were a hint that he gave out that he knew something about a bomb that was more horrible than the H-bomb and his casual statement that the loss or retention of Quemoy and the Matsus would make little difference in the long run.

While I think that he considers himself a master of public relations, he seems to have no comprehension at all of what embarrassment such remarks can cause the secretary of state and me in our efforts to keep the tangled international situation from becoming completely impossible.

MARCH 14, 1955

The discussion centered around the capacity of the Chinese Nationalists to defend Formosa during the coming weeks without active intervention on our part; alternatively, if this should not prove possible, how effective could be our cooperation without the use of the atomic bomb?[1]

MARCH 26, 1955

Lately there has been a very definite feeling among the members of the Cabinet, often openly expressed, that within a month we will actually be fighting in the Formosa Strait. It is, of course, entirely possible that this is true, because the Red Chinese appear to be completely reckless, arrogant, possibly overconfident, and completely indifferent as to human losses.

Nevertheless, I believe hostilities are not so imminent as is indicated by the forebodings of a number of my associates. It is clear that this gloomy outlook has been communicated to others because a number of articles in the papers state that the administration is rather expecting hostilities within a month.

I have so often been through these periods of strain that I have become accustomed to the fact that most of the calamities that we anticipate really never occur. No period was more illustrative of this truth than the six months following upon the outbreak of our war in 1941. Every prophet in those days was one of gloom. Only two or three of the eventualities that sprang up in the mind or in the imagination came to pass.

MAY 2, 1955

I have the Thai prime minister to entertain—he wants to play golf.

Had considered a flyer on a small basis (five hundred bucks only) in a new uranium company in which Charley Thompson is interested.[1] Told him today that I could have nothing to do with it.

Governors conference and National Chamber of Commerce, both here.

MAY 3, 1955

Ninety-two years ago Jackson was shot.[1]

Bipartisan meeting to discuss foreign aid.

From 10:00 A.M. onwards the morning devoted to "public relations" chores —meeting farm editors, deaf people, "Supreme Guardian of the Daughters of Job," etc.

Appointments go to 4:00 P.M.

MAY 10, 1955

The secretary of the navy came in to see me. His principal purpose was to describe the results of an exchange of visits between himself and staff on the one hand, and certain of the Latin American countries' comparable people and their respective staffs on the other. He promised to discuss with Mr. Holland and Mr. Streibert the success of these exchanges to see whether expanded opportunities of this kind could not be created.[1] The army, navy, air force, and marines could also participate.

He also informed me that he will not ask for an extension of the present chief of naval operations tour. He and Carney do not see eye to eye on the respective functions of their two offices—apparently Carney believes he has an authority entirely independent of his secretary and in this situation there is no point considering his retention.

I believe that he favors a man named Burke as replacement.

The Dixon-Yates affair was a complicated effort to take the government out of industry, in this case the production of electricity by the Tennessee Valley Authority, which was running out of locations for water power and proposed to build a steam plant for the city of Memphis that would be powered by coal. At that juncture, the Eisenhower administration arranged for a private syndicate, the Dixon-Yates group, to build the plant. An impropriety by a government official, together with delays by Dixon-Yates, eventually led to abandonment of the plan, and the city of Memphis opted to build its own steam plant. For a while, however, the issue was a symbol of a major administration program.

JULY 14, 1955

The Dixon-Yates contract has been abandoned because the city of Memphis has finally undertaken to construct its own facilities for electric power.

Philosophically this is a great victory for the administration because it signifies acceptance on the part of the inhabitants of that region that the federal govern-

Press conference, June 8, 1955. Eisenhower was adept at press conferences. Usually he prepared carefully. But he could handle any occasion. It is true that one time when a tricky question was anticipated, his press secretary, Hagerty, was concerned. Ike told him not to worry—that he, the president, would just confuse the reporters.

ment will not be responsible for the construction of power plants that will be needed in that area in the future.

When it was first recommended to me by the people of the TVA region that the Congress appropriate another $110 million to build another steam plant in the region something on the order of 600,000 kilowatt capacity, I urged that either through state, municipal, or private enterprise action they build their own plant.

In my office, the group that came here with Governor Clements declared this to be impossible, giving as the reason the fact that all TVA contracts in that area are exclusive in character. This they stated would deny them any use of TVA power if they bought or manufactured a single kilowatt from any other source.

At the same time, the need for power in the region by early 1958 would be some 600,000 kilowatts in excess of the prospective supply, and they argued that only the federal government could prevent their industrial growth from ceasing completely.

In this situation I conferred with the atomic energy commission to determine whether that body could not procure this amount of power from some source other than the TVA. This would release the necessary power to the citizens for industries of the region and would give them the time to work out a plan for procuring future power from some source other than the federal government. I insisted that if the federal government was to provide all the power for any region of the United States, then it should do so as a matter of policy for all regions. Therefore, until all those other regions had proportionately as much federal power within their boundaries as TVA now has, I could not see how in fairness we could further tax the American people to provide steam plants for the Tennessee Valley.

Chairman Strauss of the Atomic Energy Commission assured me that they would be glad to buy power commercially in order to accommodate this situation and give to the people of the region ample time to work out their problem.

This was the inception of the Dixon-Yates contract.

Finally it became recognized both by the politicians here in Washington and by the people in that region that I would not yield in this matter of principle. Consequently—apparently as a political move—the city of Memphis came forward to say that it intended to build its own electrical plant. Clearly this was a political move because under present arrangements they are buying the power they need from TVA at a remarkably cheap rate. By their new move they admit they will eventually have to terminate their purchases from TVA, and they have already announced a hope that eventually TVA would take over their plant. Consequently, they are going about the matter in a very clumsy and possibly expensive manner.

The contract having been terminated by my orders, the matter is closed—except for the action of two or three demagogues who are determined that they are going to make it appear to the public that there was some ulterior motive or crookedness involved in the situation. Unfortunately, their complaints have a slight appearance of plausibility because of an unnecessary and unwarranted secrecy observed by some of the executive departments in handling details of the affair.

As far as I am concerned, I repeat what I said above. It is a great victory for the theory of maximum responsibility and authority and for partnership arrangements in those public works projects where there is a federal requirement and interest or where the resources of the region are inadequate.

If the opposition can claim a political victory out of this kind of thing, it is all right with me—but it will be hard for them to make much out of anything that was so soundly conceived, earnestly analyzed, and so widely studied as was this one. The federal power commission, the securities exchange commission, to say nothing of one or two other agencies of government, all pronounced the Dixon-Yates contract sound and economical.

The four-power conference is sufficiently explained in public statements that have been made by both Foster Dulles and me over the past several weeks. One or two of these statements are attached.[1]

Krishna Menon is a menace and a boor.[2] He is a boor because he conceives himself to be intellectually superior and rather coyly presents, to cover this, a cloak of excessive humility and modesty. He is a menace because he is a master at twisting words and meanings of others and is governed by an ambition to prove himself the master international manipulator and politician of the age. He has visited me twice (in company with Secretary Dulles) to talk about establishing some basis of mediation between Red China and ourselves. I have bluntly told him, both times, that the American people will not consider using the lives and freedom of their own citizens as a bargaining material. Since Red China, in violation of her solemn word given in the Korean armistice, unjustly held some of our men prisoners—men that China herself admits were in uniform when captured—we will not make important political concessions on the grounds that this would be recompensed by the return of some of these men. We maintain that China cannot be regarded by us as a civilized nation ready to work with us in good faith until after they have released these prisoners, such release to be without any promise of concessions on our part other than the assurance that all Chinese in our country are free to go back to China whenever they may desire. This Menon does not accept.

These notes are undoubtedly filled with some of my comments upon the pettiness of many of the men who occupy political positions in this city.

With a presidential election campaign opening in just a trifle more than a year from now, this pettiness becomes more and more marked. The extravagance of political statements reaches the point of bombast or worse—personal ambition is far more important to many than is the safety and welfare of our country.

I am hopeful that in the coming years when I may have some opportunity for recreation, reflection, and repose, that I now have not, I will remember only the names of the individuals who have sacrificed and slaved for the benefit of all of us. I feel, however, that a few of them are such perfect demagogues and such unadmirable characters that it will be difficult indeed for me to forget their names entirely.

AUGUST 15, 1955*

The Blue River project has been one in which the city of Denver has been interested, to my certain knowledge, since 1923–1924.

This morning I was visited by the mayor, by an official of the water board, and two other individuals.

The fight about the Blue River project seems to be between the Justice Department and the city of Denver, since I am given to understand that the Department of the Interior is at least sympathetic to the Denver problem.

The national government apparently claims ownership of the water of the Blue River and, along about 1938, built a dam (a public power project) which uses at least most of the water coming down the Blue River.

The city of Denver wants to get part of this water by tunneling through the mountains to the headwaters of the Blue.

Of course there are other elements involved: there are equities and there are certainly involved questions as to the best use of this water and the best interests of the future of the region. As I understand it, Denver, in spite of its search for water elsewhere, simply must have additional amounts within the next five years.

The people here believe that the Justice Department man who had been assigned to this project is one of the original fanatics on federal control and ownership and of federal development of power. Consequently, they believe his mind is closed on both the legal aspects of the matter as well as the equities.

A meeting is set up in Washington for September 12.

I am not personally attempting to determine any of the issues involved. It would be inappropriate for me to do so if for no other reason than my family's modest holdings in the city of Denver.

But I do request a thorough and fair examination of this whole matter so that if any composition is possible, we can bring to a close this long drawnout effort and quarrel to the best interests of all concerned.

Incidentally, I was told that while Denver had originally requested 170,000 acre-feet annually, that the costs of tunnels and other facilities—all of which has been appropriated for—can be put in the amount of around 122,000 acre-feet.

I should very much like for you personally—or someone that you trust such as Rankin—to hold (or if it has been otherwise arranged) attend a meeting where this whole matter could be analyzed for you from both sides.

The day before the preceding diary entry, namely, August 14, the president had taken off for Denver; after arriving in Colorado, he headed for the Rockies, for Byers Peak Ranch on the western slope of the Continental Divide, some eighty miles from Denver. The days passed pleasantly, most of the time spent with golf, fishing, painting, bridge, or taking life easy in other ways. Late in the

---

*This diary entry is entitled "Memorandum of Conversation with the Attorney General," but there is no evidence that the memo ever went back to Attorney General Brownell with a recommendation for a meeting involving Brownell or Assistant Attorney General J. Lee Rankin.

month he flew back East, to New England, to observe floods in that area and to address the American Bar Association in Independence Hall in Philadelphia. On September 10, all the Republican state chairmen breakfasted with the president at the Brown Palace in Denver. The president then returned to the ranch, owned by his friend Aksel Nielsen, a Denver business executive.

The president's private secretary, Mrs. Ann Whitman, frequently made diary comments about her work with the president, and her diary account of September 29 relates what then happened.

"The president spent the four days, September 19 to the morning of the twenty-third, at Fraser [the Byers Peak Ranch]. On the morning of the twenty-third he got up at five o'clock, cooked breakfast for the guests there (George Allen, Bob Biggers—who was an unexpected added starter by Bob Schulz—and of course Aksel Nielsen).[2] He told me that that morning he did not give them wheatcakes, only eggs and bacon. At six forty-five they left Fraser and drove to Denver. President stopped for a few minutes at the Doud house and came to the office at Lowry Air Force Base. I have never seen him look or act better—which is a flat statement made not in retrospect but made a few minutes after he left the office. He was delightful, patient with the pile of work, handed me a letter from Dr. Milton, and said, "See what a wonderful brother I have." He sat and talked for a little while after he got through the work before he went to the golf course. On the way out I screamed after him (George Allen was waiting downstairs in the car), "Tell Mr. Allen I shan't forgive him for not coming up to see me." He did so the minute he got in the car—in other words, his mind was not preoccupied with anything in particular.

"He talked with the secretary of state, and arrangements were made for the secretary to call him off the golf course. This was done at about 3:00. For the record, apparently he was called off the course, the call was not ready to go through, he went back, was called off again—and was upset.

"The next morning General Snyder called me at about six forty-five to say the president would not be in early—he might be in ten o'clock or so. If Murray had to say anything, General Snyder said to call it a "digestive upset."[3] I thought it was one of the periodic upsets he has had and was not in the slightest worried. Around eleven or so Bob Clark called International News Service and said that because of Murray's reluctance to say it was not serious, the wires were blowing it up into some major illness. Could I call General Snyder and if it was not serious, ask him to tell Murray so. This was accomplished in approximately forty-five minutes. General Snyder, for reasons of his own—the president was still asleep —said his digestive upset was not serious and this was carried on the wires. This I accepted at face value—of course it was not serious, it would not be serious.

"Meantime, at the house, General Snyder was called about two o'clock because the president had a severe pain. As soon as he arrived he gave him morphine and shortly the president went to sleep, sleeping until some time after eleven. General Snyder says he suspected it was a coronary attack but believed it better to let the president sleep and his system get over the initial shock, rather than to wake him *and get him to a hospital immediately. When he did wake, the general examined him, renewed his suspicions that this was a serious thing and I believe called General Griffin and the experts at Walter Reed.⁴ I do know that they took an electrocardiogram at the Doud house before taking him to the hospital. When the decision was made that the president was to go to the hospital, General Snyder told him he thought he would be more comfortable there. They wanted to take tests but did not, I believe, tell him what it was. The general urged the president be allowed to walk, with support, down the stairs and to the car, again because of the morale factor and because it would have been extremely difficult to carry a stretcher down the Doud stairs. The president, supported heavily, did manage to walk, and chatted with General Snyder in the car on the way to the hospital. Once there he was put in a wheel chair and taken to the suite. Dick Flohr sensed the seriousness of the attack and told me later in the day.⁵*

"At one forty-five Murray Snyder, Betty Allen, Ann Parsons, and I had gone over to the Famous Chef for lunch.⁶ Murray got the first call, told us the diagnosis was a "mild anterior coronary thrombosis," and took one of the cars to beat it back to the field. I got the second call—with which we all paid for our uneaten lunch and left. General Snyder said the president wanted me to call the attorney general for an opinion as to how he could delegate authority.

"Meantime (this of course I found out later) apparently the first time the president knew that he had had a heart attack was when they put him in the oxygen tent at the hospital. General Snyder said his eyes filled with tears. Of course he knew it was serious—he mentioned his wallet to General Snyder and some money I have for him.

"But the sequence of events makes me believe that at least we—and perhaps the world—knew that he had an attack of thrombosis before the president himself knew.

"I called Bill Rogers, the attorney general being out of town.⁷ Meantime, Murray called Jim Hagerty, who called the vice-president. From that time on (I brought Ann Parsons into the room to help), I was continuously on the telephone. As I remember it, I called Dr. Milton first, then the rest of the brothers. (The telephone operators were wonderful—and I sometimes had five and six calls stacked up, so it is difficult to know in what order they came through.) I personally called the secretaries of state and of defense, General Persons (whether he called me or I him I do not know), and I talked to the vice-president. I also talked to Secretaries Weeks and Summerfield, to scores of friends, to Bern Shanley in Tokyo.⁸ At about eleven o'clock we quit, and while I tried to meet the plane bringing Dr. Mattingly and Jim Hagerty out, I did not succeed. The plane was scheduled to land at Lowry—it was a blinding downpour—actually it had to land at Stapleton. I know I was on the phone several times during the night, to whom I do not know. I tried to get the president's best friends—had great difficulty it being a Saturday afternoon and evening in the East. Finally I got through to Slats Slater and almost immediately to Cliff Roberts and Bill Robinson.⁹

"It was Mr. Roberts who insisted and arranged for a civilian doctor, Dr. Paul Dudley White, to come out from Boston on Sunday.¹⁰ His reasoning was that

while the army doctors were no doubt competent, we would be criticized for not bringing in civilian consultants—he wanted three. He was upset when Dr. White left after two days here. But Dr. White's press conference is testimony itself of his conviction that everything was being done and that the president was coming along satisfactorily.

"Sunday is already a daze—mostly telephoning. Monday morning was the first sign of good news, and each morning thereafter it has been better. When the president woke up and said, "Where's my breakfast?" I cried. When it was reported to me that he asked about me, I cried. The first three days I was strong enough—then I collapsed and still am.

"Bill Robinson arrived without warning Sunday afternoon. He decided he had to come to see for himself. Personally I am glad he did, though it did upset Dr. Milton, whom we asked not to come."

The recovery in the army hospital in Denver required nearly seven weeks; the president was not discharged until November 11. Meanwhile he rested and for the first five weeks saw virtually nothing of a public sort—he later said he had not seen a newspaper. He lounged around his suite in a pair of red pajamas and a black cowboy hat; the get-up made him feel better and encouraged the people who saw him. Sacks upon sacks of mail came in—there was so much that it had to be stored in a little auditorium in the hospital. Once in a while Mrs. Eisenhower would scoop up a batch of letters and take them in to read, and the president found them comforting, not least the frequent comment in them that the writers were praying for him. On October 14 the cabinet, meeting in Washington, tape-recorded a birthday greeting, and that too he appreciated. And so the time went until the discharge.

Upon leaving the hospital Eisenhower flew back to Washington and spent a long week end at the White House, where he practiced swings with golf clubs out on the south lawn. On November 14 he and Mamie drove up to Gettysburg to continue his convalescence. On November 22 he attended his first cabinet meeting since his illness, held at Camp David. By the end of the year he felt well again.

1956

A new year, 1956, had to be better than the year it followed, but Eisenhower's recovery from the coronary was so rapid and he appeared so untouched by the experience—he looked so well when he returned from Denver in mid-November —that by the turn of the year the speculation over what he would do politically during the new year, 1956, was taking up columns in the newspapers and occupying the attention of people everywhere, even in foreign countries. Coronaries were part of the human experience, the prognosticators were saying, and many people lived many years after such an experience—if the president paced himself *properly and had good medical care (and surely he would have such care) there could be nothing wrong with his running again. Members of the Democratic party watched the new speculation, for Eisenhower would be a formidable candidate. The members of the president's party very much wanted him to run, for they thought he would win hands down against any Democratic candidate.*

The international scene was opaque as the new year opened, and yet it showed signs of a coming crisis in the Middle East, for the Egyptians were stirring restively under the impassioned speeches of their leader, President Gamal Abdel Nasser, who had engineered a deal involving a trade of Egyptian cotton for armaments from Czechoslovakia; obviously, Nasser had arranged with this Soviet satellite to obtain virtual Russian largesse—the Czechs never could have consented to such a deal on their own. Having arranged for his own armaments, Nasser was now asking the Western nations to underwrite construction of a higher dam in southern Egypt, at Aswan, which would impound the rampaging waters of the Nile during flood times and enable the poor farmers of Egypt to have a constant water supply and therefore irrigate their lands regularly. Nasser pushed this issue with the West, particularly the United States, as if the West could not turn him down, and his countrymen felt that since the Americans were well known to possess a money tree President Nasser would be able to give it a little shake.

Uncertain where to concentrate his attention, the president opened the year 1956 by talking about foreign policy in general with Foster Dulles.

JANUARY 10, 1956

Long conference with Foster Dulles, during which I approved certain nominations for foreign posts. These included eventual removal of Nufer from the Argentines.[1] The new government does not look on him with any great favor because they feel he was too friendly with Peron.

The secretary and I discussed the whole story of our foreign operations since 1953. We have tried to keep constantly before us the purpose of promoting peace with accompanying step-by-step disarmament. As a preliminary, of course, we have to induce the Soviets to agree to some form of inspection, in order that both sides may be confident that treaties are being executed faithfully. In the meantime, and pending some advance in this direction, we must stay strong, particularly in that type of power that the Russians are compelled to respect . . . that can be carried suddenly and en masse directly against the Russian. . . . We had likewise to deal with a number of specific problems.[2] Among these were the critical 1953 situation in Iran, the British base in Egypt, the problem in Trieste and the problem in Guatemala, the difficulties in Formosa and in Indochina, and the Korean War. In all of these areas, the problem was one either of putting out or of preventing fires. In most of them a measurable degree of success was scored, but there have been other unsolved problems that have likewise engaged our attentions, efforts, and money. One of these has been the Israel-Arab situation. . . .[3]

Eisenhower had enormous respect for his secretary of state, John Foster Dulles, whom he considered one of the great men of the age.

There is probably no one in the world who has the technical competence of Foster Dulles in the diplomatic field. He has spent his life in this work in one form or another and is a man of great intellectual capacity and moral courage.

Foster's presentation was something as follows, though I write in the first person. Of course, all of the work that Foster does is in my name, since I am constitutionally charged with the conduct of foreign relations. Foster himself has been glad that he could do this because it was his conviction that no man of our times has had the standing throughout the world that seems to be mine.

Whatever prestige I have in this field is, of course, the outgrowth of many factors, but at least if Foster's estimate is in the slightest degree correct, there are two or three conclusions to be drawn that are not too pleasant to contemplate. The first is that if this country—with all of its riches and might, and with its foreign relations directed by people so respected throughout the world as Foster and myself—cannot point to a single conclusive sign that the world is actually moving toward universal peace and disarmament, then indeed it would appear that the world is on the verge of an abyss.

Second, to an individual who so earnestly wants to lay aside the cares of public office (a sentiment that I am sure Foster shares), this estimate brings the unhappy suggestion that he must try to carry on regardless of any other factor. Certainly if, with our standing in the world (and because of the corroboration from numbers of friends both abroad and Americans who have traveled abroad, I suspect that Foster's estimate concerning my own position is substantially correct), we are to be succeeded by individuals of less experience, lesser prestige, and without the ties of acquaintanceships and even friendships that Foster and I have with many of the world leaders in many parts of the globe, then the question arises, "What will happen?"

It was on a note of this type that Foster left my office after an hour and a half of earnest conversation. What he really means is that he would think it calamitous to our public relations if I should announce that I shall under no circumstances run again for the presidency. This morning Sherman Adams, for different reasons, expressed some concurrence in the same idea.

The soup thickens.

JANUARY 11, 1956

This morning, in two successive appointments, first with Dillon Anderson and second with Arthur Flemming, the question of our mobilization stockpile was raised. There seems to be some concern as to whether we should not try to economize by cutting back our five-year program, on the theory that in a limited war we could get all the strategic materials we needed, while in an all-out war the thing would be over in thirty to sixty days. I declined to cut back the program for two principal reasons.

The theory of the thirty- to sixty-day war has nothing whatsoever to back it up. While it is obvious that in thirty to sixty days the two giants in the atomic field might conceivably accomplish a mutual destruction of terrifying proportions, yet this would not in itself necessarily end the war. Wars are conducted by the will of a population and that will can be at times a most stubborn and practically unconquerable element. In ancient times the final siege of Carthage is an example—in modern times the 1940 bombing of Britain and the 1943–1944–1945 bombing of Germany are others. Another observation under this same heading is that if our nation would suffer the kind of destruction that we know to be possible today, we could, even if considered militarily victorious, be wholly dependent upon reserve supplies for a matter of several years. This would be particularly true if ports and shipping were destroyed and if the war encompassed some of the areas from which strategic materials come.

The second reason is that I cannot possibly see how the United States can possibly lose anything in storing up imperishable supplies that it does not in itself produce in sufficient quantity. The material resources of the world are constantly being depleted, and at an accelerated pace. The time is bound to come when some of these items will begin to mount sharply in price. Some may even become almost completely exhausted. Only the discovery of substitutes or even changes in the habits or the mode of living of people will provide a long-term answer. But the nation that has supplies of presently used scarce materials will obviously have more time to work out this problem than will others. This is the case where the provisioning of war reserves in raw materials does not constitute a drain upon the long-term resources of the nation.

This afternoon the secretary of state and the former deputy secretary of defense, Robert Anderson, came to see me. Our discussion centered around the forthcoming visit of Bob to the Mideast, where we hope he can make some progress in bringing about a rapprochement between Israel and Egypt. He is one of the most capable men I know. My confidence in him is such that at the moment I feel that nothing could give me greater satisfaction than to believe that next January 20, I could turn over this office to his hands. His capacity is unlimited and his dedication to this country is complete.

Because of this feeling of confidence, the secretary of state and I have requested him to have the frankest kind of talks with both Nasser in Egypt and Ben Gurion in Israel. We feel certain that if a practicable peace treaty could be arranged between these two nations, our people and our Congress would authorize almost any kind of material aid for the two of them that they could effectively use. But we are convinced that the interests of this country will not be served by attempting to arm one against the other, and we would regard it as tragic if the USSR began to arm one while we undertook to defend the other with weapons and financial support. Consequently, we are ready to do anything within reason to bring them closer together and to start between them the cooperative process, particularly in economic matters.

Bob is starting for the Mideast next Sunday.

JANUARY 12, 1956

I was amazed at the national security council meeting to find some of our people rather bitterly opposed to the plan for continuing buildup in our raw materials reserve. Their fear is inspired by a simple thing—that at some future date the government might, through unwise release of these materials on the domestic market, do untold damage to the American producers of these same items. This to me is specious reasoning. If we have a government, and a Congress, that would be guilty of this kind of action then there would be little hope for any kind of business in America. Yet the Congress would have to be a party to such action, because the law specifically provides that items from our mobilization stockpile can be used only for emergency purposes.

On the other hand, our present stockpile program does seem to me to include a few projects that are unwarranted. One example is titanium; another is the amount of copper we are planning to obtain. I think both of these could be cut back.

JANUARY 16, 1956

The director of the bureau of the budget, Mr. Hughes, visited me this afternoon to say that the time had come when he feels he must resign his post. His deputy in the budget, Mr. Brundage, is an extremely able man, and I think that this will prevent any major break in policy or method. Nevertheless, I will miss Hughes, who has been a very hardworking and efficient public servant. Strangely enough, he does not give the normal reason for wanting to leave. He merely states that ever since coming down here in 1953 he has not missed a day of duty, and he is tired to the bone. Since in the budget post it is almost impossible to take an extended leave, he sees no alternative but to resign. Moreover, he has a very bad eye, which demands continuous treatment, and he says he has had to neglect it.

Bill Jackson is coming down to join the staff, assuming that his wife agrees to the move. If he comes, he will take the place of Nelson Rockefeller, and I feel that at last I have gotten in that post a man of exactly the temperament, knowledge, and experience that I have been seeking. I expect him to do a bang-up job.

Both Arthur Burns and George Humphrey came in to see me today to talk about business prospects. Both of them feel that the economy is, for the moment, acutely balanced between clear possibilities of depression and of inflation. Both seem to think that signs point somewhat more to a recession than toward inflation.

The 1955 wage increases and resultant increases in the price of steel and so on and the certainty that there will be another rise in steel wages for the coming year are some of the factors that point toward an inflationary trend.

JANUARY 19, 1956

I saw Howard Cullman for the first time in several months. Having retired from active participation in the New York Port Authority, he is anxious to devote some of his time to public service, especially in the fields in which he is experienced. This includes primarily motor traffic, including parkways, bridges, parking areas, and so on. He asked me whether he should take his ideas and thoughts to General Bragdon or to the secretary of commerce.[1] While I told him that I thought it did not make a great deal of difference, I suggested that he go to General Bragdon first, and if the latter found that the subject properly belonged in the commerce department, he would arrange to see that it got to the right place.

I think I indicated that if he preferred first to see the secretary of commerce, it made no great difference.

JANUARY 19, 1956 (PART TWO)

Ambassador Conant came to see me to bring me personal messages from Chancellor Adenauer and the report that the chancellor's health, at eighty-one, seems to be improving daily.[1] He also expressed to me his (Conant's) great concern in establishing in Europe a six-power community for handling of activities in nuclear science in that region. He points out that in some of these countries activities could well go underground if we did not move in the direction of the community development. I agreed with him.

JANUARY 19, 1956 (PART THREE)

Meeting was to discuss ways and means of reviewing all of our activities having any effect whatsoever on our economic relations with others.[1] This includes tariffs and changes in them, customs regulations and opportunity for revision, disposal of surpluses, military aid, economic aid, technical assistance, private investments —and securing better conditions in countries with a view to increasing private investments in them, operations of the Export-Import Bank, our participation in the World Bank, and a number of other items. It was agreed that Joe Dodge would propose in a week or so the best method for attempting to bring all of these matters into coordinated aims and actions.

JANUARY 20, 1956

Wednesday evening I had dinner with Bob Woodruff and breakfast this morning (Friday). He is doing his best to keep Senator George from becoming "partisan" in anticipation of a probable primary fight in Georgia this summer. He is trying to see that Senator George operates as a statesman rather than as a politician. Indeed, he is trying to sell the senator the idea that his political strength in Georgia is based on the assumption that he is always a statesman first and a politician second. I am to have a talk with Senator George on Monday afternoon.

The United States in 1952 tested its first H-bomb and, in 1954, exploded a blockbuster of a hydrogen device that showed unexpectedly "dirty" qualities, that is, was highly radioactive. It was this bomb that showered white ash down on a Japanese tuna trawler, the Lucky Dragon, *well beyond the radius of suspected danger. When the trawler got back to Japan its catch was impossibly radioactive, and its ailing crew were hospitalized. One crewman eventually died from secondary effects of his exposure. The Soviet Union was likewise working on an H-bomb and exploded a much-publicized prototype in 1953, an explosion that to the unsuspecting and uninformed said that the USSR was catching up with the United States in what was coming to be described as the nuclear arms race. In actual fact the Soviets were on a scientific dead end with their initial H-bomb explosion and did not explode a device comparable to the American explosions until several years later, in 1956.*
The Lucky Dragon *episode brought the issue of radiation into public notice, and, if only for that reason, it seemed necessary for the Eisenhower administration to reconsider the question of American vulnerability to a Soviet attack. The successful H-bomb tests also made a reappraisal worthwhile from a strategic point of view; the invention of huge bombs meant that any aiming problem no longer existed for large targets—in the new era of huge explosions it was only necessary to bring a bomb down in the vicinity, rather than try to pinpoint. The government commissioned a high-level and top-secret study of what a nuclear attack,*

Always there were the signatures. Eisenhower's predecessor, Truman, signed his name on the average of six hundred times a day, and Ike kept it up at the same rate, and perhaps more.

presumably with H-bombs, could do to the United States and the Soviet Union; the conclusion of the George staff group was hardly reassuring.

JANUARY 23, 1956

General George (retired from the air force), assisted by a staff group, made a presentation on net evaluation of the damage that would be anticipated in the initial stages of nuclear war between Russia and the United States.[1] The date chosen was July 1, 1956.

The report was in two parts, each based on a particular assumption as to a condition under which the war might develop. The first anticipated no warning until our DEW line was reached.[2] The second anticipated a month of strategic warning, although without specific information as to when an attack would be launched by the Russians.

Under the first case, the United States experienced practically total economic collapse, which could not be restored to any kind of operative conditions under six months to a year. Members of the federal government were wiped out and a new government had to be improvised by the states. Casualties were enormous. It was calculated that something on the order of 65 percent of the population would require some kind of medical care and, in most instances, no opportunity whatsoever to get it.

The limiting factor on the damage inflicted was not so much our own defensive arrangements as the limitations on the Soviet stockpile of atomic weapons in the year 1958.

While these things were going on, the damage inflicted by us against the Soviets was roughly three times greater. The picture of total destruction of the areas of lethal fallout, of serious fallout, and of at least some damage from fallout, was appalling. Under such an attack, it would be completely impossible for Russia to carry a war on further.

For ourselves, it would be clear that there would be no shipping in and out of our country except some small or improvised vessels for many months. It would literally be a business of digging ourselves out of ashes, starting again.

Under the second case, it was concluded that the major effort of the Soviets would be made against our airbases rather than against the United States alone. Nevertheless, there was no significant difference in the losses we would take.

It was concluded that there was little we could do during the month of warning in the way of dispersal of populations, of industries, or of perfecting defenses that would cut down losses. The only possible way of reducing these losses would be for us to take the initiative sometime during the assumed month in which we had the warning of an attack and launch a surprise attack against the Soviets. This would be not only against our traditions, but it would appear to be impossible unless the Congress would meet in a highly secret session and vote a declaration of war which would be implemented before the session was terminated. It would appear to be impossible that any such thing would occur.

JANUARY 24, 1956

Today I had a conference with the members of the new president's board for intelligence activities. All were present except Bob Lovett, who is suffering from the flu. The other civilian members are Ben Fairless, Dr. Killian of MIT, and Edward L. Ryerson; on the service side are Admiral Conolly, General Hull, and Jimmie Doolittle.[1] Each will be required to take an oath to reveal nothing to any nonauthorized person of any information he may gain while on his task. The charter of the board I intend to be very broad.

1. to examine the whole intelligence effort of the United States to see that it is possible to make it under the circumstances of today;

2. to see that policies and programs pursued by the CIA and other elements of the intelligence community are sound, effective, and economically operated;

3. to report at least semiannually to the president on the conclusions they have reached in their investigations, and as often as they may desire on any special matter of importance that comes to their attention; and

4. by reason of the standing of the members in the country and their wisdom and trustworthiness, to be able to satisfy the president, the Congress, and, if necessary, the public on the value and suitability of our intelligence efforts and to do this without revealing any detail of operations or purpose.

JANUARY 24, 1956 (PART TWO)

I met the chairman of the Republican National Committee, Leonard Hall, and the chairman of the Finance Committee, Mr. Cliff Folger, who gave me some of the details on the "salute to Eisenhower" dinners held on the night of January 20. They believe they obtained a remarkable result, not merely in the amount of money collected, but in the generating of enthusiasm and morale.

Last evening Senator George came to see me. Originally I had asked for the meeting on an "off the record" basis, but through some misunderstanding the matter got into the papers and so I had Secretary Dulles come to my house at the same time Senator George was there. We talked general matters in the foreign field, and Senator George spoke very hopefully of our chances of getting approval, in general, for the program on which we are working.

The president was not in favor of desegregation of the public schools by edict of the United States Supreme Court and believed that only when people themselves changed their minds about racial matters could any progress be made. In a press conference in 1955 he had said "I don't believe you can change the hearts of men with laws or decisions." For him, therefore, Brown v. *Board of Education of* Topeka (1954) *was a problem rather than an opportunity.*

JANUARY 25, 1956

The Supreme Court has said that segregation in the public schools is prohibited by the Constitution. Of course I favor the elimination of segregation, because I believe that equality of opportunity for every individual in America is one of the foundation stones of our system of government. We have made great strides in this field and will continue that progress. We must also make progress in reducing the critical classroom shortage, and I would be disappointed if any amendment dealing with segregation should produce a stalemate that would prevent any progress being made in school legislation.

Apparently the president was concerned with Chief Justice Earl Warren for more reasons than the Brown decision.

JANUARY 30, 1956

Jim Hagerty reports that within the last day or so, he saw the chief justice at a newspaper party. It was quite crowded, but the chief justice especially wanted to talk to Jim and so they got off into a corner for a private bit of conversation.

To Jim's astonishment the chief justice seemed a bit annoyed that I had, in a recent press conference, agreed with his prior statement that "the Supreme Court and politics should not be mixed."

Certainly I believe that if the chief justice wanted to reverse what I have understood thus far to be his position with respect to running for the presidency, he not only would have a perfect right to do so, but it would be a great relief to me. However, I would stick to this one proposition—that the first time he indicated himself as receptive to the nomination, he should resign from the Supreme Court. I think it would be possibly feasible and ethical for him to say nothing until the time of the convention. At that time, if literally drafted, he could submit his resignation and accept the nomination. The difficulty with this solution is that unless I could have personal assurances in advance that he would respond to a draft, my own problem remains more difficult to solve.

FEBRUARY 8, 1956

In all three of the state of the union messages that I have sent to Congress, I have urged that the principle of home rule be extended to the District of Columbia. I was glad to learn that progress is being made toward that goal, for it is my understanding that a home-rule bill passed the Senate last year. Now I don't mean to imply that I necessarily favor that bill in its present form, because there are necessary relationships between the federal government and the district government that have always existed and that must be preserved in any home-rule legislation. The executive branch of the federal government will have to retain some degree of control, particularly over executive functions in the District of Columbia. For example, our national government has obligations to people all over the United States, it has obligations to visiting officials from foreign countries, and things of that sort, which make it necessary that there be some ultimate authority in the president to direct the police force here in the district.

As I say, I think that progress has been made and I hope that it will continue.

FEBRUARY 11, 1956

For some years I have felt that Congress should enact legislation dealing with the confusion into which our natural gas production has lately been plunged. I have wanted a bill that would make clear that the federal government does not attempt to assume authority to rule upon the prices that may be charged for natural gas at the wellhead. This seems to be a state matter, and the producer of any such well should be enabled to charge whatever he can get by competitive bidding in his particular state.

Admittedly, the natural gas business, when distributed to communities in great quantities, must be classed as a "public utility" and is therefore subject to the regulations of the state in which consumption of the gas takes place.

Connecting the field with the consuming state is a network of long pipelines, and since these are in interstate commerce, it seems reasonable that in justice to all sections, the federal government, through the federal power commission, should exercise proper regulations over these pipelines. If it did not do so then in certain areas where a good share of the citizenry became committed to the use of the gas, the long pipelines would have almost a stranglehold on the economy of that region. So everybody admits that both the state and the federal government have a responsibility in protecting the interests of the consumers.

However, some time ago the Supreme Court made a ruling which to most people was truly astonishing. This ruling was that the authority of the federal government over the interstate pipelines gave it also the authority to determine the price in which gas could enter the interstate pipeline in the state of origin. I suppose it is presumptuous for a mere layman to question the legal ruling by the Supreme Court, but at least I can record the fact that this ruling violated many conceptions of what the Constitution has meant.

On the practical side, the effect of such a ruling can be, and actually has been, curtailment of exploration for new gas production. It is an expensive business to drill for oil wells, the drilling of which is normally responsible for the production of natural gas. I know of one well in Louisiana where the driller tells me he has already spent $1.5 million. He has drilled it to a depth of more than twenty thousand feet and is still going.

This is merely illustrative of the expensive kind of work that lies behind the production of gas. Nevertheless, in spite of my belief that the federal government should not be allowed to control the price of gas at the wellhead, even though it may be sold to an interstate pipeline, I do agree that we still have the responsibility to look after the ultimate consumer. Consequently, in seeking a law I hoped, and several times so publicly stated, that the Congress would put into its bill some kind of mandate to the Federal Power Commission to keep close watch on the prices paid by the pipelines to see that "gouging" did not occur. This is especially important in those cases where pipeline owners also own the production fields. (Incidentally, I would not be astonished to see some move made by Congress—or possibly it can be done under existing law—to divorce production facilities from interstate transport companies.)

The bill that was recently passed had some good points. It did terminate the authority of the federal government directly to control the price of gas at the wellheads when sold to interstate pipeline companies. However, the only authority it gave the Federal Power Commission to see that no unfair advantage was taken of the consumers was to say that it should assure that a "reasonable market price" should govern. As before noted, when one company held the bulk of gas production in its own hands and no competition was possible, a very bad situation could result. This would be especially true if that same company owned the pipelines entering into that area.

Consequently, I was not by any means happy with the bill, although in one or two other points it also made a step forward. For example, I believe it eliminated the so-called "most favored nation" contracts. This is a term used in the gas fields to describe the practice of raising the price of gas in any contract to the highest level that the interstate transmitting company may subsequently have to pay to another producer in the same area.

The bill split party lines wide open and people in Congress divided largely along sectional lines, that is, into the producing and consuming areas. My own contention was that the consumers ought to be very much on the side of encouraging production and that they could not do this if prices in the producing areas were too tightly regulated. In the long run I think that the present system will ruin the gas industry. I know, for example, that the Continental Oil Company has not spent one cent on exploration and development since the Supreme Court decision that upheld the federal authority to govern the wellhead prices.

The fight grew very hot in Congress and the waters were muddied by political partisanship, as well as by a peculiar situation within the Congress itself. The house had passed the existing bill at the first session of the Eighty-fourth Congress —by a very narrow margin of some five votes. Everybody that was in favor of any bill of any sort therefore insisted that the Senate should act solely on the bill passed by the house, on the theory that if it went back to the house it could not pass in an election year. This, of course, is a wholly indefensible basis for the development of legislation. If the legislative process in a republic cannot correct pending legislation when mistakes are found then I firmly believe that our whole system is headed for some very rough going.

Into this situation stepped certain of the oil and gas interests with the most flagrant kind of lobbying that has been brought to my attention in three years. One senator has alleged that he "suspected" that he was offered a $2,500 bribe to vote for the bill. It would appear on the information available to the public that his suspicions were well founded. He was known to be bitterly against the bill, and yet a professional lobbyist in the employ of one of the oil companies sent him a $2,500 donation to his "campaign fund." Incidentally, the senator himself would seem to have one difficult question to answer in that he apparently did not make any statement on the matter until two or three weeks had elapsed.

The president of that same company had luncheon with two or three Republicans, among them Len Hall and Cliff Folger. At that luncheon, he announced in unequivocal terms that he had supported Senator Bush of Connecticut with funds for his first election, but because Senator Bush was trying to get the bill reasonably amended. The oilman announced that never again would he support such a fellow and referred to him in indecent language. He further stated that he had helped to see that the senator's son had been deprived of a large volume of business. In what business the senator's son is, I do not know, but the blackmailing intent of the oilman was clearly evident.

These are merely two instances of the kind of thing that is coming to light. It is clear that there is a great stench around the passing of the bill, even though it is my firm conviction that the great mass of the oil industry is completely innocent and is deserving of some relief consonant with the basic principles of the bill.

This is the kind of thing that has been raising my blood pressure lately.

Two or three years ago I appointed a man named Mansure, on the basis of gilt-edged recommendations, to the post of director of the General Services Administration. This organization, which carries forward many of the business operations of the government, spends something on the order of eight or nine billion dollars a year—so it is a very important post. All of the reports coming in from time to time indicated that Mansure was doing a splendid job in promoting efficiency and in saving money for the government. Recently, however, there began to come in disquieting reports to the effect that while he was doing a good job on the business end, he was being completely stupid and unfair in trying to use his office to promote his conception of the best interests of the Republican party. It seems he favored Republicans in the giving of insurance contracts—and so on and so on. These reports finally seemed to have enough substance that he himself realized his usefulness was over and he submitted his resignation, which I promptly accepted.

I can think of nothing more reprehensible on the part of a public servant than to operate a public business so as to favor any particular section or any special group, based on politics, religion, or anything else.

The Justice Department continues to make a thorough search of all that has happened to see whether there is anything actionable, in the legal sense. So far they report that there is nothing that would justify moving in this fashion against Mansure, but everybody agrees that his removal from office was necessary.

Recognizing that it would take a long time for the 1954 Agricultural Bill (providing for flexible farm supports) to bring about the desired results, the administration this year brought forward a very comprehensive program to take land out of production to preserve it and enrich it for future generations and, in general, to get the land used better to meet the current needs of the population while keeping it in the best shape for the future.

The bill also had a number of features that would increase farmers' incomes immediately. Their relative income has fallen badly over the past six or seven years, and the past year has seen a continuation of the drop. There seemed to be almost universal approval for the program the administration submitted. But the Senate Agricultural Committee promptly tacked on it a provision for the return to 90 percent rigid price supports. They are completely indifferent to the fact that this feature, designed to provide an incentive for increased immediate production, is in direct conflict with the rest of the bill. They seemingly want to bribe the farmers in the hope of getting this year's votes. In the committee three Republican senators voted with the Democrats to put over this feature. They were: Mundt, Young, and Thye, three weaklings. This is the kind of thing that makes American politics a dreary and frustrating experience for anyone who has any regard for moral and ethical standards. The Democrats are trying, of course, to put the Republicans in a hole because of the plight of the farmers, the cause of which plight is the 90 percent rigid price supports of the war that were too long continued. Today we have surpluses that cost us some $8 billion and are costing us something like $1 million a day to store. This means nothing to the politicians, who believe that they can extract political advantage from the circumstances. The three Republicans have acted even more reprehensibly than the Democrats, because they were acting completely for themselves, since the party as a whole is committed to direct opposition to rigid price supports.

If we do not get a reasonable, coordinated program for the farmers of the

United States, we are soon going to have nothing but a completely political hodgepodge that will help push us ever closer and closer toward the brink of complete governmental control of our economy.

MARCH 8, 1956

The attached cable does not represent any fixed plan.[1] It reflects nothing more than some "thinking aloud" by Secretary Dulles. Nevertheless—either through coincidence or because I may have talked about this matter with the secretary in the past—it does indicate one line of action we might possibly pursue in the Mideast, if present policies fail (as they have so far) to bring some order into the chaos that is rapidly enveloping that region.

Of course, there can be no change in our basic position, which is that we must be friends with both contestants in that region in order that we can bring them closer together. To take sides could do nothing but to destroy our influence in leading toward a peaceful settlement of one of the most explosive situations in the world today.

I cannot help reminiscing just a bit. In 1946 or 1947, I was visited by a couple of young Israelites who were anxious to secure arms for Israel. (I was then chief of staff of the army.) I tried to talk to these young men about the future in that region. The two of them belittled the Arabs in every way. They cited the ease with which the Turkish empire was dismembered following World War I and in spite of a lot of talk about a holy war the Arabs, due to their laziness, shiftlessness, lack of spirit, and low morale, did nothing. They boastfully claimed that Israel needed nothing but a few defensive arms and they would take care of themselves forever and without help of any kind from the United States. I told them they were mistaken—that I had talked to many of the Arab leaders and I was certain they were stirring up a hornets' nest and if they could solve the initial question peacefully and without doing unnecessary violence to the self-respect and interests of the Arabs, they would profit immeasurably in the long run.

I would like to see those young Israelites today. Their names have now slipped my mind, but they must be recorded in the records of appointments made for me while I was chief of staff. They were sent to me by one of the congresswomen —I believe either Mrs. Rogers or, more likely, Mrs. Bolton.[2]

In any event, we have reached the point where it looks as if Egypt, under Nasser, is going to make no move whatsoever to meet the Israelites in an effort to settle outstanding differences. Moreover, the Arabs, absorbing major consignments of arms from the Soviets, are daily growing more arrogant and disregarding the interests of Western Europe and of the United States in the Middle East region. It would begin to appear that our efforts should be directed toward separating the Saudi Arabians from the Egyptians and concentrating, for the moment at least, in making the former see that their best interests lie with us, not with the Egyptians and with the Russians. We would, of course, have to make simultaneously a treaty with the Israelites that would protect the territory (possibly this might be done through a statement, but I rather think a treaty would become necessary).

In fact, I know of no reason why we should not make such a treaty with Israel and make similar ones with the surrounding countries.

I am certain of one thing. If Egypt finds herself thus isolated from the rest of the Arab world, and with no ally in sight except Soviet Russia, she would very quickly get sick of that prospect and would join us in the search for a just and decent peace in that region.

MARCH 13, 1956

Late in the afternoon Mr. Anderson returned from the Mideast, where he has been serving as my personal representative in an attempt to bring about some kind of rapprochement between Egypt and Israel. This was the second trip he has made into this area.

He made no progress whatsoever in our basic purpose of arranging some kind of meeting between Egyptian officials and the Israelites. Nasser proved to be a complete stumbling block. He is apparently seeking to be acknowledged as the political leader of the Arab world.

In reaching for this, Nasser has a number of fears. First of all, he fears the military junta that placed him in power, which is extremist in its position to Israel. Next he fears creating any antagonism toward himself on the part of the Egyptian people; he constantly cites the fate of King Farouk.[1] Because he wants to be the most popular man in all the Arab world, he also has to consider public opinion in each of the other countries. The result is that he finally concludes he should take no action whatsoever—rather he should just make speeches, all of which must breathe defiance of Israel.

On the other side, the Israel officials are anxious to talk with Egypt, but they are completely adamant in their attitude of making no concessions whatsoever in order to obtain a peace. Their general slogan is "not one inch of ground," and their incessant demand is for arms. Of course, they could get arms at lower prices from almost any European nation, but they want the arms from us because they feel that in this case they have made us a virtual ally in any trouble they might get into in the region.

Public opinion on both sides is enflamed, and the chances for peaceful settlement seem remote.

To both Ben-Gurion and Nasser, Anderson held out every pledge of assistance and association that the United States could logically make in return for a genuine effort on the part of both to obtain a peace.

There is, of course, no easy answer. The oil of the Arab world has grown increasingly important to all of Europe. The economy of European countries would collapse if those oil supplies were cut off. If the economy of Europe would collapse, the United States would be in a situation of which the difficulty could scarcely be exaggerated.

On the other hand, Israel, a tiny nation, surrounded by enemies, is nevertheless one that we have recognized—and on top of this, that has a very strong position in the heart and emotions of the Western world because of the tragic suffering of the Jews throughout twenty-five hundred years of history.

It begins to look to me as though our best move is to prevent any concerted action on the part of the Arab states. Specifically, I think we can hold Libya to our side through a reasonable amount of help to that impoverished nation, and we have an excellent chance of winning Saudi Arabia to our side if we can get Britain to go along with us.[2] Britain would, of course, have to make certain territorial concessions and this she might object to violently. If Saudi Arabia and Libya were our staunch friends, Egypt could scarcely continue intimate association with the Soviets and certainly Egypt would no longer be regarded as a leader of the Arab world.

Hoover, Anderson, and I discussed all kinds of possibilities, of which the above are mere examples.[3] The emotional tensions in the area are such as to cast doubt on the validity of any proposed suggestion. Even the Jordan River plan, which would be of tremendous economic advantage to both sides in this quarrel, has really been rejected by both because of these tensions.[4] It is a very sorry situation.

MARCH 13, 1956 (PART TWO)

I urged Len Hall to obtain from the State Department the briefest kind of review of world developments since January, 1953, and then to furnish that review to all Republicans in the Congress, to all governors, and to every other Republican who could conceivably be asked to appear on the television networks in the so-called press programs. I told him that he should send out nothing elaborate —merely the briefest kind of statement with respect to Korea, Indochina, Iran, Mideast, Trieste, Guatemala, and progress in NATO, SEATO, northern tier, and the like.[1] My belief is that if such a record is made too elaborate, it will not be read. Moreover, I cautioned him against claiming too much in the way of credit for the administration—we should put out the bald facts and let them speak for themselves.

I particularly wanted to speak to General Norstad because he is almost the only logical successor that this country could put forward to take the place of General Gruenther, if the latter should decide to retire as he has several times intimated he wanted to do.[2] Schuyler, now chief of staff to Gruenther, might be a possibility, but he at present has obtained the grade only of lieutenant general.

The position is one that calls for a good personality, the readiness to cooperate with others, and, above all, a much greater comprehension of European and world social, economic, and military problems than is normally expected of the professional soldier, sailor, or airman. I regard it as the most important military post that the United States has to fill today, with the single exception of the position of chairman of the joint chiefs of staff. In their importance to this country these two posts are roughly equal.

MARCH 19, 1956

I received today a note from Eden that gives some very exact intelligence on Nasser's intentions with respect to the Arab world. Likewise, I received also an acceptance from Nehru to my invitation to visit this country. He hopes to come in early July for a few days of informal conferences.

Secretary Dulles is now on his way home from Japan. He should reach here Wednesday. He has kept me well informed of all of his conversations with various heads of government. The cables are in the appropriate file.

MARCH 23, 1956

Thursday evening, March 21, 1956, at 5:30 I had in for a conversation, Secretary Humphrey, Secretary Mitchell and David J. McDonald, of the United Steelworkers of America. We chatted, I suppose, for about an hour and a half.

We went over such problems as statesmanship in business, the need for a sound dollar to protect pensions and old-age insurance, the racial problem in the United States, factors that might lead to inflation, and the waterfront situation in New York, where the charges of gangsterism and so on have frequently been made in the papers.

In all of these subjects Mr. McDonald agreed with the rest of us. His position was middle-of-the-road. He indicated that the efforts of the miners this year in their yearly bargaining would be more for those things yielding future security than on immediate pay. He gave the experience of the unions in dealing with the racial problem and was quite clear in his assertion that the sound dollar was at the basis of our whole future prosperity. I told him that I thought that labor unions ought to help in this matter, since whenever a political leader mentioned the "sound dollar" the charge was made that he was interested only in the rich people. He agreed that the sound dollar was vital to the salaried man and to one who had to depend upon pensions for his old age. It is of much less interest to the wealthy man who can purchase equities.

He said that the steelworkers union in the South is completely integrated. No differences whatsoever are made between the races.

He made a rather astonishing statement with respect to the difficulties on the New York waterfront. He said that a man named Hoffa, who is pictured in the papers as being little better than a gangster, was a "much maligned man."[1] He said the man does not smoke, has never taken a drink, and knows only one thing in life and that is work. He works incessantly, day and night, hours that would kill any ordinary person. But he said because of the fact that Mr. Hoffa is such a hardworking fellow and has had to deal with some pretty tough problems, he got the reputation of being a bit of a gangster type, and apparently he has not yet lived it down. Mr. McDonald was a little reticent in talking about the affair on the New York waterfront. He said that it stemmed primarily from the ambition of the Teamsters Union to be the biggest in all America.

The meeting was friendly in every way, but of course produced nothing that could be called a "meeting of the mind" in the intent to support a particular program, legislative or otherwise. In fact I invited Mr. McDonald in only that he could be sure as to exactly what this administration is trying to accomplish in the economy of America and the importance of these measures to labor as a whole. He may have known all this before, but, in any event, he seemed to be pleased that he had been asked in.

MARCH 23, 1956 (PART TWO)

The senator [George] seems to be shocked that so many Democrats could vote for Kefauver.[1] He said, "I could never vote for him."

He talked about his earnest desire to help me in the foreign field. He asserted that he is an urgent supporter of the bipartisan theory, but did say that he would have to vote against certain portions of my mutual security program. I instantly told the senator that my plan was not sacrosanct and asked him for his suggestions for its improvement. He turned the subject elsewhere, but I brought it back to him and asked him again. He had no suggestions whatsoever.

He then remarked, "I am sometimes ashamed of myself when I have to vote against you." He did say that occasionally party machinery made a great point of unity in combating the administration, and in such cases he sometimes felt he had to go along.

At this point he shifted to the question of his possible retirement.

He said he was tired, but that he has a very earnest desire to be helpful to me in the things I am trying to do in the foreign field. Moreover, he is very greatly worried about the race relations problem in the South and believes that we must have moderates from both sides working on this problem. Otherwise, he feels that we will get in a pretty sorry mess.

He ventured the opinion that if he did retire from the Senate, his successor would not only be an extremist on the racial problem, but would be very antagonistic to a continuation of the mutual security programs.

He voluntarily brought up the Bricker amendment. A long time ago the senator and I had agreed that the old section 1 of the original Bricker amendment was unobjectionable, although he remarked at the time, "Actually no amendment is needed." Now the Bricker forces have taken the original amendment and inserted the words, "Any provision of" in the sentence which formerly read, roughly, "Any treaty or international agreement that is in violation of this Constitution shall have no force or effect."

The senator expressed the belief that the Supreme Court would interpret the amendment with the three words included exactly as if they were absent. But he then remarked, "Of course if this is true, then the question is why do not the proponents of the amendment agree to the omission of these words?"

After the senator had gone, it occurred to me that I had not pressed him sufficiently on this point to determine accurately whether this is one of the places where he is again going to be "ashamed of voting against me," or whether he is really going to oppose the Bricker amendment if those words are included in it.

This is one point where I wish you (Bob Woodruff) would help. I should like very much to get his commitment.

The senator seemed to be waiting for me to express an opinion about the wisdom of his running again, but I was careful to say nothing beyond the fact that I had always admired the firmness with which he stood for bipartisanship in foreign relations and for moderation in human progress. This seemed to please him very much.

I then told him that even if he desired to retire, I should like to feel free to call upon him from time to time for advice and counsel. When I suggested anything more permanent—that is, to put him in an advisory position with the title of "ambassador-at-large"—he said, "No, if I retire, I want to stay down home and rest. I am really tired." He did agree, however, that he could be available occasionally.

All in all, he talked like a man who was ready to quit but who would really like to be urged to stay. He mentioned his age two or three times and repeated more than once that he was naturally tired.

Underneath it all, he is a man who is a little bewildered that his state is not practically unanimous in demanding that he stay on; in fact, I think the way he brought up the subject indicated that he was looking for some sharing of that feeling.

MARCH 28, 1956

This memorandum was brought to me by the secretary of state in response to my request that he prepare a list of the things that might be done in the Middle East which could help stabilize the situation and give us a better atmosphere in which to work.[1]

I have authorized the State Department to start work on all of the attached points. A fundamental factor in the problem is the growing ambition of Nasser, the sense of power he has gained out of his associations with the Soviets, his belief that he can emerge as a true leader of the entire Arab world—and because of these beliefs, his rejection of every proposition advanced as a measure of conciliation between the Arabs and Israel.

Because of this, I suggested to the State Department that we begin to build up some other individual as a prospective leader of the Arab world—in the thought that mutually antagonistic personal ambitions might disrupt the aggressive plans that Nasser is evidently developing. My own choice of such a rival is King Saud. However, I do not know the man and, therefore, do not know whether he could be built up into the position I visualize. Nevertheless, Arabia is a country that contains the holy places of the Moslem world, and the Saudi Arabians are considered to be the most deeply religious of all the Arab groups. Consequently, the king could be built up, possibly, as a spiritual leader. Once this were accomplished we might begin to urge his right to political leadership. (Obviously this

is just a thought, but something of the nature ought to be developed in support
of the other suggestions contained in this memorandum.)

We had a long conversation deciding upon the kind of person who could direct
and coordinate the campaign visualized in the memorandum. He will need quite
a staff and some field organization, and it will be a real job to find the right man.

*By the middle of the 1950s some Americans began to fear that the Soviets,
apparently moving ahead with the H-bomb, might also get ahead in the means
to deliver such a weapon from the air, namely, the ballistic missile; Bernard
Baruch picked up this concern and came to see the president. Perhaps Baruch,
something of an egotist, envisioned himself in charge of a second Manhattan
Project to develop missiles. Whatever his purpose, it was easily evident to Eisenhower that President Wilson's war mobilizer of 1918 was not en courant with
the development of weaponry thirty-eight years later. Eisenhower had good
reason to feel relaxed about the American missile program. At the Bikini H-bomb
test of 1954, American scientists had managed to miniaturize the H-bomb, and
this achievement meant it no longer was necessary for the United States to try
to construct large-thrust missiles; smaller missiles would suffice to carry the
now-smaller warheads. The Soviet Union was not even able to explode a serious
H-bomb until 1956, and this said nothing about miniaturizing such bombs—that
task would take longer.*

MARCH 30, 1956

Mr. Baruch has written me or otherwise sent me messages several times concerning the need for greater progress in the guided missile field. Because he has, in
two great wars, been deeply involved in America's logistic efforts, his opinions
are certainly worth considering—if for no other reason than because of his
standing and reputation in the public mind. In any event, I have explained to
him the world situation as I see it, with special reference to the relative capabilities of the Soviets and ourselves in our capacity for inflicting destruction upon
the other.

I pointed out that if our calculations are anywhere near correct, there is no
question that in a matter of hours we could inflict very great, even decisive,
damage upon the productive power of the Soviet Union and its satellites. The
guided missile is, therefore, merely another, or auxiliary, method of delivering
over the Soviet Union the kind of destructive force that is represented in the
hydrogen bomb. Until we found the way to make a bomb of megaton size and
put it in a small package, capable of being transported by ballistic methods, the
ballistic missile was not even a serious threat.

I further pointed out that because the ballistic missile and its early production
will have greater effect on world psychological reaction because people see it as
the "ultimate" weapon and have a picture of guided missiles raining out of the
skies in almost uncounted numbers, it is extremely important that the Soviets do
not get ahead of us in the general development of these weapons. I also explained

to him the general organization of our atomic bomb effort and the money we are devoting to it. In this last point, I tried to show him that we are already employing so many of the nation's scientists and research facilities that even the expenditure of a vastly greater amount could scarcely produce any additional results.

I also explained to him that I had decided not to make a "Manhattan Project" out of the research effort. Slow and varied type of development has been going on in this field for some years, and the operating people who know most about the matter are in the services. Moreover, each of the services has in its direct employ, or through contract with large firms, the only scientists who have been constantly engaged in this work. This means that the matter must be kept in the hands of the services, but I do agree with Mr. Baruch that the civilian boss of the job should be a real boss and not a mere expediter.

The conversation then turned to trade. Since in the past he had spoken to me rather feelingly about the wickedness of any of our so-called friends who deal with the communists, I was quite astonished to find that he now really favors a general plan of removing all restrictions on all trade with the Reds. This conforms to my view, except that we know that there are a few of our types of machinery that the Soviets want as patterns and models. These I would keep on the prohibited list. Otherwise, however, I believe that the effort to dam up permanently the natural currents of trade, particularly between such areas as Japan and the neighboring Asian mainland, will be defeated.

APRIL 20, 1956

All day long I have been receiving advice to the effect that all of us must do our best to keep the Packard-Studebaker combine from liquidating, which it seems to be on the point of doing. For more than a year I have been working on this particular matter, especially urging the Defense Department to give this firm some defense contracts, in the items in which it had already established a fine production record.

The whole thing has come to the point where few people are holding out any great hope for success. However, the Defense Department is now seeking to place a contract for some five thousand trucks; manifestly this would be of some help if it could be given to Studebaker, which has a good record in truck production. Moreover, Charlie Wilson has agreed to talk to the larger automobile companies in Detroit with two things in mind: to determine whether some contracts they now have might be shifted to Packard-Studebaker (either prime or subcontract), and whether it might not be possible for one of the big companies to buy up one or two of the less efficient production units in the Packard-Studebaker combine.

It is manifestly to the interests of the big companies, as well as to the economy as a whole, to keep Packard-Studebaker operating.

This afternoon Paul Hoffman came in to see me about another matter.[1] But since he had been so long identified with Studebaker, the subject of the survival of that company came up. It appears that Paul no longer has any executive authority whatsoever in the company, but he has worked hard in an effort to preserve the dealers' organization and to get the capital whereby the two companies could have a good line of long-term credit while trying to get back into the competitive field on a better basis.

To me he talked very pessimistically, but I did urge him to keep trying.

The automobile market is very soft at the moment, largely because the big companies would not use sense in their production schedules last year. They—and the economy—are now suffering the consequences of their blind hardheadedness. If one company would go under, it might practically dry up the market for a while and we would suffer accordingly.

MAY 18, 1956

I talked to Joe Martin about the foreign aid program and the chances of enacting the bill on OTC (Organization for Trade Cooperation).

The foreign aid bill is having pretty rough sledding, mostly because of the hope on the part of a lot of opponents that their opposition will make them popular in their districts this fall. Actually the amount of money we are devoting to our mutual security program this year is very modest as compared to the huge sums we are spending for security and protection in other directions. The congressmen are fully aware of the fact that we cannot live alone in the world, but slogans such as "I am against giveaways" are so effective in stirring up prejudices and misunderstanding that it is difficult for the ordinary congressman (normally not a very big person in any event) to resist.

However, I asked Joe to come in to see me primarily because of my concern as to the general attitude toward OTC. There is a very great deal of misunderstanding concerning OTC. Attached is a memorandum that shows what OTC is.[1]

Joe understands this, as do the other congressional leaders. However, since the popular concept is that OTC is a device for lowering tariffs, the project is disliked in manufacturing districts such as Joe's. Consequently, he himself is very lukewarm.

I insisted that there be a conference called of Republican congressmen (immediately after action on the foreign aid bill is completed) to make certain that each of them understands exactly what OTC is. Moreover, I insisted that each understand how intensely interested I am in having it favorably considered. I pointed out to Joe that many of these people would, this coming fall, be asking for my blessing in races for reelection. I told him that, as always, I would stand for principles and important measures, and one of the measures I would insist was needed by our country was this OTC. This would create a very difficult situation if we found a majority of house Republicans opposing me on this point; any request of mine under these circumstances for a Republican House would be greeted with a considerable amount of justifiable ridicule.

I think that Mr. Martin got the point; he promised faithfully to get the group together and allow any congressman to present the case to the Congress whom I might consider capable of doing well.

I told Bryce Harlow to keep in touch with the matter and expressed the opinion that Charlie Halleck would probably do the best job of anyone.

Mrs. Whitman early in June recorded another presidential illness. On the morning of June 8, Eisenhower's personal physician, General Snyder, called about 7:45 and said the president had a digestive upset and the cabinet meeting should be cancelled. In midmorning a diagnosis of ileitis was made, a misfunctioning of the valve opening into the large intestine, and a decision was made to operate, which was done early the following morning. When apprised of the need of an operation the president remarked, "Well, let's go." As he was being given the anesthetic he was saying to General Heaton, "You know, Leonard, I have a lot of bills to sign and I am going to have to be able to sign them within three or four days." He added something about the Constitution, and went off.

Recovery was routine, and by the second week in the hospital he seemed much like himself. Still, there was evident a great physical and psychological depression, according to Mrs. Whitman, that lasted several weeks. Perhaps coming on top of the coronary the new attack, although not at all related, was bothersome. Actually Eisenhower had been experiencing digestive upsets for many years, and the operation ended them. But maybe he was thinking of the awkwardness of going ahead with a campaign for a second term that fall, after two hospitalizations.

On July 10, at a meeting of legislative leaders at Gettysburg, the president casually remarked that he would campaign vigorously. Not long afterward he went on a trip to Panama where an inter-American conference was in session.

JULY 25, 1956

So far as I am concerned, the meeting just concluded at Panama gave me a chance to pay my respects, in a single conference, to each of the republics lying to the south of us. From time to time I had entertained the idea of a tour of that region, but all such plans were always wrecked on the obstacle of time. No president could ever leave the country for a sufficient length of time to pay a meaningful visit to each of twenty countries.

The opportunity to make the trip came about in a rather odd way. A new secretary general of the Organization of American States, Señor Mora, was appointed and promptly requested permission to come to my office to pay his respects. He was accompanied by Mr. Holland. During the conversation at my desk, he told about the forthcoming meeting in Panama in celebration of the 130th anniversary of the signing of the Bolivar Agreement. He happened to remark, "It would be wonderful if you personally could come." I instantly replied that if other heads of state would show any interest in the matter, I thought I could come.

When the idea was suggested to the president of Panama, he picked it up and issued invitations to the heads of state and we were soon assured that most of the heads of state would attend.

The date of the meeting was June 20, but when I was taken sick and had to undergo an operation, the presidents agreed to postpone the meeting in the hope that I could come later.

It was a great success from the standpoint of public relations. Each of the presidents that I met seemed to consider my visit to Panama practically as a personal visit to his particular country. It had, of course, been my hope to inspire this feeling. Press stories from some of these countries more or less reflected the same view.

The official parts of the meeting were completed within two days. I stayed over a third day because so many of the other presidents had asked permission to make a personal call on me at the American embassy. I had an opportunity either that day or the evening before to talk privately to each, with the exception of the president of Uruguay.

As individuals I thought the president of Paraguay (Stroessner) and Nicaragua (Somoza) stood out. I was also quite taken with old General Ibanez of Chile. Kubitschek of Brazil is smart, quick, but I am a little uncertain as to his stamina if he gets into a real battle.

All in all, I would class the meeting as a very successful affair in the promotion of good will.

Welcome to Gettysburg.

AUGUST 6, 1956

Today I signed a letter directing Admiral Strauss as to the estimated amounts of fissionable material to be produced in 1957. The letter was of six pages. I initialled each one and signed the last one. It was reported to me orally the number of weapons of various sizes we now have in our possession.

AUGUST 8, 1956

The Suez affair has a long and intricate background, and at this moment the outcome of the quarrel is so undetermined that it would be difficult indeed to predict what will probably happen.

Unlike the Panama Canal, which was built as a national undertaking by the United States under the terms of a bilateral treaty with Panama, the Suez Canal was built by an international group. There seems to have been felt the need for clarifying rights and privileges of the several nations in the use of the canal, and so in 1888 a convention or treaty was signed, among a group of nations (about ten, I think), which was left open for the purpose of permitting other nations to sign later should they so choose. That treaty, among other things, made the waterway an international one forever, open to the shipping of all countries both in peace and war.

The canal was originally constructed under a concession from Egypt, which expires in 1968, but the 1888 convention specifically provided that the international character will continue no matter what the future ownership or concession arrangements might be.

Originally, I believe the stock was held largely by Egypt and by Frenchmen, but during the course of the years Egyptian rulers sold theirs. In any event a large block was acquired by the British government. I am not certain, but it is possible that the British government may have owned some of the original stock. In any event, as of today the British own about 400,000 shares.

On the morning of July 27, Gamal Abdel Nasser, the president of Egypt, made a very inflammatory speech, in which he announced the nationalizing of the canal company. This meant that the Egyptian government took over the entire resources of the Suez canal company wherever they might be located. He also issued an extraordinary order to the effect that all people working for the canal would be required to continue in their present employment under penalty of imprisonment. A further statement indicated that he expected to realize something on the order of $100 million profit a year out of the canal and this undoubtedly meant a steep increase in canal tolls, since today after the payment to Egypt of the normal ground rental of some $17 million there is only about $35 million profit. Another point in this connection is that the volume of traffic and the size of vessels is increasing so rapidly that very soon an extra $750 million must be spent to deepen and widen the canal.

Nasser said he was doing these things because of the refusal of the United

States to help him build the Aswan Dam.

When we made our first offer, I think more than a year ago, to help build the Aswan Dam, it was conceived of as a joint venture of ourselves and the British, which, once accomplished, would enable the World Bank to go in and help Nasser to completion of the work. It was felt that under this basis, the project would be feasible but would require all the resources that Egypt could donate to public affairs.

Egypt at once did two things: (1) They sent back to us a whole list of conditions that would have to be met before they would go along with this plan, and some of these conditions were unacceptable. (2) They began to build up their military forces by taking over equipment provided by the Soviets, and they went to such an extent that we did not believe they would have a sufficient balance of resources left to do their part in building the dam.[1]

We lost interest and said nothing more about the matter.

Suddenly, about a month ago, Nasser sent us a message to the effect that he had withdrawn all of the conditions that he had laid down and was ready to proceed under our original offer. Since conditions had changed markedly and we had thought the whole project dead, we merely replied we were no longer interested.[2]

By the autumn of 1956 the British and French were conspiring with the Israelis in a plan that was Machiavellian in its deceptions and simply could not have worked in the latter twentieth century. It was conceived in secrecy, without telling the United States. The plan seemed necessary because of the peculiar military conditions that would govern the attack upon Egypt, which all three nations desired to make. The British were irritated because of President Nasser's confiscation of the Suez Canal Company. The French wanted to have a go at Nasser because he had been harboring Algerian revolutionaries. The Israelis saw a chance to enlarge their territory by taking the Gaza strip and the Sinai peninsula. To accomplish these aims it was necessary to have the Israelis attack west and south, into Gaza and the Sinai; British planes would have to attack Egyptian airfields—because it was necessary to neutralize the Egyptian air force, which otherwise might attack Israeli cities. Meanwhile an Anglo-French invasion force, which had to be based on faraway Malta rather than Crete, because of the lack of suitable Cretan harbors, would be sailing eastward toward Port Said, the northern terminus of the canal. The rather transparent diplomatic ploy by which the three powers in collusion were to obtain their military way was for Israel to attack first, and for the Anglo-French then to demand that both sides, Israel and Egypt, halt hostilities—keeping away from the canal for a distance of ten miles on each side of the great ditch. When the Israelis or Egyptians or both would refuse to stay away from the canal, the Israelis because they probably would not have reached it, the Egyptians because they happened to own it, the Anglo-French would declare the need to neutralize the canal and bring in their forces, with British planes beginning with a bombardment of Egyptian airfields.

Eisenhower knew that something strange was going on in Malta, for the U-2 pilot of later fame, Francis Gary Powers, flew a plane over the eastern Mediterranean that autumn and photographed the Anglo-French buildup.

In any event the first stage of the Anglo-French-Israeli plan was for the Israelis to make a feint against Jordan.

OCTOBER 15, 1956

The secretary of state, accompanied by Mr. Hoover and Mr. Rountree of his office, came to see me about the deteriorating situation in the Israel-Jordan area.

It seems to be taken internationally as a foregone conclusion that Jordan is breaking up, and of course all the surrounding countries will be anxious to get their share of the wreckage, including Israel. In fact, there is some suspicion that the recent savage blows of the Israel border armies against the strong points within Jordan territory are intended to hasten this process of dissolution.

On the other side of the picture, there is some indication that Britain is really serious in her announced intention of honoring her pact with Jordan, which requires her to help defend Jordan in the case of outside invasion.

Should this occur, we would have Britain in the curious position of helping to defend one of the Arab countries, while at the same time she is engaged in a quarrel—which sometimes threatens to break out into war—with Egypt over the Suez question.

All this brings to the fore one particular thing we must bear in mind. It is this: as of this moment we are dealing with the existing situation—that is, with Jordan enjoying the rights of a sovereign country. At the same time, in view of the possible disintegration of the Jordanian government, we must be ready to deal with the situation in which the people and territory of that country would be absorbed by others.

For the moment we can deal only with the first problem.

The secretary of state is having a long conference with the Israeli ambassador to this country, Mr. Eban. The ambassador is about to return to his own country and is visiting Foster to discuss some of the factors in the above problem.

I have told the secretary of state that he should make very clear to the Israelis that they must stop these attacks against the borders of Jordan. If they continue them, and particularly if they carry them on to the point of trying to take over and hold the territory west of the Jordan River, they will certainly be condemned by the United Nations, and not only Arab opinion but all world opinion will be brought to bear against this little country. Moreover, should there be a United Nations resolution condemning Israel, there will be no brake or deterrent possible against any Soviet move into the area to help the Arab countries. They could bring considerable forces in under the guise that they were carrying out a United Nations mandate, the ultimate effect of which would be to Sovietize the whole region, including Israel.

There has been some disposition to believe that Ben Gurion's obviously aggressive attitude is inspired, at this moment, by three things: (1) his desire to take advantage of the gradual deterioration in Jordan and to be ready to occupy and lay claim to a goodly portion of the area of that nation; (2) the preoccupation of Egypt and the Western powers in the Suez question, which would tend both to minimize the possibility that Egypt would enter a war against him promptly, while at the same time it would impede Britain's capability of reinforcing Jordan; and (3) his belief that the current political campaign in the United States will keep this government from taking a strong stand against any aggressive move he might make.

Secretary Dulles will warn the ambassador that while, of course, we would hate to create misunderstandings and needless passion in this country over this question, at this moment he should inform his government that no considerations of partisan politics will keep this government from pursuing a course dictated by justice and international decency in the circumstances, and that it will remain true to its pledges under the United Nations.

Ben Gurion should not make any grave mistakes based upon his belief that winning a domestic election is as important to us as preserving and protecting the interests of the United Nations and other nations of the free world in that region. The secretary is to point out, moreover, that even if Ben Gurion, in an aggressive move, should get an immediate advantage in the region, on a long-term basis aggression on his part cannot fail to bring catastrophe—and such friends as he would have left in the world, no matter how powerful, could not do anything about it.

Foster will make this attitude clear and unmistakeable to Mr. Eban.

At the same time I have Foster's promise to have ready a policy or plan that would guide our action in the event that the dissolution of Jordan would actually take place and thus create a new situation in the world.

It is believed that one of the recent Israeli raids against Jordan involved two or three battalions of infantry, artillery, and jet airplanes. Incidentally, our high-flying reconnaissance planes have shown that Israel has obtained some sixty of the French Mystère pursuit planes, when there had been reported the transfer of only twenty-four. Jordan has no aviation.

Events began to move rapidly. In Europe two Soviet satellites, Poland and Hungary, rose in virtual rebellion against the Soviet Union, and the Russians had their hands full. Here the problem went back for some years because of satellite restlessness under the exploitative leadership of Moscow, but more particularly to the great speech that Khrushchev had made before the Twentieth Party Congress early in the year 1956, the speech in which he had denounced the criminal behavior of his predecessor Stalin. He had made the speech in secret, but it was leaked to the West, apparently by Poles, and became public knowledge, for the CIA arranged for copies to be published. Meanwhile the Poles and Hungarians took the Soviets at their word and chose to have more freedom. The Poles were more careful than the Hungarians, even though Khrushchev and a high-ranking delegation of Soviet leaders visited Warsaw and threatened to overturn the Polish regime of the new communist leader Wladyslaw Gomulka;

meeting in private with the delegation, the Poles promised a revolution if their Russian brothers did such a thing, and Khrushchev backed off. In Budapest the communist leader Imre Nagy let affairs get out of hand and allowed the Roman Catholic primate of Hungary, Joseph Cardinal Mindszenty, to enter the city in triumph, to the ringing of all the city's church bells broadcast for the world to hear. This was too much, and after the Soviet army feigned a withdrawal from Budapest it reappeared and, city block by city block, reconquered the capital from its own people.

The above events had not yet worked themselves out but were in course when on October 26, with some crisis obviously imminent in the Middle East and the presidential election due in a few days, Eisenhower took alarm.

OCTOBER 26, 1956

Warned both the chairman of the chiefs of staff and the director of the Central Intelligence Agency to be unusually watchful and alert during the crisis occasioned by the Hungarian revolt.

Between October 29 and November 2, 1956, the forces of Israel brilliantly finished off all Egyptian troops in the Sinai peninsula and could have cut straight to Cairo and taken all Egypt if they had not been stopped by their arrangement with Britain and France. The two Western powers gave both the Israelis and Egyptians an ultimatum on October 30, and when the Egyptians as expected ignored the ultimatum, the Anglo-French brought their forces into the canal area, shelled, and occupied Port Said. The Egyptians blocked the canal with wrecks. There followed a diplomatic, military, and economic impasse at Suez until the United Nations at the instance of Canada created an emergency force, which beginning in mid-November arrived in the Middle East and by Christmas replaced the British and French. In the course and sequels of this complex crisis the United States joined with Russia in the United Nations to oppose Britain and France; the Russians threatened to shoot missiles into the Western capitals and send "volunteers"—that is, troops—to the Middle East; there was sabotage of the Iraq oil pipeline through Syria; the British pound sterling came within an ace of devaluation; two British ministers resigned; and the British, French, and Israelis were furious at the United States.

NOVEMBER 8, 1956

Information, not yet official, indicates that both Israel and Egypt have now fully accepted the terms of the United Nations cease-fire plan, and that peaceful conditions should prevail soon in the Mideast.

If the above hope is borne out by events of the next day or so, we should be promptly ready to take any kind of action that will minimize the effects of the recent difficulties and will exclude from the area Soviet influence.

Measures to be taken under these elements would be: (1) rapid restoration of pipeline and canal operation. This might have to be done almost wholly by American technical groups, but I should think that we might also mobilize some people from Germany and Italy. This work should begin instantly. (2) Push negotiations under the United Nations so as to prevent renewed outbreak of difficulty; and (3) provide to the area, wherever necessary, surplus foods, and so on, to prevent suffering.

Simultaneously we must lay before the several governments information and proposals that will establish real peace in the area and, above all, exclude communist influence from making any headway therein. There are a number of things to do.

One of the first is to make certain that none of these governments fails to understand all the details and the full implications of the Soviet suppression of the Hungarian revolt. We should, I think, get all the proof that there is available, including moving pictures taken of the slaughter in Budapest.

We must make certain that every weak country understands what can be in store for it once it falls under the domination of the Soviets.

And beyond this, however, are the constructive things that we can do once these nations understand the truth of the immediately preceding paragraph.

For example, we can provide Egypt with an agreed-upon amount of arms—sufficient to maintain internal order and a reasonable defense of its borders, in return for an agreement that it will never accept any Soviet offer.

We should likewise provide training missions.

We can make arrangements for starting the Aswan Dam on a basis where interest costs would be no higher than the money costs ourselves. This, of course, would be contingent upon Egypt negotiating faithfully on the Suez Canal matter and in accordance with the six principles laid down by the United Nations.[1]

We could assist with technicians in the repair of damage done in Egypt in the late unpleasantness and could even make an economic loan to help out.

In Israel we could renew the compact (Eric Johnston plan) and take up again the $75 million economic loan that they desire.[2]

We could possibly translate the tripartite statement of May 1950 into a bilateral treaty with each of the countries in this area.[3]

We could make some kind of arms agreement—particularly maintenance and training—with Israel of exactly the same type we could make with Egypt.

We could explore other means of assisting the Arab states of Iraq, Jordan, Saudi Arabia, and Lebanon, and develop ways and means of strengthening our economic and friendly ties with each of these countries, either on a bilateral or group basis.

Not long after the fiasco of Suez, Prime Minister Anthony Eden relinquished the seals of his office to Harold Macmillan.

Watching nation-wide closed-circuit television on October 13, 1956, in honor of the president's birthday, which was the next day. L. to r., the president, Mrs. Eisenhower, Anne, David, Barbara, John.

1956 Republican convention.

NOVEMBER 20, 1956

I called Winthrop Aldrich and told him to let Butler and Macmillan know simultaneously that we are sympathetic with their troubles and interested in helping them out.[1]

NOVEMBER 21, 1956

I approved today the joint chiefs of staff plan for the disposal to bases, fields, and ships afloat all the present atomic stockpile, nuclear and fission.

I informed the chairman of the chiefs of staff that the State Department should be in agreement with all disposal involving overseas bases, and today's dispersal should mark the approximate number of those to be maintained permanently in the field. The bulk of those manufactured hereafter (except for air defense types) should be kept in United States reserve stocks.

NOVEMBER 21, 1956 (PART TWO)

I just finished a conversation with the Tunisian prime minister, Mr. Habib Bourguiba.

I was struck by his sincerity, his intelligence, and his friendliness. He is grateful for the help we have given him from surplus foods, particularly wheat. He says that, in addition, his country needs of course a great deal of technical assistance.

He gave as his biggest problem the existence of the French-Algerian war. He came back again and again to the expressed hope that the United States could find some way to mediate in that useless struggle. He claimed that France would have to concede very little in order to settle the proposition; on questioning, he expressed the belief that an arrangement like the British Commonwealth of Nations between France and Algeria, to become effective within a given number of years, would be most acceptable to the Algerians.

He says that if we could get this war settled, all the Western world would have a very much finer relationship with North Africa and indeed with the Arab world.

He said that the Jewish-Arab quarrel was no concern of theirs—they are not affected by it.

I assured him of America's friendliness, and particularly of its desire to deal directly with each one of the Moslem countries in the effort to promote our common interests.

DECEMBER 16, 1956

Luncheon was purely social. No political problems were brought up. Nehru seemed very pleasant and interested in the history of various items about the White House as told to him by Mrs. Eisenhower. Both Nehru and his daughter, Mrs. Gandhi, wore native costumes.[1]

UNDATED [DECEMBER 1956?]

During my term of office, unless there is some technical or political development that I do not foresee—or a marked inflationary trend in the economy (which I will battle to the death)—I will not approve any obligational or expenditure authorities for the Defense Department that exceed something on the order of $38.5 billion mark. Consequently, when yearly obligational authority exceeds the new obligational authority or the expenditure program, this must invariably be made up from "carry-over" and not by a mortgage on future appropriations.

THE SECOND
ADMINISTRATION

By the time of the second administration, beginning in January 1957, life in the White House had become routine to the man who twenty years earlier had been an army officer in the Philippines working under the imperious Douglas MacArthur. How life had changed from the trivialities of Manila!

But Eisenhower must have wondered occasionally if the heights were as attractive as they had seemed from the valleys. He had been in the most demanding of public offices since December 1941. The pressure had been intense and incessant—in personal anxieties, in nervousness, in calls for patience from a psyche that inwardly was very impatient. The physical cost had been high. He had suffered a coronary in 1955 and an operation for ileitis in 1956. If any more evidence was needed that he had reached the end of his physical capacity it appeared in November 1957 when he suffered a stroke, "an occlusion of a small branch of a cerebral vessel which has produced a slight difficulty in speaking." Recovery was quick, but the stroke raised a serious question as to whether he could make it through until January 1961. Certainly the second administration was going to be his last period of public service.

Perhaps for this reason, perhaps for others, the second administration was in no sense as satisfying as the first. The note of triumph that was close to the surface of the diary entries in 1953 and especially in early 1954 had departed from the prose of the mid-decade and it never reappeared. The entries became less philosophical, more hurried, the diarist always seems to have looked weariedly to another task. Occasionally he allowed himself the satisfaction of remarking that "we" (by which he meant his wing of the Republican party and, generally, the moderates of both parties) had managed to do this or that. From the diary, one has the feeling that he believed he had established a centrist position for the country as a whole, that he had returned American politics to an earlier simplicity based upon moral values and religion. The task, however, had its personal cost, and the man in control was far more tired than he would have wished to be.

In the second administration the American people saw more of Eisenhower personally than they had during the first. It was not that the president had changed his modus operandi, his belief that the essential task of administration is to persuade others to do their jobs and not to receive personal credit for the persuading—the belief that as president he should be the unseen hand, the guiding spirit, not an open manipulator of public opinion and balancer of forces. But in foreign relations the increasing illness of Secretary of State Dulles, evident when in the midst of the Suez crisis the secretary had to go into the hospital for a cancer operation, caused the president to get out more in front, helping Dulles visibly with the tasks of statesmanship. Dulles became so wracked by pain—his hope for life dimming—that he resigned in April 1959. The new secretary of state, Christian A. Herter, was not nearly so prominent a public figure, and Eisenhower continued to take an active part in foreign affairs.

In his last years in office the president did a great deal of foreign traveling. For a while Dulles was ill and could not travel. His successor Herter was himself a man of some physical infirmity; Herter had to walk with crutches because of osteoarthritis, which produced a postural problem at the base of his spine; the new secretary was not easily able to engage in the incessant traveling that was Dulles's style. There was nothing for Eisenhower to do but step into the breach and do some traveling himself. Perhaps then the appetite increased with the eating, for he traveled more and more. In the last two years of the second administration, he went on six international good-will trips—320,000 miles, twenty-seven countries.

As the years of the second administration passed, with sometimes awkward international developments such as the Soviet launching of the first earth satellite in October 1957, challenging the supremacy of American science, one might have thought that Eisenhower's luster as a national and world leader would have dimmed. When Khrushchev rose to the premiership of the Soviet Union and began to give nonstop orations that raised up the values of communism in comparison with the failures of the West, one might have thought that the unnamed antagonist of these addresses would have diminished in stature before his own countrymen. The American economy was not performing perfectly, and in 1957 a deep recession began that lasted into 1959. The federal budget, almost in balance during the early years, went out of balance because of poor collection of taxes because of the recession. All the while the farm problem was raising its ugly head again—surpluses on American farms were building up in an uncontrollable way, with row upon row of hastily constructed storage silos rising throughout the American West.

The president of the United States could have come in for criticism as all these things went wrong, but his reputation rose year after year. The American people liked his political behavior. Here was a man who did not say publicly until 1952

An interesting double photograph—two sides of the man.

One of Eisenhower's great
advantages in public was his
extraordinarily mobile face, and here
he unconsciously displays his talent
against another actor, Joe E. Brown.

The domestic and foreign advisors,
April 3, 1957; Sherman Adams and
Dulles; Adams would leave the
administration the next year, Dulles
in 1959.

that he was a Republican, who never had voted in a national election until that year when he, himself, was the candidate, who had never bothered to join a church until he became president. Surely he was above politics. They liked his behavior in the presidency and were satisfied until the day he left.

1957

FEBRUARY 5, 1957

Almost four years ago, the attorney general and I agreed that, except for the position of chief justice, we would confine our selections for the Supreme Court to people who had served on either minor federal benches or on the supreme courts of the various states. We also agreed that so far as possible, we would try to get a balance on the court between Democrats and Republicans. In working toward this balance (the court was eight-to-one Democratic when I was first inaugurated), I have two Republicans and one Democrat.

Yesterday I saw in the paper quite a squib concerning the qualifications of Herb Brownell himself for the Supreme Court. While I was certain the article was not "inspired," I did have a short talk with the attorney general last evening. I mentioned the article and asked him whether he was still of the opinion that we should stick to our plan of selecting Supreme Court judges from sitting judges on the lower courts, always with the rule, too, that they be under sixty-two years of age. He agreed. He did say, however, that our rule should not be inflexible, in the event we did discover some outstanding attorney who we should like to put directly on the Supreme Court. I told him that if he had any ambitions to go on the court, that we should appoint him immediately to the vacancy now existing on the appellate court in New York and then, when and if another vacancy occurred on the Supreme Court, I could appoint him to it.

He said he thought we should just let things go as they were.

It is entirely possible that he would like to be on the Supreme Court. But I think that on balance he prefers to go back to private practice some day and earn some money for himself and family.

MAY 20, 1957

The Justice Department have a number of antitrust cases pending, affecting a number of companies in which Mr. Mellon is heavily interested.[1]

The first of these is Alcoa. Mr. Mellon says that there has been a twenty-year judgment of some kind against the company, which is now practically cleared up —but that the Justice Department has just extended their jurisdiction for five years.

The next company he talked about was Gulf—there were a number of cases (five or six, I believe) but the one that seemed to involve persecution was Warren Oil. Gulf took over Warren Oil, which was engaged in a specialty business and in no way whatever was competitive with Gulf.

The next company was the Pittsburgh Plate Glass Company, against which there are six cases pending. One of these involved the pricing of paintbrush handles. He says this is so inconsequential that from his standpoint they would be delighted to give away an extra paintbrush handle with almost any sale. He says the reasoning is so inconsequential that it has the ominous look of persecution.

AUGUST 5, 1957

This morning I made two telephone calls to the Defense Department, the first to the chief of staff of the army, General Taylor.

Last week Mr. Wilson had a press conference in which he spoke very facetiously about an alleged army intention of building an eight hundred-mile ballistic missile. He spoke about it in terms implying strong disapproval, and he also implied that the army had undoubtedly acted without any authority from the secretary of defense.

A memorandum to me from the army states that the proposition that was mentioned was incorrectly described in the question addressed to Mr. Wilson. On top of this, the army has done nothing whatsoever in extending the range of the particular missile in question (I believe it is the Redpath) but requested authority to introduce a solid propellant which it is alleged would give the missile an effective range of four hundred to five hundred miles (not eight hundred as alleged in the question directed to Mr. Wilson). The army also states that its plan would be to use this weapon to get greater flexibility, but dependent completely upon the air force for reconnaissance necessary to report targets and results of findings.

Actually the whole proposition seems sensible to me, particularly in that development costs would be limited to modification for the change in fuel.

I suggested that the chief of staff seek an appointment at once with the secretary of defense, telling the secretary that he was doing so at my instruction.

I am disturbed by the implication left in the newspaper stories that the departments are operating in defiance of the secretary of defense's orders, when, as a matter of fact, it appears to me that the army did everything possible to keep this matter strictly within the limits of regular and proper procedure.

A copy of the army memorandum is filed with this account.

My second call was to General White of the air force. A newspaper story states that in a recent public speech, he made comparisons between the air force and its sister services in the matter of their readiness to appreciate modern conditions and adapt their methods and equipment to those conditions.

I told him that I had no objection to his praising his own service as much as he pleased, but I did object to any representative of one of the services comparing

Cabinet meeting, May 3, 1957.

Cabinet meeting, May 24.

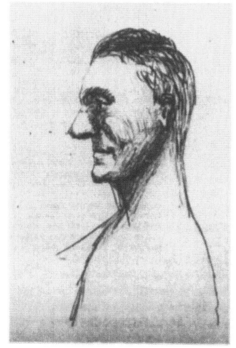

himself or his own service with the others to their disadvantage and his own advantage. This in my opinion is destructive in terms of the whole general service morale.

It is the old question of whether service men are working first of all for their own service or for the good of the United States.

General White agreed that this had been an error but stated that the document had been submitted to the secretary of defense before delivery as a public speech. He said also that he called specific attention to the paragraph that aroused my concern and that the speech was approved by the Defense Department without comment. I suggested to him that hereafter if he had any doubt about any feelings that might be hurt, he should consult with the chiefs of staff rather than with the Defense Department staff, whose concern for such remarks might not be so acute.

The city of Washington was growing rapidly in the 1950s and the question arose of another airport, with runways long enough to take the new jets. National Airport across the Potomac from the District was congested. Friendship Airport in Maryland was on the far side of the city from the suburbs in Virginia. The obvious place for the new airport was Virginia, and the place eventually chosen became the present-day Dulles Airport.

AUGUST 14, 1957

This morning I had Senator Holland in to talk to me about the project for establishing a new airport in Fairfax County, commonly known as the Burke Airport.[1] I had heard that Senator Holland was particularly hostile to the carrying out of the Burke project.

The attitude of the Commerce Department (and the CAA in that department) is reported fairly accurately in the short summary of facts attached hereto.[2]

Senator Holland has several emphatic objections, all of which appear to him, of course, to be valid. He summarized them somewhat as follows:

1. The area around Washington is being settled up rapidly as population grows, and Fairfax County is one of the regions included in this rapid residential development. Only the eastern half of that county is available for the reason that drainage from the eastern half flows into the Potomac below Washington. In the western half of the county, the drainage is into the Potomac above Washington. By law, no more storm or city sewerage can be dumped into the Potomac above Washington. Yet he points out that the Burke Airport development is in the heart of the eastern section of the county on ground that is especially valuable from a residential viewpoint. Since the airport will require a total of 4,400 acres held in fee simple and 2,000 additional acres, which will be released to prevent building in the areas used for approaches, he feels that condemnation of that amount of ground would be grossly unfair to the citizens of the area. Incidentally, he stated that the population of this particular region had more than doubled

within very recent years, going from eighty thousand to about two hundred thousand.

2. The senator says that the one million dollars invested by the government in this project back in 1951 would not be wasted, even if it should now be abandoned. The value of property has so increased in that area that he says the government could make a profit out of the deal.

3. Their committee has testimony that with an airport located at Burke, there would be interference between the stacking areas needed by the National Airport and Burke Airport. As a consequence, the full value of neither port could be realized.

4. He maintains that construction at Chantilly—some distance to the north-westward—would be much less than at Burke. Commerce denies this, saying that the difference in construction costs would not be more than a million dollars out of a total budget of some fifty million.

5. He is very much concerned with the bitter opposition to the Burke project of the four area senators. These are Byrd and Robertson of Virginia, and Beall and Butler from Maryland. The opposition of the Virginia senators is based on different reasons from that of the Maryland senators. The latter want to compel part of the Washington traffic to use the Friendship Airport near Baltimore and thus share in the cost of maintenance of that facility. The Virginia senators do not want the Burke Airport merely because the residents object and they of course are concerned politically.

6. He believes that when the new superhighway running westward from Washington is completed (it will run directly along the border of the Chantilly airport), the travel time from Chantilly to Washington or the Washington Airport will compare favorably with the travel time from the Burke Airport. In this connection he says that six major airports in the United States lie farther from the cities they serve than does the Chantilly area from Washington.

7. Finally he argues that Congress has never approved the Burke site. He says that authorization for a second airport was given by congress in 1950, but the site was picked out by CAA. They got one million dollars from Congress on the representation that they could buy all the ground they needed. Actually they got only one-fifth and that is all the government owns in this region.

In view of all these things, Senator Holland believes that the project should be restudied, and he particularly suggests that the new Aeronautics Advisory Committee, under the direction of General Quesada, restudy the whole matter.[3]

In this situation, the secretary of commerce says that we have studied all of the possible solutions to the Washington traffic problem over the period of the past four years. Always the answer of the individuals making the study has been that the Burke Airport was the best site and the Commerce Department has adopted this as their official solution.

The House of Representatives has already passed an appropriation bill to acquire the remainder of the ground necessary and to get started on construction. He says, therefore, that the Commerce Department cannot back off from the proposition and will simply recite again to the Senate Committee all of the various steps through which this study has gone through the past years. They will then say in effect, "The bill is now in your hands and with our recommendations, based on our best information and professional advice. You, of course, will have to do as you please with it."

The revealing point of self-analysis that follows was at first dictated by the president to go in a letter to Henry Luce. Then he told Mrs. Whitman, "No, don't put it in, I will say it to him sometime."

SEPTEMBER 13, 1957

Incidentally, the developments of this year have long since proved to me that I made one grave mistake in my calculations as to what a second term would mean to me in the way of a continuous toll upon my strength, patience, and sense of humor. I had expected that because of the Constitutional amendment limiting a president's tenure to two terms, I could rather definitely in a second term be free of many of the preoccupations that were so time consuming and wearing in the first term. The opposite is the case. The demands that I "do something" seem to grow.

Brown v. Board of Education of Topeka (1954) *was made to order for an Arkansas governor like Orval E. Faubus, and when trouble over desegregation of Little Rock's lily-white Central High School threatened to explode into violence, Faubus found himself a national and international figure. Eisenhower found himself with a nasty problem.*

OCTOBER 8, 1957

What he had to say was pretty well represented in the press releases given out that day [September 14]. Governor Faubus protested again and again he was a law-abiding citizen, that he was a veteran, fought in the war, and that everybody recognizes that the federal law is supreme to state law. So I suggested to him that he go home and not necessarily withdraw his national guard troops but just change their orders to say that having been assured that there was no attempt to do anything except to obey the courts and that the federal government was not trying to do anything that had not been already agreed to by the school board and directed by the courts, he should tell the guard to continue to preserve order but to allow the Negro children to attend Central High School. I pointed out at that time he was due to appear the following Friday, the twentieth, before the court to determine whether an injunction was to be issued. In any event I urged him to take this action promptly, whereupon the Justice Department would go to the court and ask that the governor not be brought into court. I further said that I did not believe it was beneficial to anybody to have a trial of strength between the president and a governor because in any area where the federal government had assumed jurisdiction and this was upheld by the Supreme Court, there could be only one outcome—that is, the state would lose, and I did not want to see any governor humiliated.

He seemed to be very appreciative of this attitude, and I got definitely the understanding that he was going back to Arkansas to act within a matter of hours to revoke his orders to the guard to prevent reentry of the Negro children into the school.

He told me of his war experiences and vigorously asserted his deep feelings of loyalty and dedication to the federal government, and repeated several times that he had shown respect for the law in all his actions.

After some twenty minutes of personal conference, we invited Governor Adams and Brooks Hays, and later, the attorney general, to join us.[1] The ensuing conversation was generally along the same lines as he had talked to me in private.

Faubus withdrew the national guard, whereupon extremist mobs prevented the black children from entering the school. Eisenhower dispatched regular army troops to protect the black pupils. Federalized Arkansas national guardsmen shortly replaced the army units and remained on duty for the rest of the school year.

OCTOBER 29, 1957

I was visited by Professor Rabi, Admiral Strauss, Gordon Gray, and one or two others.[1] The purpose was to bring to me certain conclusions reached by Professor

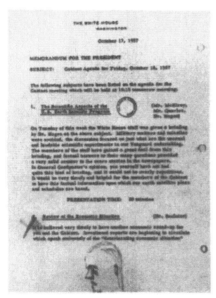

Cabinet meeting, October 18, 1957.

Rabi's committee, called the Scientific Advisory Committee to the Director of Defense Mobilization.

Briefly, their conclusion was that we now enjoy certain advantages in the nuclear world over the Russians and that the most important of these gaps can be closed only by continuous testing on the part of the Russians. Professor Rabi's committee has therefore reached the conclusion that we should, as a matter of self-interest, agree to a suspension of all tests subject only to the installation of inspectional systems that would almost surely reveal the occurrence of a test. Scientists differ as to whether certain nuclear tests can be conducted without any knowledge reaching the outside world, but the Rabi committee believes that with a half dozen or so properly equipped inspectional posts inside of Russia, any significant explosion could be detected.

While the Rabi committee agreed that certain advantages in our weaponry could be realized by advancement of testing, they say that the expected advantage would be as nothing compared with maintaining the particular scientific gap that exists in the design of the Russian H-bomb as compared to ours.

The nature of this gap is that Russian bombs are unshielded against certain types of radioactivity that could be placed around them as they approach. The effect of this would not be to destroy the bomb but to reduce its effect by something like 99 percent.

Admiral Strauss and his group of scientists do not believe some of the assumptions made by the Rabi committee. They are keenly afraid that should we discontinue our tests, the Russians would, by stealing all of our secrets, equal and eventually surpass us. So Admiral Strauss and his associates believe we should continue all of our experiments and testing out in the open, refusing to be victimized by Russian duplicity. They are quite firm in their belief that we could not protect ourselves adequately against that duplicity.

The outcome was that Gordon Gray, Admiral Strauss, and General Cutler are going to try to get (if possible) an agreement of scientific opinion in this whole matter to see what we should do about it.

Incidentally, I learned that some of the mutual antagonisms among the scientists are so bitter as to make their working together almost an impossibility. I was told that Dr. Rabi and some of his group are so antagonistic to Doctors Lawrence and Teller that communication between them is practically nil.[2]

1958

The year 1958 was no annus mirabilis, *and on the home front the economy sputtered (Eisenhower in his memoirs related how the preceding year was not merely the time when the Russians launched sputnik but also when the economy lapsed). It would not recover until the next year. Critics of the Republicans' management of the economy believed that conservative management of Amer-*

ica's economics had produced conservative results. Economists in the 1970s would have agreed. Economists of the next decade, the 1980s, uncertain of their former diagnoses, would not be so sure. The American economy was a delicate mechanism, and its forward and retrograde movements were hard to regulate—Eisenhower did his best, which did not seem effective.

In foreign affairs the country was treated to the Lebanon crisis—about which unfortunately the president made no diary entries. The ambitions of President Nasser had spilled over into Syria, which country united with Egypt to establish the United Arab Republic. The UAR gave evidence of becoming the wave of the future among the small nations of the area, and soon revolutions were brewing in Jordan, Iraq, and Lebanon. Revolution had been brewing in Jordan for years. In Iraq the government—a monarchy guided by the long-time prime minister Nuri al-Said—was very insecure. In Lebanon the president of the republic desired an unconstitutional second term, arranged it, took some money from the Americans under a legislative enactment of 1957 known as the Eisenhower Doctrine, and plunged Lebanon into civil war. Revolution broke out in Iraq in July; to avoid the spread of disorder, the president of the United States sent troops into Lebanon, and the British sent troops to Jordan. The crisis quieted.

JANUARY 14, 1958

C.D. Jackson has been talking to the secretary of state about the idea that the secretary might now be more valuable as my special assistant and advisory, and a younger man take on the duties of secretary of state. I find that C.D. Jackson now wants to talk to me about this kind of thing.

JANUARY 24, 1958

I sense a difference with Foster Dulles (in the approach to the Soviets). His is a lawyer's mind. He consistently adheres to a very logical explanation of these difficulties in which we find ourselves with the Soviets, and in doing so—with his lawyer's mind—he shows the steps and actions that are bad on their part; we seek to show that we are doing the decent and just thing. Of course we have got to have a concern and respect for fact and reiteration of official position, but we are likewise trying to "seek friends and influence people."

Therefore, I sometimes question the practice of becoming a sort of international prosecuting attorney in which I lay out all of the things that I intend to prove before the jury and make an opening statement of intention in order to make certain that people will understand.

FEBRUARY 28, 1958

From time to time I have received informal recommendations from members of the automobile industry that, in order to have an equal part in collective bargaining with the UAW [United Automobile Workers Union], there should be industry-wide bargaining on the part of the companies.

Apparently all the companies except General Motors accept this view completely.

In informal conversation with Mr. Curtice [of General Motors], he has made arguments against the proposition. It seems to me as I listen to him that he is really more interested in General Motors' competitive position vis-à-vis the other companies than he is in the establishing of an orderly industry-wide bargaining position.

I have been very careful to avoid any appearance of governmental interference into such matters, and such questioning as I have done with Mr. Curtice and others has been merely for information.

Mr. Curtice took the opportunity to describe to me some of the economic consequences of the Supreme Court order requiring DuPont to divest itself of sixty-three million shares of General Motors stock. I understand from the attorney general that he has already submitted to the Court a plan for accomplishing the divestiture, at the same time recognizing the need for avoiding economic shocks in throwing this amount of stock suddenly upon the market. The attached memorandum briefly shows Mr. Curtice's views.[1]

Again I listened and questioned only for information, but I did acquaint the attorney general verbally with Mr. Curtice's conviction that this divestiture will have to be accomplished very slowly and judiciously or some very bad economic effects will occur.

No action is indicated on any of these matters on my part.

MARCH 8, 1958

Jim Black was in to see me for some twenty minutes. I could not determine exactly the purpose of Mr. Black's visit with me. He did tell me something about a lawsuit now pending in the Supreme Court which is known as the "Memphis case." I told him that I had no interest in any lawsuits and did not have the time to study them. But he gave an economic twist to his presentation by saying that if the Supreme Court did not reverse the appeal court decision, a number of steel companies would have to cancel (and in some cases have already cancelled) contracts for making of steel pipe.

I reminded him that I had nothing to do with such cases and we would have to see what the Supreme Court said.

MARCH 17, 1958

On Saturday, March 15, I had a talk with Roger Kyes. He had two ideas that he suggested might have some virtue—one in the foreign field, the other in the domestic.

The Foreign Field. He gave only the barest outline of what he has in mind, but he has promised to send me a copy of a letter he has previously written on the subject. As I understand the matter, he wants to set up a huge international corporation, in effect a holding company.

Trading would be accomplished under the auspices of the holding company, and one of the purposes of the company would be to promote the flow of profitable trade for participants.

Each country desiring to trade with others would purchase stock in the holding company, but free enterprise would be encouraged by making it possible, in countries such as ours, for a business firm to purchase such stock directly. His idea was that countries that derived income from the export of raw materials (such as oil) could pay for their stock out of earnings. His big purpose is to get each country to have a stake in the prosperity of each of the others; in other words, to have a powerful influence for peace.

The actual financial details are something we did not go into, and I am most interested in hearing what the explanation of them will be. Moreover, I will be waiting to hear what he says on tariffs. But he is a smart man, and I am sure that he believes that he has an idea that would be most beneficial to every country involved.

Stimulation of the Domestic Economy. In this field he has been thinking about the effects of tax reduction. He is very fearful that tax reduction would leave us with such a gap in revenue that we would quickly be going into deficit spending at an indefinite rate and for an indefinite period. The inflationary effect of this would wipe out, he is sure, any beneficial effects to be expected. He seems to have this conviction whether we are talking about reducing income tax or excise tax.

So his simple idea is that we should have a percentage refund on the 1957 personal income tax. This would be a "one time" affair and would immediately put a lot of money into the hands of the population and would spur buying all along the line. He thinks it would spur the weakest phase of our consumer buying —namely, consumer hard goods—for example, automobiles, refrigerators, house and farm appliances of all kinds.

He suggested the possibility of requiring that all refunded amounts over a particular level would have to be used as venture capital of some kind. In thinking it over, I do not see how this could be done because while an individual might make a purchase of this kind, he could resell it at his own convenience. (Possibly there should be a maximum limit on any single refund.)

With the $36 billion collected in taxes on 1957 personal income, he thought that even a 25 percent refund would not be out of order. This $9 billion, he believes, would have a tremendous effect both materially and psychologically.

The Treasury Department is thinking of a similar idea, although probably on a small basis. Since I know he has been talking to Secretary Anderson, it is probable that it was by his initiative that this thought came under study.[1] In any event, I shall keep it completely secret.

I talked about the philosophy under which the administration is pushing ahead with its effort to stimulate the economy. (1) We are basically conservative. We believe, for example, that frantic efforts now to put the federal government into a large-scale building program will have most unfortunate financial consequences in the years immediately ahead. We believe in a private enterprise rather than

THE SECOND ADMINISTRATION

a "government" campaign to provide the main strength of recovery forces. (2) We want to avoid a succession of budgetary deficits because of the inflationary effect. (3) We want to do everything that has a stimulating effect on the economy, but so far as expenditure programs are concerned, we prefer to limit these expenditures to projects that are useful and needed. The idea is to do them now rather than later. We want to do everything that is feasible and practical to stimulate recovery, and at the same time keep our own financial house in order.

I told Roger that we expect to push forward with the things we have already undertaken administratively and with those we have already recommended to the Congress. (The easing of credit and reducing bank reserves slightly was, of course, done by the Federal Reserve Board, but with the approval and urgent support of the financial section of the government.) This memo does not enumerate all the particular programs, but I attach hereto two statements, one written on February 12 and the other March 8.[2]

There is one idea I have been discussing with the treasury which I believe could become important. This concerns the railways, which by every discernible statistic are in real trouble. Only a few seem to be doing well. The majority are in bad shape, and it is my belief that unless something is done, there will be bankruptcies looming for a number of railway systems within a matter of a few months.

I believe it is important for the railways to achieve a truly competitive status with respect to other forms of transportation. To my mind, success demands real cooperative studies as between the railways and other transportation systems if we are to get the highest form of efficiency from the several types. Take, for example, railways and trucks. If the public could be informed as to what is really the most efficient form of freight transportation measured by such criteria as distance of haul, bulk, weight, and conditions of delivery, it would certainly be to the benefit both of the shipper and of all transportation systems.

Here are some things to consider: (1) the elimination of the transportation tax, at least the 3 percent that is applied to the transportation on things. (2) The placing before Congress of a list of the restrictive laws that are preventing the railways from being truly competitive with respect to the other transportation systems. These laws were largely written when the railways had a monopoly on transportation and in many instances may be no longer applicable. I believe that one of their worst effects (this is possibly as much administrative as it is legalistic) is that railway complaints, protests, and recommendations cannot even be heard and acted upon within a matter of one or two years. This is unconscionable. The railways now have the right to reorganize into a fewer number of systems, so long as the attorney general does not find a reason for taking action against them under the Antitrust Act. But the ICC must find that the consolidation is in the public interest. I believe that if an application is not protested in a reasonable time, there should be a presumption of public interest in the consolidation. An appeal could be taken to a hearing. Reorganization could get rid of duplicatory service and mileage—and would be most helpful in a number of other ways. (3) The whole question of featherbedding under existing laws and union procedures should be thoroughly considered by the Congress. This would take considerable time, but it would be hopeful if the Congress would at least have the courage to undertake the examination. (4) Assuming that (1) and (2) could be done, the railways could certainly gain so much efficiency, better their service, lower costs, and increase revenues that the way would be open for them to begin the renovation and reorganization of the railroad systems. The federal government could then well undertake the same kind of responsibility that it did with both the maritime and air industries, in guaranteeing loans for new equipment and general renovation. (5) To my mind this is a project that must be undertaken promptly because of its effect on the whole transportation capacity of the country and its significance for the nation's defensive strength.

In the case of the railways, the program would be not only important in itself, but incidentally would be one of the greatest possible spurs to economic recovery because of the widespread character and the volume of the work that would be immediately necessary.

Today I have a draft of a report of the transportation study group. I find that it suggests some of the same things to which I have adverted.

Finally, I have asked Bob Anderson to confer with Dr. Saulnier to establish a committee on economic development.[3]

MARCH 18, 1958

I spoke to the secretary of state about a mistake in the public relations section of the State Department, which was reported to have said yesterday, "The State Department announces that the United States rejects the Soviet proposals on outer space." The secretary of state was already aware of the implications of such a statement and has taken steps to correct any future occurrence of the kind.

The secretary himself was at some pains at a press conference when he arrived in Washington to point out that the original proposal was mine and that I was

Cabinet meeting, June 27, 1958.

the one who had to make decisions as to acceptance or rejection of any Soviet counterproposals.

JUNE 9, 1958

This morning I noted in the papers a report that an American helicopter was down in East Germany. Some difficulty was being incurred in our attempts to get the people back because of Soviet insistence that we deal with East Germany and our insistence that we wanted to deal with the Soviets because we do not recognize East Germany.

Having forgotten the incident until about twelve noon, I called the secretary of state on the telephone to remind him that under somewhat similar circumstances we had dealt directly with Red China, which we do not recognize. When I had the secretary on the phone, he remarked that my call was a remarkable coincidence because he was just reaching for the phone to call his staff to remind them of the same circumstance and to express his opinion that we should not be too stiffnecked in our attitude. To do so might easily create a situation that could bring about a prolonged stalemate, such as we have had in China.

The gap in diary entries for the year 1958, from June 9 until December 6, concerned Mrs. Whitman, who made a notation on the latter day: "For the first time in a long time, the president dictated long notes for the diary."

A whopper, just brought in. (Fishing trip at West Greenwich, Rhode Island)

DECEMBER 6, 1958

A few days ago, in Augusta, I had a long talk with Cliff Roberts about the political situation. The general tenor of that conversation was very similar to one that I held later with the vice-president, reported below. The only point on which Cliff Roberts had a positive conviction, that is not shared by Dick Nixon and me (and certainly not by the principal members of the White House staff), is that Meade Alcorn should be removed as chairman of the Republican National Committee.[1] He also believes an effort should be made to substitute for him Chuck Percy of Chicago.[2]

I agree without reservation that Chuck Percy is a very unusual and capable young man and in my opinion would, if we could induce him to take this post, make an extraordinarily effective chairman. Further than this I did not concur with Cliff's conclusion, for reasons that appear in the following paragraph.

Meade Alcorn has been the best chairman of the Republican National Committee that I have known. His intelligence, energy, imagination, and dedication are exemplary. Cliff, while not well acquainted with Mr. Alcorn, had no reason, he said, to differ with this evaluation. Cliff's big point is that Meade Alcorn is not a "real figure" in the national scene. He says that Alcorn cannot be effective for the simple reason that people do not pay attention to him. Moreover, Cliff feels that the terrible drubbing that the Republican party took in the recent election is bound to be laid largely to Alcorn's door, even if the allegation is unjust and really represents nothing more than the effort of others to alibi their own inefficiencies. He concludes that since Alcorn's name is connected with failure and since he has not succeeded in establishing himself as a real influence in the party, we should let him go.

My final remark was that I never thought it wise to fire anybody unless I knew that I had a better person to take over. In addition, I again repeated the list of Alcorn's good qualities and I pointed out to Cliff that in four attempts to get what he or anyone else would consider a "big" man (in the sense that he was regarded nationally as an influential figure) I had not been successful. Honesty, courage, intelligence, and incessant work, after all, can be of more importance than reputation.

DECEMBER 6, 1958 (PART TWO)

The vice-president and I agreed that we should try to get a broadly based committee to analyze Republican difficulties and failures and to work out the finest possible plan we could develop for their correction. We further agreed that time is of the essence because we have to do a lot of rebuilding.

I shall attempt, below, to lay out an outline of the steps we thought should be tried and some of the problems that we think must be met and solved.

1. The committee should be organized as soon as possible. On it there should be the vice-president, Alcorn, Justin Dart, and a number of others who could

possibly include Summerfield, Chuck Percy, and at the very least one of the individuals who was in the original committee in 1951–1952 to support my original nomination and election.[1] Such a person could be Lodge, Clay, Paul Hoffman, or Dewey. (We discussed briefly the desirability of getting at least one senator and one member of the House to serve on the committee, but I believe we left the matter open.)

Two men that I would like to see brought in and very closely questioned—possibly one or both could be members of the committee—are Congressman-elect Lindsay from New York City and Governor-elect Hatfield of Oregon. Both of them ran beautiful races almost on their own and both were successful. There ought also possibly be at least one well-known businessman and another individual from the university world.

In the shakedown I believe there should not be over nine members, and possibly this might be too many. A necessary recording staff could be provided by Meade Alcorn. (With respect to favoring such a committee, a later talk with Alcorn developed that he was thinking along these same lines and indeed he has already talked with the vice-president about doing something of the kind suggested above.)

2. We should make a survey of exactly what happened on November 4 in the various areas and why. We believe that the pollsters as well as reports from county and state chairmen and others should be examined. The analysis of this report should be undertaken by someone selected by the committee, who is experienced in research of this kind.

3. The next step for the committee would be to work out procedures by which (a) an organization could be built up from the grassroots (This organization's effort should emphasize youth, vigor, and progress so that as it develops upward there will be elected as county and state chairmen the finest young leaders that we can find. The same effect will finally be noted in the type of our national committeemen, but in this case elections can be held once only every four years.) and (b) we could develop a sturdy, broadly based, and hardworking finance group which would bring in necessary revenue on a continuing monthly basis.

4. We should decide upon the form of the top organization. Here we mean not only the possible reorganization of the national committee as such, but a careful examination of the need or lack of need for the so-called congressional and senatorial committees as now organized and supported. It is reported to me that the congressional committee is particularly costly, its maintenance expense being something over $64,000 a month. This not only raises the question of getting our money's worth out of these two committees, but it raises a far more serious question of a single versus a triheaded political effort.

The national chairman is of course the alter ego on party matters of the president. This means that the proclamations and policies and plans of the national committee must, under the president's leadership, provide the guidelines for party effort, always, of course, within the limits laid down by the national platform. If the heads of the congressional or senatorial committees take a different political line and urge a different doctrine then not only is our effort

weakened, but we have the curious spectacle of the national committee supporting with very large sums of money a committee which is preaching something
that the president, the administration, and the national chairman disapprove.
This sort of thing happened in some instances in the last campaign. Incidentally,
to point up the importance of this problem we should note that the amount of
donations made to the congressional committee by the national committee in the
years 1956 and 1958 were respectively $1,600,000 and $400,000. I have no idea
how the money was used, but I was importuned to help raise money and did so.

Relating further to the question of top organization, there could be a voluntary
advisory committee to the national chairman to be made up of businessmen, and,
if the congressional and senatorial committees were either eliminated or drastically reduced, another could be made up of a combined group of senators and
congressmen—possibly six in number.

5. Throughout the organization from top to bottom there must be useful and
dedicated voluntary workers; in addition we must have, according to the need,
the necessary paid workers.

6. With this kind of an organization developed, we must have, in addition to
a clear understanding of our problems and policies and programs, the finest
possible candidates. Again these people—men and women—should be young and
vigorous and intelligent. If the preliminary organizational steps are properly
accomplished, the result in terms of good candidates will be almost automatic.
However, nothing can be taken for granted and we believe that it would be a good
move to have in the national committee two or three "traveling salesmen" who
are clearheaded people looking out for this type of candidate and able to get the
local people to carry out the necessary measures.

There were, of course, a number of other related subjects discussed between
the vice-president and myself. A later conversation with Meade Alcorn was
almost identical.

Alcorn is, at the moment (December 6) in San Francisco or Hawaii. He will
be back in a few days and he and the vice-president will start this work at once.

There was nothing significant in my conversation with Bill Knowland, except
to note that he talked more objectively and sensibly after his defeat than he did
before.

DECEMBER 6, 1958 (PART THREE)

Recently I have had several talks with the secretary of the treasury and the
chairman of the council of economic advisers, Dr. Saulnier, on these subjects.[1]
Possibly I have recorded elsewhere some of our projected difficulties in refinancing as outlined and detailed to me by Bob Anderson, the secretary of the treasury.
Unquestionably, these problems are serious, the principal factors being as follows:

In the year 1959 we have to refinance more than $50 billion of bond issues,
each of which is more than one-year term. In addition to this, we have to roll
over four times during the year something on the order of $26 billion worth of

short-term papers. Beyond this we must find $12 billion of new money because of the 1959 deficit. Still above this, we must get the additional money in November and December that will represent the difference between receipts and expenditures during that low point of the year. Finally, whatever projected deficit there will be in the 1960 budget will be overhanging the market.

In view of the fact that we are already spending more than $8 billion a year for interest alone, without any amortization, the scope of this problem and the rates of interest that we have to pay are, to say the least, serious.

On the other hand, Saulnier takes a very much more optimistic view than Anderson does with regard to the gravity of this problem. Whereas Anderson believes that, unless we have a balanced budget, we are going to have very bad effects in foreign banking circles because of a diminishing faith in the dollar, Saulnier believes that there is very little danger of this at the moment. Moreover, he is not particularly concerned about the accelerated outward movement of gold. He believes that as corporation earnings go up—and he believes that the rate of increase is going to be higher than most people feel—corporations will have to find use for their money. Many of them will be purchasing notes and short-term securities, and this will greatly strengthen the bond market and tend to minimize our interest costs.

On the other hand, Saulnier does not by any manner of means minimize the seriousness of the situation that will develop if, in addition to the obvious obstacles, we should have a disappointing performance of the economy insofar as its next twelve months recovery is concerned.

In any event, both agree that a balanced budget would have the most salutary effect on our fiscal situation that could be imagined.

The president described the following entry as a "footnote to history."

DECEMBER 17, 1958

Governor Stassen has several times informed me that it was only by his prompt and decisive action that he swung the Minnesota delegation to me in 1952 and thereby achieved nomination on the first ballot.

The other day, about December 10, 1958, Senator Thye called me on the telephone to say goodbye. (He was defeated in the last senatorial campaign.) He started off the conversation with words about like these: "Since the moment that I made advance arrangements for and did swing the Minnesota delegation to your side in 1952, thereby achieving your nomination on the first ballot . . ." Several times I have heard refuted by others Governor Stassen's claim that he took the initiative in this matter and accomplished it. Senator Thye's testimony in the matter is of a very direct and personal character.

1959

John Foster Dulles resigned in April 1959 and died the next month; Eisenhower was distressed, for he had lost a good friend as well as an able cabinet member. But on the very day of Dulles's funeral the date expired on which Khrushchev had said six months before that he would turn over the Russian sector of Berlin to the East Germans so that the United States and the other Allies in Berlin would have to deal with the unrecognized East German regime. Dulles's demise and the eventless expiration of the Soviet deadline probably were a coincidence, for the Russian leader was beginning to think of a trip to the United States—and it was no time to get into an argument with a future host. In September the premier arrived and barnstormed his way from Washington to California via several stopovers, including the Iowa cornfield of corn expert Roswell Garst, where Khrushchev stood in the middle of a field, held up an ear of corn, and grinned expansively. Peace, perhaps, had come.

The economy returned to health, and for that boon Eisenhower was grateful. His second term was moving toward its end, and for that he was grateful too.

JANUARY 27, 1959

The vice-president, in talking to me last evening, mentioned the fact that he had met a number of very fine foreign service officers in the numerous countries he

Principal actors of the era (and earlier): Dulles, Churchill, the president, Eden.

had visited in the past several years. However, from that the vice-president went on to state that an astonishing number of them have no obvious dedication to America and to its service—in fact, in some instances they are far more vocal in their criticism of our country than were many of the foreigners that Pat and Dick met.

He thought that this was possibly due to the fact that most of these men had been appointed to the career service during the New Deal years and consequently they felt no loyalty to the present government. Nevertheless, he felt that the matter was somewhat deeper than this, thinking that the tendency represented sort of an expatriate attitude toward his native country.

As an example of the kind of thing, he mentioned a statement made in many forms but with a similar general meaning to the effect, "I hope I never have to go back to the United States."

His wife, Pat, who is very sensitive to these things, was more emphatic than Dick in her expressions of belief that there was a very great deal of this kind of feeling and thinking in the foreign service.

FEBRUARY 16, 1959

Someone told me it takes about $15,000 of investment in capital goods to produce one job in industry. Since we have an average addition of 700,000 per year to our labor force, it would appear that we have to invest some $10 billion to $11 billion each year for these recruits.

I do not know the amount of money we have to put in for replacement or renovation of equipment already installed. In addition to investments for these two purposes, we must of course provide for increase in productivity per man in the entire labor force.

Over the last years our average investment in new plants and equipment has been about $28.5 billion annually. It would appear that a figure something on the order of $32 billion or $33 billion—always of course increasing a little bit each year—would be about our safe minimum.

MARCH 3, 1959

This morning the two Democratic senators from West Virginia, Randolph and Byrd, came in to see me. They were quite decent about their presentation, arguing the plight of the coal industry in competition with residual oil, and therefore arguing there must be some restrictions. I am afraid myself that restricting importation of residuals will merely mean the replacement of that much oil fuel by American oil supplies, rather than giving the coal industry an opportunity to take up some of the slack. This was brought about, I think, by the rising costs of the past twenty years in coal production.

Also this morning I had a message from George Love, another coal producer, which made some of the arguments represented by the two senators.

Other individuals, particularly the eastern seaboard consumers, are very much on the other side of the argument.

Another factor that neither side mentions is that any time we restrict imports we make it more difficult for us to export the products from our industry because we deny other people to earn the dollars they need with which to purchase our goods. This makes for an unhappy, lowered level of mutual trade and, eventually, a general decline in economic activity, including our own. It likewise has the result of driving more of our friends into other channels of trade, an increased percentage of which will be with the communist bloc.

All this is bad. Yet there seems to be no possibility of giving to the oil and coal producers of our own country some kind of assurance that they are not to be eliminated as productive industries. This we cannot afford to do, if for no other reason than in the event of emergency we shall need their facilities operating at an increasing tempo.

MARCH 3, 1959 (PART TWO)

Bob Cox, president of the junior chamber of commerce, was in to see me. I told him that I would look over the possibility of addressing the junior chamber of commerce on June 16 at Buffalo. In some ways I look upon the invitation as an opportunity because these young men are normally possessed of a real sense of civic responsibility as well as enthusiasm.

However, June is going to be a busy month for me, with many engagements already made. I promised Cox to give him a final answer no later than April 10. I do this because I want to find out whether I could get some very rough draft quickly so that I could look it over and see whether or not it would be useful as a vehicle for me to produce a talk that I would consider worthwhile.

The general theme of the convention is to be "The Dignity of Man," but these young men are hopeful that each speaker will develop his own views on this theme from the standpoint of his own current responsibility and interests. For example, they would like me to talk on the relationship between sound fiscal measures, frugality in government, and so on, in the relationship of these values to man's freedom.

At the time of Dulles's death, former Secretary of State Marshall, Eisenhower's old military mentor, was in precarious health and obviously could not live much longer. (He died in October.) The death of one secretary and the illness of another inspired the following commentary about how the president, years earlier and acting as an envoy for another president, had notified General Marshall that he, Marshall, was to be secretary of state whenever Secretary Byrnes chose to resign.

MAY 27, 1959

In April, 1946, President Truman sent for me to come to the presidential yacht, then tied up at the dock at Quantico, Virginia. The purpose of the visit was to talk to me about an impending vacancy in the office of secretary of state. He said that Secretary Byrnes, then occupying the office, had suffered a deterioration of health and wanted to resign by the middle of the year. He said that there were only two men he would even consider for the appointment, one of whom was General George C. Marshall, then in China. I told him that I was just starting on a trip through the Orient and would be happy to carry a message to General Marshall. He directed, of course, that the utmost secrecy should be observed in making known his wishes to General Marshall.

At the meeting in Chungking, General Marshall indicated his readiness to accept the offer, requesting me to keep him informed of developments. In order that we might keep our correspondence confidential, General Marshall made out, in his own handwriting, a simple code for the key words that might be used in our cabled interchanges. For some years I carried this little paper in a coin purse. This explains its dilapidated appearance.

Incidentally, the arrangement for appointing General Marshall was considerably postponed, the president informing me later that Mr. Byrnes wished to put off his resignation date for some months. Some time later General Marshall did become secretary of state.

The Code

PINEHURST: secretary of state   COURIER: president
AGENT: Byrnes   AGREEMENT: confirmation

Statesmen and diplomats from all over the world came to Dulles's funeral, among them Chancellor Konrad Adenauer of West Germany. His message was more of what was his well-known refrain that Eisenhower knew by heart—his need for reassurance that America and its allies would stand behind the new Germany.

MAY 27, 1959 (PART TWO)

Chancellor Adenauer, as usual, laid out his general thinking toward the communist menace. In this he shows no great change—indeed, if he did I would be greatly disappointed.

He seems to have developed almost a psychopathic fear of what he considers to be "British weakness." I went over with him some of my conversations with Mr. Macmillan and also described in rough fashion some of the British problems in the world. I told him that I am certain that, in basic conviction and belief, Harold Macmillan and the Conservative party leadership stand squarely with the rest of us. On the other hand, Britain has some economic and political problems that are almost unique, at least they are delicate and never ending. Since there is a very sharply divided opinion in that nation affecting such matters, Macmillan has had to tread a very careful path. In spite of this, I told the chancellor that, in my opinion, in any showdown Macmillan would stand firmly on principle.

The chancellor discussed the continuing objective of reuniting Germany. He stated, or implied, that the practicalities of the situation were such that the end would have to be achieved in a step-by-step process in which the two sides of Germany would themselves have to exhibit a clear readiness to be conciliatory and reasonable.

At the time of Dulles's death the foreign ministers of the Big Four were holding a meeting in Geneva; they adjourned and came to Washington in a group for the obsequies. During their Geneva sessions they had had trouble agreeing, prompting Eisenhower to remark after their Washington flight that he had thought of keeping them in the air until they could agree. The funeral did offer diplomatic opportunities, as the president quickly realized.

MAY 28, 1959

I had an official visit with the four ministers who had been in Geneva and later held a luncheon for all of the foreign dignitaries present for Secretary Dulles's funeral.

My purpose was to thank both groups for their courtesy in paying their respects to a man that we, here, thought to be one of our greatest and, of course, in both cases, I wanted to try to help improve the atmosphere both in general and in the specific sense. I say specific because I am referring here to the atmosphere in which negotiations are being conducted in Geneva. . . .[1] I told the group that I was personally anxious that such progress be accomplished, because only in this way could America agree to go to a summit meeting. To go without such progress would be not only an exercise in futility, but would have an adverse effect upon world thinking when it was understood that the meeting was condemned in advance to sterility. . . .[2]

Respecting the luncheon, each of the individuals present took the occasion during the coffee period to assure me of his nation's respect for Mr. Dulles and for the policies that Mr. Dulles and I have advocated and carried out. I asked each to convey to his respective head of government or state my personal thanks for the courtesy, and all in all, I think the meeting was worthwhile.

JUNE 22, 1959

In June of 1953 President Hoover came to my office, for the first time, to pay a courtesy call. He fell to discussing the character of the problems facing me, particularly those in the field of the nation's economy.

He pointed out that for twenty years the conservatives and middle-of-the-roaders had discerned a drift toward greater governmental controls—or at least interference—in the nation's economy. People who belonged to the extreme right became very worried about this and became very critical in their condemnation of the whole thing as "socialism" and so on and so on. On the other hand, there were many people who listened to the oratory of the 1953 campaign who thought that I was not sufficiently "liberal" to meet the requirements of a modern democracy. He pointed out, therefore, that I was strictly in the "middle"—the most difficult position that a political leader can take up.

I interrupted long enough to tell him that on September 3, 1949, at a time when I was certain that any thought of a political career for me was now eliminated from the public mind, I made a speech before the American Bar Association in St. Louis in which I had voiced the same convictions about the middle-of-the-road position that he had expressed to me. He went on to say that this whole matter gave to me a problem greater, in the domestic field, than any other president had ever encountered and been called upon to solve. He said that the rightists expected that on the day after inauguration there would be an immediate return to the "good old days"; some of them, he felt, would argue for a much lesser application of the antitrust laws and greater control of unions, and, indeed, some even would insist that there should be no unions except on a company level. He carried these examples into taxes and regulatory commissions and so on.

In the same way, he said that I would be beseeched by the so-called liberals to enlarge and increase every welfare program in the country and that I would be bitterly accused of being the tool of Wall Street unless I acceded to such demands. Then he said that it is quite true that the curve representing the interference of government into private life, private business, and into the responsibilities of states and cities had risen rapidly and steadily over the past twenty years. He pointed out that we have to take as a starting point in such matters the position at which we now stand. He stated flatly that it was impossible to take this curve and bend it sharply downward, as the rightists would have me do, and certainly a man who took the middle-of-the-road course could not be happy with the degree to which it was now rising. He stated, in other words, that all I could do—the very maximum any administration could bring about—would be a flattening of the curve in this particular trend. He pointed out, of course, that there had to be constant expansion of the economy to meet our increased obligations in the world and at home but that if I should be successful after my years in office in stopping future encroachment of the federal government into the field of regulation, control, and direction of the economy, this would indeed be a brilliant victory. He again repeated that no more could possibly be done and to get this much done would be an achievement that would be long remembered.

The president on September 10 gave a television and radio talk to the nation on his European trip—he had just visited Bonn, London, Paris, and Scotland— and as he was reading over the final script he noticed the date (September 10, 1959) and wrote on the covering page in pencil.

SEPTEMBER 10, 1959

Today, fifteen years ago, I met Monty at Brussels airfield. I was accompanied by Gale and Tedder. He made his preposterous proposal to go to Berlin. I asked him first to get across the Rhine and gave him all he asked for this operation. I told him that when he was across he must clear out opposition to Antwerp because of our extended supply position. He failed even to get the bridgehead.

NOVEMBER 9, 1959

On Saturday morning, November 7, the Supreme Court approved the injunction ordering the steelworkers back to their jobs for a period of eighty days.

From the very beginning of negotiations between steel management and the union, I have been indirectly—or even occasionally directly—in contact with some of the participating individuals, so as to keep in touch with the issues that seemed to be primarily at stake. My principal informant has been Secretary Mitchell.

What seems to be involved primarily is different convictions concerning the so-called "work rules."

The management seems to believe that these rules are antiquated and in

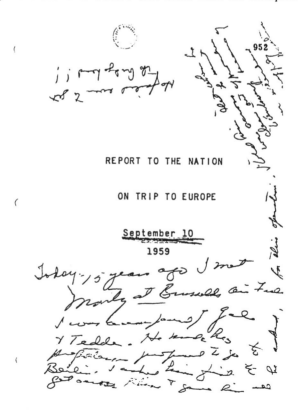

REPORT TO THE NATION

ON TRIP TO EUROPE

September 10
1959

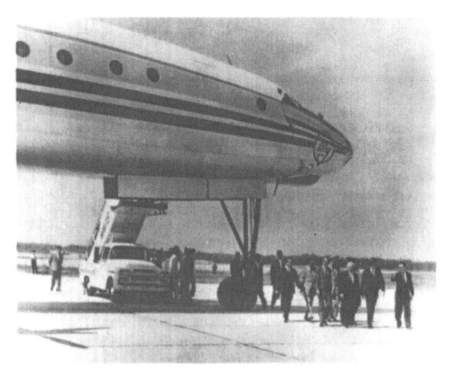

Khrushchev's arrival in the United States.

On September 15, 1959, Premier Khrushchev of the Soviet Union arrived in Washington, a short and stocky figure with an air of authority.

themselves compel an inefficient type of operation that helps to price their products out of the market, especially foreign markets.

On the other hand, the union labels as trustbusting any attempt to change these so-called work rules.

Secretary Mitchell and I believe that the management does not comprehend how seriously the union membership takes this matter. The management seems to believe that the issues are raised merely to achieve a better wage settlement. On the other hand, the union asserts that it has never stood in the way of improved technology and in achieving automation. It insists that it is quite ready to submit arguments on this point to arbitration.

On Friday evening, November 6, Mr. McDonald came to see me, off the record. He was accompanied by Secretary Mitchell. He professed himself as being very anxious for a fair and just and noninflationary settlement, and he seemed to believe that Mr. Cooper, the negotiator for the steel management, is not only very rigid and stupid but is obsessed with a distorted conviction as to the importance of these so-called work rules. I sent Secretary Mitchell to see Mr. Blough, president of United States Steel, and to keep in very close touch with the matter to see whether something might be done. Mr. Blough and Mr. McDonald met either Saturday or Sunday for a two-hour meeting and have agreed to meet again on Wednesday.

I earnestly hope that something will be done promptly.

As the second Eisenhower administration moved toward its end, the president ruminated about his entry into politics in 1952 and evidently wondered on occasion if it had been a good idea. To clear the air, apparently, and without any notion of writing to be read, he set down an account of how he reached the presidency. It was an account that if any other man would have written it would have been almost unbelievable. He was contending that he had obeyed the old rule of American statesmanship—that the office must come to the man, not the man to the office. No politician or political leader, and very few statesmen, have ever obeyed this rule; where it has had meaning in American politics is that it simply has defined a well-known fact, namely, that Americans do not like candidates to give the impression that they are eager for office—a certain reluctance, a modest carelessness for one's own personal future, must be in evidence, and after that any would-be officeholder can scramble any way he wants to. But in Eisenhower's case his protestations, one could well believe, were true. There is a sterling sort of honesty about the following account that shows that the president of the United States in 1959 actually had moved toward his high office reluctantly and waited until there had been a virtual draft from his countrymen. He had not much wanted the job, even though he saw that to take it would, as he had said at the time, constitute a duty he could not easily refuse, for much was at stake—indeed, all the things he had believed in over the years, since he had grown up in Abilene at the turn of the century.

NOVEMBER 28, 1959*

The possibility that I might one day become a candidate for the presidency was first suggested to me about June 1943. My reaction was of course completely negative, and my feeling was that the matter was never seriously considered even by the proposers. Actually the hard military campaigns of the war were at that time obviously still ahead of us, and any diverting of our attention to political matters would have been more than ridiculous.

The subject was again brought up in the middle of 1945. By this time the war was over in Europe, and there was more than idle speculation on the part of visiting friends, newspaper representatives, and noncareer soldiers. I cannot recall, at that time, of any career soldier who mentioned the matter, possibly because they had concern, all being my juniors, as to the character of my reaction. This subject became one of more lively interest when, with a number of military associates of all services, I made a tour, at the direction of the president and the War Department, through several American cities. The purpose of the tour was to establish a more personal connection between the victorious army, navy, and air force in Europe and the people at home. Incidentally, the party accompanying me had representatives of all ranks from private upward.

We visited Washington, New York, West Point, Kansas City and Abilene, Kansas. For the first time newspaper representatives began quizzing me in public press conferences, in an effort to determine my attitude. I continued, as always before, to reply in completely negative terms.

There was no question that I felt a very great sense of pride in the success of the invading forces in Western Europe. When we arrived at D-Day, June 6, 1944, there was no universal confidence in a completely successful outcome. Indeed most people thought that even should we, in some two or three years, eventually win, we would pay a ghastly price in battling our way toward Germany in the pattern of World War I, with its terrible memories of Passchendaele, Vimy Ridge, Verdun, and the like.

Some newspapers went so far as to predict 90 percent loss on the beaches themselves. Even Winston Churchill, normally a fairly optimistic individual, never hesitated to voice his forebodings about the venture. He frequently repeated that if we were successful, we could count any advance on the Allied part that would seize and hold Paris by mid-winter as one of the greatest and most successful military operations of all time.

Consequently, when on May 8, 1945, the confidence and enthusiasm of my own headquarters proved justified by completing the entire campaign in eleven months, I felt that the climax of my own personal career had clearly been

---

*This account does not differ materially from what Eisenhower later set down, albeit in more detail, in the opening pages of the first volume of his memoirs, *Mandate for Change*, and some of it appeared in his autobiography, *At Ease*. The present telling, however, has a succinctness that the other accountings do not have, and it is garnished with detail that was dropped out of the others, perhaps for diplomatic reasons.

attained. Anything that could happen to me thereafter would, in my opinion, be anticlimatic. I had some conversations with General Marshall and others about my desire to retire, but I did agree to remain temporarily as military governor of the American zone in Germany, although at that time constantly recommending to the War Department, to the president, and to Secretary of State Byrnes that as quickly as possible a civilian should be appointed to this post. My superiors expressed sympathy for the idea but said that this could not be done until the Allies, including the Russians, would agree. I kept pounding away on this matter because of my feeling that after wars are over and matters of civil government come to the fore, the executive head of all organizations governing civilians should be, under the Western tradition, a civilian.

In any event, the armistice in Europe provided an opportunity for many American visitors to come into the area. In the tradition of the past, these people almost inevitably revised the proposition that a successful general should be considered as a possible candidate for the presidency. I always had the feeling that most of these, at that time, had no interest in my possible qualifications or my personal philosophy of government. They were merely voicing interest in an individual who, because of the circumstances of the war, might finally develop into a popular public figure. At the same time, I think that they were very little impressed by my denials of any interest in politics or of any intention to get involved in political affairs. In these circumstances, while the matter never completely died out, it never reached a real crescendo of discussion and debate. One of the reasons for this was because President Truman was still in his first year of incumbency of the office.

At the end of the year, I was ordered back to Washington to become chief of staff of the army. I informed the president of my hope to retire and unless he had a positive desire that I take over the office for a period, I should like to decline the appointment. He told me that the only other individual he could consider to take General Marshall's place was General Bradley, who at that time was serving as the head of the Veterans Bureau. He informed me also that he would need General Bradley in that post for at least two years but stated that if I was still of the same mind at that time, he would accept my resignation and appoint Bradley to the post of chief of staff of the army.

Under this circumstance, I retained the post of chief of staff until early 1948.

By mid-1947 the pressure brought to bear upon me to secure my consent for seeking the presidency had many times intensified. The nature of the argument presented underwent a change. No longer was the matter completely personal; it now began to involve also governmental philosophy. Since I continued to maintain my negative attitude toward the entire matter, I declined also to outline in specific terms my own conception as to the functions of government and my own satisfaction or dissatisfaction with the political scene as I viewed it.

While my appointment book would of course give a record of those individuals visiting my office to discuss this matter, I cannot now recall many of them to my mind. Three that did stick out in my memory were Douglas Freeman, the historian, Walter Winchell, the columnist and commentator, and Mr. Wadsworth, a congressman. Each of these had a different type of approach. Douglas Freeman was deeply religious and opened his conversation with a prayer. He believed that government needed a shake-up; in his opinion complacency had overtaken the party which had been in power ever since 1932. Because of this he felt that the Democratic Party was neglectful of self-examination, and as a result there was becoming evident examples of carelessness and, even worse, in the conduct of governmental affairs. He was very earnest and he placed his accent on the word "duty." He said that recent history would show that only a popular figure could defeat any Democratic candidate—and that I had the duty to make the race. He played upon this theme for a considerable time; as I recall he stayed more than an hour and called upon history to provide examples of the need for change. I had met Dr. Freeman several times earlier and had long talks with him. He paid me the compliment of saying that he knew I was not only reluctant to accept his counsel but that the whole idea of political involvement was distasteful. But he added that because I had a sense of duty and since he believed that I was both disinterested and honest and had shown good administrative capacity, he was sure I would see my duty and perform it. These thoughts were the subject of the prayer with which he opened the conversation.

Walter Winchell put the whole matter on a personal basis. He didn't like the government then existing; he wanted it changed. He thought I was the only one who could do it. He didn't care whether I was a Democrat or a Republican.

Mr. Wadsworth was more analytical, but he was fully as thoughtfully serious as Douglas Freeman. As in the prior cases, I told him that I had decided to do nothing whatsoever about the matter.

A few others who talked to me at that time were some from the newspaper world, Senator Vandenberg, and so on. The whole affair became more difficult. At a Republican dinner, which I had supposed to be entirely social and nonpartisan, an attempt was made to portray me as an extreme New Dealer. The purpose of this was to show me as unacceptable as a Republican candidate. Whether traveling outside of Washington or in my office in the Pentagon, every day brought some new recommendation, conviction, or opinion. The purport of each was that I simply had to run for the presidency.

Finally, in January of 1948 there came a letter from a man named Finder, one of the publishers of a newspaper in New Hampshire, saying that a group of which he was a part intended to enter my name in the New Hampshire primary of that year. I knew that I was going to refuse, but I also felt a compulsion to inform the public, through my answer, of why I would not allow my name to be used. A copy of that letter is attached to this memorandum. I still believe it was sound. After its writing, I felt that I had removed myself from the political scene for once and all, and thereafter I could feel free to do as I pleased since within a month or so I was to leave the office of chief of staff.[1]

I had already accepted an invitation to become president of Columbia University, the effective date to be the one on which my term as chief of staff officially was to end—I think it was about May 5 or 6.

Very quickly my belief that I had removed myself forever from politics was shattered. Suddenly there came to me a multitude of new suggestions, recommendations, and importunities, this time almost exclusively from Democratic party members. Up until the time I had written the letter in January the pressure had come largely from the Republicans. Now it seemed that the whole experience was to be repeated, but with the other party. Numerous governors, United States senators, private citizens, and others joined the campaign. Since I had already made my position clear—and in my letter I had not mentioned party—I saw no necessity for repeating anything further. Nevertheless, as the late spring of 1948 rolled by, the pressure became almost unbearable. A telegram reaching me about July 1 seemed to demand an answer. I made another statement, which I did through the public relations officer of the university, Mr. Herron. It was again negative and is on record—I assume a copy is now in the hands of Colonel Schulz.[2]

This had the effect of stopping, for the moment, most of the pressure from the Democratic side. Strangely enough, a new flurry came from the Republicans during the course of their national convention, held that year in Philadelphia. Numerous telephone calls came into the office to the effect that certain individuals wanted to come over to New York at once to urge me to reconsider my decision and, as reported to me, to stop the trend toward Dewey. I refused to receive any calls or to discuss the matter further.

Quite naturally, after Dewey's defeat in the fall of 1948, I again began to feel the pressure.

With Dewey's failure against Truman, who was then popularly supposed to be the weakest candidate that the Democrats could put into the field, the cry began to be heard that "We must find some new faces in the Republican party if ever we are going to win a national election." Since we were again in the beginning of a presidential cycle, most of the suggestions and arguments could be pushed off without trouble. But before many months the campaign began again to intensify. When Mr. Dewey ran for reelection to the governorship of New York, he stated, in order to answer a charge that he was running again merely to enhance his standing as a candidate for the presidency, that he favored me as the Republican candidate in 1952. This really put fresh fuel on the fire—and every day contributed something new to its heat.

Finally, in December of 1950 President Truman called me on the phone to ask whether I would undertake the duty of commanding the Allied forces to be established under the North Atlantic Treaty Organization. He and I both knew that this was a thankless job, but I was in complete agreement with the president that collective security arrangements for Western Europe had to be worked out in the least possible time and that America had to participate in the effort. By this time I had become deeply interested in my work at Columbia University and it was a tremendous personal disappointment to me to have to give it up. But I reminded him that I was a soldier and subject to his orders. But he emphasized that he wanted to persuade me that undertaking this duty would be a great public service. I felt that the European post was of such importance that, so long as he thought me best fitted for the job, I should have to undertake it, at least until we had worked out its programs of raising, organizing, training, and deploying troops. It was a demanding effort.

My first move was to make a "reconnaissance" visit to every capital involved. Since I did this in mid-winter, the task was difficult, but I met with the governments of the twelve countries involved and completed the trip in some eighteen or twenty days. I came back to report to the president, made a television speech to the public, and reported also to an informal joint session of the Congress held in the auditorium of the Congressional Library. Just before departing again for Europe, I called in a couple of members of my staff and told them that I was going to make a personal move and a statement which, if successful in its preliminary parts, would take me forever, and beyond any question, out of the political scene.

My purpose was to invite Senator Taft to come to my office to discuss what we were trying to do in Europe, and I told my associates that if Senator Taft would pledge his support to the idea of collective security in Europe, I would immediately make a statement to the effect that my return to active military service precluded any future speculation about the possibility that I would ever enter the political arena and that my answer, in advance, to any further importuning along this line would be a flat negative.

I invited the Senator to my office in the Pentagon, and he came one evening around five or five thirty. My conversation with him was exclusively on the subject of NATO. I went through the whole history of the war and later developments in Europe, the operation of the Marshall Plan, the responsibilities and opportunities now lying before the Western world, and how necessary it was that we strengthen Western European defenses by welding them together in one machine. I thought also that American contingents and troops would have to be employed in Europe but as to their number I was not certain.

It happened, at that moment, there was an argument going on between the president and the Congress as to the president's unrestricted right to station American troops wherever he decided they should go in the world. Congress was further preoccupied with a debate as to whether there should be four or six divisions sent to NATO.

I told the senator that with the details either of the constitutional question or with the amount of forces to be sent abroad I had no interest at the moment. I said that until I could survey the situation more closely, I would not have any recommendation as to the size of the American forces that should come to Europe. I simply asked the Senator whether he could not agree that the collective security of Western Europe, with some American help, had to be assured. He declined to commit himself on the matter, repeating words to the effect that he was not sure whether he would vote for four or six divisions. I argued that this was of no interest to me whatsoever. I simply wanted to get his assurance of support in the work for which I was called back to active duty. He repeated his refusal to make the point clear, and so finally we parted and, of course, I did not go through with the part of my plan that would have depended upon his affirmative reply.

For the next few months the whole matter seemed to lie fairly dormant, although now and then individuals of more or less importance arrived in Paris from America to give me their views about the forthcoming campaign. Starting in the fall of 1951, the whole matter came to the fore once again and this time the clamor was more intensified than ever before. Since I had never made public my particular political affiliations, the pressure came from both parties. However, it was more pronounced on the Republican side than the Democratic. One reason for this was a speech that I had made before the American Bar Association in St. Louis on September 3, 1949. In that talk I analyzed and discussed the so-called "middle-of-the-road" approach to political activity. This represented a profound conviction on my part and I repudiated any thought that the idea comprised any namby-pamby or fence-straddling viewpoint. Indeed, I argued that in great human affairs the middle-of-the-road approach was the only one that provided any avenue for progress and the extremists both of reaction and of so-called liberalism should be abjured like the plague.

A good many people remembered this talk and felt that as opposed to the New Deal - Fair Deal philosophies of the thirties and forties, it was sound Republicanism.

These Republicans all had one battle cry, "We must win or the two-party system as we know it will be destroyed." Behind this pronouncement was always one of a secondary character which was "Only a new, respected figure can carry us to victory. Of all the figures in sight you are the one that can do this without question."

There was every conceivable kind of variation on which this theme was played and many tangential streams of argument went along with it.

As the months wore on, I stood my ground and kept on file in my office the letter I had written to Mr. Finder in January of 1948 and would insist always that the visitors familiarize themselves with the language I used in that letter.

I think the argument that began to carry for me the greatest possible force was that the landslide victories of 1936, 1940 and 1944 and Truman's victory over Dewey in 1948 were all achieved under a doctrine of "spend and spend, and elect and elect." It seemed to me that this had to be stopped or our country would deviate badly from the precepts on which we had placed so much faith—the courage and self-dependence of each citizen, the importance of opportunity as opposed to mere material security, and our belief that American progress depended upon the work and sweat of all our citizens, each trying to satisfy the needs and desires of himself and his family—and that instead we were coming to the point where we looked toward a paternalistic state to guide our steps from cradle to grave.

I believed this most profoundly, but I still hoped and believed that someone else could lead the Republican party much more effectively and to a better result than I could. But because I did believe the basic truth I did go so far, in January of 1952, to admit that I had always been Republican in leanings and had always voted that ticket when given the opportunity to do so. On the second point, the identity of the individual who could lead the Republican party to victory, was the

place where all argument was now focused. Rallies were held around the country
—cables and letters told me about their purpose. A group of about twenty
congressmen sent me a petition in February to become a candidate—and so on
and so on. What impressed me more than anything else was the the extent of
real grassroots sentiment for me to become a candidate. I had seen enough of
the presidency to realize that any serious-minded incumbent of that office is
bound to feel the weight of his burdens and soon come to feel that its frustrations
and disappointments far outweigh any possible personal satisfaction anyone could
have in holding the position. Consequently I had no struggle with any personal
ambition of my own. Beyond this, it was clear that by next election time I would
have passed my sixty-second birthday. Ever since the end of 1941, I had been
occupying posts both in war and in peace of great importance and I was eagerly
looking forward to a period when I could, with my family, live a somewhat more
restful and leisurely life.

Always with friends I brought out these points; always they were brushed aside
by people who had become in some instances almost fanatical in their conviction
as to my duty to become a candidate for the presidency.

Respecting every other candidate then campaigning actively or passively for
the office, those who came to see me were pessimistic, if not even scornful, of
their ability to win the national election.

Bit by bit my confidence that I alone should make a negative decision was worn
away—I have always been particularly sensitive to any insinuation that I might
recoil from performance of any duty, no matter how onerous. But to persuade
me that it was a duty to stand for election was an entirely different matter. I
cannot at this moment remember the names of all those who came to see me.
Among them were Lodge, Clay, Bill Robinson, Jacquelin Cochran (who brought
with her a two-hour film of a Madison Square Garden rally gotten up by private
citizens), Herb Brownell—and many others. On the Democratic side, the man
I remember best was Senator Brien McMahon, who came to see me in the late
fall of 1951 and who used much the same arguments that the Republicans did.

Finally one thing became clear. Either I had to decline flatly and unequivocally
to stand for the nomination or I had to leave my present post. Our work at NATO
had progressed satisfactorily, and in the past fifteen or sixteen months we had
gotten command and staff systems well set up, training schools started, the
European Defense Community Treaty initialed by all the governments, and
finally I decided to resign my present post and turn it over to another soldier.

I reached the United States on June 1 and informed my friends that if the
Republicans and their supporters saw fit to nominate me, I would make the race.
I refused to seek delegates—in fact to this day I have never consciously requested
any individual in the world to vote for me. But I did make myself available for
people who wanted to see me. This compelled me to make a number of talks—
the first of which was on a rainy day in Abilene about the first week in June;
thereafter, I was stampeded by invitations to speak but went back to 60 Morningside at Columbia to spend a few weeks. There, and later in Denver, where I went
about the middle of June, a number of delegations visited me, and we had

discussions about the political scene, but there was no "electioneering" as such. As time for the convention approached, I told my friends that I did not want to go to Chicago. I felt that the business of nominating a candidate belonged to the convention and its delegates. The whole prospect was completely distasteful to me. But all the friends that I have mentioned and hundreds more kept hammering that it was my duty to allow myself to be seen, to receive visitors at my hotel suite, and to chat with them on a friendly basis. This I did. By the time the voting for candidates rolled around I was completely worn out and heartily sick of the whole business.

When the balloting was all done, I was the Republican candidate for the presidency, but I still was not completely confident that my decision to allow this effort to go forward was a wise one.

1960

In 1960, a quarter-century after going out to the Philippines, Ike spent his last year in the White House, and at long last the chance of retirement loomed no longer as chance but certainty. The next years he could fish, hunt, and enjoy the outdoor life he so loved and all the pastimes that attracted him, such as bridge, golf, and reading Westerns. At Gettysburg a fine house awaited him, rebuilt from the ground up—after the Eisenhowers had discovered that the farmhouse they had bought while at Columbia was built around an old log cabin, and that the timbers were rotten and worm-eaten and had to be taken out. The prospect of going up to Gettysburg kept him going through the year, which passed quickly. There were the usual alarms and excursions, including the Paris Summit Conference in May—the meeting that was not officially a summit conference because Premier Khrushchev stalked out, allegedly because the president of the United States had allowed U-2 flights over the Soviet Union for four years and at last one of the planes had come down in the Soviet Union near the Russian Pittsburgh, Sverdlovsk, on May 1, the Soviet Fourth of July. But during the year, Eisenhower continued his travels and took much pleasure in them, and his stock was high among all the places he visited. To his delight it remained high, too, among the American people.

JANUARY 13, 1960

In the conduct of a national political campaign there are two distinct parts: (1) the support of the presidential ticket; (2) the effort to elect all other candidates, both on the congressional level and on the state and local level.

The national chairman is of course concerned with both these purposes, but principal responsibility for the conduct of the presidential campaign must be borne by the presidential nominee—or his designated representative. Many speakers may be available for both divisions of the campaign, but the nominee for the presidency should himself make sure that there is a group of speakers to support him and the vice-presidential candidate. I believe the candidate should choose these men from among people who have the knowledge and qualifications expected for one or more of the cabinet posts.

The man nominated for vice-president should, of course, have the qualifications to take over the presidency whenever circumstances might compel him to do so and should be able to speak from this broad base. Men who might qualify are, among others, Anderson, Lodge, Mitchell, McElroy, Rockefeller, Rogers, Morton, Halleck, and, if he could be induced to go into political life, General Gruenther.[1] (In this list, I have not tried to arrange names in any order of priority.)

To speak in the field of foreign affairs, likely selections would be: Lodge, Dillon, Secretary of the Treasury Anderson, possibly Dillon Anderson. (Herter not mentioned because of office.)

To discuss finance and the duties of the secretary of the treasury are such men as Anderson, Stans, Dillon, Hauge, Baird, Scribner, and George Humphrey.[2]

In the field of defense there are Gates, McElroy, Seaton, and Dillon Anderson.[3] Possibly others could be added from among the civilians now holding appointive office in the Defense Department. Brucker might be good.[4]

Speeches in these fields should never be strictly partisan, but they can properly extol Republican record and policies.

Post Office Department: Arthur Summerfield, Charlie Hook, Stans, Sessions.[5]

Agriculture: The man who stands highest, so far as knowledge of this subject and integrity of purpose are concerned, is, of course, Secretary Benson. Many Republicans think that any public appearance by him would be a detriment in the Middle West. Nevertheless, it is possible that he could be used efficiently in the metropolitan areas because his viewpoint is that of the nation and not of the local voters. Individuals who would be listened to respectfully in the farm areas would include Allen Kline, W.I. Myers (Cornell), Les Arends, Charlie Hoeven, and, if he could be induced to participate in the political campaign, Milton Eisenhower.[6]

Attorney General: There might be Rogers, Brownell, Walsh, Barnes, Dewey, and others.[7]

In interior are: Seaton, Governor Hatfield, Walter Williams.[8]

Commerce: Chuck Percy, Secretary Mueller, Hauge, Walter Williams, Harold Boechenstein, Stephen Bechtel.[9]

Labor: Jim Mitchell, Rocco Siciliano, and selected members of the labor committees in both the Senate and the House.

HEW: Flemming, Oveta Hobby, Chuck Percy, Hauge.

Two subjects not to be neglected are housing and budget. A number of men, in and out of public life, could meet the requirements. Housing could well be handled by Mason and Aksel Nielsen.[10]

Each of the individuals named above is sufficiently well-informed to talk on the whole general field of political philosophy, and in each talk his major theme should be the field assigned by the candidate. The idea of segregating these according to cabinet department is so that none of the qualifications, in the aggregate, of the speakers' bureau will be overlooked.

JANUARY 20, 1960

It has been suggested, directly in the case of Charlie McAdams of the McNaught Syndicate, and indirectly, through the *Saturday Evening Post*, and by letter from Harry Luce of *Time-Life*, that I should do some writing after leaving this office. My response has never gone further than to say that I would never engage myself to do this without letting the individual or company know of my intention.

MARCH 23, 1960

Governor Hatfield brought Senator Lusk to my office to call. I promised Senator Lusk that at the first time I had an opportunity, I would arrange a chopper trip around the city, since he used to live here many, many years ago—in fact, he is a fourth-generation Washingtonian. I told him I would try to do it when I was going to Gettysburg some day; he could go with me and, after dropping me, he could come back on the eastern boundaries of Washington.

Foreign Minister Castiella of Spain informed me very confidentially that Franco will soon give the Protestants freedom of worship in Spain, but it is taking some little bit of time to swing public opinion around to it. He seemed to think this would take place in three or four months.

JULY 1, 1960

Forty-fourth wedding anniversary. Spent weekend at Gettysburg. Came back evening of the fourth.

JULY 5, 1960

A long day. Breakfast with chairman of national committee, Len Hall, and Clif Folger.[1]

Talked finance of campaign of 1960. Decision to hold a "closed circuit" television dinner, to raise money. Undersecretary of state with secretary of the treasury and others here to discuss international situation, especially Cuba.

JULY 6, 1960

Gordon Gray to plan National Security Council meetings for rest of summer. Also to approve directive requiring all departments to study applicability of our policies in light of global unrest as evidenced in overthrow of Rhee in Korea, Menderes in Turkey, actions of Castro in Cuba, mob influence on Kishi in Japan. (Indeed, it appears that our Congress is beginning to watch and obey pressure groups—postal workers—more than it does common sense and public interest.

Approved Emergency Sugar Act and, after two long conferences today, issued applicable proclamations and accompanying statement.[1] Have warned all to be alert to Cuban reaction because when dealing with a "little Hitler" anything can happen. Have an appointment with Drummond and Krock this evening, 5:30.

In the election of November 1960, Senator John F. Kennedy of course defeated Vice-President Nixon, and President Eisenhower was not happy with this result, but there was little he could do about it. Now it was his turn to invite his successor to the White House to hear a discussion of how the administrative mechanism worked, just as Ike had done with Truman in November 1952. Fortunately, however, there was a contrast in the meetings of 1952 and 1960, for the latter had none of the awkwardness and even tenseness that marked the meeting of Eisenhower with his Democratic predecessor. Senator Kennedy came by himself, without a retinue, and seemed eager to learn about the organization of the White House—and he much impressed Eisenhower.

DECEMBER 6, 1960

I arranged for an informal military parade in front of the White House to receive the president-elect. I met him on the north portico of the mansion.

We immediately started talks in my office.

It quickly became apparent that any single meeting, no matter of what length, could do little more than hit the high spots in the problem of transferring federal control from one administration to another.

The agenda suggested in advance by Senator Kennedy (copy attached) had as its first three items: Berlin, the Far East and Cuba. He had previously been briefed by Allen Dulles a number of times and had some familiarity with the details of these three subjects. Even so, there was no point in trying to go deeply into the details of these subjects because a full morning could be easily devoted to the possibilities, both adverse and favorable, that lie before us. Three short memoranda on these subjects are attached.[1]

The senator was interested in the national security setup and its operations. He suggested also that I give him any ideas I might have about improving the Pentagon operation.

I explained to him in detail the purpose and work habits of the Security Council, together with its two principal supporting agencies—the Planning Board and the Operations Coordinating Board. I said that the National Security Council had become the most important weekly meeting of the government: that we normally worked from an agenda, but that any member could present his frank opinion on any subject, even on those that were not on the formal agenda. I made clear to him that conferences in the White House are not conducted as committee meetings in the legislative branch. There is no voting by members and each group has one purpose only—to advise the president on the facts of particular problems and to make to him such recommendations as each member may deem applicable. I described how "splits" in Planning Board papers were handled.

He, obviously, could not be expected to understand the operations of the Security Council from one short briefing, and I urged him to appoint, as soon as he possibly could, an individual that he would want to take over the duties, after January 20, of Gordon Gray. I stated that if he would do this, Mr. Gray would make it his business to acquaint such an individual in detail with the operations of the National Security Council and with the general content of the files.

Regarding the Pentagon setup, the senator mentioned a report he had just received from the so-called Symington Committee.[2] From the papers I had learned something about the report and while I consider it so useless as to be ridiculous, I was careful to say nothing about the report as such.

I did urge him to avoid any reorganization *until he himself could become well acquainted with the problem.* (Incidentally, I made this same suggestion with respect to the White House staff, the National Security Council, and the Pentagon.) I told him that improvements could undoubtedly be made in the Pentagon and the command organization, but I also made it clear that the present organization and the improved functioning of the establishment had, during the past eight years, been brought about by patient study and long and drawn-out negotiations with the Congress and the armed services. Much has been said about "streamlining" such an organization in the belief that too many advisers and assistants are impeding the making of wise and prompt decisions. I think that something along this line might possibly be done, but in a mechanism such as the defense establishment, which spends something on the order of $42 billion a year. I pointed out that the secretary of defense should be fortified with the finest military and civilian advisers he could get. I pointed out the value of our scientific experts and their counsel. The importance of scientific research is illustrated by the amount of money devoted to the designing, development, and testing of any weapons, without placing a single one of them in the operational inventory. (Incidentally, this figure is $6.5 billion. Another $23.5 billion goes to pay for maintenance of personnel and equipment.) This emphasized, I told him, the need for earnest study and thinking before making radical changes.

I spent some time explaining the difference between the functions of the White House staff as an immediate supporting body to the president on the one hand, and the relations between the president and his cabinet officers. These, both individually and collectively, are always in contact with the president on any important problem affecting one or more.

I told him that without a personal staff all the detailed problems that would arise, even after major policies had been approved, would come directly to the attention of the president—and all of this without any coordination among departments.

I told him the divisions within the White House were the military aides on the one hand and the civilian staff on the other. This civilian staff comprehends a legal section, an economic section, a liaison section and a secretarial section. The records section is a somewhat separated organism, because it is not only manned and headed by civil service personnel, but is the only permanent body in the White House.

The senator seemed to be a bit amazed when I told him about the great numbers of people that operate in the Signal Corps, Transportation and Evacuation activities, all under the military aides. I also described the functions of Camp David.[3]

Within the civilian side, many minor problems arise at the staff level among the different departments. To expect each department head to take up each of these with the president or to hold special cabinet meetings would be undesirable and indeed in the long run impossible. Consequently this coordination is achieved by the president's personal staff, operating under its chief, a man whom I have given the title, "The Assistant to the President."[4]

Aside from certain responsibilities of the president touching upon the regulatory commissions, there are ten statutory departments, each headed by a cabinet officer and, in addition to these, we have the Bureau of the Budget, the Atomic Energy Commission, the Office of Civil and Defense Mobilization, the Council of Economic Advisers, the General Services Administration, the Federal Aviation Agency, and the Veterans Administration.

In addition we have the Central Intelligence Agency, the Civil Service Commission, and the United States Information Agency. The assistant to the president, the director of the Bureau of the Budget, and the director of the Office of Civil and Defense Mobilization have been accorded cabinet rank, as has the president's representative to the United Nations.

With all these agencies officially and directly subordinate to the president only, and with every problem engaging the attention of any agency normally affecting others, it is easy to see that there is a vast volume of staff coordination required. All of this is done by the president's personal staff.

I said nothing to him about the ceremonies, making of engagements, confidential correspondence, and many other activities which of course are handled normally by the president directly with the responsible individual.

Senator Kennedy wanted to get my personal thinking about Macmillan, De Gaulle, and Adenauer. I gave him my opinions concerning these people as I have formed them over many years of association with them. I told him that I did not believe that my own comments would mean too much. I did venture the opinion that if he would take the trouble to meet them and talk with them individually and collectively, he would be impressed by their ability and their integrity, even though there would be many instances where he would disagree with their stated opinions.

I voluntarily brought up the question of NATO and our ballistic missile proposal to that organization.[4] I told him that De Gaulle has created a number of difficulties in the operation of NATO. I gave Senator Kennedy my opinion that it was the most important alliance to which we belong, one whose maintenance and strength was vital to our own security and prosperity.

In this context I brought up the subject of dealing more closely with our allies in the matter of atomic weapons. I told him that our hands were somewhat tied .

because the Joint Committee of Congress dealing with atomic matters was formed and is operating under a law that was written at a time when we had a true monopoly of atomic manufacture. Today the international club is growing and I think it is worse than silly to allow America's interests and responsibilities in this field to be handled by a committee whose principal purpose is to stand watch over the *operations* of the Atomic Energy Commission—which is an operative and *not* a policy-making organization. I told him that our relations with the Congress on this subject should be handled through the foreign relations committees and the defense committees in both Houses. Frankly, I see no need for the continuance of the Joint Committee on Atomic Energy.

I talked to the senator for some twenty minutes on the present situation and the balance of payments and foreign confidence in the dollar, and the way that confidence is affected by the balance or imbalance of budgets. I attach a copy of a short memorandum on the matter,[6] but after I had talked to him Secretary Anderson gave him a much longer briefing on the whole matter, lasting some forty-five minutes. I pray that he understands it. Certainly his attitude was that of a serious, earnest seeker for information and the implication was that he will give full consideration to the facts and suggestions we presented.

Partly because of the outflow of gold caused by the great deployments we have abroad, but also because of other reasons, including my conviction that America is carrying far more than her share of free world defense, I told him that I was going to warn the NATO community of the United States's intention of redeploying some of its troops from Europe unless other arrangements could, at the very least, stop this drain on our gold. I told him that I informed him of this so he would not be surprised, and the decision was made and the announcement would be made in such a way as to leave him a free hand in reversing this policy if he so chooses. I told him that while I believe thoroughly that the European nations, all of which have been so vastly strengthened by the billions we poured out through the Marshall Plan and since, were reaching a level of economic productivity that is for them unprecedented, they still seem to be unwilling to pick up what seemed to us to be their fair share of the defense burden. This government has pointed out to them often that we have taken the responsibility for the creation and maintenance of the free world's deterrent. We provide a vast portion of the navies and most of the bombing force in the free world. And we think that the European nations and Canada should be prepared to maintain a much larger proportion of the ground defense formations.

On the personal side, Senator Kennedy asked me whether I could be prepared, upon call from him, to serve the country in such areas and in such manner as may seem appropriate. I told him that, of course, the answer was obvious, but I did say that I thought I had the right, after many long years of service and in view of my age, to suggest that if he should request anything from me, it should be normally in terms of conferences and consultations on subjects on which I have had some experience, rather than errands which might necessitate frequent and lengthy travel. While I did not exclude the possibility of making some trip for some extraordinary reason, I did say that in the main I would like to have this restriction on my understanding.

Senator Kennedy was very much concerned with the activities of General Goodpaster, and said he would like to hold Goodpaster for two months into the new administration. I told him that I thought a better solution would be for him to appoint a man right now who could take Goodpaster's post (the duties of which I detailed at some length) and allow Goodpaster to leave with the rest of us on January 20. He said he would be handicapped unless he had Goodpaster for a month or two, really favoring the second. Of course I had to say that he would soon be the commander-in-chief and he could order General Goodpaster to do anything, and those duties would be efficiently performed; but I told him, also, of Goodpaster's great desire to go to active line duty and that a particular spot was being held for him.[7] I asked the senator if he would assure me that that spot would be held. (That evening I called General Decker and told him the details of this conversation and asked him, as a personal favor to me,[8] to make it his business to protect Goodpaster's future to this extent. He said there would be no trouble about this.)

Later in the conversation with the three secretaries, Senator Kennedy repeated this promise, and I think there should be no difficulty in fulfilling it.

Finally, I told the senator that this hurried description of his many functions and duties would possibly be confusing, but if he should like to come back at any time all he had to do was give my secretary a ring and we would set up an appointment promptly.

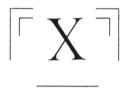

RETIREMENT

Leaving the presidency of the United States on January 20, 1961, was no chore, for Eisenhower had done his best and the time had come. Because of the Presidential Succession Act passed back in the Truman administration there could be no thought of a third full term. The president sensed that physically he could not make it through another term. He had agonized in 1955 and 1956 and finally accepted the second nomination, feeling that the tasks were not yet done. In January 1961 he was satisfied, feeling that even a change in parties would not this time turn clocks back. The closeness of the election of November 1960 between Senator John F. Kennedy and Vice-President Richard M. Nixon made a centrist Democratic presidency certain, whatever new slogan the new Democratic incumbent might produce to fool the unwary.

This time, unlike leaving the army in 1948, it was not necessary to move into a barny house in some strange environment such as Columbia University in the City of New York. Gettysburg provided a house designed by Mamie that was full of charm and capable of holding the presidential and military trophies and the paintings; moreover, the estate also was a dude farm, where Colonel Arthur Nevins could put everything in order for the general. Eisenhower could look over the stock and the fields and think back to the simplicities of Abilene in the 1890s and the turn of the century.

The years of traveling around, never long in some post before getting another, of moving for a long period out to the Philippines, where everything was impermanent, the years of the war, and then Quarters Number One at Fort Myer (a place that could never be home, because it looked like the entire row of red-brick houses), had done away with any ability to settle down; the attractiveness of Gettysburg palled as the months and years went by. Before long, Eisenhower looked to other pastures, and he enjoyed the attractions of California, where Palm

Desert with its golf courses and retired friends made the rigors of a Gettysburg winter unattractive. And there always were the moves around the country for speeches and receptions and awards and banquets in honor of the Republican party or the Republican faithful or the old army friends.

The general, as he was known (rather than "the president"), could not sit still, and time seemed to hang on his hands. People noticed the golf games, which were easily reported, and there was talk of much card playing.

What people did not notice was the correspondence, which ran on and on, year after year, a stream of letters to friends and acquaintances, recalling this or urging that, congratulating upon anniversaries, offering condolences—with more of the latter as the 1960s went on.

The general tried his hand at literary composition, and the result was two thick volumes of reminiscence, The White House Years, subtitled Mandate for Change, and Waging Peace. Published by Doubleday in 1963 and 1965, the books were elaborately detailed; if one took the time to read them, there was much to learn.

A more interesting accounting for the general reader was the little book that appeared in 1967, entitled At Ease: Stories I Tell to Friends. Doubleday published the hardcover, and Avon the paperback—tens of thousands of these little books were not merely sold but read, and more than once. At Ease was an autobiography, gracefully told. The modesty of Dwight Eisenhower again came from the pages, the long journey through life's tasks from Abilene to West Point, Panama, the Philippines, Washington State, Washington, D.C., London, Versailles, Frankfurt, Washington, New York, France again, all the years down to the presidency.

The readers of this delightful volume hoped that Eisenhower would take his stories through the presidency and into retirement, but this was not to be, for the book represented the last extended literary effort of which he was physically capable. About this time, his health began to fail. The years of responsibility had taken their toll, and the book, like the life itself, had to stop.

Dwight D. Eisenhower died in Washington at Walter Reed Hospital, after a long illness, on March 28, 1969. The general of the army and former president of the United States was seventy-nine years old. He was buried in Abilene, Kansas.

1961

In April 1961 the invasion of Cuba by a group of Cuban exiles trained by the CIA in Guatemala proved an abject failure, and President Kennedy asked the advice of General Eisenhower, in whose administration the operation had been planned. Eisenhower's successor also was concerned about Laos, which little Asian country he wanted neutralized.

APRIL 22, 1961

Mr. Kennedy met me when I landed from the helicopter at Camp David. We went to the terrace at Aspen cottage to talk. He began by outlining the Cuban situation, including a description of the planning, the objectives, and the anticipated results. This outline agreed exactly with that given me by Allen Dulles yesterday morning.[1]

He explained in detail where things began to go awry and stated that the whole operation had become a complete failure. Apparently some men are still hiding in the "bosque" and possibly have made their way to the mountains. Apparently about four hundred prisoners were taken.

The chief apparent causes of failure were gaps in our intelligence, plus what may have been some errors in shiploading, timing, and tactics.

It appears that too much specialized equipment was carried in a single ship and, when this ship was damaged, the troops on the beach were left fairly helpless. I inquired whether or not the troops had had the equipment immediately with them (in platoons and companies) to establish effective roadblocks on the three avenues of entry into the swamp area. He was under the impression that this equipment was properly distributed and the troops well trained in its use. Therefore, the reason for the quick penetration of the swamp into the vulnerable beachhead was unknown.

The press has mentioned a great deal about MIGs [Soviet fighter planes]. The president is not certain, and neither was Allen Dulles, that these were MIGs. They could easily have been T-33s, equipped with rockets and guns, but, at least, they shot down a number of our airplanes and apparently operated effectively against our troops in the beachhead.[2]

He is having General Taylor come to Washington to analyze all phases of the operation, including all of the planning and the methods so as to see whether there are lessons to be learned. He has the feeling that we can be faced with some similar situation over the next decade and thinks we should do our best to be prepared to meet it. (He did not say that this report would be made public— but I did get the impression that it would.)

The next thing that he wanted to talk about were the direction and prospects for future action. I was unable to give him any detailed suggestions but did say that I would support anything that had as its objective the prevention of communist entry and solidification of bases in the Western hemisphere.

He believes that the two great powers have now neutralized each other in atomic weapons and inventories but that in numbers of troops, and our exterior communications as opposed to the interior communications of the communists, we are relatively weak. He did not seem to think that our great seapower counteracted this situation completely.

The only real suggestion I could give him regarding the Western Hemisphere was to do his very best to solidify the OAS against communism, including a readiness to support, at least morally and politically, any necessary action to expel communist penetration. I said that this was something that had to be worked on all the time. I told him, also, that I believed the American people would never approve direct military intervention, by their own forces, except under provocations against us so clear and so serious that everybody would understand the need for the move.

The president did not ask me for any specific advice. I contented myself with merely asking a few questions about the tactical action, including the timing of the support that I understood the navy air had given to the landings. He said that in the first instance they were so anxious to keep the United States hand concealed that they accorded no such support, and when they finally did get word of its need, it was too late. This situation was complicated by the fact that all communications went out. I understood that the communication equipment was on the ship that sank, but this is hard to believe because each unit carries some light communication equipment, including the ability to send radiograms to a distance of some fifty to a hundred miles.

There are certainly factors, now unknown, that will finally come to light under searching scrutiny. The purpose of this scrutiny is not to find any scapegoat, because the president does seem to take full responsibility for his own decision, but rather to find and apply lessons for possible future action.

The president brought up Laos. He outlined the situation and said that the British were very reluctant to participate in any military intervention, and, of course, the French positively refused to do so. . . .[3]

The president was quite sure that there was no possibility of saving Laos by unilateral military action. Consequently he looked forward to a cease-fire, which is promised for this coming Monday, the twenty-fourth. He remarked that he was not so much concerned about Laos as Thailand. I replied that, in that event, it would seem the part of wisdom to begin immediately the strengthening of the Thai forces and positions. My former reports led me to believe that the Thai might be very sturdy soldiers. . . .[4] I asked him whether the ICC was to be allowed, coincidentally with the cease-fire, to survey the whole country and see exactly what the situation was.[5] He said our people would insist upon that.

Again I told him that from my own position I could not offer any advice— I could just say that as a generality in order to keep your position strong at the conference table you had constantly to let the enemy see that our country was not afraid. We believe in what is right and attempt to insist upon it.

Quite naturally a conversation such as this had no definite conclusion. We talked throughout most of the luncheon and afterward strolled through the camp and continued discussing various aspects of each situation, but nothing of a dramatic character came up.

Finally we met with a group of newspaper reporters and photographers in front of Aspen cottage. I enjoyed meeting so many of my old friends among the crowd. He made a very short statement and said that he had just outlined for me the situations in these two parts of the world and had asked for my counsel. Nothing else was said.

When the reporters turned to me I said that it was rather fun to be in the

Camp David, April 22, 1961.

position of not having to make a statement and having nothing to say. They then asked me whether I supported him. I repeated a generalization that I had expressed on other occasions—that when it came to problems of foreign operations, then an American traditionally stands behind the constitutional head, the president.

This, of course, was said with respect to purposes; no one outside government is committed to support details of timing, tactics, selection of operation sites, and methods. These are not even yet known to outsiders.

After all this, he took me in his car to the heliport and suggested a golf game in the near future. Dick Flohr was driving, and John Campion was riding in the front seat.[6]

JUNE 5, 1961

Attached hereto is a rough sketch of the Cuban coastline on which the attack was made by insurgent Cubans on April 7 of this year.

The sketch was made by one member of the attacking force, who was one of some half dozen who succeeded in getting back to a ship and was rescued from the debacle.

The sketch was handed to me by Mr. William Pawley, who had been closely associated in an advisory capacity with the attack. The man who made the sketch did so in Mr. Pawley's presence, and the latter guarantees the authenticity of the

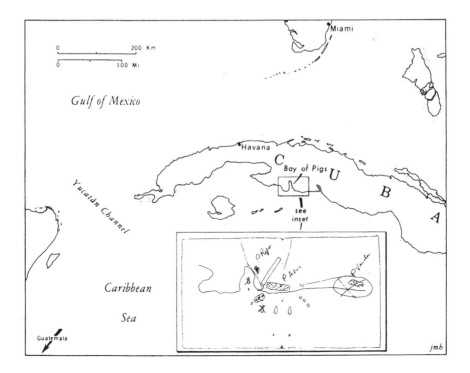

sketch as well as the following story.

The man accompanied the attacking expedition from a port of embarkation in Central America. According to the orders received by him (and my understanding is by all other members of the force), the time of landing was designated as midnight. The invasion force was escorted by a carrier and a couple of destroyers and was carried in three or four small ships secured from the United Fruit Company. There were landing craft present, but I am not certain whether they were big enough to come under their own power or whether they were carried aboard ship.

In any event, the attack plan was to be formed up according to the attached sketch and involved Red, Blue, and Green objectives. Apparently the two flanks were about one mile distant from each other.

The attack was to be supported by an air strike at first light the following morning. There were some fifteen to twenty aircraft involved and these were to attack Castro's military airfield and tank park in the near vicinity.

These support strikes were not made, and, as a result, the hostile air was permitted to operate freely and succeeded in sinking our principal supply ship, carrying heavy signal equipment and a load of ammunition.

In spite of these handicaps, the man said that the force attacked efficiently and effectively and were finally forced to surrender by lack of support and when their ammunition was completely exhausted. He said at that time their casualties in killed and wounded were not over a couple of hundred, whereas the defending force had some one thousand killed and two to three thousand wounded. Moreover, he reports that the militia was very sympathetic to the attacking personnel, and the latter, when they saw the necessity of surrendering, released all the militia prisoners they had so that they could make their escape.

Mr. Pawley went on to say that the airplanes based on the carrier were over the attacking ships at the proper time but were recalled by the admiral on what were said to be "orders from the White House."

Thereafter, Mr. Pawley related a story of a meeting at the White House between the president, Mr. Stevenson, Secretary Rusk, Secretary Bowles, and possibly others.[1] According to the story, Mr. Stevenson made strong representation against any participation by American forces in the attack. This support had been previously promised both as to the strike above mentioned and the overhead cover to be provided by the airplanes on the carrier.

Due to Mr. Stevenson's representations, the president revoked the order involving this air support. Of course, the attacking forces knew nothing about this and were in effect abandoned to their fate.

If this whole story is substantially correct, it is a very dreary account of mismanagement, indecision, and timidity at the wrong time.

I am told that part of this story has already leaked to the press, but if the whole story ever becomes known to the American people (and always on the assumption that it is substantially correct), there will be a terrible outcry and I should think a virtual repudiation of the present administration.

If true, this story could be called a "Profile in Timidity and Indecision."[2]

1962

The Cuban missile crisis of October 1962 was on its way to a settlement when Kennedy consulted Eisenhower.

OCTOBER 29, 1962

Yesterday, Sunday morning, President Kennedy called me on the phone to tell me about certain messages that he had received from Khrushchev dealing with the efforts to solve the Soviet-American differences in the Cuban situation. He did not quote to me the exact language of the messages that he had received from the Kremlin but did give their substance. The basic proposal was that Russia would dismantle all its bomb sites in Cuba if, in return, the United States would guarantee that it would not invade Cuba.

The messages received from the Russians contained different provisions but the final one seemed to be very simple and, the president thought, quite acceptable in general intent. I concurred but told him that I thought our government should be very careful about defining exactly what was meant by its promises. I observed, since we make a point of keeping our promises, that they should not imply anything more than we actually meant. It would be a mistake, I said, to give the Russians an unconditional pledge that we would, forever and under all conditions, not invade regardless of changing circumstances. For example, I said that if Castro should attack Guantanamo, or if he became active with agents and provocators in Latin American countries, it might become necessary for us to occupy the island.

My impression was that the president understood this and would make certain that we would not be overcommitted.

I then called John McCone, head of the Central Intelligence Agency, who is normally my contact with the president on matters involving national security and gave him the gist of the conversation, particularly about the reservations that I thought should accompany any all-out promise of ours.

I said to the president that my own estimate of what might happen would be a Russian effort to drag negotiations to such an extent that we would feel stymied and might be, by world opinion, held on dead center. I therefore said that, in my opinion, the government should by all means hold the initiative that it had finally seized when it established the quarantine.

He obviously agreed with this thinking because he said this was probably just the first step in a long series of efforts that will have to come about before the thing is settled.

NOVEMBER 2, 1962

This morning I returned from a trip to New York City and was disturbed to find, in a number of conversations with rather well-read people, that in their opinion the United States was making an unwise commitment to Russia respecting the Cuban problem. I assured the people that the president had the need for reservations in mind and I was quite sure that the apprehensions of my New York friends were unfounded. However, to reassure myself I called John McCone last evening about five or six o'clock and I feel certain that the matter is being carefully handled.

NOVEMBER 5, 1962

I called John McCone last evening from my room in Walter Reed Hospital. My question to him was, "Do the conditions laid down by Castro possibly constitute a repudiation of any implied agreement between the United States, Soviets, and (I had thought) Castro?" Is it not our intent to insist that any inspection be fully satisfactory to us, and, thereafter, must it not be of a kind to prevent any return of missiles to Cuba?

Since obviously we could not make an agreement with Khrushchev that could bind Castro, did we not owe it to ourselves and to Latin America to (1) first, make

In France at Omaha Beach for the filming of D-Day-plus-twenty years (CBS), August 5–10, 1963. (With Walter Cronkite, August 7.)

certain all missiles are gone; (2) to assert our right to take such action, at any time, against Castro as would assure Latin America and ourselves protection against subversion, sabotage, etc.?

1964

SEPTEMBER 11, 1964

John McCone came to see me this morning to give me a general briefing on the world situation. The trouble spots to which he referred were Laos, where things seem to be looking a little better; South Vietnam, where anything can happen; Indonesia, where Sukarno may have to be slapped down; and information on the military programs of both Russia and China.

Apparently in Russia progress is being made in producing bigger and more destructive weapons and anti-missile missiles. China seems to be making definite efforts to produce atomic weapons.

The CIA director's information on Russia's anti-missile program was perhaps exaggerated, for at the end of the decade an American anti-missile program got underway on a note of crisis and then ground to a halt when it became clear that the Russians were not moving rapidly and were willing to compromise in a SALT-I agreement. McCone's news about the Chinese nuclear program, alas, was quite correct; the Chinese exploded a nuclear device within a little more than a month after the conversation with Eisenhower.

NOVEMBER 20, 1964

I talked with Robert B. Anderson on November 17 and 18. It appears that he is still preserving close contacts with the president and keeps an index of the matters that he hopes to discuss with the president. I suggested one of the matters he should take up was the reported swindle in the road construction program as reported in the *Reader's Digest* of November. That story is almost hair-raising, and I would hope that something could be done about it.[1]

Another subject was a report (from Slats Slater) that there is being considered by the administration a proposal submitted by Walter Reuther to establish federal control over all of the $69 billion private pension funds in this country. I could think of nothing more terrible than its effects if this should be taken up seriously.

Another subject was the hope that the budget could soon be balanced and it was suggested that Bob recommend against any further tax cuts until we could show a budget surplus.

1965

OCTOBER 16, 1965

The only important thing that the president spoke to me about at our meeting on the airplane at Andrews Field on the morning of October 5 was the problem placed before the government in continuing economic aid to Pakistan and India. He wanted me to think about the problem and be ready to confer with him when an opportunity arose.

1966

President's Johnson's budget director, Charles Schultze, asked former Secretary of the Treasury Anderson to talk to Eisenhower about the forthcoming budget.

(Eisenhower with President Johnson)

The fisherman in California, 1967.

Gettysburg.

NOVEMBER 23, 1966

The gist of the request was that Mr. Anderson would confer with me to determine whether we were in agreement with a number of budgetary reductions that
the administration plans to make in the 1968 administrative budget. Mr.
Schultze gave Mr. Anderson the amounts of specific cuts that were to be made
in certain areas and apparently wanted general approval from the two of us.

My reply to Mr. Anderson was that in all foreign problems I was always ready
to do the best I could to help out the government. However, it was clearly
understood between the president and me that in domestic policies and programs
I was flatly opposed to many of the things that he had succeeded in having
enacted into law. Some of my opposition was as a matter of principle and in other
cases it was the size of the program and its costs.

Mr. Anderson and I agreed that we were not in a position to make any specific
recommendations because we knew nothing about income expected, the actual expenditures to be made, or the necessity for many of the programs. Consequently, I told Mr. Anderson that he could quote me as saying that for six years I have
been publicly opposing a number of the "Great Society" programs and the high
cost—in my opinion unnecessarily high—of the numbers of these activities.

Therefore I would repeat only what I have said publicly that I am philosophically opposed to the level of expenditures we now have and any step to reduce
these would be to my mind a very beneficial act. However, I refused to suggest
that I would approve of a budget merely because it might be somewhat lower
than the unconscionably high one of 1967.

1967

MARCH 14, 1967

At an impromptu press conference at the gate of the Eldorado Country Club
yesterday in which Governor Reagan and I were both present, a number of
reporters were talking simultaneously in order to get their own particular questions answered. The meeting was a very friendly one between the governor and
me and I expressed my pleasure at meeting him and complimented him on his
early work as governor.

While there was considerable conversation one individual directed to me a
question involving Mr. Nixon and my opinion of him. I remarked that he was
one of the ablest men I knew and a man that I admired deeply and for whom I
had a great affection. The reporters present obviously did not hear Mr. Nixon's name
included in the question and therefore reported my answer as referring to Governor
Reagan. Later this error was repeated by Walter Cronkite and when I talked to
him on the phone I made the correction. He was chagrined to admit that his information came from a newspaper and he hoped sometime to change it.

NOTES

December 27, 1935

1. Jimmy Ord and Dwight Eisenhower were great friends and became confederates in the business of standing up to General MacArthur—for which see the pages that follow—but Jimmy's career came to a tragic end. One day in 1938, when Ike was in the hospital for a brief stay, Jimmy came by to say so long and mentioned that he was taking a Filipino student as pilot on a trip to the Philippine summer capital of Baguio. "No you won't," said Ike. "Get one of the American flight instructors. They'll be glad to do it." Jimmy laughed and said, "Our Filipino boys are doing really well. I'll use one of them. I won't be gone more than a few hours. See you late this afternoon." As the plane neared Baguio, up in the mountains of northern Luzon, Jimmy decided he would drop a note near the house of a friend and asked the pilot to circle the place. In circling, the plane lost speed and crashed, Jimmy was whipped around and incurred grave injuries; he died within hours. Dwight D. Eisenhower, *At Ease: Stories I Tell to Friends* (New York: Doubleday, 1967), p. 223.
2. Captain (later Brigadier General) Thomas Jefferson Davis later served in Eisenhower's head-quarters in North Africa and Europe as adjutant general during the Second World War.
3. This plan, worked out by MacArthur's aides in Washington rather than by the general himself, showed some signs of reality in that it looked forward to what was virtually guerrilla warfare and the maintenance of what, some years later, might have been called unsinkable aircraft carriers; MacArthur and his aides were hoping to defend at least some of the perhaps four thousand Philippine islands and to sell their eventual surrenders at high prices. The United States Navy in the Far East, of course, was a very weak force throughout the 1930s, and despite the labeling of this force based upon the Philippines as a "fleet" it was not much more than it had been in the days of Commodore George Dewey—that is, a squadron. The largest surface ship was a heavy cruiser. To depend on such a force was, MacArthur knew, sheer folly. His real dependence was the battleships and carriers and heavy and light cruisers of the United States Pacific fleet, based upon Pearl Harbor. The governing plan of the army and navy during the 1930s, until adoption of Rainbow 5 (calling for attack by a coalition of enemies, rather than simply Japan), looked to the sending of a relief expedition to the beleaguered Philippines, a battleship force that would push its way through by the weight of metal hurled from its fourteen- and fifteen-inch guns.

4. When the B-17 bombers became operational in the late 1930s this hopeful plan of defending the Philippines by air power received much attention, and the army and navy came to rely upon it, foolishly as matters turned out, for the B-17s were caught on the ground on December 7, 1941, and in subsequent days the bomber force was reduced to a nullity.

5. Here is the first diary mention of what was to be the Achilles heel of the American military plan for the Philippine commonwealth—money was to dominate all the calculations. Never did the ideal plans work out, because of lack of money. There does not seem to have been any large understanding of this problem by MacArthur, at the outset of his Philippine duty, and the general liked to ignore the problem, hoping that something else would turn the ideal into the real, but his assistants found their work plagued by the money problem.

5. The Philippine peso then equalled fifty cents in American currency.

7. Manuel L. Quezon remained president of the Philippines after the Japanese invasion and occupation. Having been evacuated by submarine from Corregidor, he died in the United States in 1944.

8. The Philippine Scouts, a native constabulary officered by regular officers of the United States Army, had been created years before. It was an efficient force, and one of the problems of MacArthur and Eisenhower was to ensure that the Scouts would not be so weakened, perhaps by amalgamation, that in the process of obtaining a new national force the Philippines would eliminate the only native force it had.

9. It is impossible to calculate the dates, if there were more than one, on which the preceding diary accounting was written, but the presumption of course is that the diarist either had begun by a backdating or else had gotten behind gradually and was trying to catch himself.

10. Colonel (later Major General) Paulino Santos; Brigadier General (later Major General) Basilio Valdez; Colonel (later Major General) Guillermo B. Francisco. The almost immediate fuss over ranks for Filipinos was, as Eisenhower sensed, an ill omen for the American advisers, for it raised the ugly problem of face, rather than defense.

11. The ellipsis points indicate a page missing in the original typescript—this portion of the diary was in typescript—in Abilene.

January 20, 1936

1. The mid-1930s were no congenial time for individuals such as Eisenhower who were trying to increase the level of armaments anywhere. The agitation of earlier years in favor of disarmament had come to focus in the United States on the so-called merchants of death, the private manufacturers of arms; congress, beginning in 1935, passed a series of neutrality acts that tied the hands of President Roosevelt in advance of any war—appropriations for the army and navy became very difficult, and it was virtually impossible to export American-made arms anywhere, even to the Philippine commonwealth.

2. The high commissioner, Frank Murphy, former mayor of Detroit, later associate justice of the supreme court, was an unfortunate choice. His Catholicism made him available, but his political background was entirely domestic. He knew no Spanish nor had the slightest knowledge of local problems. Roosevelt appointed him to Manila because of his prominence in Michigan and his Irish-American and Catholic prominence. He was to be followed by Paul V. McNutt, an amiable and ambitious Indiana politician. Both men were handsome figureheads.

3. Major Eisenhower's jaundiced view of the American political scene had some basis in fact. The first Roosevelt administration, 1933–1937, was not distinguished by any large move in international relations, other than declarations of American distance from international problems. In the second administration the president turned increasingly to foreign affairs.

February 6, 1936

1. Eisenhower's first intimation of Quezon's emotional instability apparently came at this time. Manuel Quezon never was able to hold a straight line with his feelings, and his highs and lows produced consternation among friends and associates. For his deplorable attempt to declare the Philippines neutral early in 1942, presumably under Japanese supervision, see below. In 1944,

as he lay dying from tuberculosis, he grew irrational and critical especially of his obvious successor, Sergio Osmeña. "Look at that man," he said. "Why did God give him such a body when I am here struggling for my life? I am Manuel L. Quezon—I am the Filipino people—I am the Philippines." When Quezon died in August, and Carlos Romulo brought the news, Osmeña burst into tears. Theodore Friend, *Between Two Empires: The Ordeal of the Philippines, 1929–1946* (New Haven: Yale University Press, 1965), p. 237.

February 15, 1936

1. The precedent here was the colonial armies of all Western nations, and in the case of the United States, the Philippine Scouts. It almost goes without saying that in the case of an army like that of the United States in the interwar era, the prospect of suddenly increased rank was enticing.
2. In the instance of machine guns, the American Browning came into use just at the end of the World War. Superseding the Lewis, it was the standard gun of its type in the Second World War and the Korean War.

September 26, 1936

1. Arthur Hurd was an Abilene lawyer whom Eisenhower had known since his boyhood.

November 15, 1936

1. The chairman of the Scripps-Howard newspaper chain was much in evidence in the Philippines in these years and was close to Quezon. Because of MacArthur's strained relations with Roosevelt, anything that Howard might have communicated about the general's enthusiasm for Landon could have produced serious personal results for the new Philippine field marshal.

January 23–May 30, 1937

1. "H" refers to Dr. Hutter, the MacArthur group's medical adviser and physician. "Q" refers to Manuel L. Quezon, then president of the Philippines.

June 23, 1937

1. "B of B" apparently refers to the Philippines Bureau of the Budget.

June 24, 1937

1. Brigadier General (later Lieutenant General) George Grunert was later commander of the Philippine department of the United States Army.
2. Colonel (later General) Courtney H. Hodges; Brigadier General Charles F. Humphrey, Jr.

June 26, 1937

1. Segundo later became Brigadier General Fidel V. Segundo.
2. Jorge Vargas was personal secretary to Quezon.

July 13, 1938

1. Major General Charles D. Herron was commanding the Hawaiian department.

July 18, 1938

1. Paul A. Hodgson was Eisenhower's roommate at West Point.

July 22, 1938

1. Lieutenant (later Brigadier General) William L. Lee was one of the American instructors in the Philippines. Early in 1936, Ike at the age of forty-six began to take flight training, and at the end of his Philippine tour had logged 350 hours. "After World War II, I had ceased to

fly altogether, except that once in a while, on a long trip, to relieve my boredom (and demolish the pilot's), I would move into the co-pilot's seat and take over the controls. But as the jet age arrived, I realized that I had come out of a horse-and-buggy background, recognized my limitations, and kept to a seat in the back." *At Ease*, pp. 226–27.

2. Eisenhower wanted to know whether shipment of fifteen planes on the *Meigs* would displace Philippine Army equipment.

July 28, 29, 30, 1938

1. Walter Beech was head of the Beechcraft Company, airplane manufacturers.
2. Lieutenant (later Major General) Hugh A. Parker was another of the Philippine group's flight instructors and also one of Ike's teachers.

July 31, 1938

1. "Dick" probably refers to Lieutenant Colonel (later Lieutenant General) Richard K. Sutherland, who came from Tientsin to be MacArthur's deputy chief of staff after Ord's death and succeeded Eisenhower as chief of staff.

September 7, 1938

1. General Malin Craig, chief of staff; Major General Emory S. Adams, the adjutant general; Brigadier General (later Lieutenant General) Stanley Embick; Brigadier General George P. Tyner, assistant chief of staff, G-4 (supply); Brigadier General (later General of the Army) George C. Marshall, chief of war plans; Major General George A. Lynch, chief of infantry; Major General (later General of the Army) Henry H. Arnold, assistant chief of the air corps; Major General Oscar W. Westover, chief of the air corps.

October 10, 1938

1. Edgar Eisenhower was Ike's brother; Mark Wayne Clark later became a commanding general in Italy, Austria, Korea. The question mark was in the original diary.

January 1, 1942

1. Magnet was the code name for a buildup of American forces in the British Isles; Gymnast looked to an offensive into French North Africa in 1942.

January 5, 1942

1. Brigadier General Wade Hampton Haislip was known as Ham.
2. The last three sentences were omitted in the edited version of this entry and show the sort of comment that Eisenhower later believed should not see the light of day. In the early months of American entry into the war he doubtless was tempered, and comments about the British were a relief to his frustrations. He also would comment about his erstwhile commander, MacArthur, and about the navy's uncooperativeness and inefficiency, with special attention to the egotism of Admiral King. But in long retrospect these commentaries do not seem out of line—they were just the result of overwork and, actually, of embarrassment at the unreadiness of American forces, despite nearly two and a half years since the outbreak of the Second World War in Europe.

January 6, 1942

1. Lieutenant General Hugh A. Drum had been chief of staff of the American First Army in the First World War, a powerful position, as his superior Lieutenant General Hunter Liggett let Drum run the details of headquarters, and First Army comprised the bulk of Pershing's front-line troops. The army's humdrum affairs of the 1920s and 1930s had bored Drum, who waited impatiently for higher authority; in 1939 he was a leading candidate for chief of staff.

According to President Roosevelt, who related his own impatience to subordinates, Drum "beat his drum" too much, and the appointment went to Marshall. Drum was vastly disappointed and unwilling to take any inferior command unless it was very special. In the present instance, as appears in Eisenhower's diary entry of the next day, Secretary of War Henry L. Stimson was offering Drum a command in China, and Drum proved reluctant to take it.

2. Brigadier General Leonard T. (Gee) Gerow was chief of war plans; Lieutenant General Henry H. Arnold was commanding general of the United States Army Air Force.

January 12, 1942

1. Brigadier General (later General) Carl A. Spaatz was deputy commander and chief of the air staff.
2. Major General (later General) Brehon B. Somervell was chief of army supply.

January 13, 1942

1. Major General Lewis H. Brereton had been MacArthur's air chief in the Philippines and was now in Australia; General Sir Archibald P. Wavell was commander of the joint American-British-Dutch-Australian forces against the Japanese.
2. Here Eisenhower refers to the manner in which on December 7 the Philippines, because of the time lag, had several hours of darkness after the dawn attack on Pearl Harbor—7:30 A.M. Hawaiian time was 2:00 A.M. Manila time. There was time to prevent the planes in the Philippines from being caught on the ground. Unfortunately, because of confusion in MacArthur's command setup, they were caught on the ground.

January 15, 1942

1. Because of Drum's reluctance to accept the China command it went to Major General (later General) Joseph W. Stilwell.

January 17, 1942

1. Colonel (later Major General) Patrick J. Hurley had been secretary of war in the Hoover administration.

January 19, 1942

1. Brigadier General John Magruder was chief of the military mission in Chungking.
2. The American Volunteer Group—the "flying tigers"—had been organized to aid China by allowing United States Air Force pilots to go on inactive status and join the group, and its leader was Claire L. Chennault, soon to be a brigadier general (later major general) and head of the Tenth Air Force in the China-Burma-India theater.

January 22, 1942

1. Brigadier General (later General) Matthew B. Ridgway was chief of the Latin American section of war plans.

January 23, 1942

1. Major General (later Lieutenant General) Sutherland was MacArthur's chief of staff from 1939 to 1945.

January 25, 1942

1. Major General Ralph Royce was en route to the Southwest Pacific.
2. General and Mrs. Mark Clark.

January 27, 1942

1. Colonel (later General) Thomas T. Handy was then one of Eisenhower's subordinates in war plans.
2. Major General (later General) Joseph T. McNarney was chairman of a War Department committee to reorganize the army.

January 29, 1942

1. Eisenhower evidently believed that MacArthur had inspired Quezon to write a letter proposing the neutralization of the Philippines; the letter created consternation in Washington, as neutralization was virtually a surrender—the United States was dealing from a position of weakness, and the Japanese could have construed neutralization to mean anything they said it did. Vikdun Quisling was the Nazi-supported governor of occupied Norway, and during the war his name became a synonym for traitor. As for America's old antagonist of the Spanish-American War era, Emilio Aguinaldo, he was in the process of going over to the Japanese.

January 30, 1942

1. "Ireland movement" refers to a convoy headed for Northern Ireland.

February 2, 1942

1. William C. Bullitt, former ambassador to the Soviet Union and to France, was then ambassador at large.

February 8, 1942

1. MacArthur was forwarding a proposal from President Quezon that if the United States would withdraw its troops from the islands and grant the Philippines immediate independence (according to the arrangement then in force, independence was to come in 1946), he would seek to persuade Japan to do the same. The high commissioner, Francis B. Sayre, approved the plan, and MacArthur did not oppose it.

February 16, 1942

1. "Gee" Gerow, promoted to major general, took command of the Twenty-ninth Division.

February 17, 1942

1. Here Eisenhower means the United States Army Air Force, which had developed from the army signal corps many years earlier. During the Second World War the air force was autonomous, but did not become independent until the Unification Act of 1947.

February 22, 1942

1. Dr. Soong was Chinese foreign minister and brother-in-law of General Chiang Kai-shek.

February 23, 1942

1. Major General Edwin M. (Pa) Watson was President Roosevelt's military aide.
2. Admiral Harold R. Stark remained chief of naval operations until March, when he relinquished the post to Admiral King.
3. Major General John Pope during the Civil War and General Horatio Gates during the Revolution challenged the authority of their commanders-in-chief, Lincoln and Washington.

February 28, 1942

1. Lieutenant Colonel Charles W. McCarthy was a member of Eisenhower's staff.

NOTES [403]

March 8, 1942

1. The Australian proposal was precedent breaking, the first instance of a member of the British commonwealth in effect proposing to withdraw, for purposes of defense.

March 9, 1942

1. Lieutenant General Andrew G.L. McNaughton.
2. Rear Admiral Emory S. Land, chairman of the Maritime Commission, was in charge of constructing a merchant marine.

March 10, 1942

1. See below, footnote 1 for entry of March 14.

March 14, 1942

1. Sometime later Eisenhower replaced this last sentence with: "Must have been someone on the admiral's staff, as he's too big to let a little thing like that bother him." After the war and upon return to Washington, Ike discovered the diary notes of 1942, which he had left behind, and was chagrined to observe his treatment of King: "In glancing back over old notes I see that Admiral King annoyed me. In justice I should say that all through the war, whenever I called on him for assistance, he supported me fully and instantly." Papers of Kevin McCann.

March 28, 1942

1. One of the United States Army's old saws was that there was a right way and a wrong way and the army way, and nowhere was this point better taken than in regard to rank in wartime. So as to avoid a future peacetime army that was so overranked it would resemble that of some Latin American country, the United States Army made most wartime promotions "AUS," that is, Army of the United States, rather than RA, or Regular Army. This as compared with the Civil War custom of the brevet. But the army then played games with the distinction between AUS and RA and during the war managed promotions on both tiers—which, of course, fascinated the people involved and probably subtracted considerably from attention given to wartime duties. Ironically, all the care about wartime promotions did not prevent gross overranking in the subsequent years of peace, when the army was chockful of colonels and there was a general where every colonel once had been.

March 30, 1942

1. Major General (later General) Jonathan M. Wainwright was MacArthur's successor in the Philippines.

April 20, 1942

1. Secretary of Commerce Harold L. Ickes and Undersecretary of State Sumner Welles.

May 5, 1942

1. Bolero was a code name for the buildup of United States forces and supplies in the United Kingdom for a cross-Channel attack.

May 25, 1942

1. Brigadier Vivian Dykes was British secretary of the combined chiefs of staff in Washington and had accompanied Eisenhower to the United Kingdom.

May 26, 1942

1. Major General James E. Chaney was US Army commander in England.
2. Colonel (later Lieutenant General) Lucian K. Truscott, Jr., was then attached to the British combined operations headquarters; Marshal of the Royal Air Force Sir Charles F.A. Portal was chief of the air staff.

May 27, 1942

1. Lieutenant General (later Field Marshal) Bernard L. Montgomery was, of course, to be associated with Eisenhower for the rest of the war.
2. Major General Montagu Burrows commanded the Ninth Armored Division; Major General Sir Michael Creagh served in the Middle East from 1939 to 1944.

May 28, 1942

1. Roundup was the code name for a cross-Channel attack, 1943.
2. General Sir Alan F. Brooke was chief of the imperial general staff.
3. For Bolero see above, May 5, 1942, footnote 1.
4. Admiral Lord Louis Mountbatten was chief of combined operations.
5. The diagram showed a supreme commander reporting to the combined chiefs of staff, and below the commander were the operating forces. Combined staff work was nicely boxed up in a deadend box to the side—that is, the combined staff worked by itself—and simply reported to the supreme commander; it had no operating forces.
5. These complicated box plans are referred to in the text above.
7. General Sir Bernard Paget was commander, home forces.
8. The "tentative estimate" is not in the original of the diary in Abilene.

May 29, 1942

1. Herbert Evatt was Australian minister to the United States, and was in London at the time.
2. Colonel Arthur S. Nevins, younger brother of the historian Allan Nevins, had been serving in the operations division of the War Department.
3. When Admiral King became chief of naval operations in March 1942, Admiral Stark was shunted off to be commander of American naval forces in England. During the First World War this post was occupied by the formidable Vice-Admiral William S. Sims and was a major assignment, indeed the best the navy offered in that war. In the Second World War it was a ceremonial place.

May 30, 1942

1. Colonel Ray W. Barker was head of a planning group in General Chaney's headquarters; Colonels Josef R. Sheetz and Archelaus L. Hamblen had been serving in Washington.

June 4, 1942

1. Admiral Sir Dudley Pound was first sea lord and chief of naval staff; Major General Archibald Nye was vice-chief of the imperial general staff.

June 20, 1942

1. It was standard practice for American army personnel serving with the Philippine Commonwealth forces to receive additions to their pay, and Eisenhower received a monthly stipend of $500 while in the islands. When he left in 1939, President Quezon presented Ike with a $100,000 annuity, but he diplomatically refused it. Many years later an historian working with the Richard K. Sutherland papers in the National Archives came on an explanation of how Quezon early in 1942—when the decision was pending on whether to remove him from Corregidor by submarine—presented cash awards to several members of General MacArthur's

staff. MacArthur himself received a half million dollars; his chief of staff Major General Sutherland, $75,000; his deputy chief of staff Brigadier General Richard J. Marshall, Jr., $45,000; and his personal aide Lieutenant Colonel Sidney L. Huff, $20,000. Carol M. Petillo published her discovery as "Douglas MacArthur and Manuel Quezon: A Note on an Imperial Bond," in the *Pacific Historical Review*, vol. 48 (1979), 107–17, and some months later the article came to the attention of a newspaper editor who saw its news value, whereupon the gist of the article was published in most newspapers in the United States—thus, many years afterward, corroborating the judgment of Major General Eisenhower in 1942. Among other revelations, the article related that Secretary of War Stimson and President Roosevelt knew of these payments. The author of the article rightly asked how such payments squared with Army Regulations 600–10, Par. 2e (9), of December 6, 1938: "every member of the military establishment . . . is bound to refrain from . . . acceptance by an officer of a substantial loan or gift or any emolument from a person or firm with whom it is the officer's duty as an agent of the government to carry on negotiations."

June 22, 1942

1. Harry Hopkins, head of the lend-lease program, was presidential alter ego.
2. Milton S. Eisenhower had worked with the Department of Agriculture since 1926 and then was director of the War Relocation Authority, charged with moving Japanese-Americans from the West Coast to the interior. It was, of course, doubtful if Milton was the subject of a "war"; the president was exaggerating.

June 23, 1942

1. Brigadier General (later Major General) Charles L. Bolté, Chaney's chief of staff in England; Major General (later Lieutenant General) John C.H. Lee, former commander of the Second Infantry Division, later Eisenhower's head of theater services of supply; Brigadier General (later Major General) Robert M. Littlejohn, a Philippine comrade, who became theater quartermaster general.

June 25, 1942

1. The conference notes are unavailable.
2. Lieutenant General Sir Hastings L. Ismay was chief of staff to the minister of defense (Churchill).

June 26, 1942

1. John G. Winant was former governor of New Hampshire.
2. Brigadier General Donald A. Davison.
3. Major General Russell P. Hartle was commanding V Corps and the First Armored Division, then training in Northern Ireland.

June 27, 1942

1. Colonel Everett S. Hughes was an ordnance officer.

June 29, 1942

1. During the First World War the organization of the SOS was one of the most intractable problems confronting Pershing. It was exacerbated by the bad relations between him and the chief of staff in Washington, General Peyton C. March, and by Pershing's cavalryman's sense that supply problems could be worked out—because fighting, not fooling around with supply, was the task of the army. March wanted to send the builder of the Panama Canal, Major General George W. Goethals, to take charge of the SOS in France, but Pershing saw the proposal as poaching on his command prerogatives. He then arranged for his close friend and

subordinate, Major General James G. Harbord, to take over the SOS; another friend, Colonel (later Brigadier General) Charles G. Dawes, became Harbord's assistant. Harbord and Dawes performed miracles of supply, but down to the armistice on November 11, 1918, supply problems were barely under control, and Goethals and other highly competent men believed that the system would have collapsed if the war had continued much longer.

2. Colonel (later Major General) William J. (Wild Bill) Donovan had established the office of strategic services, an intelligence organization that was the forerunner of the CIA; his assistant was Whitney Shepherdson.

3. Sledgehammer was the code name for a cross-Channel attack in 1942.

June 30, 1942

1. Major General Alexander D. Surles was head of the War Department's public relations.

July 1, 1942

1. Major General Charles W. Ryder commanded the Thirty-fourth Division.

July 2, 1942

1. Brigadier General (later Major General) Robert A. McClure was a military attaché in the London embassy and later Eisenhower's chief of intelligence.

2. The army's staff organization, the so-called "G" system, was as follows: G-1, personnel division; G-2, intelligence division; G-3, operations division; G-4, supply division.

3. Colonel Homer Case.

4. H. Freeman Matthews.

July 3, 1942

1. Brigadier General (later General) Ira C. Eaker.

2. Here is the first diary mention of Lieutenant Commander (later Captain) Butcher, who as Eisenhower's naval aide was to keep the headquarters diary. The Eisenhowers and Butchers had been friends since 1927, when they met at Milton Eisenhower's house in Washington. Butcher had been a radio executive in New York. Colonel Davis was of course TJ, of Philippine days. George E. Allen, insurance executive, former commissioner of the District of Columbia, was a member of President Roosevelt's circle who in 1942 had arranged an appointment in the American Red Cross. Allen had a remarkable way of moving around, and because his wife, Mary, had known Mamie Eisenhower in Washington, he wangled himself into the general's company in the summer of 1942, even though he had not met Eisenhower until then. Later he became an intimate of President Truman. When Ike became president in 1953 the wily Allen, to Truman's disgust, soon was playing golf with the new president. Allen was the author of a witty book entitled *Presidents Who Have Known Me* (New York: Simon and Schuster, 1960).

July 5, 1942

1. Gymnast later was to be called Torch (the invasion of North Africa in 1942).

July 6, 1942

1. For Roundup see above, May 28, 1942, footnote 1.

2. Major General Thomas T. Handy, operations division of the War Department; Colonel (later Major General) Haywood S. Hansell, Jr., appointed commander of the first Bombardment Wing of the Eighth Air Force.

July 26, 1942

3. Colonel William Stirling was a member of the secretariat of the British chiefs and later joined Eisenhower's staff.

July 27, 1942

1. For Sledgehammer see above, June 29, 1942, footnote 3.
2. Captain (later Colonel) Ernest R. (Tex) Lee, aide.
3. For Gymnast see above, January 1, 1942, footnote 1; for Roundup, May 28, 1942, footnote 1.

September 2, 1942

1. For Torch see above, July 5, 1942, footnote 1.

September 13, 1942

1. Lord Frederick J. Leathers was minister of war transport.
2. For Torch see above, July 5, 1942, footnote 1.
3. Convoy around Norway to Murmansk.

September 15, 1942

1. Brigadier General Claude M. Thiele, anti-aircraft commander; Brigadier General (later Lieutenant General) Walter Bedell Smith, Eisenhower's chief of staff.

November 8, 1942

1. General Charles E. Mast was chief of staff of the French XIX Corps in Algeria.

November 9, 1942

1. Portion deleted in accord with the donor's deed of gift.

December 10, 1942

1. Lieutenant General Sir Kenneth A.N. Anderson commanded the British First Army.
2. Brigadier General Lunsford E. Oliver was commander of combat command B, part of the United States First Armored Division.
3. Portion deleted in accord with the donor's deed of gift.

January 19, 1943

1. Peyrouton was a former member of the Vichy government; Yves Chatel was governor of Algeria.

February 25, 1943

1. Major General (later Lieutenant General) Lloyd R. Fredendall was commander of II Corps.
2. The combined chiefs of staff were the American chiefs and a group of high-ranking British officers detailed to Washington.

June 11, 1943

1. The Royal Air Force was created largely by Lieutenant General Sir Hugh Trenchard, who was the British equivalent of Brigadier General William (Billy) Mitchell. Trenchard was a keen personality during the First World War and managed to split off the RAF from the army many years before the American air force could even have contemplated such an arrangement. Eisenhower apparently was a believer in the importance of keeping air power under the army's wing.
2. Clark did not hesitate to express himself to the press, and Eisenhower might have been talking about that. Or he might have been speaking about Clark's unwillingness to take any field command except that of an army—an unwillingness the general next relates.

July 1, 1943

1. In January 1943, Roosevelt and Churchill met at Casablanca to discuss the progress of the invasion.
2. Brimstone was the code name for the capture of Sardinia.
3. Malta.

November 12, 1943

1. In his message of September 8, Eisenhower said he wanted Italian cooperation in the armistice, else he would "publish to the world" that Badoglio had reneged. Alfred D. Chandler, ed., *The Papers of Dwight David Eisenhower: The War Years*, five volumes (Baltimore: Johns Hopkins University Press, 1970), III, 1402–1403.
2. Pointblank was the code name for the air offensive against Germany.
3. Overlord was the code name for the invasion of France in the spring of 1944.

December 6, 1943

1. Frank Knox was secretary of the navy.
2. Late in November, en route to the Teheran Conference, Roosevelt and Churchill stopped in Egypt. Just outside Cairo, at the Mena House, almost literally in the shadow of the great pyramid of Cheops, they held a conference with General Chiang Kai-shek and his staff.
3. The first Quebec Conference, August 11–24, 1943. A second conference was held there in September, 1944.
4. Harriman in 1941 had been expediter of lend-lease in London and that year went to Moscow to negotiate for lend-lease. In December 1943 he had just become ambassador to Russia.

February 7, 1944

1. Eisenhower asked for a five-division assault, which would extend the frontage and afford a greater opportunity of finding a weak spot to exploit. For the cable of January 23 see Chandler III, 1674–75.
2. Anvil was an Allied operation in the Mediterranean against southern France; for Overlord see above, November 12, 1943, footnote 3.
3. Anzio.

March 22, 1944

1. When the hope to rally the French of North Africa to Giraud quickly faded, the star of General Charles de Gaulle rose; the general's French National Committee became the only serious representative of French resistance. No one, of course, knew whether De Gaulle's claims to represent sentiment in occupied France could be substantiated.
2. For Pointblank see above, November 12, 1943, footnote 2.
3. Air Chief Marshal Sir Trafford Leigh-Mallory was head of the Allied Expeditionary Air Force, comprising the Royal Air Force tactical air force and the United States Ninth Air Force.
4. Somewhat confusingly, Tedder was Eisenhower's deputy in charge of Leigh-Mallory, Spaatz, who commanded the United States strategic air force in Europe (Eighth Air Force), and Air Chief Marshal Sir Arthur T. Harris, who commanded British bomber command. One has the impression that not merely did the diplomacy of Allied command force upon Eisenhower a topheavy command arrangement, but personality differences compounded the complexity.

April 12, 1944

1. CAS is the British chief of air staff, that is, Portal.
2. CIGS is the chief of the imperial general staff, that is, Brooke. Eisenhower did not send the telegram.

May 22, 1944

1. Here Eisenhower meant Vice Admiral Sir Bertram Ramsay, the top naval planner for Torch, and Air Chief Marshal Leigh-Mallory. Chandler III, 1881.

June 3, 1944

1. De Gaulle was in Algiers.
2. The duplex-drive tank carried a canvas flotation device that could be pulled up around the tank's sides, in effect putting the tank in a waterproof sack. Unfortunately the device made the tank vulnerable to mines and objects floating in the water.

August 6–7, 1944

1. Chandler IV, 2057, so guesses the date. The entry clearly was written before August 8, the date under which Butcher filed the entry in his diary.
2. Montgomery's latest directive, M-517, looked to a wider swing by the Third Army. Chandler IV, 2058.

September 5, 1944

1. The Germans began bombarding England with V-1 bombs, drone aircraft fitted with explosives, on June 12, shortly after D-day, and early in August they began sending over the V-2 missiles. The former were fairly easy to shoot down, once the Allies realized what they were up against, but the latter weapons were impossible to intercept. It was difficult to know what variety was the more fearsome. The V-1 weapons made a terrible racket as they came down and exploded. As for the V-2s, no one heard them until they struck. If they hit an open place, they were relatively harmless. But if they hit a building, they would penetrate to the cellar and obliterate everything. The launching sites of these weapons now lay near the lines of the Allied advance.

   To avoid confusion with army numbering, the army groups were named Sixth, Twelfth, and Twenty-first. The Sixth (Devers) comprised the French First Army and United States Seventh (Lieutenant General Alexander M. Patch); the Twelfth, the United States First, Third, Fifteenth (Gerow), and Ninth (Lieutenant General William H. Simpson); the Twenty-first, the British Second and Canadian First.

December 23, 1944

1. The line was more fiction than reality, but constituted a rough set of positions in front of the Rhine, protected by hills and other natural strong points.
2. Field Marshal Karl von Rundstedt was German commander in the Ardennes battle.

December 15, 1945

1. The ellipsis points are in the original text—likewise in the subsequent material from the papers of Kevin McCann, diary entries from December 15, 1945, through January 15, 1948.

March 29, 1947

1. General Francis W. De Guingand had been Montgomery's chief of staff for operations and intelligence; Brigadier James F. Gault was Eisenhower's British military assistant.

December 1, 1947

1. Robert Schuman later served as foreign minister and was the author of the Schuman Plan for the economic reorganization of Western Europe; Edouard Herriot was a long-time French political leader, prominent in the interwar period.

December 2, 1947

1. In the early summer of 1943, Kay Summersby was engaged to Colonel Richard R. Arnold, who was killed in the explosion of a mine.

December 31, 1947

1. John S. D. Eisenhower married Barbara Jean Thompson on June 10, 1947, and the grandchild proved to be Dwight David Eisenhower II.

January 4, 1948

1. "Tex" Lee had named his son Dwight Eisenhower Lee.

January 15, 1948

1. Leonard V. Finder was publisher of the Manchester *Union-Leader*. For the letter that Eisenhower wrote Finder declining nomination in the New Hampshire primary in 1948, and the circumstances surrounding the letter, see above, p. 371, and below, p. 425.

December 13, 1948

1. Stuart Symington, secretary of the air force; General Hoyt S. Vandenberg, chief of staff of the air force; Admiral Louis E. Denfeld, chief of naval operations; Admiral William H. P. Blandy, commander in chief of the Atlantic fleet; Wilfrid J. McNeil, Forrestal's assistant; Major General (later General) Alfred M. Gruenther, director of the joint staff of the joint chiefs of staff.

December 17, 1948

1. Harold B. Hinton was the new Military Establishment's director of public relations; Marx Leva, Forrestal's assistant; William Webster, chairman of the military liaison committee to the Atomic Energy Commission; Major General Grandison Gardner, special assistant to the secretary of the air force; Lieutenant General (later General) Lauris Norstad, deputy chief of staff, air force, for operations; George B. Woods, special assistant to the undersecretary of the air force.

January 27, 1949

1. Vice-Admiral Arthur W. Radford, vice-chief of naval operations.

February 2, 1949

1. Lieutenant General Albert C. Wedemeyer, director of plans and operations; Major General Lyman L. Lemnitzer, deputy commandant, National War College; Lieutenant General Leroy Lutes, director of staff, munitions board, National Military Establishment.
2. Vice-Admiral Forrest P. Sherman, commander of the Sixth Fleet.
3. Rear Admiral Richard L. Conolly, commander in chief, Eastern Atlantic.

March 19, 1949

1. Vice-Admiral Arthur D. Struble, deputy chief of naval operations.
2. Louis Johnson, a lawyer from West Virginia, former assistant secretary of war, past president of the American Legion, had been treasurer of the Democratic party in 1948 and thereby performed yeoman service for President Truman, whose campaign initially was very poorly supported within the party. Forrestal had become so emotionally distraught that Truman had to replace him.

June 4, 1949

1. James E. Webb was undersecretary of state.

July 7, 1949

1. Here is a tantalizing statement, for it is capable of only one interpretation, namely, that Truman had inquired about Eisenhower's possible political ambitions when the two men met at the time of the Potsdam Conference. Later rumor had it that Truman in a burst of admiration for the general had offered Eisenhower the chance to run for the presidency in 1948, presumably on the Democratic ticket—that Truman had said he would give Eisenhower anything the general desired, and that included the Presidency. Truman later denied having made such an offer.

September 27, 1949

1. Paul E. Fitzpatrick, New York state Democratic chairman
2. Because a newspaper publisher wanted to enter his name in the New Hampshire primary of March 1948, Eisenhower had released a letter taking himself out of the race. After remarking that "Politics is a profession; a serious, complicated, and, in its true sense, a noble one," he added unmistakably: "my decision to remove myself completely from the political scene is definite and positive."
3. Wife of Henry Luce, publisher of *Time, Life*, and *Fortune*. Mrs. Luce was a conservative Republican and former congresswoman and coiner of the word "globaloney," which she had pinned on the Democrats. After he achieved the presidency Eisenhower appointed her ambassador to Italy.
4. Senator Arthur H. Vandenberg of Michigan had been interested in the presidential nomination of the GOP in 1948, but the party went to Dewey. The senator was the uncle of General Hoyt Vandenberg.

November 3, 1949

1. Admiral Forrest Sherman. Admiral Denfeld, Sherman's predecessor, had proved unable to control his subordinates, who "revolted" against the pretensions, as they described them, of the other services. For the Truman administration it was bad enough to deal with the ambitions of the air force; a navy revolt was too much, and Denfeld gave way to Sherman. The latter maintained better control, but his personal luck did not last, for he collapsed and died of a heart attack while negotiating for bases in Spain in 1952. As for Indonesia, whose independence was arranged by American envoys aboard a United States Navy ship in Indonesian waters, the new nation fared poorly under its recklessly nationalistic and dictatorial president, Ahmed Suekarno. The country's Chinese residents fared very badly in the mid-1960s, when tens of thousands of them were massacred because of their supposed involvement in a communist plot. The independence of Indonesia thus brought a time of trouble.

c. January 1, 1950

1. The head of International Business Machines, Thomas Watson, Sr., had given him a new electric typewriter.
2. Ferdinand Eberstadt was an investment banker; Herbert Brownell, lawyer, was later an attorney general.

March 22, 1950

1. Dean John Krout of Columbia was a well-known historian; Dean Dunning headed Columbia's new engineering center.

undated

1. Eisenhower's doctor and friends constantly sought to reduce appointments and engagements and provide blocks of leisure, for the general had a history of hypertension.

April 5, 1950

1. For many years Barnard College for women has been closely associated with Columbia, and Columbia's president was ex officio a trustee of Barnard.

April 29, 1950

1. The so-called China White Paper, a huge volume compiled in the Department of State and published in 1949 by the government printing office, contained two parts—a long chronology of American relations with China and a documentary portion giving telegrams to and from China by American officials. The most widely read part of the White Paper was the letter of transmittal, written by Secretary of State Dean Acheson to President Truman. In the letter Acheson said that nothing the United States had done or not done could have made any difference in the outcome in China, that the communization of the Chinese mainland was necessarily a result of local forces. It is difficult to know whether publication of the White Paper was a good idea, as most of the critics tended to argue from the letter of transmittal. Historians at the time and later were thankful for the documentary annex, which showed the inability of Americans to influence the course of events, short of a massive military intervention, which no American, Republican or Democrat, proposed—it would have been political suicide in the immediate years after the Second World War, when the veterans wanted just one thing, and that was to be let alone.

May 2, 1950

1. The general's mother, Ida Stover Eisenhower, had died in September 1946. He had been devoted to her, even though as a member of Jehovah's Witnesses she had rejected the use of force in human relations. None of her sons believed as she did, but she did not try to push her beliefs on them.

June 30, 1950

1. Apparently Eisenhower went to the Walter Reed Hospital for a checkup.
2. General Wade H. Haislip, vice-chief of staff of the army; General Collins, chief of staff; Lieutenant General (later General) Matthew B. Ridgway, deputy chief of staff for administration; Lieutenant General (later General) Gruenther, deputy chief of staff for plans; General Bradley, chairman of the joint chiefs.
3. The Korean War had broken out on June 25, and by the day that Eisenhower arrived the military services had received full authority to intervene by land, sea, and air.

July 6, 1950

1. Thomas K. Finletter was secretary of the air force; John A. McCone was undersecretary of the air force; Lieutenant General Norstad was acting vice-chief of staff of the air force; Harriman had been European representative under the Economic Cooperation Administration (Marshall Plan) and was special assistant to the president.
2. The decision to go all-out to aid the South Koreans.

October 28, 1950

1. The French advanced a plan by which the Germans would not maintain any forces larger than brigades, so that no Nato divisions would be German divisions. Multilingual units, of course, might not work together easily in combat, but such a detail did not detain the French, who wanted to avoid any German military revival, which would carry political overtones. As a result

of the London recommendations of early June 1948, the Germans in the three Western zones and in West Berlin had been encouraged to form larger political organizations—provincial governments looking toward a West German government. The latter was organized in Bonn in 1949. Not until 1955 did West Germany receive full independence. The French saw the handwriting and were much agitated, and hence the plan to brigade German units.

2. Theoretically the general's position was impeccable, but like all American logic about German rearmament it failed to understand French amour propre. The latter phrase had been a part of the English language for a long time but was easy to forget, if applied to the wayward French. Moreover, the loss of national resolution that came with the fall of France to Nazi Germany in 1940 was to afflict an entire generation, and not to begin to disappear until the magic phrases of General Charles de Gaulle, who returned to power in the 1960s, were combined with a remarkable French economic growth during those same years, coupled with the appearance of a new postwar generation. By 1950, too, the Indochinese quagmire was taking a dreadful toll of French lieutenants and captains, and about the time the French in 1954 passed Indochina to the United States they were engaged in another quagmire in Algeria. Only De Gaulle proved large enough in leadership to take France out of Algeria. By that time, the 1960s, the French not only had failed to prevent the rearmament of West Germany, but also had failed to contribute hardly any land forces to NATO.

3. The general may have overestimated his wife's heart condition, but Mrs. Eisenhower's trouble with her physical balance, the condition attributable to a malady of the inner ear, mentioned in the introduction to the present volume, was a constant concern. Mamie's aged parents were in poor health, and her father died within months of Ike's accepting the NATO assignment.

November 6, 1950

1. The memo is not in the original diary. The American Assembly was a continuing popular forum to discuss problems of American life. Its headquarters was at the former Harriman estate, Arden House, an hour's drive from New York City.
2. The conference was over West Germany's role in NATO—how to include West German forces without alienating France.
3. James G. Conant was president of Harvard; Robert S. Lovett was undersecretary of defense.
4. For the military budget.
5. Marshall had replaced Louis Johnson as secretary of defense in September 1950.

November 19, 1950

1. Russell Leffingwell was a lawyer.

December 5, 1950

1. Amon Carter was publisher of the Fort Worth *Gazette*.

December 16, 1950

1. Eisenhower meant that he soon would be going to Europe.
2. The memos are no longer in the original diary.

January 1, 1951

1. Senators James H. Duff and Joseph Clark of Pennsylvania; James R. Forgan, investment banker; William Benton, senator from Connecticut; Russel Davenport, writer.
2. Major (later Brigadier General) Robert L. Schulz was an aide.

March 2, 1951

1. Admiral William D. Fechteler.
2. Admiral Robert B. Carney.
3. Brigadier James Gault, wartime personal military assistant; Colonel Paul T. Carroll.
4. Robert Schuman, foreign minister; Jules Moch, minister of war.

March 3, 1951

1. The officer was Rear Admiral Leslie C. Stevens. His paper, referred to, is not in the original diary.

April 27, 1951

1. Upon returning home, for the first time since 1937, MacArthur had addressed a joint session of Congress; his case then went officially to a joint hearing of the Senate's committees on foreign affairs and military affairs. The country watched while a galaxy of military and civil officials came before the committee to testify. President Truman (who did not of course testify) years later said that never before had a major nation spilled so many of its high-level secrets, revealed so much of its tactics and strategy, to a foreign foe or to anyone who wanted to read, as did the American government in the so-called MacArthur hearings. A great debate the hearings decidedly were not, as the arguments tended to proceed ad hominem. Gradually the country and the Senate lost interest in the proceedings, and they came to an end. The hearings afterward were published by the government printing office in five huge volumes.

May 15, 1951

1. Conrad Hilton, of the Hilton hotel chain.

May 30, 1951

1. Major General Courtney Whitney was a former Philippine businessman who became one of MacArthur's principal aides in the wartime and postwar era, and who accompanied him into retirement.
2. The examples are not in the original diary.

June 14, 1951

1. John S.D. Eisenhower and wife, Barbara, their children, David and Ann, and Mamie's mother, Mrs. Elivera Carlson (Min) Doud.
2. William C. Foster was with the Economic Cooperation Administration (Marshall Plan).
3. Senators Robert A. Taft (Ohio), Kenneth Wherry (Kansas), James P. Kem (Missouri), Joseph R. McCarthy (Wisconsin).

June 25, 1951

1. Portion deleted in accordance with the donor's deed of gift.
2. Jacob Potofsky, labor leader.

July 2, 1951

1. At that time Eisenhower and Clay were military governor and deputy governor, respectively, of the American zone of Germany.

August 6, 1951

1. Hoffman was Economic Co-operation Administration administrator and a Republican; Cowles, the publisher of the Minneapolis *Tribune*.

October 4, 1951

1. Governor Harold Stassen of Minnesota; Senators James H. Duff (Pennsylvania), Frank Carlson (Kansas), Henry Cabot Lodge, Jr. (Massachusetts); General Mark W. Clark; Roy Roberts of the Kansas City *Star;* George N. Craig of Indiana.

November 9, 1951

1. Senator Kenneth McKellar of Tennessee resembled a cartoon character of the era, known as Senator Snort, who possessed a string tie, bulbous nose, and flying hair. In the cartoons Snort was always sounding off, and a copy of his book was ostentatiously on his desk, with the title visible, *The Old Rocking Chair Got Me.*

November 16, 1951

1. Governor Alfred E. Driscoll of New Jersey.
2. Bengamin Gayelord Hauser was the author of *Better Eyes Without Glasses* (New York: Tempo, 1938), *Diet Does It* (New York: Coward-McCann, 1944), and notably *Look Younger, Live Longer* (New York: Farrar, Straus, 1950).

November 24, 1951

1. The evangelical French economist Jean Monnet had been present at the Paris Peace Conference of 1919; ever since that experience he had propagandized for the economic collaboration of the nations of Europe. In a long life that lasted into the 1970s, and through not merely his own hard work but such disciples as George Ball, undersecretary of state for economic affairs during the Kennedy administration, Monnet sought to get the Europeans together. Part of his program took the name of the Schuman Plan, after French Foreign Minister Robert Schuman, a plan for unification of steel and coal in France, Luxembourg, the Saar, Belgium, and Western Germany. The reference to "European army" is to the Pleven Plan, named after French Premier Rene Pleven, which was the old French idea of brigading German units into a European army.
2. The Military Defense Assistance Plan followed the Marshall Plan and undertook to reequip the Europeans militarily.

January 22, 1952

1. Charles Sawyer was secretary of commerce; Dan Kimball was secretary of the navy.

February 11, 1952

1. Jacquelin Cochran was a well-known aviatrix and wife of the industrialist Floyd B. Odlum.

February 12, 1952

1. Henry R. Luce was publisher of *Time, Life,* and *Fortune.*

January 5, 1953

1. Senators Hugh Butler (Nebraska), Arthur V. Watkins (Utah), Cordon (Oregon), and William F. Knowland (California).

January 5, 1953 (part two)

1. Herbert Brownell had been designated attorney general. He had favored Randolph A. Crossley for governor.
2. Charles F. Willis, Jr., special assistant on President-elect Eisenhower's staff, favored Samuel W. King for governor, and King received the appointment.

January 6, 1953

1. John Foster Dulles, of course, had been designated secretary of state.
2. The prime minister of Iran, Mohammed Mossadegh, was negotiating to get more oil revenue from the British-controlled petroleum company.

January 7, 1953

1. Senator John Williams (Delaware).

January 16, 1953

1. Martin P. Durkin, designated secretary of labor. Durkin was president of the plumbers union. He did not last long in the cabinet and resigned after eight months because of a misunderstanding, for he had believed that Eisenhower would sponsor amendments to the Taft-Hartley Act, which generally was considered hostile to the interests of American labor.

February 1, 1953

1. The National Presbyterian Church at 1764 N Street, NW. Its minister was Dr. Edward L. R. Elson.

February 2, 1953

1. Until the Twentieth Amendment to the Constitution, effective with the inauguration of President Roosevelt for a second term in January 1937, the president was inaugurated on March 4, and the state of the union speeches came in December. Elimination of a possible interregnum from November until March was a good idea, but the incidental change in the major annual address could cause problems.

February 7, 1953

1. Senators H. Styles Bridges (New Hampshire), Homer Capehart (Indiana), Everet McK. Dirksen (Illinois).
2. Representatives Joseph W. Martin, Jr. (Massachusetts), Charles Halleck (Indiana), John Tabor (New York).
3. Senator Frank Carlson (Kansas).
4. Senator Leverett Saltonstall (Massachusetts).
5. John W. Davis was a Wall Street lawyer and Democratic candidate for president in 1924.
6. Sinclair Weeks, Massachusetts manufacturer, former senator (replacing Henry Cabot Lodge, Jr., in 1944–1945, when Lodge served in the army).
7. Lodge was ambassador to the United Nations; Stassen, director of the Foreign Operations Administration; Joseph M. Dodge, director of the budget; Oveta Culp Hobby, secretary of Health, Education, and Welfare.

February 13, 1953

1. The talk of Churchill's age was not so much numerical as physical—he had aged rapidly, though he was only seventy-nine in the year 1953. Compared to the longevity of some of his contemporaries in power—Konrad Adenauer, Syngman Rhee, Chiang Kai-shek—he was not unduly old. In the past, British statesmen had flourished into their eighties, and Palmerston held power until the day he died, in 1865, when he was eighty-one.
2. Portion deleted in accordance with the donor's deed of gift.
3. Portion deleted, as above.
4. Holmes bore the title of minister, serving under the ambassador. Such titles were coming into vogue for the larger embassies.

April 1, 1953

1. In his effort to create a responsible, forward-looking Republican party, Eisenhower often had to move in gingerly ways, and no more so than in the case of the Bricker amendment—where he had to placate the Ohio senator and yet oppose him.
2. Confirmation of Charles E. Bohlen as ambassador to Russia. A foreign service officer, Bohlen had served as interpreter for President Roosevelt at the wartime conferences, notably Yalta, also for Truman at Potsdam, and these associations seemed suspect. Bohlen was uncontrite about his diplomacy.
3. Barry Goldwater (Arizona).
4. Senator George Malone (Nevada).

May 1, 1953

1. Eisenhower refers here to the National Security Council.
2. Secretary of the Treasury George M. Humphrey, Directors Dodge and Stassen, and Undersecretary of Defense Roger Kyes.

May 14, 1953

1. Brigadier General Wilton B. Persons, special assistant to the president; Gabriel Hauge, administrative assistant for economic affairs; Stephens was appointments secretary.
2. Portion deleted in accordance with the donor's deed of gift.

June 1, 1953

1. Wayne Morse (Oregon) was about to cross the aisle to the Democratic party.

July 24, 1953

1. Eisenhower had known James F. Byrnes when the latter during the war was "assistant president" for the home front, and when he was secretary of state in 1945–1947. Politically Byrnes had broken with Truman over domestic politics, perhaps partly Byrnes's desire to reenter politics on the state level as governor of South Carolina, where both personal and public inclination moved him in the direction of the Dixiecrats of the persuasion of former Governor Strom Thurmond, now senator. President Truman detested the "Republicats," as he called them, who along with the followers of former Vice-President Henry A. Wallace had divided the Democratic party and nearly given the 1948 presidential election to the Republicans. In January 1950, Truman was led to believe that Byrnes had tricked him in the summer of 1944 when the Democratic party was about to choose a vice-presidential nominee, really a successor to the mortally ill Roosevelt, and from that point onward there was a complete break, personal as well as political, between Truman and Byrnes. It was interesting, therefore, to observe the fast friendship between Byrnes and Eisenhower, which said that perhaps Eisenhower's hope to found a new party might succeed (that is, if Eisenhower was willing to take a few members who joined out of belief in Southern civil rights).
2. *Brown versus Board of Education of Topeka (1954)*, the landmark case, was before the court. Because of a preceding decision (*Sweatt* v. *Painter* [*1950*]) that a separate law school established for blacks by the state of Texas satisfied neither the standard of genuine equality in legal education nor the requirement of the equal protection clause of the Constitution, and because a comparable case involving the University of Oklahoma made southern state universities begin admitting blacks to their professional and graduate schools, it was only a matter of time before similar reasoning would be extended to the high schools and grade schools.
3. President Syngman Rhee.

July 31, 1953

1. Portion deleted in accordance with the donor's deed of gift.
2. Leonard W. Hall, chairman of the Republican national committee.
3. Portion deleted in accordance with the donor's deed of gift.

August 1, 1953

1. Bernard M. Shanley, special counsel to the president; Samuel K. McConnell, Jr. (Pennsylvania).
2. Rocco C. Siciliano, later special assistant to the president for personnel management.

August 19, 1953

1. John M. Wisdom, New Orleans attorney was Republican national committeeman from Louisiana.

October 24, 1953

1. Senators Duff and Edward Martin; Gilbert Mason Owlett, Wellsboro, Pa. attorney, Republican national committeeman; Governor John S. Fine of Pennsylvania.

October 26, 1953

1. Albert M. Cole was housing and home finance administrator.

December 2, 1953

1. Rear Admiral Lewis L. Strauss, New York banker was chairman of the Atomic Energy Commission.
2. Brigadier General Robert Cutler, Boston banker, was special assistant to the president for national security affairs; Allen W. Dulles was director of the Central Intelligence Agency.

December 11, 1953

1. Howard Cullman was a New York tobacco merchant and Port Authority commissioner.

December 11, 1953 (part three)

1. Roy Roberts was publisher of the Kansas City *Star.*

December 17–19, 1953

1. Congressmen Rees (Kansas), Short (Missouri); Senator Alexander Wiley (Wisconsin).

January 18, 1954

1. After eight months in the cabinet Durkin had resigned because Eisenhower would not go along with his ideas about amending the Taft-Hartley Act. He was replaced by James P. Mitchell.
2. William E. Jenner (Indiana), Eugene D. Millikin (Colorado), and William Langer (North Dakota).
3. Sherman Adams was former governor of New Hampshire, chief of staff. When Eisenhower visited Truman in the White House shortly before taking office, he said to the then president that he wanted a chief of staff. Truman thought poorly of the idea, as he believed it would prevent easy access to the president by his assistants and therefore would choke off ideas and problems, but he also disdained it because it was a military notion—that all commanders have, if only for purposes of prestige, chiefs of staff. *Off the Record: The Private Papers of Harry S. Truman* (New York: Harper and Row, 1980), p. 274.
4. James C. Hagerty was press secretary; C.D. Jackson was special assistant for psychological strategy.

5. I. Jack Martin, administrative assistant for congressional liaison, had been for years Taft's righthand man; Gerald D. Morgan was a special counsel; Bryce N. Harlow was administrative assistant for congressional liaison; Arthur Minnich was administrative assistant for general correspondence and activities pertaining to domestic issues.
5. Emmet Hughes was a former articles editor of *Life*.
7. Brigadier General Carroll, secretary of the White House staff, died September 17, 1954.

January 27, 1954

1. Lieutenant Governor Lloyd H. Wood ran for governor and was defeated in the November election.

Week of February 7, 1954

1. American prisoners taken during the Korean War.

February 8, 1954

1. Saltonstall was chairman of the Senate Armed Services Committee.

February 10, 1954

1. James S. Kemper, mutual insurance executive, American ambassador to Brazil.

February 10, 1954 (part two)

1. The president did not place a copy of the Rhee letter in his diary, and at the present writing (1981) the letter has not been published elsewhere. The pertinent Far Eastern volume of the department of state's series, *Foreign Relations of the United States*, has not yet appeared.

February 26, 1954

1. Nothing eventually came of the Bricker amendment—or the amendment to the Bricker amendment by Senator Walter F. George (Georgia)—but in the course of devolving down to nothing the whole business caused a lot of trouble. Simply remembering what the details were all about must have consumed great amounts of time. The Senate rejected the Bricker amendment on February 25, by a vote of forty-two to fifty. This narrowed the fight to the George amendment and the revised administration amendment sponsored by Knowland and others. The president was saved embarrassment when next day, February 26, the Senate voted down the George amendment by a single vote, thirty-one to sixty.

March 5, 1954

1. Senator McCarthy was chairman of the committee on government operations and of its permanent subcommittee on investigations.
2. Flynn was a possible candidate for the Senate from Oklahoma.
3. The Republican primary in New Jersey involved Clifford Case.
4. Henry Carbaugh of Tennessee was a candidate for the chairmanship of the TVA.
5. Bedell Smith was undersecretary of state. The issue concerned foreign aid in the Far East, especially in Indochina.
   John J. McCloy, wartime assistant secretary of war, was a New York banker. The Chase National Bank and the National City Bank financed the Anaconda Copper Company, which controlled the Montana Power and Light Company. The question was whether the Chase and the National City could help elect a senator, presumably in Montana. If so, they were to get in touch with Senator Dirksen.
   The army was buying broiler chickens in Virginia and North Carolina instead of Delaware, where Senator Williams was worried.

April 8, 1954

1. Dr. Arthur Burns was chairman of the Council of Economic Advisers.
2. Dr. Burns's suggestions of April 2 recommended a careful stimulation of the economy and stressed the need to avoid any measures that would compete with private enterprise.

May 11, 1954

1. McCarthy temporarily had relinquished the chairmanship of the Permanent Investigations Subcommittee to his friend Senator Karl E. Mundt (South Dakota).
2. General Ridgway was army chief of staff.

October 22, 1954

1. General Doolittle was investigating the secret operations of the CIA.

November 9, 1954

1. Robert B. Anderson was deputy secretary of defense, successor to Roger M. Kyes.

November 16, 1954

1. The draft resolution is not attached to the diary entry in the Eisenhower Library.

November 20, 1954

1. Representative Fred A. Hartley, Jr. (New Jersey); Robert R. McCormick, publisher of the Chicago *Tribune.*
2. Americans for Democratic Action (ADA): Senators Paul Douglas (Illinois), Hubert Humphrey (Minnesota); former Secretary of Agriculture Charles Brannan, John A. Carroll, candidate for senator from Colorado; former President Truman; former governor Adlai E. Stevenson; Stewart A. Mitchell, chairman of the Democratic national committee.

January 10, 1955

1. By complicated agreements at Paris that brought West Germany and Italy into a so-called Western European Union, a way at last opened by which West Germany could join NATO. In the course of this arrangement the West Germans received complete independence. The path to compromise had been tedious, for Eisenhower at SHAPE had tried to push the French into the Pleven Plan, named for their own premier, which looked to a European Defense Community. After quite a lot of pushing, including a shove by Secretary of State Dulles who in December 1953 spoke of an agonizing reappraisal of American commitments to Europe in event the French national assembly turned down EDC, the assembly did exactly what it was not supposed to do. There followed a hasty diplomacy in which the Germans and Italians joined the Brussels Pact of 1948 in place of EDC and all the signatories created WEU and everyone was happy. The French then asked for a summit conference.

January 10, 1955 (part two)

1. The minority leader of the Senate announced that the Republican party did not want a reluctant presidential candidate in 1956 and said he would not join in a "draft-Eisenhower" movement.

January 17, 1955

1. Robert W. Woodruff of Atlanta was chairman of the executive committee of the Coca-Cola Company.
2. For the Dixon-Yates affair see below, pp. 297–300.

January 17, 1955 (part two)

1. Portion deleted in accord with the donor's deed of gift—all subsequent ellipsis points for the same reason.

March 14, 1955

1. The meeting was held on March 11.

May 2, 1955

1. Major General Charles F. Thompson.

May 3, 1955

1. Attending a funeral in the rotunda of the Capitol, Jackson came within range of an assassin who fired at him twice, at pointblank range, but each time the cap of the pistol failed. The chance of such a failure, later reckoned, was almost nonexistent, but Jackson's luck held. After the first crack of the pistol the general lunged for his assailant, for Jackson knew a pistol's sound as well as anyone, but a young army officer got there first and subdued the man.

May 10, 1955

1. Henry F. Holland was assistant secretary of state for inter-American affairs.

July 14, 1955

1. The statements are not attached to the diary entry in the Eisenhower Library.
2. Krishna Menon was foreign minister of India.

September 29, 1955 (Ann Whitman diary)

1. The Byers Peak Ranch was near Fraser, Colorado.
2. Robert L. Biggers, automotive executive; Colonel (later Brigadier General) Robert L. Schulz, aide.
3. Murray Snyder was assistant press attaché.
4. Major General Martin E. Griffin was commanding general of Fitzsimons General Hospital on the outskirts of Denver.
5. Deeter B. Flohr was Eisenhower's personal secret service bodyguard.
5. Snyder, Allen, and Parsons were secretaries.
7. William P. Rogers was deputy attorney general.
8. Arthur E. Summerfield was Postmaster General; Bernard M. Shanley was appointment secretary.
9. Ellis D. Slater, president of Frankfort Distillers Corporation; C. Wesley Roberts, former chairman of the Republican national committee; William E. Robinson, president of the Coca-Cola Company.
10. Dr. White was a renowned heart specialist at the Massachusetts General Hospital, Boston.

January 10, 1956

1. Albert F. Nufer was ambassador to Argentina.
2. Portion deleted for security reasons.
3. Portion deleted for security reasons.

January 19, 1956

1. Major General John S. Bragdon was special assistant to the president for public works planning.

January 19, 1956 (part two)

1. James B. Conant, president of Harvard, was ambassador to West Germany. A chemist, Conant had been one of the leaders in the Manhattan Project during the war.

January 19, 1956 (part three)

1. Attending the meeting were Secretaries Dulles and Humphrey; Undersecretary of State Herbert Hoover, Jr.; John C. Hollister, head of the State Department's International Cooperation Administration; Budget Director Dodge; Sherman Adams; and Gabriel Hauge.

January 23, 1956

1. Lieutenant General Harold L. George was a former commanding general, air transport command.
2. The Distant Early Warning line was a radar network in northern Canada, to catch hostile planes coming over the pole.

January 24, 1956

1. Robert A. Lovett, former secretary of defense; Benjamin Fairless, president of the United States Steel Corporation; James R. Killian, president of the Massachusetts Institute of Technology; Edward L. Ryerson, iron and steel manufacturer; Rear Admiral Richard L. Conolly, Lieutenant General John E. Hull, Lieutenant General James H. Doolittle.
3. As head of the GSA, Edmund F. Mansure had testified that "practical politics" dictated that a large brokerage contract should not go to a firm that did "not help this administration get into office."
4. Senators Mundt (South Dakota), Stephen M. Young (Ohio), and Edward J. Thye (Minnesota).

March 8, 1956

1. The cable is not attached to the diary entry in the Eisenhower Library.
2. Edith Nourse Rogers (Massachusetts).

March 13, 1956

1. King Farouk was expelled from Egypt in 1952.
2. The oil discoveries in Libya had not yet occurred.
3. Undersecretary of State Hoover.
4. To impound the waters of the Jordan and use them for irrigation.

March 13, 1956 (part two)

1. At the end of the Second World War the Trieste problem had flared up, and in 1949 Yugoslavia occupied one portion of the territory and British and American troops remained in another; after Tito defected from the communists a settlement became possible, which was made in 1954. That same year Guatemala had suffered a revolution in the course of which a leftist government was overthrown with the help of rebels assisted by the CIA. Secretary of State Dulles was engaged in promoting some kind of solidarity, perhaps an alliance, among the northern tier of states beginning with Turkey and moving east—Iraq, Iran, Pakistan. The four nations together with Britain already were allied in the Baghdad Pact, to which the United States in 1958 promised a relationship that would be similar, the Americans said, to membership. In 1959 the Baghdad Pact was converted into the Central Treaty Organization (CENTO).
2. Gruenther was Eisenhower's successor at SHAPE.

March 23, 1956

1. James Hoffa was head of the teamsters union.

March 23, 1956 (part two)

1. Senator Estes Kefauver of Tennessee.

March 28, 1956

1. The memorandum was entitled "Near Eastern Policies," and accompanying Secretary Dulles were Undersecretary Hoover; George V. Allen, assistant secretary for Near Eastern, Asian, and African affairs; William Rountree, deputy assistant secretary; Reuben B. Robertson, Jr., deputy secretary of defense; Secretary of Defense Wilson; Admiral Arthur W. Radford, chairman of the joint chiefs.

April 20, 1956

1. Paul Hoffman was former administrator of the Marshall Plan and former president of the Studebaker Corporation.

May 18, 1956

1. The memorandum, entitled "Important Facts on OTC," showed how OTC would increase American trade without touching the right of Congress to control the tariff.

August 8, 1956

1. One of the advantages of the proposed dam had been that it would tie up Egypt's credit for years to come and make it impossible for the Egyptians to purchase arms to use against the Israelis.

2. The Egyptians did not seem to feel that their barter agreement with the Czechs, whereby they would mortgage their cotton crop for an unpredictable number of years in exchange for arms, made any difference in their relations with the West. Moreover, the Egyptians were saying that if the United States and other Western nations did not come across with money for the dam, President Nasser would go to the Soviets for help (which is what he eventually did, after which he expelled Soviet advisers from Egypt).

November 8, 1956

1. The United Nations had entered the Aswan Dam-Suez Canal imbroglio at the request of the parties, and insisted upon peace and justice.

2. The head of the Motion Picture Distributors Association had proposed an international arrangement to control the waters of the Jordan River.

3. Among other things the statement of Britain, France, and the United States promised to prevent any border changes by the Arab states or Israel: "The three Governments, should they find that any of these States was preparing to violate frontiers or armistice lines, would, consistent with their obligations as members of the United Nations, immediately take action, both within and outside the United Nations, to prevent such violation." This part of the declaration proved a dead letter, but another part provided a virtual arms embargo, a careful measuring of requests for arms by the Arab nations or Israel, so that there would be no arms competition by these small nations.

November 20, 1956

1. Harold Macmillan replaced Eden as prime minister. R.A. Butler was the number-two man in the Cabinet.

December 16, 1956

1. Indira Gandhi, who later became prime minister.

May 20, 1957

1. Paul Mellon, financier, was the son of Andrew W. Mellon.

August 14, 1957

1. Spessard L. Holland of Florida.
2. Civil Aeronautics Administration (CAA). The document referred to is not attached to the diary entry in the Eisenhower Library.
3. Lieutenant General Elwood R. Quesada was one of Eisenhower's tactical air commanders in Europe during the Second World War.

October 8, 1957

1. Brooks Hays was an Arkansas congressman and well-known liberal.

October 29, 1957

1. I.I. Rabi was professor of physics at Columbia University; Gray was special assistant for national security affairs.
2. Ernest O. Lawrence was head of the radiation laboratory at the University of California at Berkeley, inventor of the cyclotron; Edward Teller was co-inventor (with the mathematician Stanislas Ulam) of the hydrogen bomb.

February 28, 1958

1. The memorandum is not attached to the diary entry in the Eisenhower Library.

March 17, 1958

1. Robert B. Anderson had replaced George M. Humphrey as secretary of the treasury in 1957.
2. The statements are not attached to the diary entry in the Eisenhower Library.
3. Raymond J. Saulnier had succeeded Arthur F. Burns as chairman of the council of economic advisers.

December 6, 1958

1. Meade Alcorn was successor to Leonard Hall.
2. Charles Percy later became senator from Illinois.

December 6, 1958 (part two)

1. Justin Dart was president of Rexall Drug, Inc.

December 6, 1958 (part three)

1. Reference is made to budgetary struggles and the outlook for refinancing.

May 28, 1959

1. Portion deleted for security reasons.
2. Deleted, as above.

November 28, 1959

1. In the letter to Finder, publisher of the Manchester *Union-Leader*, of January 22, 1948, Eisenhower said, "I am not available for and could not accept nomination to high political office." He considered it a good idea for military officers to stay out of politics—a complicated profession for which he thought a military man could not easily qualify—and hence, "I could not accept nomination even under the remote circumstance that it were tendered me."
2. Colonel Robert L. Schulz (later Brigadier General) was an aide.

January 13, 1960

1. Neil H. McElroy, successor to Wilson as secretary of defense; Nelson Rockefeller; Senator Thruston B. Morton (Kentucky), chairman of the Republican national committee.
2. Maurice Stans, successor to Dodge as director of the budget; Undersecretary of the Treasury Julian Baird; Undersecretary of the Treasury Fred C. Scribner, Jr.
3. Secretary of the Interior Fred A. Seaton.
4. Secretary of the Army Wilber M. Brucker.
5. Postmaster General Arthur E. Summerfield; Deputy Postmaster General Edson O. Sessions.
6. Former American Farm Bureau Federation President Allen B. Kline; Congressmen Leslie C. Arends (Illinois) and Charles B. Hoeven (Iowa).
7. Deputy Attorney General Lawrence Walsh.
8. Governor Hatfield of Oregon.
9. Boechenstein and Bechtel were leading industrialists.
10. Norman P. Mason, administrator of the housing and home finance agency.

July 5, 1960

1. Senator Morton was chairman, Len Hall was one of his predecessors, and J. Clifford Folger was chairman of the finance committee.

July 6, 1960

1. Reference is made to the abolition of the special arrangement under which Cuban sugar was admitted duty-free to the United States.

December 6, 1960

1. Senator Kennedy's list is not in the manuscript diary. As for the memoranda, they dealt with Soviet "whittling away" tactics in Berlin, that is, salami tactics—cutting down the Western position; the need to use the Organization of American States to replace Castro in Cuba; and the importance of the Republic of China on Taiwan as a beacon of freedom, "a symbol of hope for Chinese everywhere."
2. The Symington Committee of the Senate, chaired by Stuart Symington of Missouri, had investigated American security commitments abroad.
3. The president had discovered that Camp David served an important diplomatic function, and probably mentioned it to Kennedy. The camp, to be sure, was an informal place, and had advantages in negotiation, for anyone taken there could hardly create a diplomatic crisis in the easy atmosphere of overstuffed furniture and the out-of-doors. It also had become a place of prestige—Eisenhower had found that his important visitors, and many minor ones, desired to be invited to Camp David because someone else, from some other country, had been invited there.
4. Until 1957, Governor Adams had been assistant to the president, and Adams's place had been taken by General Persons.
5. A proposal to share American missile know-how in some way or other was before the NATO allies. It was an awkward proposition, as it tended to result in two kinds of proposals—one was the sort that the British made, for a special relationship with the United States, meaning

bilateral arrangements to give the British missiles (this they obtained when they received Polaris missiles in 1962); the other was to place operational control of American missiles in NATO hands somehow or other, without relinquishing American authority over the missiles; the result here was the ill-fated proposal for a "multilateral force" on the high seas, a joint manning of ships—a proposal that came to naught during the Kennedy administration.

6. The memorandum is not attached to the manuscript diary.

7. Goodpaster went back to command positions and eventually became commander of NATO. Years later, at the end of the 1970s, he returned to active duty as superintendent of West Point, where there had been a cheating scandal.

8. General George H. Decker, chief of staff of the army.

April 22, 1961

1. The president had asked Eisenhower to talk to Dulles.
2. T-33s were American training planes.
3. Portion exempted for security reasons.
4. Exempted, as above.
5. Reference is made to the International Control Commission.
6. Campion was a secret service agent.

June 5, 1961

1. Adlai Stevenson was ambassador to the United Nations; Chester Bowles was undersecretary of state.
2. The president was, of course, the author of *Profiles in Courage*.

November 20, 1964

1. In "Let's Clean Up This Highway Mess," Kenneth O. Gilmore attacked the federal-aid highway program in what he described as the story of national disgrace—collusion, chiseling, bureaucratic incompetence. In Arizona an employe was asked if he was aware that to falsify records was a crime. "I kind of had an idea," he answered, "it wasn't exactly right."

SOURCES

In the Dwight D. Eisenhower Library in Abilene the Eisenhower diaries are mostly in four distinct locations in the archives and are easy to find. A single archival box entitled Diaries Miscellaneous —a gray cardboard box four inches wide, with papers stored vertically in file folders—holds the Philippine diary, the account of the trip to Yellowstone Park in 1938, most of the Second World War diary for the first half of the year 1942, and the diary for 1948–1953. The wartime diary for the remainder of 1942 together with 1943–1944 is almost all in the Harry C. Butcher headquarters diary, Boxes 141–146 in a series known in the library for the years it covers, the 1916–1952 ("16–52") series. The third location of the diaries is a miscellany for the presidential years known as the DDE Diaries—fifty-five boxes of telephone conversations, memoranda not necessarily by the president, letters, accounts of meetings, in which are interspersed folders of diary entries and occasional single entries. The fourth is the Ann Whitman Diary—eleven boxes of material preserved by the president's private secretary that include her own diary entries, copies of Eisenhower diary entries in the DDE Diaries, and some unique presidential entries that Mrs. Whitman managed to secure. In addition I have used entries from the papers of Kevin McCann, Eisenhower's aide and speechwriter. A few diary items are from the post-presidential files; for the most part those files are closed, but a few items have been released by request either through security declassification or by a review under the donor's deed of gift.

The somewhat longer descriptions that follow are the formal descriptions, the proper citations of materials mentioned above, together with the box numbers and, where necessary, the names of folders.

One last preliminary explanation, about the folder names. In the citations that follow, everything after the box number is the folder name. Consider the following citation: Eisenhower, Dwight D.: Papers as President of the United States, 1953–61 (Ann Whitman File [DDE Diaries series]), Box 9, Diary-Copies of DDE Personal 1953–54 (3). The folder name is "Diary-Copies of DDE Personal 1953–54 (3)." Originally the presidential papers were in four-drawer file cases, and when the papers were shipped to Abilene they were simply taken out of the cases and packed in containers. At the Dwight D. Eisenhower Library the archivists put the papers in the gray cardboard archival boxes and numbered the boxes. But the papers were left in their original folders, or if placed in new folders the names of the original folders were used, hence, the inconsistent and sometimes complex titles, hurriedly invented by Mrs. Whitman and her assistants—such as "Diary-Copies of DDE Personal 1953–54 (3)." In citing materials I have dropped folder names for boxes where everything therein is chronological, as in the Butcher headquarters diary. In most cases, however, the names are essential, and for two reasons. For one, the archivists sometimes redistribute material and change the box numbers (between two of my visits to Abilene the archivists xeroxed the original DDE Diaries and increased the box numbers from thirty-six to fifty-five, vastly confusing my researches as I had failed to make note of the folder names). For another, without the folder name it is frequently necessary to look through an entire box for a single item.

The Philippines. December 27, 1935–November 5, 1938: All diary entries for chapter I, The Philippines, are in Eisenhower, Dwight D.: Diaries Miscellaneous.

The War Department in Crisis. January 1–July 6, 1942: All entries for this period (with exceptions noted below) are from Diaries Miscellaneous. Two typed versions of the diary for these months survived, and the version edited by Eisenhower appears in Alfred D. Chandler, ed., *The Papers of Dwight David Eisenhower: The War Years*, five volumes (Baltimore: Johns Hopkins University Press, 1970), volume I. Chandler supplemented this expurgated version with a few entries published in Kevin McCann, *Man from Abilene* (Garden City, New York: Doubleday, 1952). The present book offers the unedited diary, for which I have used original handwritten entries in the papers of Kevin McCann, supplemented (the entries are incomplete) by a typescript in the Eisenhower Library. Three handwritten items in the McCann papers are not in the library's typescript—the final sentence for the entry of March 14 (Eisenhower later replaced it with another sentence, now in the typescript) and entries for March 21 and March 31.

North Africa and Italy. Entries from May 23 through May 30 are in Eisenhower, Dwight D.: Papers, Pre-Presidential, 1916–52, Box 153, Operations-Bolero-1942. (Note: "Operations-Bolero-1942" is the folder name.) They were published in Chandler I, 318–22 and are an account of Eisenhower's first trip to the British Isles that year. An entry for June 20 concerns a meeting with President Quezon of the Philippine Commonwealth, and is in Eisenhower, Dwight D.: Papers, Pre-Presidential, 1916–52, Box 87, Quezon, Manuel. It likewise was published in Chandler I, 349–50. July 20, 1942: The original manuscript of this entry is in the massive compendium constituting the Harry C. Butcher headquarters diary, now at the Eisenhower Library. The citation is Eisenhower, Dwight D.: Papers, Pre-Presidential, 1916–52, Box 141. (Note: as mentioned, no folder name is necessary because the Butcher headquarters diary is chronological.) Butcher's book, *My Three Years with Eisenhower* (New York: Simon and Schuster, 1946), consisted only of a selection of his own diary entries and has none of Ike's. July 22, 1942: Box 141; Chandler I, 405–6. July 26, 1942: Box 141; Chandler I, 417–18. July 27, 1942: Box 141; Chandler I, 420–21. September 2, 1942: Box 141, Chandler I, 524–27. September 13, 1942: Box 141; Chandler I, 557. September 15, 1942: Box 141; Chandler I, 559–60. November 8, 1942: Box 142; Chandler II, 675. November 9, 1942: Box 142; Chandler II, 679. December 10, 1942: Box 142; Chandler II, 822–25. December 15, 1942: Box 142; Chandler II, 842–44. January 19, 1943: Box 143; Chandler II, 909–10. February 25, 1943: Box 143; Chandler II, 987–92. June 11, 1943: Box 143. This entry is not in Chandler. July 1, 1943: Box 143; Chandler II, 1230–33. September 14, 1943: Box 144; Chandler III, 1418–19. November 12, 1943: Box 144; Chandler III, 1560–63. December 6, 1943: Box 144; Chandler III, 1585–88.

Victory in Europe. February 7, 1944: Box 144; Chandler III, 1711–12. March 22, 1944: Box 145; Chandler III, 178–285. April 12, 1944: Box 145; Chandler III, 1820–21. May 22, 1944: Box 145; Chandler III, 1880–81. June 3, 1944: Box 140, Crusade in Europe; Chandler III, 1903–6. August 6–7, 1944: Box 145; Chandler III, 2057. September 5, 1944: Box 145; Chandler III, 2121–22. December 23, 1944: Box 146; Chandler IV, 2371–75.

Chief of Staff. December 15, 1945–January 15, 1948: All entries are from the papers of Kevin McCann.

Columbia University; NATO. December 13, 1948–February 28, 1952: All entries are in Diaries Miscellaneous.

The First Administration. January 5–February 2, 1953: Diaries Miscellaneous. February 7, 1953: Eisenhower, Dwight D.: Papers as President of the United States, 1953–61 (Ann Whitman File [DDE Diaries series]), Box 9, Diary-Copies of DDE Personal 1953–54 (3). February 9, 1953: Ibid. February 13, 1953: Diaries Miscellaneous. April 1, 1953: DDE Diaries series, Box 9, Diary-Copies of DDE Personal 1953–54 (3). May 1, 1953: Diaries Miscellaneous. May 14, 1953: Ibid. June 1, 1953:

DDE Diaries series, box 9, Diary-Copies of DDE Personal 1953–54 (2). July 2, 1953: Ibid. July 23, 1953: Ibid. July 24, 1953: Ibid. July 31, 1953: Diaries Miscellaneous. August 1, 1953: DDE Diaries series, Box 9, Diary-Copies of DDE Personal 1953–54 (2). August 19, 1953: Diaries Miscellaneous. August 19, 1953: Ibid. October 14, 1953: DDE Diaries series, Box 4, DDE Diary Oct.-Dec. 1953. (Note: in the preceding citation there is not a diary within the diaries, but the folder title is "DDE Diary Oct.-Dec. 1953.") October 24, 1953: Ibid. October 26, 1953: Eisenhower, Dwight D.: Papers as President of the United States, 1953–61 (Ann Whitman File [Ann Whitman Diary series]), Box 1, ACW Diary Aug-Sept-Oct 1953 (1). October 27, 1953: DDE Diaries series, Box 3, DDE Diary October 1953 (1). November 11, 1953: DDE Diaries series, Box 4, DDE Diary Oct.-Dec. 1953. December 2, 1953: Ibid. December 3, 1953: Ibid. December 10, 1953: Ann Whitman Diary series, Box 1, ACW Diary, Nov-Dec 1953 (2). December 10, 1953 (part two): DDE Diaries series, Box 4, DDE Diary Oct.-Dec. 1953. December 11, 1953: Ibid. December 11, 1953 (part two): Ibid. December 11, 1953 (part three): Ibid. December 14, 1953: Ann Whitman Diary series, Box 1, ACW Diary Nov-Dec 1953 (1). December 17–19, 1953: DDE Diaries series, Box 4, DDE Diary December 1953 (1). January 12, 1954: DDE Diaries series, Box 4, DDE Personal Diary Jan.-Nov. 1954 (2). January 18, 1954: Ibid. The president revised the original entry and it was retyped on January 31; the retyped version appears here. January 27, 1954: DDE Diaries series, Box 5, DDE Diary-January 1954 (1). Week of February 7, 1954: DDE Diaries series, Box 4, DDE Personal Diary Jan.-Nov. 1954 (2). February 8, 1954: Ibid. February 10, 1954: Ibid. February 10, 1954 (part two): DDE Diaries series, Box 5, DDE Diary February 1954 (1). February 15, 1954: Ibid. February 26, 1954: DDE Diaries series, Box 4, DDE Personal Diary Jan.-Nov. 1954 (2). March 5, 1954: Ibid. April 3, 1954: Ann Whitman Diary series, Box 2, ACW Diary April 1954 (3). April 8, 1954: DDE Diaries series, Box 4, DDE Personal Diary Jan.-Nov. 1954 (2). April 27, 1954: DDE Diaries series, Box 4, DDE Personal Diary Jan.-Nov. 1954 (1). May 11, 1954: Ibid. May 24, 1954: Ann Whitman Diary series, Box 2, ACW Diary May 1954 (1). June 15, 1954: DDE Diaries series, Box 7, DDE Diary June 1954 (2). June 18, 1954: DDE Diaries series, Box 7, DDE Diary June 1954 (1). July 10, 1954: DDE Diaries series, Box 7, DDE Diary July 1954 (2). July 13, 1954: DDE Diaries series, Box 7, DDE Diary July 1954 (1). October 5, 1954: DDE Diaries series, Box 8, DDE Diary-October 1954 (2). October 22, 1954: Ibid. October 26, 1954: DDE Diaries series, Box 8, DDE Diary-October 1954 (1). November 9, 1954: DDE Diaries series, Box 8, DDE Diary-November 1954 (2). November 16, 1954: DDE Diaries series, Box 8, DDE Diary-November 1954 (1). November 20, 1954: DDE Diaries series, Box 4, DDE Personal Diary Jan.-Nov. 1954 (1). January 10, 1955: Ann Whitman Diary series, Box 4, ACW Diary January 1955 (4). January 10, 1955 (part two): DDE Diaries series, Box 9, Diary-Copies of DDE personal [1955–56] (2). (Note: the bracketed dates are part of the folder title.) January 11, 1955: Ibid. January 17, 1955: DDE Diaries series, Box 9, DDE Diary January 1955 (1). January 17, 1955 (part two): DDE Diaries series, Box 9, Diary-Copies of DDE personal [1955–56] (2). January 26, 1955: Ibid. February 7, 1955: DDE Diaries series, Box 9, DDE Diary-February, 1955 (2). February 15, 1955: Ibid. February 19, 1955: DDE Diaries series, Box 9, Diary-Copies of DDE personal [1955–56] (1). March 12, 1955: Ann Whitman Diary series, Box 4, ACW Diary March 1955 (6). March 14, 1955: DDE Diaries series, Box 10, DDE Diary March 1955 (2). March 26, 1955: DDE Diaries series, Box 10, DDE Diary March, 1955 (1). May 2, 1955: DDE Diaries series, Box 10, DDE Diary May 1955 (2). May 3, 1955: Ibid. May 10, 1955: Ann Whitman Diary series, Box 5, ACW Diary May 1955 (6). July 14, 1955: DDE Diaries series, Box 9, Diary-Copies of DDE personal [1955–56] (1). August 15, 1955: Ann Whitman Diary series, Box 6, ACW Diary August 1955 (3). September 29, 1955 (Ann Whitman Diary): DDE Diaries series, Box 9, DDE Personal Diary 1/1/55–[11/10/55]. January 11, 1956: DDE Diaries series, Box 9, Diary-Copies of DDE personal [1955–56] (2). January 12, 1956: Ibid. January 16, 1956: DDE Diaries series, Box 12, Jan '56 Diary. January 19, 1956: DDE Diaries series, Box 9, Diary-Copies of DDE personal [1955–56] (2). January 19, 1956 (part two): Ibid. January 19, 1956 (part three): Ibid. January 20, 1956: Ibid. January 23, 1956: Ibid. January 24, 1956: Ibid. January 24, 1956 (part two): Ibid. January 25, 1956: DDE Diaries series, Box 12, Jan '56 Diary. January 30, 1956: DDE Diaries series, Box 9, Diary-Copies of DDE personal [1955–56] (2). February 8, 1956: DDE Diaries series, Box 12, Feb '56 Diary. February 11, 1956: DDE Diaries series, Box 9, Diary-Copies of DDE personal [1955–56] (1). March 8, 1956: Ibid. March 13, 1956: Ibid. March 13, 1956 (part two): Ibid. March 19, 1956: Ann Whitman

Diary series, Box 8, Mar. '56 Diary-acw (2). March 23, 1956: DDE Diaries series, Box 9, Diary-Copies of DDE personal [1955–56] (1). March 23, 1956 (part two): Ibid. March 28, 1956: Ibid. March 30, 1956: DDE Diaries series, Box 13, Mar '56 Diary. April 20, 1956: DDE Diaries series, Box 9, Diary-Copies of DDE personal [1955–56] (1). May 18, 1956: DDE Diaries series, Box 15, May '56 Diary. July 25, 1956: DDE Diaries series, Box 9, Diary-Copies of DDE personal [1955–56] (1). August 6, 1956: DDE Diaries series, Box 17, Aug. '56 Diary. August 8, 1956: DDE Diaries series, Box 9, Diary-Copies of DDE personal [1955–56] (1). October 15, 1956: Ann Whitman Diary series, Box 8, Oct. '56 Diary-acw (1). Published in *The White House Years: Waging Peace, 1956–1961* (Garden City, New York: Doubleday, 1965), pp. 676–77. October 26, 1956: DDE Diaries series, Box 8, Oct. '56 Diary. November 8, 1956: DDE Diaries series, Box 19, Nov. '56 Diary. November 20, 1956: Ibid. November 21, 1956: DDE Diaries series, Box 9, Diary-Copies of DDE personal [1955–56] (1). November 21, 1956 (part two): DDE Diaries series, Box 19, Nov. '56 Diary. December 16, 1956: Ann Whitman Diary series, Box 8, Dec. '56 Diary-acw. Undated (December 1956?): Ibid.

The Second Administration. February 5, 1957: DDE Diaries series, Box 21, Feb. '57 Diary. May 20, 1957: Ann Whitman Diary series, Box 9, May '57 Diary-acw (1). August 5, 1957: DDE Diaries series, Box 25, DDE Diary-7/1/57–8/31/57. August 14, 1957: Ibid. September 13, 1957: Ann Whitman Diary series, Box 9, September '57-acw Diary. October 8, 1957: Ibid. October 29, 1957: DDE Diaries series, Box 28, October '57 D.D.E. Dictation. January 14, 1958: DDE Diaries series, Box 29, DDE Diary Jan 1958. January 24, 1958: Ibid. February 28, 1958: DDE Diaries series, Box 30, D.D.E. Diary February 1958. March 8, 1958: DDE Diaries series, Box 31, DDE Diary March 1958. March 17, 1958: Ibid. March 18, 1958: Ibid. June 9, 1958: DDE Diaries series, Box 34, June 1958-DDE Dictation. December 6, 1958: DDE Diaries series, Box 38, DDE Diary-Dec. 1958. December 6, 1958 (part two): DDE Diaries series, Box 37, DDE Dictation-Dec. 1958. December 6, 1958 (part three): Ibid. December 17, 1958: Ibid. January 27, 1959: Ann Whitman Diary series, Box 10, ACW Diary-Jan 1959 (1). February 16, 1959: DDE Diaries series, Box 39, DDE Dictation February 1959. March 3, 1959: Ann Whitman Diary series, Box 10, [ACW] Diary March 1959 (2). March 3, 1959 (part two): Ibid. May 27, 1959: DDE Diaries series, Box 41, DDE Dictation May 1959. May 27, 1959 (part two): Ibid. May 28, 1959: Ibid. June 22, 1959: Ann Whitman Diary series, Box 10, [ACW] Diary June 1959 (1). September 10, 1959: Ann Whitman Diary series, Box 11, [ACW] Diary September 1959. November 9, 1959: Ann Whitman Diary series, Box 11, [ACW] Diary November 1959. November 28, 1959: DDE Diaries series, Box 45, DDE Dictation November 1959. January 13, 1960: Ann Whitman Diary series, Box 11, [ACW] Diary January 1960. A copy of this entry was given to Vice-President Nixon on February 12, and much of it was published in *Waging Peace*, pp. 591–92. January 20, 1960: Ann Whitman Diary series, Box 11, [ACW] Diary January 1960. March 23, 1960: Ann Whitman Diary series, Box 11, [ACW] Diary March 1960 (1). July 1, 1960: Ann Whitman Diary series, Box 11, [ACW] Diary July 1960 (2). July 5, 1960: Ibid. July 6, 1960: Ibid. December 6, 1960: Ann Whitman Diary series, Box 11, [ACW] Diary December 1960. This entry was published in *Waging Peace*, pp. 712–16.

Retirement. April 22, 1961: Eisenhower, Dwight D.: Papers, Post-Presidential, Augusta-Palm Desert series, Box 11, Kennedy, John F. June 5, 1961: Box 10, Cuba. October 29, 1962: Ibid. November 2, 1962: Ibid. November 5, 1962: Ibid. September 11, 1964: Box 10, McCone, John. November 20, 1964: Box 11, memoranda for the record. October 16, 1965: Box 10, Pres. Johnson, 1964 (1). November 23, 1966: Box 10, Pres. Johnson, 1966. March 14, 1967: Box 7, Nixon.

INDEX

Printed in the United States
79959LV00003B/7

9 780393 331806